THE LIFE OF JOHN LANCASTER SPALDING

MAKERS OF AMERICAN CATHOLICISM
General Editor, John Tracy Ellis
Volume One

JOHN LANCASTER SPALDING

THE LIFE OF JOHN LANCASTER SPALDING

First Bishop of Peoria, 1840–1916

DAVID FRANCIS SWEENEY, O.F.M.

HERDER AND HERDER

1965
HERDER AND HERDER NEW YORK
232 Madison Avenue, New York 10016

Imprimi potest: Francis Hoag, O.F.M.
                      Minister Provincial
Nihil obstat: Brendan Lawlor
                      Censor Deputatus
Imprimatur: †Robert F. Joyce
                      Bishop of Burlington
                      August 25, 1965

The *Nihil obstat* and *Imprimatur* are official declarations
that a book or pamphlet is considered to be free of doctrinal or moral error. No implication is contained therein
that those who have granted the *Nihil obstat* and *Imprimatur* agree with the contents, opinions, or statements
expressed.

Library of Congress Catalog Card Number: 65–13480
© 1965 by Herder and Herder, Incorporated
Manufactured in the United States of America

Contents

FOR
JOHN PATRICK AND CLAIRE SWEENEY

Foreword

In a sermon on the parable of the unjust steward preached by John Henry Newman in July, 1870, he spoke of the varied gifts that God gives to every man, whether he be in a high or a low station of life, and he then stated:

> He has given us a certain power of influencing others. He has given us a certain circle of persons, larger or smaller, who depend on us, whom our words and our actions affect for good or for evil. . . .[1]

Of very few men of high station in the Catholic Church of the United States can it be more appropriately said than of the subject of this biography, that his "power of influencing others" was quite beyond the ordinary. Every human being exercises some influence on those whom he encounters along the road of life, but with most men one is left to wonder and to surmise what that influence may have been. In the case of John Lancaster Spalding, however, the historian does not need to fall back on surmises, for the evidence of his influence, through the medium of the spoken and written word and of the institutions that he brought into being, has long been recognized as an authentic part of the American Catholic story.

A quarter of a century ago one of this country's most distinguished Catholic figures, John A. Ryan, offered a striking example of Spalding's influence. Of the latter he wrote, "For many

[1] "Stewards and Also Sons of God," a sermon preached on July 31, 1870, *Faith and Prejudice and Other Unpublished Sermons of Cardinal Newman*, edited by the Birmingham Oratory (New York, Sheed & Ward, 1956), p. 101.

9

years he exercised a greater influence upon my general philosophy of life, my ideals, my sense of comparative values than any other contemporary writer."[2] Those who knew how alien to the spirit of Monsignor Ryan were fulsome praise and exaggeration, will agree that this was an impressive tribute to the first bishop of the Diocese of Peoria. It is now over a decade, incidentally, since the present writer had occasion to speak of having been born in that diocese in the year when Bishop Spalding suffered his first paralytic stroke (1905). On that occasion I stated that I had known at first hand something of the imprint left by him on what I called "the intellectual tastes, the good reading, and the careful preparation of sermons of many of his priests." It was a subject of comment in my youth, and from a personal acquaintance with several of these venerable priests I could verify, as I said, "the effect that these intellectual habits had upon their lives."[3] If, therefore, there should be any need—which there is not—to justify the prolonged and scholarly labors of Father David Sweeney extending over almost a decade, the single fact of Spalding's widespread, deep, and abiding influence on the lives of his contemporaries and on those of succeeding generations would furnish that warrant.

What was the secret of Spalding's influence, and to what particular areas of human endeavor was it directed? Each reader of his life will answer the first part of this question in accordance with his own norms and standards, and in the light of what he conceives are the qualities that should constitute greatness, or the approach to greatness, in an American Catholic bishop. In this introduction the present writer would invoke his right to do the same. As a consequence of my independent study of Spalding's career, and of a close and critical reading of Father

[2] John A. Ryan, *Social Doctrine in Action, A Personal History* (New York, Harper & Brothers, 1941), p. 29.

[3] John Tracy Ellis, *American Catholics and the Intellectual Life* (Chicago, Heritage Foundation Inc., 1956), pp. 39–40.

Sweeney's pages, where to a greater richness of factual detail he has added a more balanced and realistic interpretation than is to be found in any other publication on the first Bishop of Peoria— I gradually reached the conclusion that while there were numerous facets that explain the man, as is true of every educated and sophisticated churchman, it seemed to me that the principal factors might be reduced to three: 1) a strong and articulate native American tradition inherited from family ties and nurtured by youthful training; 2) an extraordinarily acute mind that was exploited to the utmost in response to a deep sense of dedication to a lofty ideal; 3) a resolute will that when once fixed on an objective, and convinced that its course was the right one, had not only the courage to encounter opposition but the perseverance to stand against it and often the power to overcome it.

John Lancaster Spalding was a true American. Thomas Spalding, the earliest member of the family of whom there is record in colonial Maryland, arrived around 1658 from England where he had been born about 1640.[4] When one reflects that the latter date was just two centuries before the subject of this biography saw the light of day in Kentucky, it can be more readily comprehended why Spalding should have thought, spoken, and acted as one "who belonged here." As the citation for Columbia University's honorary degree conferred in 1902 phrased it, the fact that he was the "descendant of a house honored among two peoples . . . ,"[5] would help to explain his attitude toward many of the great questions that agitated both Church and State during his mature years. Spalding never suffered from the handicap of most of his contemporaries among the Catholic bishops of the United States in being either of foreign birth or of immi-

[4] Hughes Spalding, *The Spalding Family of Maryland, Kentucky and Georgia from 1658 to 1963* (Atlanta, Privately Printed, 1963), p. 11.
[5] The degree of doctor of letters, *honoris causa*, was conferred on Spalding on June 11, 1902.

grant parentage. No bishop nominated to an American see after John Carroll's founding of the hierarchy in 1790—including Carroll himself—had a more thoroughly native lineage than Peoria's first ordinary. That would account in good measure for the surety of tone in which Spalding often made public pronouncements as, for example, when in 1894 he defied the bigotry of the American Protective Association by forthrightly declaring in the pages of the *North American Review* that he saw no reason for Catholics to proclaim their loyalty to the Republic. "To protest is half to confess," he said, "as to exhort is to reproach. . . ." To Spalding the patriotism of his coreligionists was to be taken for granted, and thus he saw no need, as he remarked, for Catholics "to hold the flag in our hands when we walk the streets [and] to wave it when we speak. . . ."[6]

The same deep American strain enabled Bishop Spalding to criticize public officials freely and without misgiving when he felt that their policies and actions were at fault, as happened in 1889 when his own State of Illinois enacted a school law that, he maintained, embodied features that threatened the rights of Catholic parents and children. Nor was he frightened off by the angry fulminations against the Catholic Church on this issue then emanating from Joseph Medill's Chicago *Tribune*. On the contrary, he used the inaugural issue of the weekly newspaper established for the Archdiocese of Chicago and its suffragan sees, the *New World* (September 10, 1892), to state the Church's case against the Edwards Law in forceful detail.

Yet there was no Catholic of Spalding's lifetime who was prouder of his country and who rose to its defense more fearlessly when he thought its merits and interests had been slighted. Thus in his address at the dedication of Holy Cross College in Washington in October, 1899, he championed the United States against Europe toward which, he believed, too many of his fel-

[6] "Catholicism and APAism," *North American Review* CLIX (September, 1894), 285.

low Catholics looked back with nostalgic glances. "What sacredness is there in Europe more than in America?" he asked, and thereupon proceeded to inquire, "What country ever had fortune like ours? Where else has the Catholic Church ever had a wider or a freer field?"[7] These words assume added significance when it is recalled that they were uttered nine months after Pope Leo XIII's letter, *Testem benevolentiae,* which had condemned the errors of the so-called heresy of Americanism, and that they were spoken in the presence of Sebastiano Martinelli, O.S.A., Apostolic Delegate to the United States. Moreover, less than six months later Spalding carried the public support of his country and its way of life to the Eternal City where in March, 1900, in the Church of the Gesù he delivered what was probably the most famous sermon of a long and distinguished preaching career. In language that would almost suggest Pierre Teilhard de Chardin, he declared:

> The law of man's life . . . is growth. He must continue to grow, or he will lose vital force; and as he develops, the institutions whereby his life is sustained and fostered must adapt themselves to his increasing wants. As in order to live he must renew himself, and therefore change, the environment in which he is placed must lend itself to his widening needs, and therefore change.[8]

On this same occasion he championed, as he had done so many times before, the intellectual freedom of his fellow Catholics, making it clear that while he held fast to what he termed "the principle of authority," he would at the same time insist that "man's mind is free, and . . . he has the right to inquire into and learn whatever may be investigated and known." Disciples of the current *aggiornamento* at work within the Church would

---

[7] "The University: A Nursery of the Higher Life," in *Opportunity and Other Essays and Addresses* (Chicago, A. C. McClurg & Company, 1900), pp. 107–108.

[8] "Education and the Future of Religion," a sermon preached on March 21, 1900, *Religion, Agnosticism and Education* (Chicago, A. C. McClurg & Company, 1902), p. 149.

13

echo these sentiments as they would the preacher's words when he told his Roman listeners on that March day of 1900, "If the Church is to live and prosper in the modern world, Catholics must have not only freedom to learn, but also freedom to teach."[9] The leading Protestant weekly of the United States, *The Independent,* was enthusiastic about Spalding's ideas. In an editorial it was said, "For the intelligence, courage and sound Americanism of this admirable sermon Catholics and Protestants may equally be grateful."[10]

It is one thing to have the "proper" national and family background, combined with a superior mind that generates ideas of an original character; it is quite another thing to employ these advantages for the Church's welfare in so attractive a way as to earn a respectful hearing in learned circles. There was never any question, however, about a sophisticated audience for the arresting ideas that came from the resourceful brain of Peoria's first ordinary, and John A. Ryan gave the reason in part when he stated, "Bishop Spalding was undoubtedly the greatest literary artist in the entire history of the American Hierarchy."[11] And if one were to inquire of his biographer in what particular aspects of life the bishop expended his best talents, Father Sweeney would probably reply in behalf of religious education and social betterment.

As for the former, virtually every important educational problem that came before the national forum, or that circulated within the confines of the Catholic community, in the forty years between Spalding's return from his European studies in 1865 and 1905 when he was incapacitated by a stroke of paralysis, was the object of his critical scrutiny and analysis. What the present writer published on this point four years ago,[12] as well

[9] *Ibid.,* p. 158.

[10] "Bishop Spalding on Americanism," *The Independent* LII (September 20, 1900), 2287.

[11] Ryan, *op. cit.,* p. 28.

[12] John Tracy Ellis, *John Lancaster Spalding, First Bishop of Peoria, American Educator* (Milwaukee, Bruce Publishing Company, 1961).

as what others had written about the bishop's educational theories and activities, have now been superseded by Father Sweeney's work where all these matters are treated with a wealth of documentary evidence available to no previous student of Spalding's career. Here one may read the account of the latter's first practical educational efforts as a priest directed toward his Negro parishioners at St. Augustine's Church in Louisville. Here, too, there is related the story of his persistent campaign for improved clerical education in the American Church that finally resulted after a struggle on his part of nearly a quarter century in the opening of the Catholic University of America in November, 1889, of which, said John Ireland, Archbishop of St. Paul, at Spalding's silver jubilee in 1902, "He is the founder . . ."[13] Thirteen years later the University marked its own twenty-fifth anniversary at a time when the shadows had already begun to darken over the stricken figure of John Lancaster Spalding. On the latter occasion the University's Chancellor, Cardinal Gibbons, affirmed the judgment of his friend from St. Paul when he said:

All great works have their inception in the brain of some great thinker. God gave such a brain, such a man, in Bishop Spalding. With his wonderful intuitionary power, he took in all the meaning of the present and the future of the Church in America. If the Catholic University is today an accomplished fact, we are indebted for its existence in our generation, in no small measure, to the persuasive eloquence and convincing arguments of the Bishop of Peoria.[14]

Tributes of a like kind might be cited for Spalding's many other educational understandings, to mention only two, the notable sermon on seminary education preached during the Third Plenary Council of Baltimore in November, 1884, and his able

---

[13] *Souvenir of the Episcopal Silver Jubilee of the Rt. Rev. J. L. Spalding, D.D., Bishop of Peoria* (Chicago, Hollister Brothers, 1903), p. 76.

[14] "Address on the Occasion of the Silver Jubilee of the Catholic University, delivered at St. Patrick's, Washington, April 15, 1916" [*sic*], James Cardinal Gibbons, *A Retrospect of Fifty Years* (Baltimore, John Murphy Company, 1916), II, 195.

direction of the Catholic educational exhibit at the World's Columbian Exposition at Chicago in 1893.

Meanwhile Bishop Spalding frequently spoke and wrote on the problems of public education as well, and on their relation to the private religious school, always making clear his strong preference for the latter and yet stating that preference in a manner that avoided alienating fair-minded educators outside his own Church. For example, William Harris, noted United States Commissioner of Education, was a warm admirer, and on one occasion in 1899 he referred to him publicly as "the most beloved of American educational leaders." More than a generation later Merle Curti declared that it was Spalding who had done more than any single individual "to convince Catholics, and even Protestants, that the parochial school could provide a secular education equal to that which prevailed in the best public institutions."[15] Indeed, the views of the Bishop of Peoria on parochial schools would be regarded as highly conservative by some Catholics today. Thus during the heated debate over Archbishop Ireland's Faribault-Stillwater plan Spalding showed himself as distinctly hostile to the Minnesota experiment which he feared as a threat to the Church's schools.

John Lancaster Spalding was a complex personality, a controversial figure who was looked upon by some as "near great," by others as "something of a disappointment." His literary output was tremendous, considering the numerous distractions under which he labored. Moreover, his books and articles, to say nothing of his memorable and graceful sermons that later found their way into print, did a great deal of good in influencing the opinion of his age on grave questions in both Church and State.

---

[15] Merle Curti, *The Social Ideas of American Educators* (New York, Charles Scribner's Sons, 1935), p. 356.

[16] *Ceremonies of the Golden Sacerdotal Jubilee of His Grace John Lancaster Spalding, Titular Archbishop of Sciotopolis* (Chicago, Ringley Company, 1913), p. 17.

[17] *Ibid.*, p. 31.

Yet the time that has elapsed since Spalding's death would seem to have confirmed the judgment expressed to the present writer by John F. Fenlon, S.S., at the time Provincial of the Sulpicians in the United States, a few days before his own death in July, 1943. Father Fenlon was a discerning observer of men and he wrote appreciatively of the bishop's literary work in general, but he added, "I do not think that any large body of his writings will have a permanent place in the history of American literature." It is no disparagement of Bishop Spalding's memory to state that Father Fenlon's judgment was a true one.

Zealous for a thousand good causes, Spalding's enthusiasm sometimes outran his prudence, and it is difficult to escape the impression of a strong element of pride behind his merciless scorn of mediocrity. In the words of the old saying, the first Bishop of Peoria "did not suffer fools gladly." That this was sensed by men of his own generation was reflected a few days after his death when *The Record* of Louisville stated, "Magnetism was not his great quality, for he frequently repelled as well as attracted" (August 31, 1916). While Spalding often accurately assessed men and issues, this was not always the case, and the fact that his way of doing things was disliked at times by others, probably contributed to the pain that he suffered during a career that displayed from the outset a curious vulnerability and an overly sensitive reaction to criticism. Possessed of an unusually clear vision of the role that the Catholic Church should play in American pluralistic society, disappointments in the realization of the bishop's ideals occasionally put him in a somewhat rebellious mood against the established order, but, be it added, a mood that was induced by a deep and abiding devotion to the cause of truth. Not infrequently overworked and overwrought by the intensity of his own nature and his almost too eager mind, in the final analysis it was in his utter dedication to truth that the memory and knowledge of Spalding's life will ever remain an inspiration. What the bishop said of John P.

17

Altgeld, former Governor of Illinois and fellow crusader for justice, at the latter's death in 1902, might well have been used fourteen years later as his own epitaph—"His eye was everywhere, and saw . . . through shams and shows into the heart of things."[18]

Few biographers could have succeeded in balancing the numerous merits and accomplishments of the first Bishop of Peoria against the several but real defects of his character and personality, all of which came to light in the abundant documentation through which Father Sweeney had to pick his way. The highest compliment that can be paid to the manner in which he executed his task is to say that in his judicious weighing of the evidence and in his graceful manner of expression, in this writer's judgment Father Sweeney has written a story that Bishop Spalding would have himself approved, while at the same time limning a literary portrait that will withstand the test of time.

JOHN TRACY ELLIS

Professor of Church History in the University of San Francisco
General Editor of "Makers of American Catholicism"

---

[18] "An Orator and Lover of Justice," in *Socialism and Labor and Other Arguments* . . . (Chicago, A. C. McClurg & Company, 1902), p. 191.

Introduction

FACTS are a severe taskmaster. Especially is this so in the field of biography, where the facts of a man's life, the whole panorama of his existence, will occasionally upset the *a priori* conceptions held by his contemporaries, as well as by those who come after him.

The present writer's purpose is to tell the story of John Lancaster Spalding, the first Bishop of Peoria, Illinois; to set forth, in other words, the facts about a man who was perfectly sincere and peculiarly himself, a man absolutely honest, often impolitic, but never expedient, a man who, through his bold and candid speech, shattered his own ecclesiastical career. Spalding was a victim of the flaws of his character, yet his ambiguities and ambivalences were separable, nevertheless, from his immense contribution to the Catholic Church in the United States.

John Spalding was an intellectual aristocrat whose independent mien and views differed widely from that of his more liberal confreres in the resolution of many of the basic issues that divided the American hierarchy during his episcopal career. Spalding was a defender of both the American and the Catholic tradition; he saw the need for American Catholics to meet the challenge of their age in their pluralistic society, and to assimilate the culture in which they lived. But unlike an Archbishop Ireland or a Bishop Keane, his response to the crises that beset the "Church of the immigrants" in the years following the Third Plenary Council of Baltimore was essentially conservative.

19

Though the Bishop of Peoria despised certain connotations of the word "career," we may be pardoned for saying that it has been necessary to trace his career, for only within the framework of what the man did can later writers and historians evaluate the Prelate who became in his generation the most articulate spokesman for Catholic education in the United States, and who waged what was at times a solitary crusade until at last the Catholic University of America became a reality.

It is a truism to say that this biography could never have been completed without the guidance and encouragement of the Right Reverend John Tracy Ellis, former Professor of Church History in the Catholic University of America, now at the University of San Francisco. Grateful acknowledgement is due also to the Reverend Robert J. Trisco, Associate Professor of History in the Catholic University of America, and to Professor John T. Farrell of the same institution, for their close and critical reading of this work.

Archivists and librarians both at home and abroad have been most generous in their help. Without their permission to use books, letters, manuscripts, and other library and archival material, the life of the first Bishop of Peoria could not have been told so completely. I am particularly indebted to the Reverend Nicholas Kowalsky, O.M.I., Archivist of the Sacred Congregation for the Propagation of the Faith, for copies of letters by or about Bishop Spalding which are housed in that rich depository. Grateful thanks are likewise due to the Reverend Henry J. Browne, former Archivist of the Catholic University of America; to the Reverend Thomas T. McAvoy, C.S.C., Archivist of the University of Notre Dame; to the Right Reverend Jeremiah J. Brennan, former Archivist of the Archdiocese of New York; to the Reverend Paul Love, former Archivist of the Archdiocese of Baltimore; to the late Eugene P. Willging and the staff of the Mullen Library in the Catholic University of America; and to Mr. Rodney Armstrong and the staff of the Davis Memorial Library in the Phillips Exeter Academy, Exeter, New Hampshire.

Finally, to the Very Reverend Donald Hoag, O.F.M., Minister Provincial of the Province of the Most Holy Name of Jesus, and to the Reverend Reginald A. Redlon, O.F.M., Rector of St. Francis College, Rye Beach, N.H., I will be always grateful.

DAVID FRANCIS SWEENEY, O.F.M.

Christ the King Seminary
St. Bonaventure University
St. Bonaventure, New York

THE LIFE OF JOHN LANCASTER SPALDING

1

Years of Preparation

"ALREADY they have toppled the Appalachian Mountains. From thence they behold an immense plain. . . . Over this would they wander without a possibility of restraint. . . ."[1] Thus Edmund Burke characterized the beginnings of the era of the American frontiersman. Men, women, and children would soon fill a great new country in the land beyond the mountains, foreshadowing, as did Burke's splendid protest, the course of American history and the westward growth of the nascent Republic. There was the Old Northwest, soon to be peopled by intrepid pioneers, but far bolder and braver was the more dramatic story of the Old Southwest, where the founding of Kentucky became the "great pioneer achievement of the time" with "Hundreds Travelling hundreds of Miles," as Moses Austin wrote, "they know not what for Nor Wither, except it's to Kentucky . . . the Promis'd Land . . . the Land of Milk and Honey."[2]

Long before Kentucky became in 1792 the first of the new states in the trans-Appalachian area, the movement into the Blue Grass region had been well advertised by the hunters who had been seeking deer skins there since the 1760s. By far the most famous of these wanderers and pathfinders was Daniel Boone, prototype of the westward frontiersman, whose talk of

[1] E. J. Payne (ed.), *Burke, Select Works* (Oxford, 1874), I, p. 188.
[2] Richard M. Ketchum (ed.), *The American Heritage Book of the Pioneer Spirit* (New York, 1959), p. 207 and *passim*.

the beauty and the richness of the Kentucky country fired Judge Richard Henderson's imagination and his dream of a colony in the land he called Transylvania. Kentucky remained inaccessible to colonization, nevertheless, since the less valiant lacked the stamina to scale the mountains; and there were other barriers. Even after Boone discovered that at the bottom of a great valley the western mountain wall breaks down into the Cumberland Gap, an open path through the mountains to the interior, settlers still hesitated to move so long as the Shawnees and the Cherokees justified the land's renown as "the dark and bloody ground." With Lord Dunmore's victory in 1774, however, the Indian menace for the time no longer threatened, and in the quarter-century after 1775 there passed through the Cumberland Gap, where later Henry Clay would stand and listen to "the tread of coming millions," some 300,000 restless Americans beckoned by the call of cheap land and the promise of a new life in the lands where no white people had settled before.[3]

Among the pioneers who looked hopefully to the frontier were a group of Catholics in southern Maryland where, in addition to the recent memories of political and religious discrimination, economic conditions were uncertain enough to make them susceptible to the contagion of Kentucky fever. Both in Maryland and in Kentucky it has been traditionally believed that at least sixty Catholic families from St. Mary's, Charles, and Prince George's counties formed neighborhood pacts to emigrate to the West. They were not, however, to go all at once, but within specific periods of time, and they were to settle in the same region in order "to make better provision for the early establishment of a church and to afford mutual protection against the Indians."[4] Thus it was that Catholic laymen, united

[3] *Ibid.*, p. 129 and *passim*.

[4] Sister Mary Ramona Mattingly, *The Catholic Church on the Kentucky Frontier* (*1785–1812*) (Washington, 1936), p. 8.

in what would come to be known as the Maryland Colonization League, were to inaugurate Catholic life in the Old Southwest, and to make Kentucky the cradle of Catholicity in the West. "We shall form a Catholic League," they were later reported to have said, "and we shall hold together for the sake of the Catholic faith. It is strong enough in us to survive, even though we have to wait for years for priests and bishops to come."[5] It was a chapter not unique in the history of American Catholicism where the laity would come first, "a Catholic people calling for their ministers to come among them."[6]

Basil Hayden was the leader of the first of these Maryland pioneers who set out for the West, though it is possible that Peter Abell, Stephen Jarboe, and perhaps Raphael and John Lancaster acted as an advance guard for those who left St. Mary's County in 1785.[7] Soon thereafter other Catholic groups followed, so that before Kentucky was admitted to the Union as the fifteenth state in 1792, there were at least five different colonies of Catholics, all within the vicinity of Bardstown. One of the earliest settlements was that of the Rolling Fork, where Benedict Spalding, who left Leonardtown, Maryland, in 1790 to follow his brother-in-law, Robert Abell, ultimately made his home. Here, in 1797, Spalding purchased six hundred and seventy-nine acres of land in the small river valley on both sides of the Rolling Fork, reserving ninety-five acres which he sold to Father Michael Fournier at two dollars an acre for a church.[8] Later, he bought more than 1,000 acres at a tax sale held by

[5] *The Record* (Louisville), October 9, 1902. John Lancaster Spalding spoke these words at the banquet held in Louisville, October 2, 1902, on the occasion of the golden jubilee in the priesthood of William G. McCloskey, Bishop of Louisville.

[6] Henry J. Browne, "The Layman in Perspective," *Commonweal,* LXIII (February 24, 1956), p. 537.

[7] Mattingly, *op. cit.,* p. 22.

[8] Ben J. Webb, *The Centenary of Catholicity in Kentucky* (Louisville, 1884), pp. 102–110 and *passim.*

27

Sheriff Sam Grundy, and acquired other tracts of land from the state. Characterized as wealthy, intelligent, and highly respected, Spalding was soon prominent in local affairs; he was made a justice of the peace and was several times a member of the Kentucky Legislature. Richard Spalding, his oldest son, married three times and was the father of twenty-one children. In a strange little book which traces the origins of "allied families" of Maryland and Kentucky, Richard Spalding is listed as being at various times a farmer, auctioneer, sheriff, and "guardian and the discounter of notes of his less prosperous neighbors, opprobriously called 'shaving' and then believed to be very sinful." It is said that his pious relations, though they looked to him as their leader, considered him "too devoted to money-making, the fair sex, and general worldliness."[9] His eldest son, Richard M. Spalding, was the father of the future bishop, John Lancaster Spalding.

Little is known of the early years of the younger Richard Spalding. He was born June 7, 1808, in his father's home along the Rolling Fork, in sight of the house that his grandfather had built twenty years before.[10] In all likelihood, he attended classes with his younger brothers Leonard and Martin in the log-cabin school of a certain Mr. Merrywether. Later, Richard and his brothers were among the first to enroll in St. Mary's College, a country school about five miles from the town of Lebanon. It was there in 1821 that Father William Byrne, frustrated in his efforts to teach catechism by the inability of the Kentuckians to read, had resolved to turn an old distillery into a primary school. His main endeavor was to further the religious training of the sons of the Catholic pioneers, to prepare them for their First Holy Communion, but some instruction likewise was to be given in the three Rs. Unfortunately, the college was destroyed by fire in 1822, and Leonard and Richard Spalding

[9] J. W. S. Clements, *Origin of Clements, Spalding and Allied Families of Maryland and Kentucky* (Louisville, 1928), p. 61.

[10] *The Record* (Louisville), October 20, 1883.

returned home; their younger brother, Martin, remained behind to continue his studies with Father Byrne in the school, which was later reconstructed.[11]

To continue their education, Leonard and Richard enrolled in St. Joseph's College in Bardstown, which had come into existence in the Fall of 1819. In time, Richard resolved to study for the priesthood, and on September 8, 1826, he received clerical tonsure at the hands of Bishop Benedict Joseph Flaget, S.S., in St. Joseph's Cathedral in Bardstown.[12] While continuing his studies, Richard taught mathematics at the college, for at the time the seminarians were intermixed with the lay students. Soon after graduating from the new St. Mary's in Lebanon, Martin joined his older brother at St. Joseph's, as did their still younger brother, Benedict Joseph. Since Martin showed unusual ability, Bishop Flaget decided to send him to Rome to complete his theological studies at the Urban College of the Propaganda, and it was planned that Richard should follow at a later time when he was no longer needed at the college.[13]

Apparently, however, the young seminarian was of a different mind. Although Richard Spalding, Sr., was anxious that young Richard and Benedict should follow in Martin's footsteps, less than two months after the latter's arrival in the Eternal City the younger Richard wrote quite emphatically: "I do not desire to go to Rome."[14] Bishop Flaget readily understood, for writing to Martin in the summer of 1831, he said:

[11] J. L. Spalding, *The Life of the Most Rev. M. J. Spalding, D.D., Archbishop of Baltimore* (New York, 1873), p. 23.

[12] University of Notre Dame, Bruté Papers, John B. David to Simon Bruté, Bardstown, November 13, 1826. Hereafter the manuscript collections in this depository will be cited as UND. Cf. also *The Record* (Louisville), July 18, 1912.

[13] Spalding, *op. cit.,* p. 33.

[14] Archives of the Archdiocese of Louisville. Richard M. Spalding to Martin J. Spalding, Bardstown, August 18, 1830. Hereafter these archives will be cited as AAL.

As for Richard, he is still more necessary at the College than Benedict; but he is far from being desirous as his brother to go to Rome. His vocation is not firm and irrevocable. Everyone believes that he will follow Leonard as his model.[15]

Flaget's prophecy proved correct, and not long after Richard abandoned his studies for the priesthood and became a full-time instructor at the college. Not only did he follow Leonard as a model, but on July 22, 1839, he married Mary Jane Lancaster, a sister of Leonard's wife.[16]

Shortly after his marriage, Richard M. Spalding moved with his wife to Lebanon, which was almost in the center of the state, and there he found employment at the Spalding store which had been established by his grandfather in 1813.[17] As early as 1789, a colony of settlers from Campbell County, Virginia, arrived in the knob-hill country. They were all Presbyterians and their first thought, it was said, after building their own primitive homesteads, was to erect a church. Their farms were miles apart and there were no roads, only a few footpaths and a buffalo trail that stretched east and west through the forest and made passage on horseback possible. It was along this trail that the settlers elected to build their house of worship which for many years served all the denominations. Eventually, the buffalo trail became Main Street, and as the settlement grew into a village it was called Lebanon by a certain John Handley, so its early historians wrote, because of the abundance of cedars on the surrounding hills.[18] Lebanon was incorporated into a town in 1815 and at the time had three stores, the first of which had been built by Ben Spalding. Springfield merchants who had been enjoying the business of the Lebanon folk noticed a dif-

[15] AAL, Benedict J. Flaget to Martin J. Spalding, Baltimore, Summer, 1831.

[16] *The Record* (Louisville), October 10, 1907.

[17] Clements, *op. cit.,* p. 61.

[18] The Marion *Falcon* (Lebanon, Kentucky), March 21, 1934.

ference in their trade, but they reassured themselves that these country stores would not last long. They were wrong, however, for Lebanon continued to grow, and in 1818 the town's first bank with a capital of $100,000 was established with Ben Spalding as president.[19]

As Catholic families, primarily from the Rolling Fork settlement, moved into the vicinity of Lebanon, there was need for a house of worship. Just before his departure for Europe on a begging tour in 1814, Father Charles Nerinckx, pioneer missionary and founder of the Sisters of Loretto at the Foot of the Cross, had spoken of Lebanon and his plans for a church there. He called the settlement "an incipient town composed almost entirely of Presbyterians and Catholics," and the strangest thing about the place was the fact that the Presbyterians, anxious for the Catholics to have their church, had already subscribed one-third of the total cost. Nerinckx was anxious about the matter, for he feared lest his Catholic families move on to Springfield, where the moral theology of the Dominican friars at St. Rose-Priory was too lenient for his taste. On his return from Europe, Nerinckx pushed forward the construction of St. Hubert's, the name he intended for the church, but as he again went off to Europe the following year, it was left to Father David A. Deparcq to finish the edifice which was eventually dedicated under the title of St. Augustine's.[20]

By 1840, Lebanon could boast of an "urban population" of 750.[21] It was on June 2 of the same year that Richard Spalding's wife, Mary Jane Lancaster, gave birth to their first child, a son, whom they named John Lancaster after his maternal grandfather who had died the year before. Ten days later, on June 12,

---

[19] Clements, op. cit., p. 61.

[20] Samuel J. Boldrick, "Bishop and Priests," St. Mary's Sentinel, XXXV (November, 1915), p. 54. This issue of the Sentinel commemorated the centenary of St. Augustine's Church, Lebanon, Kentucky.

[21] The Marion Falcon (Lebanon, Kentucky), March 21, 1934.

1840, the infant was baptized at St. Augustine's by Father Augustus Thébaud, S.J., who frequently attended the congregation while the pastor, Father Deparcq, visited the other mission stations in his care.[22] Life as a merchant was evidently not to Spalding's liking, and in 1843 he moved his family to a farm two miles distant from the town on the road to Springfield. It was at Evergreen Bend, as the farm was called, therefore, that John Lancaster spent his early years. There are few, if any, records of the Spalding household for those years, but it was probably typical of the Kentucky Catholics described by Thébaud when he reminisced:

I often visited them in their homes, and was the happy witness of their virtues. It was impossible not to be struck with their simple and unaffected manners. It would have been difficult to find a single one of their houses in which prayers were not recited in common every evening. On Sundays all those who could leave the house went to church; and it was a pleasure to see around the sacred edifice, often in the woods, or at some crossroad, hundreds of horses tied to the trees or to a fence whilst the riders, men, women and children, were devoutly hearing Mass or listening to the sermon. . . .[23]

[22] Archives of St. Augustine's Church, Lebanon. Register of Baptisms, Book I, 1835–1899, p. 17. Local tradition varies as to the actual location of Spalding's birthplace. Some maintain he was born in the frame house that was razed years ago to make way for the high school in Lebanon; others claim the site of the old Masonic Lodge. Catherine Lancaster, Spalding's maternal grandmother, and David A. Deparcq, the pastor, were the godparents. Deparcq was born in Belgium in 1795, came to America in 1818, and was ordained at Bardstown in 1819. He labored in the Kentucky missions for forty-four years, and died in 1864. Thébaud was born in Nantes, France, in 1807; ordained a secular priest, he entered the Society of Jesus in Rome in 1835. In 1839 he came to Kentucky and labored at St. Mary's College, outside Lebanon, where in 1846 he was made rector. When the Jesuits left St. Mary's, Thébaud became rector of St. John's College, later Fordham, in New York, where he died in 1885.

[23] Augustus J. Thébaud, S.J., *Forty Years in the United States of America (1839–1885)* (New York, 1904), pp. 89–90.

32

Childhood, it has been said, is all heritage, a dowry of personality. For many people a consciousness of childhood means very little beyond a vague and half-erased memory, while for others it is an overture to real performance, full of promise and anticipation of the future. For young John, or Lank, as he was called, his early years were a time of untroubled happiness, and the past would ever remain in the period of a troubled maturity the essential picture of his true and valid self. While the Spalding household was a happy one which John Lancaster would often recall in quite sentimental prose, the intense family spirit that prevailed at Evergreen Bend was, perhaps, akin to the spirit that the English Catholics brought with them first to Maryland and thence to Kentucky, and which has been called a heritage that was "both their strength and their weakness:"

> Their strength . . . since . . . it provided the theater for those noble cultural developments, which, in turn, gave birth to great statesmen like the Carrolls, jurists like Taney, prelates like Archbishop Carroll and the Spaldings, religious women like Mother Hardey. . . . Their weakness since the family tended to become self-centered . . . and by reason of its very intimacy and perfection, the family tended to discourage effective social development. . . .[24]

Many years later, the future Bishop would write of his great fortune in having brought "into the life-struggle pure memories of a happy home." Yet even as he wrote, he would remark that there was the desolate feeling that "he had lived in paradise

[24] John LaFarge, S.J., "The Survival of the Catholic Faith in Southern Maryland," *Catholic Historical Review*, XXI (April, 1935), p. 7. John Carroll (1735–1815) was the first bishop of Baltimore and later the first archbishop when in 1808 Baltimore became an archdiocese. Roger Brooke Taney (1777–1864) succeeded John Marshall as Chief Justice of the United States. Mother Aloysia Hardey, related to the Spaldings through her mother, was at the time of her death in 1886 an assistant mother general of the Society of the Sacred Heart.

and had been driven forth into a bleak world."[25] If a happy childhood means more than a childhood paradise, then here was the essential weakness for Spalding, and his early years were a mere idyll before real life became, as it were, only a temporary shelter from the raw reality that is existence.

As a small boy, Lank is said to have been sickly and little given to play; yet in the Kentucky tradition, he and his younger brother Richard became in time expert horsemen.[26] He was the favorite of his Uncle Martin, who after a brilliant career as a student in Rome had returned to Kentucky in 1834. When John was only a boy of eight his uncle was consecrated, on September 10, 1848, as coadjutor bishop to the beloved Flaget. "I shall never forget," John wrote as a young priest, "the pleasant journeys, which, when quite a small boy, I had the happiness to make with him." Frequently, he accompanied his uncle on episcopal visitations of the diocese, recalling in later years "with what warmth and reverence and love he was received everywhere, and how his presence was never connected in my mind with anything morose or severe."[27]

The earliest schooling that the youngster had was from his mother, who had been the first graduate of Loretto Academy in 1837. It was she, he would always remember, who turned his thoughts to the world of spiritual things, who taught him that men were born upon this earth for no other purpose than "to know truth, to love goodness, to do right, that so, having made ourselves god-like, we may forever be with God."[28]

[25] J. L. Spalding, *Education and the Higher Life* (Chicago, 1890), p. 151.

[26] Interview of Sister Mary Evangela Henthorne, B.V.M., in 1929 with Mother Henrietta Spalding, R.S.C. Cf. Henthorne, "The Life and Career of Bishop John Lancaster Spalding" (Urbana, 1930), p. 7, microfilm copy.

[27] Spalding, *Life of the Most Rev. M. J. Spalding,* p. 223.

[28] Spalding, *Education and the Higher Life,* p. 151.

At the age of twelve, John left home for the first time, and in September, 1852, entered St. Mary's College on the outskirts of Lebanon.[29] The Jesuits who had been in charge of St. Mary's from 1833 had left the diocese in 1846, and thereafter the college was administered by the few secular priests who could be spared amid the pressing needs of a missionary diocese. Still little more than a preparatory school, the "college" curriculum ranged from the primary grades to the high school level. During the tenure of the Jesuits at St. Mary's, Thébaud had observed of his Kentucky students:

All our Western boys wanted to shine as orators. In their estimation, no one in the whole world was superior to the great Henry Clay or to John C. Calhoun. If they thought they could not aspire to so high a place, they wished at least to shine in their native country among those who knew them. . . .[30]

To encourage the boys in this endeavor, the fathers had organized a debating club which bore the ponderous name, "The Philomanthian Society for the Improvement of the Students in Oratory," an honor society which admitted students only after two years at the College. On December 6, 1855, the students reorganized the society, and on this occasion Lancaster Spalding was elected recording secretary while the post of

[29] Archives of St. Mary's College, St. Mary, Kentucky. Records of the Philomanthian Society. All the evidence points to the fact that Spalding attended St. Mary's from 1852–1857. It is safe to say that he never attended St. Joseph's College, his father's alma mater, in Bardstown. Professor Alphonse Lesousky, the archivist at St. Mary's, is certain that the Bardstown School would have claimed Spalding as an alumnus if he had spent one semester there. The present writer found varying reports on Spalding's attendance at St. Joseph's, and there was the name of a John L. Spalding in the lists of those receiving premiums at various exercises for 1846 and 1848. There is, however, no evidence that the aforesaid is the subject of this biography. Hereafter the archives of St. Mary's will be cited as ASt.M.

[30] Thébaud, op. cit., p. 337.

treasurer went to his friend and fellow townsman David Russell. It was the same month in which John debated the question: "Which has caused most misery to mankind, War or Intemperance?"—the future temperance advocate successfully defending the latter.[31] At the society's spring elections in the following year, John Spalding was chosen president, and at the next meeting David Russell, now the recording secretary, dutifully noted: "Lancaster Spalding gave his inaugural address. It would have done honor to more experienced speakers."[32] Sometime later, Lank ended his first term in office, and the minutes stated:

> The President, Lank Spalding, then delivered his valedictory in his usual ciceronian manner, and as some of the members have lately withdrawn, he gave us every encouragement to continue and keep up the former fame of the society. Showing us the many advantages which are derived from such an organization, he at last descended from his stand in the midst of enthusiastic cheering.[33]

In his senior year at St. Mary's, Spalding assumed the role of prefect for the younger boys and also acted as an assistant teacher. There is a tradition at St. Mary's, however, that young Spalding was not always amenable to college discipline himself. Proud and sensitive, ever conscious that he was a Spalding and that a Spalding was the bishop, he had, so it was believed, settled ideas on many subjects and not infrequently clashed with both superiors and equals. In his early years at the college, beset with homesickness, he more than once ran off to Evergreen Bend. Even as a senior, he evidently asserted his spirit of independence, though often enough in a refreshingly normal way, since on October 24, 1856, the daybook read: "All present except Mr. Lank Spalding who has taken his flight to the Bardstown Fair."[34] Spalding persisted nonetheless, and on July

[31] A St. M., Records of the Philomanthian Society, December, 1855.
[32] Ibid., p. 169.
[33] Ibid., p. 172.
[34] Ibid., p. 189

2, 1857, he graduated from St. Mary's, and with a classmate, William Burke, took part in the graduation debate on the question: "What is necessary to make this permanently a truly great and flourishing country?" Prizes were then awarded, and while the band played the "Congratulation Song," composed for the occasion, Lank Spalding advanced to the center of the stage in Philomathian Hall to receive first honors from Father Peter J. Lavialle, President of the college.[35]

After spending the summer at Evergreen Bend, young Spalding again left his family home, this time to continue his education at Mount St. Mary's College in Emmitsburg, Maryland. It was here in the beautiful valley of the Blue Ridge on the eastern prominence of the Catoctin Spur that Father John Dubois, abandoning his plan to establish a home for old and ailing priests, had established the *petit séminaire* which was to develop into a college and major seminary. When John Lancaster arrived at Emmitsburg in August, 1857, the "Old Mountain" school, as it was to be called, was nearing its golden jubilee under the firm guiding hand of its seventh president, Father John McCaffrey. Classes began in early September with one hundred and sixty boys in the college and twenty-eight in the seminary.[36] Shortly after, Lank wrote to his mother:

I have been waiting for some time for letter writing day in order that I might have time to write you a long letter. . . . To begin with, I feel well, better than I have felt for two years. I am no longer the frail specimen of humanity I was when last you saw me but I have grown to be a robust hardy mountaineer . . . As to my education, I think I might say that I am learning very fast. My mind is developing itself. And what I saw confusedly is now becoming clear as the crystal light

[35] *Ibid. A Catalogue of the Officers and Students of St. Mary's College, Near Lebanon, Ky., for the Academic Year, 1856–1857* (Louisville, 1857), pp. 5–16. The total number of students for the academic year, 1856–1857, was 149.

[36] Mary M. Meline and Edward F. X. McSweeney. *The Story of the Mountain* (Emmitsburg, 1911), I, p. 527 and *passim*.

of day . . . I have received today a letter from Rich [Richard] . . . He says he heard I was not satisfied. I cannot have imagined how this can have reached him. He must have dreampt it. Or I think he has merely devised this by way of exordium to a piece of sage advice which he gives me, "Study hard, Lanc, and you will never regret the time spent." . . .[37]

Some weeks later, Lank described the many improvements that were then being made at the Emmitsburg school—a recently completed stone building contained a dormitory, refectory, and some private rooms. If all went well, they would move into the new building at Christmas. It was to be his first Christmas away from home, and while his parents suggested he spend the holidays with his distant relatives, the Lancasters of southern Maryland, he did not think well of the idea since, as he said, "the connection is to [sic] remote (if there is any at all) to render it proper that I should go there without knowing any of them." He preferred to spend the vacation either at the college or at home, but he left the choice to his parents. There were busy days ahead, he continued, "since I am one of the speakers upon Saint John's day, one of the greatest collegiate festivals, since the name of the Pres. and the Vice-Pres. is John." He therefore begged to be excused if his letters were not four pages long.[38]

Spalding's first Christmas away from home was also to be his last at Emmitsburg. On January 14, four days after the students had moved into the new building, there occurred what has been called the "rebellion of '58," and apparently Lank was involved. One of the students had smuggled what was regarded as an immoral book into the house and had been caught. After the collegians had retired for the night, the prefects,

[37] UND, Spalding Papers, Lancaster Spalding to Mrs. Richard M. Spalding, Emmitsburg, November 11, 1857.

[38] *Ibid.*, Lanc. J. Spalding to Mrs. R. M. Spalding, Emmitsburg, December 2, 1857. John McCaffrey became the seventh president in March, 1838, and served until April, 1872. John McCloskey, vice-president of the college since February, 1842, succeeded McCaffrey as president in November, 1872.

students of the seminary, had searched the desks of all the students for other contraband. In the morning the search of the previous night was, of course, found out, and some of the students immediately got indignant and formed a committee that called upon the president, Father McCaffrey. The students formally demanded of him a promise that further searches of this kind would not take place without first informing the student body and asking for their keys like gentlemen. McCaffrey, renowned as a stern disciplinarian, not only refused to be dictated to, but ordered the protesting committee to be sent to the "Jug." With this, the rebellion began. A large number of students stampeded from the campus into the village and there, in comic-opera style, formed a regiment and marched on the college. However, the revolt was quickly suppressed by the remaining loyalists under the leadership of Uncle Bush Althoff, blacksmith to the Mountain, whom Father McCaffrey dubbed "the noblest Roman of them all." In the sequel, the leaders of the "rebellion of '58" were expelled, and forty-five sympathizers left with them in protest. Of these, nearly all were sent back to the college by their parents. Whether Lank Spalding was one of the ten leaders expelled, or whether he was one of the sympathizers, is not known. It is certain, however, that he left Mount St. Mary's on January 18, 1858, never to return.[39]

There is no record that, in the months that followed, Spalding attended any other school. More than likely, he remained home at Evergreen Bend until September 1, 1858, when he entered Mount St. Mary's of the West in Cincinnati.[40] Only two years

[39] *The Catholic Mirror* (Baltimore), January 30, 1858. Cf. also Catholic University of America, Ellis Papers, Hugh J. Phillips to John Tracy Ellis, Emmitsburg, October 26, 1843. Spalding "entered the Mountain on 22nd August, 1857 and left in Jan. 18, 1858. It seems . . . he was mixed in some student trouble and was expelled."

[40] Archives of the Archdiocese of Cincinnati, "Day Book to 1878," no pagination. Under date: 1858, September 1, Spalding, John L. Lebanon, Ky. Hereafter these archives will be cited as AAC.

before, September 15, 1856, the "junior" Mount, as it was called, had opened its doors, with the hope that its close proximity to the seminary of the same name would be a means of fostering vocations to the priesthood. Shortly after Lank departed for Cincinnati, a letter appeared in the Louisville *Guardian* which seemed to reflect on the recently established college in Cincinnati, and, so some maintained, on a newly enrolled student from Kentucky. A number of Catholic newspapers had carried as an advertisement the prospectus of Mount St. Mary's of the West for the school year beginning September, 1858, which read in part: "The discipline of the college is paternal and vigilant—the object being to Guide rather than to Drive along the Path of Duty."[41] A correspondent of the *Guardian*, known only by the initials S.M.C. with the address of Lebanon, Kentucky, took sharp exception to the statement. Attributing the kindness of the professors at Cincinnati to their need for students, S.M.C. caustically continued:

If a good-for-nothing idle disposition should happen to be the most distinguishing feature in a young man's character, and should he become discontented with college life, all in the world to be done is to write an exaggerated (or vulgarly speaking, a lying) statement of how matters are conducted at the college to good natured "Old America," mentioning at the same time that it is "Young America's" intention to leave the 'darned old college.' This is sufficient; without further inquiry "Old America" gets into a thundering passion with the President, the professors and teachers of said college and the dear boy is hastily taken home to recover his spirits and recruit his shattered health . . . At length his father, thinking it would not pay to have "Young America" doing nothing but loafing, determines to send the boy to another college (lately established), where his feelings will be better respected than heretofore and where the good professors will not want to 'drive' but to lead the young gentleman along the flowery paths of knowledge and virtue. . . .[42]

[41] *The Catholic Telegraph* (Cincinnati), September 4, 1858.
[42] *The Guardian* (Louisville), September 11, 1858.

A reply was soon forthcoming. A professor of the Western college, who identified himself as "One Who Can Be Kind Without a Motive," answered the attack in the *Catholic Telegraph and Advocate*.[43] Strangely enough, young Spalding also took the opportunity to reply to S.M.C., but in another way. On September 15, 1858, the second anniversary of the Cincinnati college was celebrated with a free day. After the morning was spent in noisy recreation, an assembly of the faculty and students was held in the hall beneath the chapel. First, the "Mountain Hymn" was sung in procession; then the president, Father Sylvester H. Rosecrans, spoke to the students, asking God's blessing on them and their work during the coming year. He then called on John Lancaster Spalding to make a brief address—an extraordinary if not auspicious introduction of a new student to his professors and fellow students. Spalding seized the occasion to respond to the critic from Lebanon in an eloquent defense of "Young America" and his new alma mater. He stressed the need for discipline in any college and its effects on the minds and hearts of the students, but he was at pains to emphasize that a more cheerful atmosphere was produced by a system of kindness and affection, by an obedience that was engendered without any element of sternness or harshness. This, he said, was to be one of the superior attractions of the new Mount St. Mary's; hence the "fullness which the College promised to the Catholic educational need." Reminding the audience of their duty to Mount St. Mary's of the West, Lank Spalding concluded with an oratorical flourish:

Then considering all her advantages, I may safely say our College will prove more beneficial than the mines of California. For she will send forth not corrupting metal but the priceless jewels of knowledge to enlighten and make our people better . . . She shall be called a second Trojan horse from which leaders will go forth to burn and obliterate—

[43] *The Catholic Telegraph* (Cincinnati), September 18, 1858.

41

not cities—but vice and crime, not with fire and sword but by the power of the immortal mind.[44]

It was, surely, an unusual speech from a student who had not been in the institution more than two weeks. In the stilted phrases and exaggerated figures of speech one might perhaps, see the embryonic writer striving to learn the might and scope of the English language. But beneath it all it was not difficult to discern in the boy of eighteen the forthrightness that was to characterize the mature man.

Spalding's year in Cincinnati was a busy one. The course of studies had recently been revised; and as a senior in the classical program, he attended classes in logic, metaphysics, and ethics, studied the Latin of Tacitus and Juvenal, the Greek of Thucydides and Sophocles, together with mathematics and chemistry.[45] Yet, despite the pressure of many classes, he found time to write. During the first semester, he published an essay in the Louisville *Guardian* entitled, "God, the Source of True Love," which was soon followed by another on "The True Patriot," and yet another on "Adversity, Often a Real Blessing."[46] On October 13, 1858, he and his fellow students attended the celebration of the silver episcopal jubilee of John Baptist Purcell, Archbishop of Cincinnati. For Lank Spalding, it also meant a visit with his favorite Uncle Martin, who as Bishop of Louisville had come to the Mount to pay honor to his metropolitan.

At Mount St. Mary's of the West, unlike the institutions he had attended at Lebanon and Emmitsburg, there was no record or tradition that Spalding proved to be in any way a

[44] Michael J. Kelly and James M. Kirwin, *History of Mt. St. Mary's Seminary of the West, Cincinnati, Ohio* (Cincinnati, 1894), pp. 109–110.

[45] AAC, Record Book I, Meeting of the Faculty, July 1, 1858.

[46] *The Guardian* (Louisville), September 9, October 9, November 6, 1858.

42

disciplinary problem. With the end of the second semester, the faculty voted that "Mr. John Lancaster Spalding be designated Valedictorian of the graduating class," and nominated him for the rhetorical honor.[47] Graduation exercises were held June 30, 1859, and after a Solemn Mass celebrated by Father Rosecrans the graduates received their degrees of bachelor of arts from the president in the presence of Archbishop Purcell. It was on that day that the college historians noted that Spalding said farewell to Mount St. Mary's of the West with "his graceful and touching valedictory, 'The Spirit of English Literature'."[48]

There is no record of the date when Lancaster Spalding resolved to follow the paths of his uncles, Martin and Benedict, but shortly after graduation from college, he began to make plans to study for the priesthood. It was a resolve that may, indeed, have come only after a long period of time, but his intention had become focused during his year at Cincinnati. In his first published essay, the eighteen-year-old had written:

All things in this world are sought more eagerly than enjoyed because possession carries within itself its own principle of destruction. Whatever we seek that has its beginning and end in this world seems desirable to us only because the mind in its delusion invests it with beauties that it has not. Love, wealth, fondness for fame—all desires that animate men in their desire and pursuit of happiness can satisfy for a time but in Him and in Him alone can the cravings of the heart for love be satisfied.[49]

If there had been much musing along these lines, it is not difficult to see how under the personal guidance of his uncle, the bishop, Lank Spalding should have become a candidate for the Diocese of Louisville. Martin was naturally pleased, and he told Archbishop Purcell late that summer: "I am sending my

[47] AAC, Record Book of Mt. St. Mary's of the West, June 25, 1859.
[48] Kelly-Kirwin, *op. cit.*, pp. 126–127.
[49] *The Guardian* (Louisville), September 9, 1858.

43

nephew, J. Lancaster Spalding, to Louvain."[50] Only two years before, the newly established American College of the Immaculate Conception had opened its doors to train priests for the missions of the Catholic Church in the United States. Largely through the zeal of the elder Spalding and of Bishop Peter Lefevere, the Coadjutor Bishop of Detroit, the idea of an American college in Belgium had become a reality.[51] "A hundred young men educated at Louvain for the American Missions!" Bishop Spalding had written some seven years before. "Is not the thought enlivening? And yet, it is very far from impossible. . . ."[52]

The day of departure soon arrived for John Lancaster. After fond farewells with the family, he travelled to Cincinnati to spend one last day at his alma mater with Father Rosecrans and his friends, and there he was joined by his mother and Uncle Martin for the trip to New York.[53] Young Spalding sailed on September 24, 1859, in the company of two priests from the Diocese of Louisville, Francis Chambige and Patrick Bambury.[54]

[50] UND, Cincinnati Papers, II-4-0, Spalding to Purcell, Louisville, September 2, 1859.

[51] J. Van der Heyden, *The Louvain American College* (Louvain, 1909), pp. 9–21.

[52] Spalding, *Life of the Most Rev. M. J. Spalding,* p. 163.

[53] Archives of the Archdiocese of Baltimore, 37–E–7, Martin J. Spalding to Mary Jane Spalding, Louisville, August 19, 1859. Hereafter these archives will be cited as AAB.

[54] AAB, Martin J. Spalding to Francis Patrick Kenrick, New York City, September 25, 1859. Francis Chambige was born November 16, 1807, near Clermont, France, came to America in 1825, and was ordained in 1834. Besides missionary work in various counties of Kentucky, he taught for a time at St. Joseph's College, Bardstown, and was for nineteen years director of St. Thomas' Seminary. In 1869 he took up residence at Nazareth Convent where he died on December 30, 1877. All that is known of Patrick Bambury is that he was suffering from consumption when he made the trip to Europe where he died shortly after his arrival.

44

Chambige accompanied Lank as far as Paris, where they parted company when Spalding took the train to Brussels and thence proceeded to Louvain by coach. He arrived in Louvain on October 12, 1859, the last student to arrive for the new term and the last to be admitted by the first rector of the college, Father Peter Kindekens.[55]

The late arrival was greeted by his old friend David Russell, who had been the first American to enter the college. There were fifteen seminarians, and classes began almost immediately. Spalding's talent, especially his aptitude for languages, soon became apparent to the faculty, and it was decided that he should follow the *cours profondes* of the *schola major,* that is, the higher courses in the Catholic University of Louvain. After hearing from his nephew, the Bishop of Louisville told the young man's father: "I am glad that Lancaster is well & so well satisfied." Strangely enough, in the light of the "rebellion of '58," only one item seemed to bother the new seminarian at Louvain —a desire for stricter discipline. It was a situation that Martin Spalding assured his brother would soon be corrected, since, as he said, "a new rector has just been appointed & has probably already entered on his office."[56] He was referring to the fact that a month previously Father John De Nève, pastor of St. Francis of Assisi Parish in Niles, Michigan, had been informed by Bishop Lefevere that he had been chosen to continue the work

[55] Archives of the American College of the Immaculate Conception, Louvain, Liber C., October 12, 1859. The writer is grateful to the Reverend John Sauter of the Archdiocese of Cincinnati for examining these archives for references to Spalding. Before assuming the foundation of the American College, Kindekens had served as vicar-general of the Diocese of Detroit. Hereafter these archives will be cited as AAC-L.

[56] AAB, 37-E-13, Martin J. Spalding to Richard Spalding, Louisville, December 24, 1859.

45

which Peter Kindekens had begun.[57] A week later, Bishop Spalding informed Lank's father with great enthusiasm:

> I am now more and more convinced that Louvain is the very place for him. The atmosphere & diet will develop his constitution and make him strong . . . while the intellectual food will be the very thing he needs & is adapted for. When he will have finished at Louvain, it is my intention to send him for a year to Rome, where, without being under the rigid discipline of the Colleges, he may be able to study the antiquities and perfect himself. . . . For this purpose it will probably be necessary for him to be previously ordained at Louvain; so that he may be more free in his movements. God grant that he may persevere. In any event, I intend to spare no expense to bring him out with all possible advantages, more greater even than I had. . . .[58]

Lank's first year at the American College has been characterized by the historian of the institution as the "great year," for in December, 1859, the new rector, De Nève, arrived in Belgium to build firmly on the foundation laid by Father Kindekens.[59]

Little is known of Spalding's activities during his initial year at the seminary, for as he himself later remarked: "The life of a seminarian is necessarily uneventful." From his rising early at dawn to his going to rest at night, everything was fixed by rule, and thus, he wrote, the seminarian "prays, meditates, assists at Mass, studies, goes to class, takes recreation, at the same hours, day by day, year in and year out."[60] A view quite prosaic perhaps, and not necessarily an inaccurate one, but at the time it

[57] Van der Heyden, *op. cit.,* p. 64. De Nève, second rector of the American College, had been in the United States three years as a priest of the Diocese of Detroit. He began his first administration of the College in January, 1860, and served until 1871; after a lapse of a decade he was again rector during the years 1881–1891.

[58] AAB, 38-E-14, Spalding to Spalding, Louisville, December 30, 1859.

[59] Van der Heyden, *op. cit.,* p. 84.

[60] J. L. Spalding, Introduction to James J. McGovern, *The Life and Writing of the Rt. Rev. John McMullen* (Chicago, 1888), p. xviii.

was written it was the view of a man who, approaching the middle years, had become somewhat disenchanted and would cry out: "*Ego dixi in dimidio dierum meorum, vadam ad portas inferi. . . .*"[61]

There were, undoubtedly, in Spalding's years at the American College events that were of more than passing interest at the time, for in the life of every seminarian little things often loom large and give color to what in later life may be the remembrance of a happy existence. During the first Spring vacation, Lank and David Russell travelled to Germany[62] and on their return shared in the joy of seeing William Wiseman, the first Irish student at the college and its first student to be ordained to the priesthood, celebrate his first Mass in the college chapel. When the new academic year opened in October, 1860, two new professors greeted the students, Florimond De Bruycker and Canon Charles Van Kerckhove. De Bruycker became the vice-rector while Van Kerckhove, preparing for the Louvain doctorate, lectured on sacred Scripture. Amid the crowded hours of the seminary schedule, Spalding found time to write the words of the first college song, which was set to music by another candidate for Louisville, Alphonsus M. Coenen.[63] In December of that year, Lank went on retreat in preparation for tonsure and minor orders, and on December 22, 1860, he entered the clerical state with eight other students who were promoted to sacred orders in the church of the Dominicans, Notre Dame aux Dominicains. By permission of Engelbert Cardinal Sterckx of Malines, the ordaining prelate was John Theodore Laurent, formerly Vicar Apostolic of Luxembourg and now titular Bishop of Chersones.[64] And on the same day, David Russell was ordained

[61] *Ibid.,* p. xxi.

[62] *The Guardian* (Louisville), April 28, 1860.

[63] Van der Heyden, *op. cit.,* p. 90.

[64] AAC-L, Liber C., December 22, 1860.

to the priesthood. "Praise be God's Holy Name," exclaimed Bishop Spalding of Louisville, "for the blessings showered upon an institution that has begun to 'reap in joy'."[65]

In the Spring of 1861, Lank elected to spend his Easter vacation at the college. He was well and content, he told his uncle-bishop, and could not ask for anything more than to serve God, except to serve Him better. He informed his uncle that he had just written to his brother Richard to say that he expected him to come to Louvain after graduation from Mount St. Mary's of the West, for, as he said, "it is certain that if we try we can have American priests enough for our diocese."[66] But the companionship of his brother was not to be one of John Lancaster's joys at Louvain. On June 12, 1861, Richard Clement Spalding had graduated from the Cincinnati College, and like his older brother he had won the rhetorical honor. Before returning to Lebanon, the youth decided to spend a few days with his seminarian friends. Three days after graduation, while swimming in the Ohio River, Richard was drowned during a storm in a futile attempt to save his companion, Maurice Garde.[67] Bishop Spalding had been in Cincinnati for the graduation exercises, and with a heavy heart he wrote to the boy's mother: "I should have taken Richard with me."[68] Years later, John Lancaster recalled this family tragedy:

. . . the first time death came within the circle of those I knew and loved. It seemed to me to be an absurdity, an impossibility, a contradiction of the nature of things. All, as the world revealed itself to me, was

[65] Van der Heyden, *op. cit.,* p. 128.

[66] AAB, 37-A-1, Spalding to Spalding, American College, Louvain, April 2, 1861.

[67] *The Catholic Telegraph* (Cincinnati), June 15, 1861.

[68] AAB, 37-E-21, Martin J. Spalding to Mary Jane Spalding, Louisville, June 17, 1861. AAB, 37-E-22, Same to Same, Louisville, June 20, 1861. In the latter the bishop remarked, "I have written to J. Lancaster about the sad affair."

life or related to life, and when I was forced to try to reconcile this view with the presence of death, I was stunned and stupefied.[69]

Saddened by the sudden tragedy, Lank reflected his heartache in the journal or diary which he had begun to keep shortly after the reception of tonsure and minor orders. "Live to die" was to be his constant refrain in the pages of what he called a *"Libellus Conscientiae vel Luminum,"* for, as he put it, "the philosophy of death is the philosophy of life."[70] It was not an unusual sentiment for a seminarian far from home whose sensitivity was tinged with a melancholy that pervaded his entire being.

After a time, classes and community life helped revive Lank's spirits as he entered on his third year at the college. There were twenty students now, one of whom was to be a lifelong friend, Patrick W. Riordan of Chicago, the future Archbishop of San Francisco. The year also saw the birth of *The Missionary,* a short-lived school paper directed by Father David Russell, who had returned to the college after ordination to teach the courses in English.[71] In the middle of the year, Spalding fell prey to worry, first about his health, then about the public trial he would undergo at the close of the semester for his bachelor's degree in theology. As the semester drew to an end, he recorded reflections that seem to suggest an inner struggle. And yet they were the kind of thoughts that occur to many students as they approach the priesthood.

[69] J. L. Spalding, Introduction to Peter M. Abbelen, *Venerable Mother M. Caroline Freiss . . . A Sketch of her Life and Character* (St. Louis, 1893), p. 11.

[70] Archives of the Diocese of Peoria, Journal of J. Lancaster Spalding, 1861–1867. The writer is indebted to Monsignor Robert C. Peters, editor of the Peoria edition of *The Register,* who informed him through the late Baldwin Schulte, O.F.M., formerly pastor of Sacred Heart Parish, Peoria, of the existence of the diary. Hereafter these archives will be cited as ADP.

[71] Van der Heyden, *op. cit.,* p. 107

... I almost feel like losing heart. When I think that I am here three years and apparently as ignorant of myself as in the beginning! But with the grace of Jesus, I will never despair of success. ... Why be proud of a great reputation? It is so rare that it is due to our merit. Occasion, hazard, defect of competition, caprice of the public, some external advantages accompanied with much presumption, birth, rank, favor, intrigue—such are the things which make great reputations. Humility, humility, if I had the world I would give it for thee.[72]

It was the want of humility, he continued, that earmarked all heresiarchs, of whom the majority had been priests of God, and he prayed, therefore, for the grace ever to preach Christ and not himself. He was often tempted, after almost three years away from home, to ask permission to leave; but he knew it was the result of fatigue and the desire for distraction. He resolved, therefore, "never again to listen to this temptation."[73]

The day of the public defense of his thesis was at last upon him. Spalding had as his subject, "The Divine Inspiration of the Scriptures," upon which he spoke before the rector of the American College, his professors, and fellow students. His principal antagonist was his classmate, Gustave Limpens. Fortunately, the manuscript edition of *The Missionary* recorded the proceedings. After noting that Spalding and his fellow contenders seemed to be "a little nervous," the writer continued in military parlance:

The defendant, Mr. Spalding, first stationed himself behind a strong breastwork of preliminaries showing the opponents how dangerous it would be to transgress the limits indicated. He then shook his fist through a porthole at Mr. Limpens and dared him to attack. Mr. Limpens immediately began to sap the foundations and would probably have overturned the whole structure of defense had not the professor stuck his head out above the walls and told him that he was not allowed to carry on the war on that system. Sapping the walls of the fortresses, he said, was an antiquated method of warfare. At present it was only al-

[72] ADP, Journal, June, 1862; there is no pagination to the manuscript journal.

[73] *Ibid.,* June, 1862.

lowed to cast shells over the walls. Mr. Limpens had not prepared any shells so he could only throw over what little grape-shot he had brought along. The other opponent marched right up to the breastworks, and thought to frighten Mr. Spalding out of his citadel by force of numbers, crying out repeatedly that he was more than 600,000 strong besides the women and children he had along. Ed. note—Our correspondent does not say what was the result of the fight. We are inclined, however, to believe that the defendant could never have been induced to quit his fortifications as he seemed to have a horror of a field engagement. We believe that neither party was injured beyond, perhaps, some slight scratches. *Hic spatium deficit.*[74]

Spalding came through the examination successfully, and with Jean B. Abbeloos, Henry Gabriels, Gustave Limpens, and Jean F. Van Rossum, he received the bachelor's degree in sacred theology on July 7, 1862.[75] Retreat for the subdiaconate began ten days later, and afforded him another opportunity for self-analysis and scrutiny of his spiritual state. The customary doubts, discouragements, and temptations appeared again, but his chief anxiety centered on his lack of humility. "There is," he wrote, "a secret seed of pride in my heart. . . . It is useless to hide it to myself, to deceive my own heart: I am proud and if misery ever comes upon me that will be the cause."[76] It was a noble admission, but it did not kill his spirit, for several days later in quite another vein Spalding recorded a sentiment that was to be characteristic of his entire life:

[74] AAC-L, *The Missionary,* I (n.d., no. 8), p. 12.

[75] *L'Annuaire de l'Université Catholique de Louvain, 1863* (Louvain, 1863), p. 155. In the list of students for the year 1862, Spalding's name appeared as a subdeacon from the Diocese of St. Louis. Limpens was ordained in 1863 for the Diocese of Detroit. Gabriels became the second Bishop of Ogdensburg in September, 1891. The future Monsignor Abbeloos became in 1887 the Rector of the Catholic University of Louvain, a post which he held until his resignation in 1900. Van Rossum was not identifiable.

[76] ADP, Journal, July 17, 1862.

My God, I will not care what men say, let them say what they will, let them think as they please. With thy grace I will serve Thee for no man is my judge but Thou alone my God. Oh God, I implore Thee, give me the grace to be independent and to serve Thee with a free and fearless heart. Let cowards fear man; I wish to fear Thee alone.[77]

On July 21, he made his general confession to the retreat master and promised to despise all scruples about his past. "*Factum est,*" he wrote.[78] On the eve of the trip to Malines, the doubts seemed to have vanished, and with a note of determination he observed:

I am to become a priest . . . I see now clearly as I see that I live that it is folly and madness to become a priest unless I acquire piety and fervor in thy service. Then with thy grace, come what will, I will become pious and fervent. If I must neglect all my studies, it is well. If I must injure my health, it is well. Health is only good in as much as it helps us to serve Thee. A Saint need not be a Doctor of Theology. . . . I know how weak I am. I know I will fall often. . . . I, myself, am my own greatest enemy. Therefore, I will fight hardest against my pride; it is a terrible foe and I tremble when I think of it. My second enemy are my own scruples, a fearful, melancholy foe. I have fought long against the monster and I never gained the victory. Now I commence with new strength and courage and promise to fight at least till one of us is dead.[79]

Spalding was ordained a subdeacon on July 26, 1862, by Cardinal Sterckx in the cathedral at Malines,[80] and shortly after he told his father and mother: "I am a Subdeacon, must say my breviary every day and with the grace of God can never get married; yet I do not ask anyone to weep over my fate. What I did, I did freely . . . and if there be anything for which I thank God with my whole soul, it is for this, that he gave me the grace to consecrate my life to him." It was easy for him to detect the note of sadness in the communications from home. The death of

[77] *Ibid.,* Sixth Meditation: On Death.
[78] *Ibid.,* July 21, 1862.
[79] *Ibid.,* Conclusion of Retreat.
[80] AAC-L, Liber C., July 26, 1862.

Richard, the War between the States, the sickness of the children —all were reflected in the letters that reached him from Kentucky in these months. "You all seem," wrote the new subdeacon, "to be losing your good humor. If things are bad now they will not always be so, I pray for Rich every day of this world and try to gain a plenary indulgence for him at least once a week. It would be strange if I did not for I have nothing else to do."[81]

The Summer vacations began that year on August 13. At first, Spalding had chosen to remain in Belgium to visit with friends and to catch up on his reading,[82] but on Father De Nève's invitation he went to Aix-la-Chapelle to attend the meeting of the Catholic Union, the general assembly of all the popular unions under the name and patronage of Pope Pius IX, the Pius-Vereine. These social groups had been formed throughout the German states with the primary object of annually bringing together for a week large numbers of the Catholic laity from all walks of life. At these meetings, the questions of the day, insofar as they touched on the Church's interests, were freely discussed, and thus there was assured a more intelligent and enlightened Catholic public opinion. The first of these general assemblies had taken place at Mainz in October, 1848. Every village in the land was represented, if not directly then through some central union, and no Catholic interest was overlooked. Side by side the cardinals, bishops, princes, and the learned professors there sat mechanics, carpenters, shoemakers. And as Spalding said some years later:

. . . not as in the act of worship, in which the presence of the Most High God dwarfs our universal littleness to the dead level of an equal insignificance, but in active thought and cooperation for the furtherance of definite religious and social ends. The brotherhood of the race was there, an accomplished fact, and one felt the breathing as of a divine

[81] UND photostat, Spalding Papers, Spalding to Mr. and Mrs. R. M. Spalding, American College, Louvain, August 12, 1862.
[82] *Ibid*

53

Spirit compared with whose irresistible force great statesmen and mighty armies are as the puppets of a child's show.[83]

The impression made on Spalding at Aix-la-Chapelle was an abiding one. He found in the joint action of these German unions an example for his own country, and he urged that nothing could be more replete with lessons of practical wisdom for American Catholics since, as he put it,

> Organization is precisely what we most lack . . . The great need of the church in this country is the organization of priests and people for the promotion of Catholic interests. Through this we will learn to know one another; our views will be enlarged, our sympathies deepened, and the truth will dawn upon us that, if we wish to be true to the great mission which God has given us, the time has come when American Catholics must take up works which do not specially concern any one diocese more than another, but whose significance will be as wide as the nation's life.[84]

Enriched by his experience at the Catholic congress, Spalding returned to Louvain where he was among the thirty-four seminarians who reported to the American College at the opening of the new academic year in October, 1862. His friend David Russell had once again returned to Kentucky in May of that year, and Lank now kept his friend posted on the latest news from the Rue de Namur. There were, he said, many new Germans at the college, and Spalding now had the title of "Prof." of the "profound course" in English, although, he hastened to add, he gave class only twice a week. Ordinations were scheduled for Christmas, but he did not know whether he would be ordained a deacon or not, since he would be "two or three days too young to become a priest at Pentecost." He also informed Russell concerning the various bishops who had stopped at the college during the summer months. In speaking of the Civil War, Jean Marie Odin, Archbishop of New Orleans, had assured him that

[83] J. L. Spalding, *Essays and Reviews* (New York, 1877), p. 246.
[84] *Ibid.*, pp. 247–248.

his Uncle Ben [Father Benedict J. Spalding, brother of the Bishop of Louisville] was not a rebel; to which Lank said he had replied: "Neither am I, although the South is the land of my heart."[85]

Meanwhile, in addition to his regular courses, Spalding pursued studies for the licentiate's degree in theology. As the new year approached, he was preoccupied with his health, but he resolved to banish all thoughts of leaving the College for home, and he wrote:

I will remain here where I am for another year. I think no more of leaving . . . If God wishes that I remain here why will I not do it . . . ? Fool that I am, how do I know what is for my own good? How do I know that in leaving now I would not perish on the sea or be overtaken by some great misfortune? I would leave here on account of my health; how do I know that this very step would not be the destruction of my health?[86]

In a New Year's Day letter of 1863 to his uncle, he alluded to what was occasionally a source of annoyance to the Bishop, namely the young man's tendency to philosophize. "You would almost say," he wrote, "I am German, I am so mysteriously and deeply philosophical . . . I am a dreamer and there is nothing practical in me . . . I am excentric [sic] and become more so every day . . . like a nervous music box with the wind, the sunshine and the rain playing upon me . . . now joyous, now sad, now full of life, now half dead." The Bishop of Louisville, a man of more practical turn of mind, was rightly annoyed, for he was interested in news, "not speculations," and the nephew, realizing this, characterized himself as being like many others "who are carried away by the charm of saying something nice, do not say what they wish to say and what they should say." As for news, he simply added that the Bishop of Boston, John B. Fitzpatrick,

[85] AAB, 37-A-2, Spalding to Russell, American College, Louvain, December 6, 1862.

[86] ADP, Journal, January, 1863.

had been a guest at the College, as had been Father Charles H. Stonestreet, S.J., who gave the seminarians the latest news of the war and of the good that was being done among the soldiers by the Sisters of Charity.[87]

Of the years 1863–1868, the historian of the College remarked that ". . . nothing of particular interest occurred to be recorded in the history of the institution."[88] But in the personal life of Spalding that could not be said for the months that followed the New Year's letter to his uncle-bishop. Retreat for the diaconate began on May 24, and as he prepared once again for the trip to the cathedral at Malines, he admonished himself: "Be indifferent as to whether you are ordered to do this or that. Whatever it may be, do it for the love of God. Always remember that a shoeblack can serve God equally as well as a bishop."[89] It was on May 30, 1863, that Cardinal Sterckx ordained John Spalding a deacon, the only American in the group.[90] He then returned to his studies in preparation for the licentiate's degree and ordination to the priesthood. Although he loved Louvain, the Kentuckian had never fully acclimated himself to the cold winters, yet, as he said, he was determined not to ask to be ordained before his superiors called him. "I will not even hint that I desire it sooner. I will not complain of anything."[91]

In October, 1863, Father De Nève informed Lank Spalding that his ordination was planned for the Christmas season. In his enthusiasm over the prospect, he was fairly bursting with zeal

[87] AAB, 37-A-3, Spalding to Martin J. Spalding, Louvain, January 1, 1863. John B. Fitzpatrick (1812–1866) was the third Bishop of Boston. Charles H. Stonestreet, S.J. (1813–1885) was the twenty-third president of Georgetown College.

[88] Van der Heyden, *op. cit.*, p. 139.

[89] ADP, Journal, May 24, 1863.

[90] AAC-L, Liber C., May 30, 1863.

[91] ADP, Journal, October, 1863.

and good resolutions. "I will take 25 minutes to say Mass," he wrote, "15 minutes preparation and 15 minutes Thanksgiving. I will ask for a low and poor place in our diocese, if for no other reason than to give good example. *I will have no privilege.*"[92] But as the weeks went by, Spalding again grew restive. In mid-November, he confessed that a word, even a look, from another at times destroyed the harmony of his life for as long as a month. He simply could not stand to be humiliated, and the merest slight could cause him to rebel, and thus instead of advancing he had taken a step backward in the way of virtue. He was determined, therefore, to be more stable and never to show exteriorly that he was displeased. If anyone should offend him, he would not reason on it, but would immediately strive to forget it.[93] Retreat for the priesthood began on December 13, and in the fervor of that final period of preparation there were other resolutions against visiting his family any more than would be necessary, to be moderate in the use of wine and beer and also snuff, and not to pamper his vanity by gazing into the mirror except for shaving. He resolved as well to have a Catholic school if he should be named a pastor, and to teach catechism to the children himself. This idealism of the days before ordination probably brought on a change in Spalding which was observed by his fellow students. He admitted that one of them had said that the change he had made would not last, and with a consciousness of his own weakness he had written: "Blessed Mother do not let that be true."[94] On December 19, 1863, the Cardinal Archbishop of Malines ordained John Lancaster Spalding to the priesthood in his cathedral.[95] "I will never say 'I can-

[92] *Ibid.*

[93] *Ibid.,* November 15, 1863.

[94] *Ibid.,* "Practical Resolutions," December, 1863.

[95] AAC-L, Liber C., December 19, 1863. Spalding was ordained with a dispensation *in aetate.*

not,'" Father Spalding noted in his journal, "for I can do all in Him who strengthens me."[96]

Shortly after ordination, Spalding returned to his studies. In May, 1864, he gave a brilliant defense of his thesis for the licentiate's degree at the University, and he then outlined for Uncle Martin his plans for the coming year. He intended to leave about the middle of July for Germany, where he would remain for three or four months, and then proceed to Italy and down to Rome, where he would spend the remainder of the academic year.[97] By this time, however, the Bishop had more pressing things to think of than his nephew's studies abroad, for on June 11, Martin Spalding had received the papal rescript appointing him seventh Archbishop of Baltimore.[98] Young Father Spalding was naturally delighted, and he wrote to his parents: "I suppose his successor in Ky. will soon be known. Whoever he may be, for us at least, he will not be Uncle Martin, but though we lose I hope others will gain . . ."[99] On July 11, 1864, he received his degree of licentiate in sacred theology from the Catholic University of Louvain,[100] and on the next day Father De Nève simply noted in the college record: "July 12, 1864, J. Lancaster Spalding, *sacerdos, Roman tendit*."[101]

Freed at last from the routine life of the seminary, John Lancaster set out on his journey, lingering in various places as fancy dictated. First he traveled to Trier in the Rhineland, where he said Mass in the cathedral only after he had convinced the authorities that he was not suspended. Heidelberg, famed for its

[96] ADP, Journal, December 19, 1863.

[97] UND photostat, Spalding Papers, Spalding to Mr. and Mrs. R. M. Spalding, Louvain, May 3, 1864.

[98] Spalding, *Life of the Most Rev. M. J. Spalding,* p. 255.

[99] UND photostat, Spalding Papers, Spalding to Mr. and Mrs. R. M. Spalding, Louvain, May, 1864.

[100] *L'Ammuaire de l'Université Catholique de Louvain, 1864* (Louvain, 1865), p. 192.

[101] AAC-L, Liber C., July 12, 1864.

university, was the next stop.[102] Then, traveling southward, he arrived at Freiburg im Breisgau in the Grand Duchy of Baden situated at the foot of the Schwarzwald. Freiburg, in 1864, was the third largest city in Baden, and was a delightful place, Spalding wrote to Father De Nève, about twenty miles from the Rhine with about 17,000 inhabitants. In the center of the city was the cathedral, one of the finest examples of Gothic art, and also the university, which was the principal reason, he remarked, why he had come to that part of Germany. The University of Freiburg im Breisgau, called the "Albertina," had been founded in April, 1455, by Albrecht VI of Austria, the brother of the Emperor Frederick III, with the sanction of Pope Callistus III, but through the years the university had all but lost its Catholic character, and efforts to regain control had proven ineffectual when in 1859 the concordat between the Holy See and Baden had been rejected. Spalding naturally had wondered how the population of the city could have remained predominantly Catholic while the university, with professors and students recruited from the north of Germany, was, with few exceptions, Protestant and rationalistic. That the people had remained steadfast in the faith, he was told, had been due to the zeal and the vigor of the 92-year-old archbishop, Herman von Vicari, who for many years had valiantly resisted the encroachments of the civil authorities and had successfully routed the remnants of Josephinism from the archdiocese.[103]

For three weeks, Spalding attended lectures in the University, and it was there that he met Johann B. Alzog, the church historian, and also Alban Stolz, professor of theology and former rector of the institution whom the young priest had character-

[102] AAC-L, Spalding to De Nève, Freiburg, July 18, 1864.

[103] AAB, 37-A-5, Spalding to Spalding, Venice, September 19, 1864. Josephinism, so called from the Emperor Joseph II whose policies and legislation embodied the ideas of the "Enlightenment," claimed the right to subordinate religion to or make it part of the state.

ized, in a rare attempt at humor, as being Stolz in name only. The latter had invited Spalding to take walks with him, and had spoken of the apparent revival of the faith in Baden.[104] Some twenty or thirty years before, the general sentiment among the Catholics there had been that the pope was a foreigner, almost as "foreign as the Grand Turk," but now even Baden, Stolz asserted, had contributed to the support of the Holy Father. Spalding was greatly impressed with the former rector and with the Germans in general, and he wrote to Uncle Martin that he had found the priests zealous and the bishops "introducing as fast as possible the disciplinary ordinations of the Council of Trent regarding the life and education of priests." "I think I have passed my time well," he said, and "learned a great deal that will be useful to me."[105] Young Father Spalding had undoubtedly profited from his short stay in Baden, and in time he would prove the gain when he would show his concern for the higher education of the American clergy and press for a Catholic university.

From Freiberg im Breisgau, Spalding moved on to Switzerland and thence to Italy. He spent three weeks in Venice, and he remarked that he found the signs of the coming revolution too obvious to be misread. "I am now living under the Austrian government," he wrote to the Archbishop of Baltimore, "the most truly catholic government that now exists," and he hoped that Venice would remain Austrian "until all the apostate priests, petty lawyers and lowbred freemasons have played out their game in Turin."[106] The game, as Spalding phrased it, was the unification of Italy while the prize was Rome, the fundamental dilemma which would remain unsolved. As an historian has remarked: "For the Italian nationalist, there could be no Italy without Rome; for the Vatican there could be no Catholicism

[104] *Ibid.*
[105] *Ibid.*
[106] *Ibid.*

without the territorial independence of the Papacy."[107] The Roman Question was highly complex, but for Father Spalding "all this cry and hurrah about nationality and freedom," as he told Uncle Martin, was "only the work of some worthless men who wish to rise in the world and are too weak and ignorant to do so by honest means." In the same vein of oversimplification, he noted that whatever concessions Pius IX might make in the cause of Italian unity, he believed they would be discounted beforehand, since "Italy is sick . . . , and publicly the Pope has no defender."[108]

Leaving Venice, Spalding traveled to Padua, Ferrara, Bologna, and Florence, and reached Rome in early October, where he took up residence at the Belgium College at the Quattro Fontane.[109] Years later, the future bishop would recall his stay in Rome and write:

> To see the illumination of St. Peter's is to have ever after the memory of a heavenly vision: to listen to the *Miserere* in the Sistine Chapel on Good Friday is to realize the depths of sorrow which only God can console, to realize the infinite agony which human souls may know: to hear the silver trumpets in the dome amid the skies break forth on Easter morning . . . is to have some faint foretaste of the bliss angelic natures know.[110]

Shortly after his arrival, he called on Father Bernard Smith, O.S.B., then a professor in the Urban College of the Propaganda. The Archbishop of Baltimore had already informed Smith of the nephew's coming, and had ventured, he wrote,

> . . . to refer him to you for advice & direction. I wish him to gain practical knowledge as to the Roman manner of conducting business,

[107] Joseph N. Moody, *Church and Society. Catholic Social and Political Thought and Movements, 1789–1950* (New York, 1953), p. 38.

[108] AAB, 37-A-5, Spalding to Spalding, Venice, September 19, 1864.

[109] AAB, 37-A-6, Same to Same, Belgian College, Rome, November 15, 1864.

[110] Spalding, Introduction to James J. McGovern, *The Life and Writings of the Rt. Rev. John McMullen,* pp. xviii–xix.

the Roman Canical [*sic*] decisions, the practical formularies necessary for a bishop's secretary, the Roman rites when they might differ from our own. I know of no one better qualified to direct him in these practical studies than yourself.[111]

On Smith's advice, Spalding told his uncle that he decided to devote himself exclusively to the practical study of Canon Law, though he hastened to add: "I have already seen a good deal of Canon Law at Louvain where it is undoubtedly better and more profoundly taught than here in Rome." On his own, he would review what he had already studied at Louvain, but he would also follow the lectures at the Sapienza and would assist at the discussions of the Congregation of the Council of Trent, where he might occasionally present a case or two for decision. In any event, he assured his uncle, he hoped to pass his time usefully.[112]

During the Winter and Spring that Father Spalding spent in Rome, it was already apparent to him that Uncle Martin's emphasis on the practical was inspired not only as a check on the nephew's tendency toward excessive speculation, but more practically to qualify him as a bishop's secretary, and specifically secretary to the Archbishop of Baltimore. From Venice, John Lancaster had written: "As to my coming to Baltimore I am willing to do anything that you desire me, dear uncle. I will never be able to repay you for all that you have done for me but I will try to do all that I can." He left his possible transfer from Louisville to Baltimore in Uncle Martin's hands, but he then added in the style which irked the Archbishop: "It is not place or circumstance that can make us happy. Happiness dwells within the soul which in itself can be heaven or a hell." For the rest he thought he would be a poor secretary, "but as to this

[111] Archives of the Abbey of St. Paul Outside the Walls. Spalding to Bernard Smith, Baltimore, September 3, 1864. Hereafter these archives will be cited as AASPOW.

[112] AAB, 37-A-6, Spalding to Spalding, Belgian College, Rome, November 15, 1864

also," he added, "I let you judge."[113] Shortly after the New Year, 1865, John Lancaster called on Alessandro Cardinal Barnabò, Prefect of the Congregation de Propaganda Fide, with a letter from his uncle to the Cardinal about the proposed transfer. Barnabò told Father Spalding that he would speak to the Pope on the matter, and then write to the Archbishop. "I suppose," Lancaster wrote to his uncle, "there will be no difficulty in obtaining my incorporation into the Diocese of Baltimore."[114] To his mind, it seemed a foregone conclusion that Baltimore and not Louisville would be the scene of his labors, and to David Russell he remarked: "I appertain to the Diocese of Baltimore."[115] It came as a surprise to Russell, and, disconcerted as he was, he immediately wrote to Archbishop Spalding:

Of course this is very little of my business but I do not believe it fair to take him from where he properly belongs, and from a place where his services are so much needed, and with due respect, I hereby enter my protest, *"in quantum possum."* Who is to defend us here, in case we should be assailed, if whenever a man of ability is found belonging to us, he is immediately transferred. True, we have a David here, but he has no sling, nor is it probable that Goliath could always be slain with a pebble. . . .[116]

Russell's fears were temporarily quieted when, shortly afterward, he heard that Lank had written to the Archbishop: "Card. Barnabò thinks it better to wait until your successor in the diocese of Louisville be appointed before asking the Holy Father to incorporate me into the diocese of Baltimore. *Sede vacante, nihil innovandum.*" Barnabò had also informed Lank that his Uncle Ben, the administrator of the diocese, was first on both the lists for the Diocese of Louisville, but he did not know whether he

[113] AAB, 37-A-5, Same to Same, Venice, September 19, 1864.

[114] AAB, 37-A-7, Same to Same, Belgian College, Rome, January 5, 1865.

[115] AAB, 35-W-11, Russell to Martin J. Spalding, Louisville, February 8, 1865.

[116] *Ibid.*

would be appointed. The Cardinal insisted, however, as Lancaster stated, that nothing could be done until the new bishop had been designated,[117] and so the question as to the whereabouts of his first assignment would remain unanswered until his return to the United States.

Meanwhile, young Father Spalding became keenly aware of the tensions that arose in Rome and elsewhere when on December 8, 1864, Pope Pius IX issued the encyclical letter *Quanta Cura,* which proclaimed a jubilee year, and to which was attached the Syllabus of Errors—a summary of views that were considered contrary to Catholic teaching. "The Propositions annexed," he told Archbishop Spalding, "make a good deal of noise here in Europe from the fact that many find in them a condemnation of the Catholic liberal school . . . of which Montalembert is the leader in France. . . ."[118] The term "liberal Catholic" was associated chiefly with such thinkers as Félicité Robert de Lamennais, Félix Dupanloup, Charles Forbes Comte de Montalembert, and others who believed that not all the new movements that were shaping the world were essentially bad, and who contended that the Church had nothing to fear from the liberal ideas of freedom of worship, freedom of speech and the press, and that it ought to see and utilize the good in such ideas for the benefit of both Church and state. They cited in their own defense the Catholic minorities in Protestant countries who had benefited from these ideas, for example the Catholic Emancipation Act in Great Britain in 1829 and the Belgian constitution of 1830 wherein Catholics had cooperated wholeheartedly with liberals in drafting a document that, while based on the new principles, had guaranteed complete freedom for the Church. On the other hand, the conservatives, then called Ultramontanists, were uncompromisingly hostile to the new develop-

[117] AAB, 37-A-8, Spalding to Spalding, Belgian College, Rome, March 13, 1865.

[118] AAB, 37-A-7, Same to Same, Belgian College, Rome, January 5, 1865.

ments in the world, and held that the new liberties were dangerous and unsafe and would only further a non-Christian state of
society.[119] It was a speech at the Malines Congress in 1863, in
the judgment of one historian, that brought to a head the tensions between these two groups when Montalembert pronounced
his political testament with the plea for

A free Church in a free state . . . Can one today demand liberty for
the truth . . . and refuse it to error?, that is, to those who do not think
as ourselves? I answer clearly: No . . . The Spanish Inquisitor saying
to the heretic, *Truth or Death,* is as odious to me as the French terrorist
who said to my grandfather, *Liberty, Fraternity, or Death.* The human
conscience has the right to demand that no one pose those hideous
alternatives.

Cardinal Sterckx had congratulated the orator, who, he said, had
spoken like a "true theologian," but many in Belgium and Rome
had not shared this opinion and had not been hesitant about expressing their objections.[120] Pius IX, no longer the liberal-
minded Giovanni Cardinal Mastai-Ferretti, but the Pope who
had returned from the exile at Gaeta on the strength of foreign
bayonets, sided with the conservatives and responded with the
Syllabus, the last proposition of which seemed to be destruc-
tive of all Catholic liberal hopes when it concluded that it was
false to say "that the Roman Pontiff can and ought to reconcile
himself to, and agree with, progress, liberalism, and modern
civilization."[121]

The Syllabus, characterized as an unusual form of papal
teaching and couched in statements declared to be false, was
subject to many and varied interpretations, and young Father
Spalding was not diffident in expounding his own view. He advised Uncle Martin that the school of liberal Catholicism was

[119] Moody, *op. cit.,* p. 232.

[120] *Ibid.,* p. 293.

[121] *Henrici Denzinger Enchiridion Symbolorum Definitionum et
Declarationum,* ed. by Carolus Rahner, S.J., ed. 28 augmentata (Freiburg im Breisgau, 1953), p. 490.

65

not to be condemned if it were to be considered merely as a practicable system applicable to Belgium, France, and the greater part of the civilized world, and here he included the United States since, as he said, "this school is the only practical school in this age and probably for ages to come," although he hastened to add that ". . . American principles are fundamentally false as is the general tendency of modern society."[122] Even when a school boy, he assured his uncle, he had never had much faith in what the spirit of the age called liberty, and he had less now as he saw more clearly that liberty, as he wrote,

. . . is only one of the many means which crafty and strong men make use of to tyrannize over the people. The people is the most gullible animal on earth and where it is Kings inevitably rule . . . The human race has always lived for the few and in this respect things have not changed in the nineteenth century. The people labors, sweats and dies in order to satisfy the lust and pride of a few worthless men who themselves are slaves. I am not a socialist. But when I see tyrants and constitutional fools and liars seeking to tear religion from the hearts of the people . . . under pretext of making them free, I wish we had an age of faith and strength like that of Gregory VII and a friend of the people to anathematize those base tyrants and to send them crouching from the face of an outraged world.[123]

He abhorred those men who talked of liberty and progress and sovereignty of the people, and when he looked over to the United States he saw that those same principles had ruined it, torn it asunder, made Americans exiles and beggars in their own homes because the "American people is today a King . . . a nation without any right except that of Self murder." That was why he believed the North was right in principle in the War between the States because, as he said, "every shot fired is a protestation against the right of *Rebellion,* the omnipotence of the people, and the deification of the vulgar many."[124] Spalding's view of

[122] AAB, 37-A-7, Spalding to Spalding, Belgian College, Rome, January 5, 1865.
[123] *Ibid.*
[124] *Ibid.*

the Syllabus and the condemnation of the liberal school of Catholicism was, to say the least, confusing. In one sense, it was an interpretation that would seemingly range him on the side of the ultramontanists—which has led one historian to state that "Spalding in his early years as a priest had disavowed all compromises with secular culture."[125] Yet, in the very same analysis of the falsity of American principles, and of liberalism in general, it seemed to the young priest that "the present state of Society is a fact which we cannot get rid of; consequently we must accept it and try to make the best of it."[126] It was the latter view that would characterize his later years, and thus cause him to be labeled "liberal" as he sought for a *rapprochement* between American Catholicism and the spirit of the age.

Meanwhile, the Archbishop of Baltimore had likewise become concerned over the effect of the Syllabus on the Catholic Church in the United States, and in February, 1865, he wrote: "I have just finished my Pastoral on the Jubilee. I attempt to defend the Pontiff and the Encyclical from the American standpoint. In view of the howl of indignation which has gone forth from England and America, I thought a vindication opportune." With the publication of the Syllabus in the United States, the outcry was that the Pope had condemned the most sacred principles of the American way of life. To this Archbishop Spalding replied that "to stretch the words of the Pontiff, evidently intended for the stand-point of European radicals and infidels, so as to make them include the state of things established in this country by our Constitution in regard to liberty of conscience, of worship and the press, were manifestly unfair and unjust."[127] He sent copies of his pastoral to Lancaster with instructions to give the one "for his Holiness to Cardinal Barnabò," and asked

[125] Robert D. Cross, *The Emergence of Liberal Catholicism in America* (Cambridge, 1958), p. 40.

[126] AAB, 37-A-7, Spalding to Spalding, Belgian College, Rome, January 5, 1865.

[127] Spalding, *Life of the Most Rev. M. J. Spalding,* p. 272.

the nephew to see Giacomo Cardinal Antonelli, the Secretary of State, and to "please ask explanations of the Nos. 55, 77 & 79—which will be construed here as condemning our system of religious toleration so advantageous . . . to Religion." He feared that "these & some other propositions will furnish pretext to the fanatics to persecute us," which, he added, they would probably do anyhow.[128] Following his uncle's instructions, Father Spalding saw Cardinal Antonelli, who told him to inform the Archbishop that the Cardinal himself would write to Baltimore on certain points pertaining to the American Church.[129]

Not long after, Lancaster informed Uncle Martin of Antonelli's reply in a letter that gave evidence of the young priest's desire to return home. The Roman Winter had been wet and cold, and since there was no way of making a fire he had been visited, as he put it, "by all kinds of ruhmatic [sic] pains and indeed I have not been very well." Then the food at the Belgian college was not the best, whereas he felt that he needed "a great deal of substantial matter" to keep going.[130] The news from home had also been disheartening with his mother having written of the death of his young brother Martin. The question of Lank's homecoming had been discussed before, and in a manner that must have caused the Archbishop to smile when earlier in the year the nephew wrote: "I am endeavoring to follow your very good counsel of being practical and letting the theoretical alone. . . ." This was more the vocation of every American, he remarked, "for we do not believe in ideas and knowledge for us is good only in as much as it is commutable with dollars and cents." And since an American was worth only as much as he had, this made him think how little he was worth, and helped to turn him to another subject.

[128] AAB, Letterbook, Spalding to Spalding, Baltimore, February 20, 1865.

[129] AAB, 37-A-8, Same to Same, Belgian College, Rome, March 13, 1865.

[130] *Ibid.*

The subject, of course, was money. He had only 1,600 francs, and while he had paid his rent at the college for six months, there were some clothes and books that he would like to buy. Nevertheless, if the times were too hard, he would try to get home without troubling anyone for more money. Yet, if Uncle Martin could by chance conveniently send him some, "I might be able to pay you back some day or other should I ever become more practical in the U.S."[131] Whether John Lancaster ever received the little extra is not known, for he simply ended his last letter from Rome in March, 1865, by saying: "I will leave immediately after Easter and be in Baltimore about the middle of May if nothing prevents me. . . ."[132] On the way, he stopped at the American College in Louvain to pick up some books that he had left there, and on the evening of his departure Father De Nève called Spalding to his room. "John," he is reported to have said, "you are entering on your life's work now, and the field that lies before you offers abundant opportunity to do God's work; yet one thing I ask you: consecrate the first years of your priestly life to those poor people who as you know have been only too long neglected and often oppressed—to the Negroes." Spalding is said to have reflected for a moment, and then to have replied: "Father John, I shall do it."[133] His priestly mission having been thus designated for him by the rector of the college wherein he had spent the previous five years, Father John Lancaster Spalding left Louvain on the following day for home.

[131] AAB, 37-A-7, Same to Same, Belgian College, Rome, January 5, 1865.

[132] AAB, 37-A-8, Same to Same, Belgian College, Rome, March 13, 1865.

[133] Jules De Becker, "Golden Jubilee," *American College Bulletin* (January, 1914), p. 5. De Becker, who became rector of the college in 1898, said: "Father De Nève himself told me of this conversation."

2

The Priest

"THE life of a priest . . . , in ordinary times," John Lancaster Spalding wrote less than ten years after his ordination, "is necessarily uneventful. There are no 'battles, sieges, fortunes, disastrous chances . . .' to be told of . . . and men, now, as in ages past, will make heroes of the successful butchers of the race, whilst its benefactors are forgotten."[1] And yet, when Spalding sailed for the United States in May, 1865, the times were hardly ordinary. Appomattox naturally brought rejoicing to a land where for four long years brother had fought against brother. Hostilities had ceased, it was true, but the rejoicing was short-lived. And for good reason had most of the American people bowed in sorrow on that April day when Lincoln died. The War between the States was over, but Appomattox had not brought peace.

After six years of study and travel in Europe, Spalding arrived in New York City during the first week of June. Following a brief visit with Father Arthur J. Donnelly,[2] pastor of St. Michael's Parish, the young priest set out for Baltimore, where on June 8, 1865, he presented himself at the cathedral rectory.[3]

[1] Spalding, *Life of the Most Rev. M. J. Spalding,* pp. iv–v.

[2] Archives of the Abbey of St. Paul Outside the Walls, Donnelly to Smith, New York, June 27, 1865, microfilm copy. These archives will be hereafter cited as AASPOW. Father Donnelly had met Spalding in Germany in the Summer of 1864. Cf. New York *Tribune,* May 1, 1877.

[3] AAB, Letterbook, Spalding to De Nève, Baltimore, June 8, 1865.

Archbishop Spalding then greeted his nephew as a priest for the first time. John Lancaster was his favorite nephew—the one on whom he had centered hopes and plans for the future, the one whom he had determined to afford even greater advantages than he had known himself. It must have been with great reluctance that he saw Lancaster, after an all too short week, leave for Louisville, where at least temporarily he would report for an assignment. Spalding arrived in Louisville on June 16. Uncle Ben, the administrator of the diocese, *sede vacante,* was hesitant about assigning his nephew to any particular duty. He stated the problem to his brother, the Archbishop, thus:

Lanky with Leonard his brother left for their father's yesterday morning. Lanky reported for duty & I gave him 2 or three weeks to visit his parents and rest. What should be done with him? I am at a loss about it, especially under the present circumstances. If he is placed at the Cathedral now, complaints might be made that partiality was shown. I do not know of any congregation in the country that would suit him. If Father Russell were sent to Louvain to a post in the Amer. College, Lanky might be brought here to take his place. Fr. Russell as you already know has been asked to go by the V. Rev. Fr. De Nève & he is willing to go if he is sent. What do you think of it?[4]

The Archbishop was embarrassed. While he was still Bishop of Louisville, the question of Russell's return to Louvain had been discussed, and so he advised his brother: "I do not think you run any risk in sending Fr. Russell, especially, if you should do so for a short time on the plea of his health." Then, he thought, there would be no serious difficulty in bringing Lank to Louisville at least until a bishop should be appointed for the diocese.[5]

Temporarily, then, John Lancaster became a member of the staff of the Cathedral of the Assumption. Meanwhile, Uncle Martin was confident that his nephew would ultimately come to

[4] AAB, 37-B-14, Benedict J. Spalding to Martin J. Spalding, Louisville, June 17, 1865

[5] AAB, Letterbook, Martin J. Spalding to Benedict J. Spalding, Baltimore, June 21, 1865.

Baltimore. "While I might repeat," he wrote to Lank, "that you are not assigned to any particular duty, a little touch of self-interest—enlightened I trust—makes me less sad at the contingency as it may possibly induce the new Bishop to give you to me. I could employ you & both constantly and usefully." The Archbishop passed on a rumor that had reached him through a letter from William McCloskey to Archbishop Purcell to the effect that Father Peter Lavialle had been appointed; but he wondered about the reliability of McCloskey's source, since he had just heard from Cardinal Barnabò and not a word had been mentioned about Louisville by the Prefect of Propaganda.[6] As a matter of fact, the information of the Rector of the American College in Rome proved very shortly thereafter to be correct. In July, 1865, Peter J. Lavialle was appointed Bishop of Louisville. Martin Spalding congratulated his former diocesan, thanked God that Lavialle had accepted the onus of the miter, and told him that he would be delighted to preach at the consecration. Then, touching on a matter that was close to his heart, the Archbishop continued:

I should be very happy to be able to bring back with me my nephew Lancaster upon whom I have many claims which I stated to Card. Barnabò who said that according to the adage—*Sede vacante, nihil innovandum*—I should wait the appointment of a bishop who would decide. I mention this early that you might have time to decide.

The Archbishop of Baltimore seemed quite anxious and in the postscript he added one final argument: "He would be of very great help to me as a private secretary particularly in case we should hold a Plenary Council this year & I consider it probable."[7]

Father Lavialle was consecrated as the fourth Bishop of Louis-

[6] AAB, 37-E-40, Martin J. Spalding to J. Lancaster Spalding, Baltimore, July 26, 1865.

[7] AAB, Letterbook, Spalding to Lavialle, Baltimore, September 6, 1865.

ville in his See city on September 26, 1865, by Archbishop Purcell of Cincinnati. Martin Spalding preached the sermon on that occasion, but Father Lancaster did not return with him to Baltimore. Instead, his beloved nephew remained in Louisville as secretary to the new bishop and as a curate in the cathedral parish. Undoubtedly, the Archbishop was disappointed, yet he had already wisely provided for that contingency. As early as June of that year, perhaps fearing that he would not succeed in securing his nephew, Spalding had already suggested to one of his youngest pastors, Father James Gibbons of St. Bridget's Church, the possibility of his joining the cathedral household and acting as his secretary.[8]

Kentucky, therefore, was to be the scene of John Lancaster's first priestly labors. There had been many changes since he had last seen his native state. The armies had only recently been disbanded, and during the protracted struggle Kentucky had played a part that was peculiarly its own. It was a border state and that in all that the phrase implied. "The Civil War," it has been remarked, "its causes and its results, gave additional proof that Kentuckians were not like other people."[9] Kentuckians boasted of their strong nationalism which favored the Union, yet this in no way minimized their insistence on the rights and powers that belonged to Kentucky as a sovereign state. It strongly defended the institution of slavery, yet in the face of it fought to preserve the Union. The state had undergone a grim internal struggle before it entered the war on the side of the North, but when once in the conflict the men of Kentucky fought with determination and bravery. Long before the war was over, however, realizing that the purposes and the premises of the conflict had been radically altered in their concept by the Emancipation

[8] John Tracy Ellis, *The Life of James Cardinal Gibbons* (Milwaukee, 1952), I, p. 57.

[9] E. Merton Coulter, *The Civil War and Readjustment in Kentucky* (Chapel Hill, 1926), p. 1.

Proclamation and the threat of a constitutional amendment to abolish slavery, Kentucky adopted a highly critical attitude toward the federal authorities, and that attitude eventually came to influence nearly all the views of its people when peace was declared. Kentuckians became more Southern in habits of thought and sympathy than, perhaps, any part of the Confederacy. Posed as a champion of the states beset by carpetbaggers, Kentucky refused to ratify the Thirteenth Amendment, and went so far as to bring reconstruction down on its own head—a sovereign state that had fought for the preservation of the Union. As Coulter observed, "It was often remarked that Kentucky waited until after the war to secede from the Union."[10]

At the time of Spalding's return home, then, the Confederate tradition had already become the dominant feeling in society, in politics and likewise in religion. War animosities had cut deeply into the churches and had greatly retarded growth. Congregations had been split apart, and many of the sects had plunged into the political turmoils of the war—and now, in the post-war period, they could not hope to escape the consequences. The Presbyterian Church had been the greatest offender, and it now became the greatest casualty with a permanent split of the Kentucky Synod into a northern and southern branch. Sectionalism and war antagonism also affected the Methodists. Only the Roman Catholic Church seemed to escape the ravages of internal dissension. Six months prior to the outbreak of war, the Louisville *Guardian,* the official diocesan paper, had blamed the Protestant clergy for the sorry state of the nation:

There is little doubt that the Protestant sects have had at least as much to do with the present unfortunate state of things as the excited sectional politicians. In the North, the Protestant preachers have long been in the habit of bitterly inveighing, Sunday after Sunday, against the evil and sin of slavery; this has, in fact, formed the chief burden of their discourses from the pulpit. . . . The religious fanaticism has evidently

[10] *Ibid.,* p. 439.

74

led the way to that political excitement which now threatens to sever our glorious union and leave it a mass of ruins. Take away the Protestant element from the discussion and little would remain.[11]

Allowing for some exaggeration, there was a grain of truth in the charge. Meanwhile, the *Guardian* had urged moderation. Catholics being on both sides should counteract the fanaticism of the abolitionists, and in the South they should strive to prevent secession until all means of justice proved ineffectual. Martin Spalding, while still Bishop of Louisville, had succinctly summarized the predominant Catholic point of view when he wrote: "My diocese is cut in twain by this unhappy war, and I must attend to souls without entering into the angry political discussion."[12]

And now, in the aftermath of war, the Catholic Church in Kentucky was faced with a new problem, namely, what to do about the emancipated Catholic Negro slaves. Soon after the Emancipation Proclamation, which did not touch the border states, Lincoln came to the conclusion that slavery should be abolished throughout the entire country forever, and to that end he set his heart on a constitutional amendment. After considerable debate and one defeat in Congress, the amendment finally received on January 31, 1865, the required majority in both houses of the national legislature and was immediately submitted to the states for ratification. On December 18, 1865, Secretary of State William H. Seward formally proclaimed the Thirteenth Amendment ratified by the vote of twenty-seven states, and thereby legally embodied in the Constitution. But Kentucky refused to ratify.

Even before the formal proclamation of Secretary Seward, great moving masses of Kentucky's freed Negro slaves, taking advantage of their new found freedom, abandoned their homes in the country and sought out the cities, where they congre-

[11] *The Guardian* (Louisville), January 5, 1861.
[12] Spalding, *op. cit.,* p. 246.

gated in menacing numbers. The two favorite centers, becoming increasingly biracial as each straggling slave slipped in, were Lexington and Louisville. The latter drew from all parts of the state, for it was the headquarters of the military, and the army had little patience with slavery. Louisville meant freedom for the slave who sought a home there. As General Joseph S. Brisbin remarked: "Having become restless and dissatisfied the slaves leave their homes and setting their faces toward Louisville, journey for days over long miles to these Headquarters, as the Mecca where freedom may be found. . . ."[13]

The Louisville to which Spalding returned was likewise in the midst of a new wave of vitality. Before the Civil War and after, traffic glutted the canal around the falls. There were packet steamers running on regular schedule between Louisville and Liverpool, and one could buy a ticket to Havana direct, for Louisville was a busy place. There was, moreover, the Louisville and Nashville Railroad, which controlled all traffic headed South. Liederkranz Hall and Macaulay's Theatre were on Main Street, also Nicholas Biddle's United States Bank. To the city's wharfs came the Southern planters to buy—cotton gins, sugar mills, pork, hay, and flour; and out of Louisville, northbound, went sugar, molasses, coffee and cotton. It was, in addition, a countinghouse and a broker's paradise. Now at the close of the war, Louisville could count a population of little less than 100,-000, of whom 14,956 were of the Negro race.[14] Among these Negroes there were not a few Catholics. Having been an integral part of Catholic households on the plantations, they had been, in the ideal and the spiritual sense, on an equal footing with their masters. But left to themselves in the cities, they became sheep without a shepherd. Prejudice against these recently freed slaves now became even stronger. No building was set

[13] Coulter, *op. cit.*, p. 263.
[14] George R. Leighton, *America's Growing Pains* (New York, 1939), p. 65.

apart for them to attend divine services, and no space was allocated to them in the existing parishes of the white people. In the Cathedral of the Assumption in Louisville, the Negroes were huddled together in the choir loft, while Northern sympathizers had already provided Protestant Negroes with "meeting houses" of their own.

Father Lancaster Spalding had grown up in the midst of the Negro slaves at Evergreen Bend. He knew their good qualities, and therefore was not daunted by the uncomfortable characteristics of this then backward race. As the Negroes congregated in larger numbers in Louisville, he saw the dangers that would beset them, left as they were without the care of priests to guide and instruct them. Without proper facilities for a church for them, little progress could be made. Ringing in Lank's ears was the parting advice of Father De Nève, his superior and friend at Louvain, when he had asked him to build a church for the Negroes, "who though of a different color, have like us been redeemed by the Precious Blood of Jesus Christ."[15] When Spalding first broached the subject, many attempted to dissuade him, saying that the Negroes lacked the means and the initiative to build and support a church; they were shiftless and unreliable; the time was not opportune. At first discouraged, he told his Uncle Martin: "Nothing has been done towards procuring a church for the Negroes, nor do I suppose that anything will be done."[16] But in the meantime, he became more determined than ever in his insistence that the church was needed and that the funds could be found. Several years might pass, he confessed, but "though all be against me, I will make the effort to do all that will keep these people true to the Faith that they have received and still prize highly."[17]

A year after his return to Louisville, while still cherishing his

[15] De Becker, "Golden Jubilee," p. 5.
[16] AAB, 37-A-9, Spalding to Spalding, Louisville, February 4, 1866.
[17] *Ibid.*

77

hopes for the Catholic Negroes, an unusual distinction came to John Lancaster, unsolicited but—perhaps—not unexpected. On the first Sunday in October, 1866, the Second Plenary Council was formally opened in Baltimore under the presidency of Archbishop Spalding as the apostolic delegate of Pope Pius IX. Seven archbishops, thirty-eight bishops, three mitred abbots, and more than one hundred twenty theologians met in the largest conciliary assembly that the American Church had then witnessed. It was a moving scene that Autumn day when, as John Lancaster later described it,

The bishops, clad in splendid robes, with mitred heads, each bearing the crosier in hand, attended by a throng of priests and acolytes, recalled, as they moved in solemn procession through the streets to the cathedral, what we read of the religious pageants of the middle ages. The whole city had crowded to behold the glorious scene . . . Every window and available spot, even the housetops from which a view of the procession could be had, were filled with eager spectators who looked on in silent reverence.[18]

The nation had emerged only a year and a half before from the Civil War. Only the Catholic Church had remained united, and it was only the Church that could now walk forth in the person of its leaders from both North and South before the eyes of the nation in undiminished strength. Father Spalding was privileged to be part of this historic gathering, and he, too, walked in procession as theologian to Francis Norbert Blanchet, Archbishop of Oregon City, and it was in that capacity that he took part in the deliberations of the Council.[19]

While the younger Spalding played a quite minor role in the deliberations of the Second Plenary Council, he was, nevertheless, selected to preach on October 10, 1866, at the Vesper serv-

[18] Spalding, *op. cit.,* p. 305.
[19] Archives of the Archdiocese of New York, William G. McCloskey to Michael A. Corrigan, Baltimore, October 19, 1866. These archives will be hereafter cited as AANY.

ice in the cathedral. He chose as his theme, "The Visible Head of the Church." The mission of the Church, he told the hierarchy and the faithful, is an essentially conservative one. Peter was to preserve the faith and teach it to all nations. Hence, Christ chose Rome, the great venerator of antiquity, the representative of law and order, as the center of His spiritual empire. Nonetheless, Spalding proposed, it was the privilege of the Church, notwithstanding her immutable constitution, to adapt herself, without harm to her unity and catholicity, to the various modifications of human society. "She is to adapt herself to all forms of government," he said, "to live and become acclimated in every land, among all the nations of the earth, with their differences of laws, customs, education and sentiment." In the organization of the Church in the United States, by way of example, he maintained there was nothing different from that which existed in Europe; yet her social milieu here was so unlike that found abroad that, as he put it, "our church polity cannot be expected to be altogether the same as that which is the outgrowth of circumstances wholly dissimilar from those in which we are placed." It seemed to the young preacher that "precisely because the Church is so fixed in faith and essential discipline, she can therefore allow a certain liberty where circumstances demand it."[20] Unfortunately, there remains no record of what the American bishops thought of this forthright discourse of the 26-year-old priest from Louisville. The term "Americanism," in its theological connotation—of which Spalding would later be accused—had not, of course, as yet been invented. Did some of the prelates, perhaps, murmur "Gallicanism" as they listened to one who in less than ten years would join their company and reveal himself a forceful figure in attempting to solve the problems arising from the demands of American liberty and American

[20] *Sermons Delivered During the Second Plenary Council of Baltimore, October, 1866 and Pastoral Letter of the Hierarchy of the United States* (Baltimore, 1866), pp. 102–103.

79

Catholicism? In any event, it is certain that at a remarkably early age, the nephew of the Archbishop of Baltimore had been given an opportunity rare for one of his years, and that he had acquitted himself in creditable fashion.

At the conclusion of the Council, Spalding returned to Louisville and continued his work as secretary to Bishop Lavialle, and with him traveled throughout the diocese on frequent episcopal visitations. Lavialle, however, who did not have good health, had been exhausted by the Council and the efforts to rebuild his diocese after the war, and in the Spring of 1867 he became gravely ill. Father Francis Chambige, veteran missionary and member of the Bishop's council, immediately informed Archbishop Purcell, head of the Province of Cincinnati to which Louisville belonged as a suffragan see:

> With a heart heavy with grief, I address your Grace. I know you will share our affliction. Our beloved Bishop is here at Nazareth, prostrated by a very dangerous disease, so much so that we will administer to him the last Sacraments this evening. Poor church of Louisville. God tries her with sore afflictions. She expected from her zealous and young Bishop "une brilliante carriere" and now she is going to lose him. I know you will sympathize with us and beg with us the mercy of God to spare him and us.[21]

Bishop Lavialle was not to be spared, however, and he died at Nazareth Convent on May 11, 1867, and was buried five days later from the cathedral in Louisville.[22] Upon the death of Lavialle, Benedict J. Spalding once again was appointed as administrator of the diocese, and John Lancaster continued his rather uneventful life as curate and secretary to his uncle, the administrator.

Yet, the Summer and Fall of 1867 could hardly be described as dull in the life of Spalding. As a seminarian, he had been

[21] AAC, Francis Chambige to John B. Purcell, Nazareth, Kentucky, April 28, 1867.

[22] Louisville *Journal,* May 17, 1867.

characterized by a classmate as one who always seemed to have a horror of a field engagement. And Spalding himself had promised: "never for a moment will I dispute. If by chance I do, I will immediately stop."[23] But five years later, he so forgot his resolution as to engage in battle with an opponent who was the veteran of many a journalistic war, James Alphonsus McMaster, the redoubtable editor of the New York *Freeman's Journal*. The stage had been set for battle in the winter of 1865 while Spalding was still in Rome. At this time, he had written to Uncle Martin:

> You have probably heard . . . that the philosophy of Louvain has been condemned. This however is entirely false. . . . Prof. Ubaghs must change some of his propositions because they are ambiguous and susceptible of a false meaning if interpreted by a party spirit, but the real doctrines of Louvain are not condemned and never will be, although as you know I suppose, there be a strong party in Belgium itself which has serious doubts as to the orthodoxy of the Louvain teaching. There is nothing so sad as this prurient eagerness for finding heresy in every Catholic writer of talent and originality who does not happen to think on every point as our own little selves.[24]

This passion for heresy-hunting, Spalding believed, was not only the source of divisions and disputes among Catholics, but it also weakened, if it did not kill, the efforts of the best and noblest champions of the Catholic cause. "Probably one of the reasons why Brownson fell into so many errors," he told the Archbishop, "was there was no ignorant and self-conceited newspaper editor in the U.S. who did not take it upon himself to denounce him to the world as a heretic."[25]

The controversy between Spalding and McMaster was conducted in a series of articles published in the Baltimore *Catholic Mirror* and the New York *Freeman's Journal* between August

[23] ADP, *Journal*, February, 1862.

[24] AAB, 37-A-7, Spalding to Spalding, Belgian College, Rome, January 5, 1865.

[25] *Ibid.*

81

and November, 1867. It revolved about the problem of ontologism in general, and specifically the teaching of Canon Gerard Casimir Ubaghs, one of Spalding's professors at the Catholic University of Louvain, where the quick and receptive mind of the young seminarian had imbibed a philosophical orientation that influenced his entire career. While Spalding was in attendance at the American College, he had also followed the lectures in the University of such men as Johann T. Beelen, Jean B. Lefebve, and Nicolas J. Laforêt.[26] These scholars were the leaders of two philosophical trends that fused at Louvain and were, for their day, an authentic response to the currents of thought then stirring among non-Catholic philosophers. Both of these trends, ontologism and traditionalism, were later condemned by the Church and ultimately died out, but not without leaving their mark upon the later movement of modernism.

Reaction against rationalism was the keystone of these two vastly different approaches. To begin with, this was the time of romanticism, an age that revealed hostility against the formal in poetry, the classic in art, and the rationalistic in thought. The thought of many was dominated by the question: What method will lead us to infallible truth? And in their desire to bolster certitude, they sought to place its basis on a solid foundation and an invulnerable position with the unifying master idea that human reason is of itself incapable of attaining truth. Thus, for a number of these thinkers traditionalism placed the ultimate basis of truth in a primitive revelation without the aid of which man could never acquire metaphysical and moral ideas. Ontologism, on the other hand, placed certitude in an intuitive vision of God in Whom we know all things.[27]

[26] *L'Annuaire de l'Université de Louvain, 1860* (Louvain, 1860), pp. 20–21. Ubaghs and Laforêt were members of the Faculty of Philosophy while Beelen and Lefebve taught in the Faculty of Theology.

[27] While it is not our purpose here to trace the origin and development of these two movements in the thought of western Europe, it was

The point that aroused Spalding, keenly aware of the Louvain controversy, was when he read in the summer of 1867 in the *Freeman's Journal* that Professor Ubaghs' works had been prohibited as textbooks in the Belgian seminaries "because they contain ontological teaching condemned in the seven propositions."[28] The seven propositions were a synthesis of the entire question of ontologism which, quite apart from the question of Ubaghs' teaching, had been reprobated by the Congregation of the Inquisition in September, 1861.[29] The battle opened on Au-

---

at Louvain that Spalding came in contact with and was strongly influenced by these views, and thus it is necessary to present at least an outline of their history. Traditionalism first made its appearance at Louvain in 1835 in the person of Professor Ubaghs. His theories were embodied in a vast collection of writings to which he devoted the best years of his life in an effort to prove the fundamental thesis that the acquisition of metaphysical truths is inexplicable without a primitive divine teaching and its oral transmission. According to Ubaghs, therefore, the first act of man is an act of faith, and the authority of others becomes the basis of certitude. The question then arises: is our assent to fundamental truths of the speculative and moral order blind, and if so, is the existence of God impossible of rational demonstration? In his *Natural Theology* (St. Louis, 1891), Bernard Boedder, S.J., wrote that "Ubaghs thought we are born with the idea of the infinite God, and this idea is in the beginning uninformed, but becomes formed by reflection, to which we are led by our education in human society." This was the core of ontologism, and at Louvain it was wed to traditionalism. The gist of the Louvain teaching on the subject of ontologism was that ideas, universal ideas endowed with the characteristics of necessity and immutability, cannot be known except by an intuition of God present to the mind and perceived by our intelligence. It was against a background of this kind that Spalding later told Orestes Brownson: "I expect to read with much advantage to myself your proofs of the existence of God, the more so since I was brought up in a school which did not admit this can be proven in a strict and logical sense" (UND, Spalding Papers, Spalding to Brownson, New York, January 14, 1874).

[28] New York *Freeman's Journal*, August 15, 1867.
[29] *Acta Sanctae Sedis*, III, p. 216.

gust 24, 1867, when Spalding's first communication, simply initialed "S," appeared in the *Catholic Mirror*. "It is a woeful thing," he wrote, "when politicians try to write on Metaphysics. The arrogance of a man who thinks himself an oracle in every branch of knowledge is insufferable."[30] Spalding informed McMaster that he had been in Rome when Ubaghs' teaching was under discussion and had even seen the secret documents of the process. He hoped the editor would not take him for one of those "gossiping and petulant Roman ecclesiastics of whom he speaks." But regardless of what McMaster thought, the chief matter under discussion was not Ubaghs' ontologism, but rather "his doctrine *de intuitionis necessitate*."[31] At the outset, McMaster had apologized to his readers for devoting so much space to what he termed a "frivolous discussion of the schools—card houses built up and blown down by school boys of various growths." The sentence irked Spalding. Flippant school boys might speak of metaphysics as an idle, useless thing, but that a man of sense should call philosophical discussion mere frivolities was, to say the least, a mystery. In the case of McMaster, however, the mystery was explainable, since he considered philosophy nothing less than "sophistry," a subject which he treated, said Spalding, "in the style of a man who all his life has been the hero of a newspaper squabble, who jumbles things together, true and false, and leaves the reader with the vague impression that Ontologism is a phantastic heresy, taught by a few men who give themselves out as God-gazers."[32]

McMaster replied on August 31 with an article entitled "Fooleries." In one sense, it was a retraction, for the New York editor claimed that the printer made him say what he had never intended to say. He had not intended to condemn Professor Ubaghs because of his ontological teaching since, to McMaster's

---

[30] *The Catholic Mirror* (Baltimore), August 24, 1867.
[31] *Ibid.*
[32] *Ibid.*

84

mind, Ubaghs' error "lies in a direction very different from that of the neo-ontologists." He had intended the words of condemnation to come after what he had said of the former Abbé Flavian Hugonin, now the Bishop of Bayeux.[33] Spalding could not accept this explanation. Grammatically, he claimed, there was no place for these words following the name of Hugonin, whereas they came naturally after the close of the paragraphs on Ubaghs. To Spalding it was just another instance of McMaster's "philosophy of assertionalism—asserting whatever may happen to please him, and whatever, therefore, he asserts is true, and none of his former assertions limit him with regard to any contradictory assertions which he may see proper to make in the future."[34] Spalding insisted that McMaster had affirmed that ontologism was condemned in the case of Ubaghs, and the strategic move of bringing the printer into the controversy was unsuccessful. "The printer in the case of McMaster," he concluded, "was a *deus ex machina*, but he was not introduced into the affair according to the rules of Horace."[35]

Spalding continued the fight. McMaster was doing great harm, he maintained, by the confused and illogical manner in which he was attempting to set limits to philosophical thought and inquiry in the Church. "Ontologism," said Spalding, "the fundamental doctrine of which affirms the intuition of the infinite—of God, has not been condemned, and I as a Catholic priest am free to hold this doctrine. Whoever calls me a heretic is himself a heretic, because he makes that an article of faith which the Church does not hold and has not defined as such."[36] He had asked his opponent to state clearly exactly what had been condemned with regard to ontologism, but instead, Spalding remarked,

[33] New York *Freeman's Journal,* August 31, 1867.
[34] *The Catholic Mirror,* September 14, 1867.
[35] *Ibid.*
[36] *Ibid.*

. . . he talks about many things in a cant-orthodox tone with the greater part of his argument, devoted to the only kind in which he excels—the *argumentum ad vulgus.* He talks of vile speculations, of school-boys who have heard the tattle of ecclesiastical gossips, of the chattering of the unconsidered hangers-on, of insects that buzz around the flanks of splendid horses, of young ecclesiastics who, having been in Rome, circulate whispering and foolish stories over the world.[37]

He suggested that if McMaster were to go South and after this fashion "harangue the freeman," it might be pardonable, but to write on so serious a subject in this manner, he thought, "shows a want of good sense."[38] McMaster might see heretics lurking in the dark, and, like the watchman in Israel, make rules for them if they wished to read his paper. But Spalding, for one, would be afraid to address the public through the pages of the *Freeman's Journal* lest, as he said, "the editor should make me take divers oaths, should make me swear to receive and interpret the Promulgation of Pontifical Authority only in the sense in which Mr. James A. McMaster received and interprets them."[39]

The editor's fury knew no bounds. "We have a right," he wrote, "to demand of whoever is responsible for the *Mirror* a retraction of the charge of willful falsehood that it has made against us."[40] The following week, Spalding foolishly came back: "McMaster's humility has not been able to bear correction. He is furious, he rages, he pours forth that ever-ready, terrible torrent of abusive language which during the late war mighty generals feared more than the sword of the enemy." When writing to the *Mirror,* he said, "I have asked myself why Mr. McMaster has become so angry, so madly furious. I think I have found the reason." In the discussion concerning ontologism, McMaster had shown himself a poor logician, Spalding was convinced, and moreover a blunderer who was given to loose as-

[37] *Ibid.*
[38] *Ibid.*
[39] *Ibid.*
[40] New York *Freeman's Journal,* September 21, 1867.

sertions. "He has seen this picture of himself, as it were, in a Mirror, has recognized the likeness and is furious."[41]

The conflict was now bordering on the inane, but it was Mc-Master's turn. He declared that "S" had a muddy head, and not only a muddy head, but a head too ridiculously muddy. It was the thrust of an expert. Spalding was hurt. "Does not any educated theologian, who takes the trouble to read this," he exploded, "see that I have a right to get mad?" If Spalding's head was muddy, he intended to get a closer view of what was going on inside McMaster's head. He first postulated the general principle: "Clear ideas find clear expression. If the outward expression be obscure, the interior view is dark. If the interior view is dark, the head is muddy."[42] To show how things looked in Mc-Master's head, he intended to examine a few sentences of Mc-Master's article on "Reconstruction." On that subject the editor had written: "We think it a thing, not only that *ought* to be done, but that, if possible, *must* be done, *so far as possible.*" Consider the "not only," said Spalding, and ask yourself the meaning of it. "How in the world *ought* a thing to be done, or how *must* it be done, if it be not *possible,* or how must it be done farther than it is possible?" This, he argued, was an example of McMaster's strong and logical sentences. "How can a paper whose editor scribbles in this manner live, or how is it that it comes to be published at all? I think I can answer for the benefit of the *Freeman.* Because it finds readers which every paper will find whose columns are filled with violent language, strong epithets and dogmatical assertions." Do you not think, Spalding asked the readers of the *Mirror,* that "McMaster's head looks rather muddy?"[43]

At this point, McMaster had already called for the identifica-

[41] *The Catholic Mirror,* September 28, 1867.
[42] *Ibid.*
[43] *Ibid.*

tion of "S." In an effort to palliate, perhaps, after having pushed the editor a bit too far, Spalding replied:

Mr. McMaster seems to glory in the fact that he stands before the world whilst the muddy-headed writer of these trivial remarks, lurks in the dark. It would be useless for me to sign my name to these communications. I am unknown outside of the little circle in which I live, and whatever I have said is neither more important nor more worthless because I have said it. My sole object in writing is to teach a lesson of modesty and moderation. I respect Mr. McMaster and probably like him more than others who write less roughly concerning him. I surely wish to say nothing derogatory to his character as a Christian or a gentleman. I have been repeatedly told by those who have the pleasure and the honor of his personal acquaintance that they have never met a more perfect gentleman or more obliging friend.[44]

On October 12, 1867, the *Catholic Mirror,* in reply to McMaster's "harsh and arrogant demand," identified "S" by telling their New York contemporary that if he would call on the Reverend J. L. Spalding of Louisville, Kentucky, he would, perhaps, receive a photograph.[45] Far from pacified, McMaster awaited what he called "the explanation that one Christian gentleman owes to another," and he hoped that he would not have to wait too long. All that Spalding had to say was that "he did not *mean* what his words did import." McMaster believed that for one such as "S," a man not accustomed to writing for the public, it would be no great humiliation to declare he had not meant what he had said. With such an acknowledgement, then they could be friends.[46]

When the identity of "S" became known in Louisville and proved to be none other than the favorite nephew of both the Archbishop of Baltimore and the administrator of the Diocese of Louisville, the latter, greatly annoyed, entered into the fray. He

[44] *Ibid.*
[45] *The Catholic Mirror,* October 12, 1867.
[46] New York *Freeman's Journal,* October 19, 1867.

wrote to McMaster to apologize for the words of his nephew, and assured him that the young man had no intention of questioning his statements. If such an interpretation had been attached to his words, Benedict Spalding would see to it that his nephew should make amends. He authorized the editor to state in the *Freeman's Journal* that he had received assurances from a reliable source that the statements made by the writer in the *Catholic Mirror* were not meant to be a reflection on McMaster's honesty. Benedict Spalding insisted, however, that his name was not to be published with the unpleasant affair.[47]

During most of the controversy, Archbishop Spalding had been in Europe, arriving home in mid-October. Shortly after, the Archbishop had a letter from his nephew, who presumed that Uncle Martin had heard of his encounter with McMaster. Since the latter had demanded a retraction in the *Mirror*, John Lancaster sent his uncle an apology—"the only one which I can or will make." He was in duty bound to insist on its publication in the *Mirror* since the editors had published his name without his consent. The whole dreary affair had now become a matter of public record, so that, as he told his uncle, "I must and will justify myself."[48]

But Spalding's "apology" was hardly a retraction.[49] He reviewed the entire ontological question, apologizing only to the public for engaging in a controversy which in itself was of no importance. As for having accused McMaster of deliberate falsehood in saying that his assertion about Ubaghs was not a printer's mistake, he insisted: "I said, I could not believe it. I repeat again what I said and do most solemnly affirm that I *can not* believe it. I do not by this assertion accuse Mr. McMaster of

[47] UND, McMaster Papers, Benedict J. Spalding to James A. McMaster, Louisville, October 26, 1867.

[48] AAB, 36-A-U2, Spalding to Spalding, Louisville, October 26, 1867.

[49] AAB, 39-B-M1, "An Apology," J. Lancaster Spalding to James A. McMaster, a manuscript of ten pages.

wilful falsehood."[50] He had said nothing with regard to Mc-Master's state of mind, but had only stated the actual condition of his own. Did McMaster wish to make Spalding a criminal because he could not "believe a thing which I really and sincerely cannot persuade myself of? I, myself, would be a hypocrite and a liar, if I should say to Mr. McMaster that I believe it. . . ."[51] He now realized how presumptuous he had been to engage McMaster in controversy. "When I began it," he confessed to his uncle, "I thought I would be able to lurk in the dark and that he would never get a fair view of me in plain daylight. But who can hide from the biting breath of Mr. McMaster?"[52] Nevertheless, he concluded:

If I have said anything that might have better remained unsaid, attribute it to inexperience rather than to malice. I assure Mr. McMaster again that I have not intentionally said anything derogatory to his character as a Christian or a gentleman. If I write at all I must write as I feel. He has forced me to write and I have written honestly as I felt.[53]

Fortunately, the Archbishop of Baltimore was a prudent man, for, evidently, he forbade the publication of Lancaster's "Apology." Instead, the whole affair ended on a quiet note when the *Mirror* warned its correspondents:

The Most Reverend Archbishop, having requested us not to admit into our columns articles invoking or provoking discussions of a personal character, we hereby request our numerous correspondents to regulate themselves accordingly. While the utmost liberty of statement and discussion should be encouraged so far as principles and even lawful opinions are concerned, controversies which are likely to lead to angry personal discussions should be discountenanced. They offend charity and do no good, but rather much harm.[54]

[50] *Ibid.,* p. 3
[51] *Ibid.,* p. 4.
[52] *Ibid.,* p. 5.
[53] *Ibid.,* p. 10.
[54] *The Catholic Mirror,* November 9, 1867.

Thus ended Spalding's first field engagement in the realm of controversy, and that rather ingloriously. And it had all been unnecessary. McMaster would have had no need to invoke a printer's mistake and Spalding, perhaps, would not have provoked the tempest if they had both read the decree of the Congregation of the Index which on March 2, 1866, prohibited the use of Ubaghs' textbooks precisely because they contained opinions similar to those of the seven propositions which had previously been condemned in September, 1861, by the Congregation of the Inquisition.[55]

The Diocese of Louisville in the meanwhile was still awaiting the appointment of a new bishop. Finally, in March, 1868, William G. McCloskey, the first Rector of the American College in Rome, was named to the See that had been vacant for almost a year. Consecrated in Rome in May, McCloskey did not arrive in his diocese until early October. In the interim, Father Benedict Spalding had continued as administrator, but on August 4, the Spalding family and the diocese endured a severe shock and loss when the administrator met a tragic death in a fire in the cathedral rectory.[56] Archbishop Purcell, as head of the ecclesiastical province, was then called on to name an administrator until McCloskey's arrival. Purcell appointed Father Hugh I. Brady, "*in quantum possum*," as he said, but not before he had suggested John Lancaster Spalding for the position. Farther Francis Chambige told the Archbishop of Baltimore that he had vetoed the idea, and that he had informed Purcell that, although Lancaster Spalding was a worthy priest, he was too young, and his appointment might be considered as an insult by the older clergy.[57]

After Bishop McCloskey's installation in Louisville, Spalding

[55] *ASS*, III, 215–216.
[56] Louisville *Courier*, August 6, 1868.
[57] AAB, 36-A-C4, Chambige to Spalding, Saint Thomas Seminary, Kentucky, August 24, 1868.

continued as secretary to the new bishop, and, in addition, Mc-
Closkey placed him in charge of the cathedral school which was
staffed by the Xaverian Brothers.

For the next several years, life was busy but not especially
eventful for John Lancaster. He continued to carry out his duties
at the cathedral until June, 1869, when he was relieved and authorized to build a church for the Catholic Negroes of Louisville.[58] Shortly after, he left on a fund-raising tour of the East—
Cincinnati, Philadelphia, and New York—returning in late September to draw up plans for his church.[59]

Meanwhile, on June 29, 1868, Pius IX had convoked an Ecu-
menical Council to meet in Rome on December 8, 1869, and in
anticipation of the Council, in a brief of April 11, 1869, the
Holy Father had proclaimed an extraordinary jubilee *ad instar*
from the first of June, 1869, to the close of the Council. Like
other priests of the Diocese of Louisville, Spalding therefore
spent the next few months after his return preaching the jubilee
throughout the diocese. Finally, on February 20, 1870, Bishop
McCloskey dedicated the new two-story church and school under
the patronage of St. Augustine. It had been paid for by the
young pastor of seventy-five Negroes in the short time of only
seven months.[60] "I am now living in my new parish," he later
wrote Father De Nève, "attending to the Negroes and myself.
And I do not think that . . . I have ever been so happy. I am
poor and content, but that is rich and rich enough."[61]

<hr/>

[58] AAB, 36-A-U3, Spalding to Spalding, Louisville, June 21, 1869.

[59] *The Catholic Advocate* (Louisville), October 9, 1869.

[60] *1870–1945, Diamond Jubilee, Parish of St. Augustine* (Louisville,
1945), *passim.* In 1870, John L. Spalding baptized fifty-nine and
officiated at one marriage; in 1871, he baptized sixty-nine and officiated
at four marriages. In 1911, on the occasion of the laying of the cornerstone of the present church, Spalding returned to St. Augustine's and
was greeted by a number of old parishioners, many of whom he called
by name, much to their delight.

[61] AAC-L, Spalding to De Nève, Louisville, May 4, 1870.

Poor and content he was, but not, however, unaware of the interest that had been aroused with the convocation of the Vatican Council. The definition of papal infallibility, it was apparent from the outset, would be the main topic of discussion and controversy. The chancellories of Europe were agog with excitement, the press was in ferment, and there were rumors of intrigues of statesmen and possible interference of governments. The direst consequences for Church and state, it was predicted, would follow the definition of the dogma of papal infallibility. Among the assembled bishops, the infallibilists and the inopportunists engaged in learned debates, and Gallicanism, bolstered by German "scientific" theology, brought to bear all the strength it could muster against Archbishop Henry Edward Manning and his following. It was a contest such as only the Catholic Church could allow, witness, and withstand. Catholics, nevertheless, were at liberty to voice their opinions, and Spalding was never tardy in expressing his. While he assured Father De Nève at Louvain that he had not the slightest intention of provoking a controversy, he wished merely to state in a modest way

. . . that nothing but a definition of the Church will ever elicit an act of faith from me in the infallibility of the Pope or that of any man. I know that the easy and prosperous way is to float along with the currents both in religious and worldly matters; but I do not know that the various winds of doctrine should have the power to make us veer round whenever they see fit to blow in a new direction.[62]

Realizing that he had probably startled his old friend and professor, he hastened to add that his faith in the Church was unbounded; nevertheless, Spalding continued, "I have little confidence in the opinions of men, and still less in the opinions of parties or cliques, and least of all in those cliques that sacrilegiously arrogate to themselves the mission of guiding aright in the Church of Jesus Christ." As for the controversies over infallibility that were then filling the air, he felt that they were conducted in a

[62] *Ibid.*

93

bitter and un-Christian spirit, with the great effort of both sides directed to victory and not truth. With the McMaster affair evidently still rankling, he concluded by telling De Nève: "Do not think, however, that I waste my time in disputes. I write nothing for publication. And I rarely ever speak of these matters except as pastime when others suggest them."[63] It was plain, however, that if Spalding had been a member of the council then in session at Rome he would have ranged himself on the side of the inopportunists.

The following June, Father Spalding left Louisville for an extended vacation in California, and was away from the diocese until the following December.[64] Soon thereafter, on October 24, Bishop McCloskey appointed him Chancellor of the diocese with residence in the Bishop's house. However, Spalding was not destined to remain Chancellor for long. Shortly after Christmas of the same year, Archbishop Spalding fell gravely ill, and for six weeks hovered near death amid great pain. A few days before he died, his nephew arrived in Baltimore and remained with him until the end.[65] Then, on February 7, Archbishop Spalding died, after having received the last rites from Bishop Becker; after the funeral, on February 12, John Lancaster returned to Louis-

[63] *Ibid.*

[64] AAB, 37-A-12, Spalding to Spalding, Louisville, June 20, 1871. On January 21, 1872, Spalding lectured on "Views and Persons and Things in California" at Weisiger Hall for the benefit of St. Vincent's Home. Among other things, he voiced a prediction which proved to be quite false when he said that "San Francisco is not likely ever to be of much greater importance than it is at present. It has undoubtedly been injured by the opening of the Pacific railroad. . . . When we add to these considerations the fact that the class of people who build up our great cities are deterred from coming to San Francisco by the detrimental competition of Chinese labor, it would seem that the Queen of the Golden Gate is not destined to fulfill the promise of her early days." Cf. Louisville *Courier-Journal*, January 22, 1872.

[65] *The Catholic Advocate*, February 15, 1872.

ville. The death of his uncle, however, was to mark a turning point in his career. In a list of private instructions left with Bishop James Gibbons, who at the time was Administrator of the Diocese of Richmond, as well as Vicar Apostolic of North Carolina, the Archbishop had directed Gibbons to give over all the necessary documents for the writing of his biography to Isaac T. Hecker of the Paulist Fathers,[66] a long-time friend. However, Hecker's ill health prevented him from undertaking the proposed biography. Instead, he suggested the nephew of the late Archbishop for the task. Gibbons agreed, and in July, 1872, Spalding obtained a leave of absence from the Louisville Diocese and left for New York, where he was to undertake the writing of the biography in the residence of the Paulist Fathers.[67]

Spalding realized, he wrote, that he was chosen for the task "less from the conviction that I was fitted for the work than from the belief that what I lacked in ability might in some measure be supplied by zeal and industry." Yet, by April, 1873, Spalding had completed the first draft of the manuscript, and in September the biography was published—though James Roosevelt Bayley, Archbishop Spalding's successor in the See of Baltimore, did not like it and complained of its "corduroy" style. Orestes Brownson, on the other hand, hailed the book as "almost the only biography worthy of the name to be found in our American Catholic literature."[68]

With the completion of the biography, it was expected in the ordinary course of events that Father Spalding would naturally return to his diocese and his position as chancellor. However, a dispute between his late Uncle Martin and Bishop McCloskey over the deposition of Benedict L. Spalding's estate[69] precluded

---

[66] Ellis, *op. cit.*, I, pp. 113–114

[67] AAB, 34-B-13, Gibbons to Spalding, Richmond, July 12, 1872.

[68] "Archbishop Spalding," *Brownson's Quarterly Review*, Last Series, I (January, 1874), p. 108.

[69] Cf. UND, Cincinnati Papers, II-5-f.

any further contact with a Bishop who had grown to have less than reverence for the name of Spalding. John Lancaster did return to Kentucky, in May, 1873, but it was only to say goodbye.[70]

Obtaining an indefinite leave of absence from the diocese but not a permanent *exeat,* Father Spalding chose to continue his priestly career in the Archdiocese of New York, where he was assigned to St. Michael's Parish as an assistant to his friend, Father Arthur J. Donnelly.[71] The New York of this time was

[70] New York *Times,* May 10, 1873. It must be admitted, however, that McCloskey had from the start always recognized Father Spalding's abilities. In his first report on the Diocese of Louisville made to Alessandro Cardinal Barnabo, Prefect of the Congregation de Propaganda Fide, McCloskey spoke of St. Mary's College as "another thorn" in his side, that the reputation of the college in the eyes of Catholics was completely ruined, and that "only one thing could take the College of S. Mary from so wretched a state." That one thing would have been the acceptance by John L. Spalding of the Presidency of the College. McCloskey added:

. . . I had confidence in his ability, and I knew that his name would have contributed much to the success of the enterprise, since many of his family had ceased to aid the College that formerly they had protected, and he himself was educated there, another spur why he should make every effort. I promised the Rev. Spalding every assistance should he undertake the Herculean labor. At first he consented, but after reflecting, seeing, I imagine, the vain hope of raising the College from its fallen state, and fearing lest his own reputation would have to suffer in not succeeding, he begged me to excuse him from accepting, nor could I blame him.

Cf. Archives of the Sacred Congregation de Propaganda Fide, Scritture originale riferite nei congressi, Report on the Diocese of Louisville made by William G. McCloskey, Bishop of Louisville, to Alessandro Cardinal Barnabò, Prefect of the Congregation de Propaganda, n.d. Internal evidence leads to the conclusion that McCloskey wrote this report shortly after his arrival in Louisville.

[71] AAB, 72-0-1, Spalding to Gibbons, New York, June 4, 1873. That Spalding did not obtain an *exeat* from the diocese, that is, a complete withdrawal, may be inferred from a letter of Father Anthony B. Schwenninger to his ordinary, Archbishop Purcell of Cincinnati (AAC,

famous for its Vanderbilts, Fisks, and Goulds; and for Boss Tweed, who only a year before had been indicted for looting the city treasury of an estimated $45,000,000. Horace Greeley, for thirty years editor of the powerful New York *Tribune,* had been nominated as candidate for the presidency on the Liberal Republican ticket by a group of reformers who had come to regard Ulysses S. Grant as totally unfit for office. The mid-1870s was also a time of nationwide religious tension, when the oft-heard no-popery cry would this time revolve around the school question and the taxation of church property.

Two years later, in his annual message to Congress on December 7, 1875, President Grant urged an amendment to the Constitution which would compel all the states to adopt a public school system, "to forbid all religious, atheistic, or pagan instruction in them," and to prohibit all distribution of federal funds among the denominations for the support of private schools.[72] Grant's proposal was quickly framed as a joint resolution of both houses of Congress on December 14 by James G. Blaine, representative from Maine and formerly Speaker of the House who introduced what came to be called the Blaine Amendment,[73] an amendment to the Constitution which was to be the means whereby the sponsor would secure the coveted Republican presidential nomination.

Grant's message to Congress had also recommended that all

---

unclassified) in which he stated: "I ask your Lordship kindly to give me permission of absence from the Archdiocese *ad libitum* as many priests have from their diocese in the old country. The young Father Spalding is here in New York under the same conditions from Louisville." Cf. Archives of St. Michael's Church, New York City, Baptismal Records. Father Spalding's name occurs in the parish records for the first time on June 17, 1873, as having baptized Jane Sherry, daughter of Patrick and Mary Sherry.

[72] *Congressional Record,* 44th Congress, 1st Session, 1875–1876, p. 175.

[73] *Ibid.,* p. 205.

church property should be subject to taxation. Catholic opposition to the proposal was, of course, widespread, and Spalding, too, opposed this "experiment of a purely secular education."[74] It would not, however, be for some years, particularly as first Bishop of Peoria, Illinois, that the voice of Lancaster Spalding would extend beyond the scope of personal letters and take on national importance in the matter of Catholic parochial education.

In July, 1876, shortly after the Republican convention nominated Rutherford B. Hayes for the presidency—the Blaine Amendment having in the meantime failed in its double purpose to tax church property and propel Representative Blaine into the nomination—John Lancaster escaped the city's sweltering heat by sailing for a vacation in Europe. After a week in London, he crossed to Paris where he visited with Mother Aloysia Hardey, then the Assistant General of the Society of the Sacred Heart.[75] From France he went to Scotland, and then over to Ireland, where at Queenstown he boarded a steamer for home.

As Spalding sailed for Europe, the United States was in the midst of celebrating its hundredth year of independence. Prompted by the occasion of the centennial year, Spalding traced for the readers of the *Catholic World* the history of the Catholic Church in the new world. Like the history of the American Republic, the external development of the Church during the first century had been characterized by a phenomenal growth. All individual energies had been concentrated to accelerate this expansion, but the next century, he believed, would bring an opportunity and a duty for more than mere external growth. There were pressing needs, and among these Spalding noted the necessity for a more thorough organization of the Catholic edu-

[74] J. L. Spalding, *Essays and Reviews* (New York, 1877), pp. 38.

[75] UND, unclassified, Spalding to Richard Spalding, London, July 24, 1876. Mother Aloysia Hardey was related to the Spaldings through her mother, Sarah Spalding, who had married Frederick Hardey. Born at Piscataway, Maryland, Mother Hardey died at Paris, June 17, 1886.

cational system. "Catholic universities must be created," he insisted, "which in time will grow to be intellectual centres in which the best minds of the church in this country may receive the culture and training that will enable them to work in harmony for the furtherance of Catholic ends."[76] A more vigorous and independent press, one not weakened by want or depraved by human respect, must also be brought into existence, and Catholics must prepare themselves to enter more fully into the public life of the nation, "to throw the light of Catholic thought upon each new phase of opinion or belief as it rises; to grapple more effectively with the great moral evils which threaten at once the life of the nation and the church."[77] All this and more, he maintained, must be done in the century ahead if the God-given mission of the American Church was to witness its fulfillment.

By September, 1876, Spalding had returned to New York and St. Michael's. In addition to his parochial duties, he continued to write for the *Catholic World,* and found time to edit two Catholic readers for the elementary grades.[78] His reputation as an orator grew, and he was often called on to preach and to lecture throughout the archdiocese and in the neighboring diocese of Newark and Brooklyn. James McMaster, still of the New York *Freeman's Journal,* occasionally gave extracts from the eloquent sermons of his erstwhile opponent, and, perhaps, with tongue in cheek, not forgetting the printer's mistake in the ontological controversy of yesteryear, constantly referred to the "Reverend Doctor James Lancaster Spalding." Worth noting, however, is McMaster's account of the sermon Spalding delivered on the

[76] J. L. Spalding, "The Catholic Church in the United States, 1776–1876," *Catholic World,* XXIII (July, 1876), p. 450.

[77] *Ibid.*

[78] The reading books, published by the Catholic Publication Society in 1875, were entitled: *The Young Catholic's Illustrated Fifth Reader* and *The Young Catholic's Sixth Reader and Speaker.*

occasion of the dedication of St. Michael's Church in Jersey City in October, 1876. Spalding was the preacher at the Pontifical Mass, and McMaster noted how for nearly an hour he held the audience in hushed attention with an eloquently delivered sermon which

. . . was practical and addressed to the popular understanding throughout; but it grazed the surface of the metaphysical just enough to refute in clear and adequate terms the condemned notion of the pseudo-ontologists who dreamed of a man, here below, having a direct vision of the Infinite Being Who is God. We know God only by the Revelation He has made of Himself, and this knowledge is addressed to the intellect through sensible representations and is recognized by the intellect when presented, because God has given the intellect the capacity to know truth, and to distinguish it from error. This was the distinct thesis the preacher developed in more eloquent words.[79]

At last, apparently, Spalding was capitulating and acknowledging that ontologism was a condemned notion, or at least he was implying it. He had to, for on the subject of ontologism—their old difference—time had proven McMaster correct, printer's mistake or not.

Quite unknown to Spalding, a series of events was about to reach its climax which would afford him an opportunity to employ his talents on a broader front for Church and country in the years ahead. In 1872, Thomas Foley, the Administrator and Coadjutor Bishop of Chicago, realizing that the territory under his jurisdiction was too large to be properly cared for by a bishop living so far north as Chicago, petitioned the Holy See for a division of the diocese, a request which was not acted on immediately.[80] Two years later, on March 11, 1874, Peter Richard Kenrick, Archbishop of St. Louis, met with a majority of his suffragan bishops at his home in St. Louis. As a result of this meeting, a letter was dispatched to Alessandro Cardinal Franchi,

[79] New York *Freeman's Journal,* October 14, 1876.
[80] *The New World* (Chicago), April 14, 1900.

Prefect of the Congregation de Propaganda Fide, asking the Holy Father for a division of the vast Province of St. Louis into three separate provinces and a further division of the Diocese of Chicago.[81] This petition was favorably received, and on February 12, 1875, Pope Pius IX, on the advice of the cardinals of Propaganda, created two new ecclesiastical provinces with metropolitan sees at Milwaukee and Santa Fe, and on the same day the territory of the Diocese of Chicago was limited by the establishment of a new episcopal See in the city of Peoria, Illinois, as a suffragan of the Province of St. Louis. Six days later, Michael Hurley, pastor of St. Patrick's Parish in Peoria, was appointed the first bishop of the new diocese.[82]

Although Father Hurley, by virtue of his location and knowledge of the new diocese, seemed to be the most appropriate candidate for the office of bishop, he himself believed that he was not suited for the burdens of the episcopacy. His whole life, his customs, his habits, everything about him proved to Hurley that he was not the man for the place.[83] As soon as the bishop-elect

[81] AAB, 41-Y-23, Peter Richard Kenrick to Bayley, St. Louis, March 13, 1874.

[82] Archives of the Sacred Congregation de Propaganda Fide, Scritture originale riferite nelle congregazioni generali, vol. 1004 (1875). The cardinals of Propaganda met on January 11, 1875, in general congregation or sessions in which questions were discussed that required formal sanction by the Pope. This sanction was given on January 17, although the actual brief creating the Diocese of Peoria is dated February 12, 1875. Cf. *Pii IX Acta Pontificis Maximi* (Romae, 1889), VII, 20–22, 23–25. The *terna,* or the list of three nominees, for the Diocese of Peoria, included Michael Hurley in the first place or *dignissimus,* Edward M. Hennessy of the Congregation of Saint Vincent de Paul in the second place or *dignior,* and John Ireland of the Diocese of St. Paul (and its future archbishop) in the third place or *dignus.* Hereafter the Propaganda archives will be cited as ACPF.

[83] New York *Freeman's Journal,* February 20, 1875. Michael Hurley was born in Tipperary, Ireland, in 1826. After his theological studies, he came to the United States and worked as a priest in Lockport,

had been notified of his nomination to the See of Peoria, he immediately went to Chicago to see Bishop Foley. "No power on earth," he told the Bishop, "can induce me to accept a mitre." Bishop Foley thereupon notified the Archbishop of St. Louis and the suffragans of the Province, and a new list of names was then drawn up. On the second *terna* forwarded to the Holy See, Father Frederick Wayrich, C.SS.R., of New York City was placed first, John L. Spalding of Louisville, second, and the third name was that of John J. Kain of Harper's Ferry.[84] "Imagine our surprise," Foley later wrote to Cardinal McCloskey, "when Bulls came to Fr. Hurley, though I had written to Card. Franchi that he would not accept even under a command." Some time later, Hurley informed Bishop Foley that he had received a letter from a certain Father X who, although he had abandoned the priesthood four years previously, had been consulted by Cardi-

---

Bloomington, and Springfield before coming to Peoria as pastor of St. Mary's Church in 1864. During his stay at St. Mary's, Hurley organized the parish of St. Patrick in what was then the lower end of town, and at his own request Hurley was transferred to the new parish and remained pastor there until his death in 1892.

[84] ACPE, Scritture orig. . . , vol. 1004 (1875), Foley to the Cardinal Prefect, Chicago, July 12, 1874. Frederick Wayrich was born August 19, 1834, in the village of Huttigweiler in Trier. In the early 1840s he came to this country with his parents. Ordained a Redemptorist in 1858, he filled many important positions in the congregation, but was known more widely as a retreat master. In 1898, Wayrich secularized and was incardinated into the Archdiocese by Archbishop Corrigan. He died on March 7, 1907. Four times during his life he was mentioned for the mitre, viz., for Newark, Savannah, Charleston, and Peoria. Cf. Henry Brann, "The Reverend Frederick William Wayrich," *Historical Records and Studies,* V (November, 1907), p. 231. John Joseph Kain was born at Martinsburg, West Virginia, May 31, 1841. Ordained July 2, 1866, he was stationed at Harper's Ferry for nine years and on May 23, 1875, he was consecrated the second Bishop of Wheeling. In early Summer of 1893, he was named Coadjutor Archbishop of St. Louis, succeeding to the See in May, 1895. Kain died in 1903. Cf. Ellis, *Life of Gibbons,* II, p. 414 and *passim.*

nal Franchi about Peoria. Father X had recommended Hurley so earnestly that the Cardinal was determined to make him a bishop.[85] Nevertheless, Father Hurley remained steadfast in his refusal until finally on April 23, 1876, Pope Pius IX accepted the resignation of the first Bishop-elect of Peoria.[86]

Meanwhile John J. Kain had been promoted to the See of Wheeling, vacant since the death of Richard Vincent Whelan.[87] The Archbishop of St. Louis thereupon forwarded a third *terna* for the Peoria bishopric with Spalding now in first place, Wayrich in second, and John J. Keane, pastor of St. Patrick's Church, Washington, D.C., as the third candidate.[88] When the Cardinals

[85] AANY, A-22, Foley to McCloskey, Chicago, September 10, 1875.

[86] The briefs appointing Hurley to Peoria were accompanied by a letter in which the Bishop-elect was exhorted in the name of the Holy Father to accept the honor conferred on him. On April 21, 1875, Hurley replied that he was obliged by conscience to decline the episcopacy since he was unable to perform the duties involved, because, as he said, he did not know an iota of Canon Law, he was little versed in theology, and felt himself unable to resolve the difficulties with which the priests of the diocese might present him and thus become the object of their contempt rather than of their respect. Finally, physical weakness would make it impossible to sustain the burdens which he would necessarily have had to face in a newly founded diocese. Hurley's refusal was made known to Pope Pius IX in an audience held on May 16, 1875, but a further delay ensued when the Holy Father asked for further information since he believed that the Bishop-elect had been prompted by sentiments of humility. When Peter Richard Kenrick, Archbishop of St. Louis, forwarded the second *terna* of Wayrich, Spalding, and Kain and informed Propaganda that the aforesaid names were submitted only after all hope of acceptance by Father Hurley had been exhausted, further investigation was considered useless.

[87] Kain, it will be remembered, was third on the second *terna* for Peoria. He succeeded Richard Vincent Whelan (1809–1874), second Bishop of Richmond (1841–1850) who became first Bishop of Wheeling in 1850. Cf. ACPF, Scritture orig. . . . , vol. 1004 (1875), n. 12.

[88] ACPE. Scritture orig. . . . , vol. 1005, folio 1073, Peter Richard Kenrick to the Cardinal Prefect, St. Louis, November 4, 1875.

of Propaganda met in general congregation on May 22, 1876, to discuss the latest list of candidates for the See of Peoria, Cardinal Franchi recalled that at the general congregation held on January 11, 1875, the name of Father Spalding had appeared on two lists for two different bishoprics, first of all for Peoria, and then on the *terna* submitted by the bishops of the Province of Baltimore for the bishopric of Wheeling. Information supplied by the prelates of both provinces, the Cardinal Prefect noted, had been satisfactory in every respect. Only the Bishop of Wilmington, Thomas A. Becker, had reported at the time to have heard that Spalding had published certain philosophical writings that seemed to agree closely with certain propositions that had been condemned at the University of Louvain.[89] It had also been rumored that at least before the definition of papal infallibility at the Vatican Council, Father Spalding had declared himself not in favor of the doctrine. Franchi had then written to John Cardinal McCloskey of New York for further information and the Cardinal had replied:

> Before the definition of the doctrine, while everybody was discussing *opportuneness* and *inopportuneness,* he [Spalding] declared himself in intimate circles to be an "inopportunist," knowing this to be the opinion of his venerable uncle. Mgr. Spalding and other American prelates, although they were very strong supporters of Infallibility. Nevertheless, he did not stress it, and he never allowed himself to stir up the issue in preaching or in writing. He confined himself to duty and awaited the solution in the council.

After the decision had been handed down, Father Spalding had not failed to sustain and defend it when the occasion was opportune, McCloskey added, and thus showed himself to be "a true and sincere Catholic, a docile and obedient son of the Church and most whole-heartedly devoted to the Holy See."[90]

---

[89] *Ibid.,* vol. 1004, folio 49, Becker to the Cardinal Prefect, Wilmington, September, 1874.

[90] *Ibid.,* John Cardinal McCloskey to the Cardinal Prefect, New York, March 24, 1876.

Despite McCloskey's recommendation, the cardinals of the Propaganda decided once again to delay the appointment of a bishop for Peoria until they had more precise information on the orthodoxy of John Lancaster Spalding, specifically on his views on ontologism and his submission to the decrees of the Vatican Council.[91] Cardinal Franchi then wrote to James Roosevelt Bayley, the Archbishop of Baltimore, to attempt to discover the truth of the charge that Spalding was an ontologist and to inquire whether or not the candidate had fully submitted to the decrees of the Council.[92] Bayley turned the investigation over to Bishop Becker of Wilmington who informed the Holy See on August 2, 1876, that he had employed divers means to arrive at the truth "fully realizing," he said, "that the burden laid upon us was fraught with risks, due to the bitter hatred of Americans for informers...." The investigation, Becker continued, had shown:

I. No published writings of a philosophical nature by the priest in question are in circulation, and whatever he did say on the doctrine of ontologism was the result, no doubt, of the intimate association between him and Prof. Ubaghs and his followers at Louvain. Indeed, he was merely the object of a few suspicions, since it is an acknowledged fact that he was not overly given to studies of this sort.

II. Our investigation has not at all been able to discover whether or not he was of a mind with the Vatican Council before its decrees were published. The most probable opinion is that he, along with his uncle, the Archbishop of Baltimore (of happy memory).... was in complete agreement with the decrees of the aforesaid Council.

III. James A. McMaster, an outstanding newspaperman, and easily the leading Catholic editor here in the United States, was questioned about this same priest and recently reported to us: "I know him to be a priest well received by people and sufficiently endowed with preaching ability; in Theology not more than sufficiently versed, even somewhat superficial, but yet orthodox, that I can hardly deny.

[91] *Ibid.*, vol. 1005 (1876), folio 1136, *Appendice alla Relazione del Maggio 1876. Sulla scelta del Vescovo di Peoria.*
[92] *Ibid.*

Moreover, added Becker, it was he as secretary of the bishops of the Province of Baltimore who had introduced into the reports to Propaganda certain charges against Spalding which had been leveled against him by the bishops and others, but these charges now seemed to be lacking in any firm foundation. A large number of the bishops who at one time harbored suspicions, or at least regarded Spalding with a wary eye, now openly speak of their great respect and high admiration for him. It was the opinion of all the bishops of the Province, therefore, that Father Spalding was a worthy candidate for the episcopacy.[93]

On November 26, 1876, the Cardinals of Propaganda agreed with Becker's conclusion and recommended John Lancaster Spalding to the Holy Father as their choice for the See of Peoria. Pope Pius IX gave his approval on December 3,[94] and it was not long before Miss Ella Edes, Rome correspondent of the New York *Herald* and the *Freeman's Journal,* informed her employers by cable that "John Spalding of Kentucky has been made Bishop of Peoria." Elsewhere it was announced that the Reverend Benedict J. Spalding of Lexington, Kentucky, had been made bishop of the new diocese, but McMaster of the *Freeman's Journal* assured his readers: "Not by cablegram, but only announcing what is well understood in certain quarters, we can say that the eloquent and esteemed Rev. Doctor James Lancaster Spalding [*sic*] (native of Kentucky, nephew of the late Martin J. Spalding, Archbishop of Baltimore) and at present resident in the diocese and city of New York, has been appointed to the Diocese of Peoria by our Holy Father the Pope."[95]

Congratulations began to reach the assistant pastor of St. Michael's, and to Bishop Gibbons the Bishop-elect wrote thanking him for his kind letter, but adding:

[93] *Ibid.,* vol. 1005 (1876), folio 1137, Becker to the Cardinal Prefect, Wilmington, August 2, 1876.

[94] *Ibid.,* vol. 1005 (1876), folio 1140.

[95] New York *Freeman's Journal,* January 1, 1877.

. . . I am sure you are too wise to think that I am really to be congratulated upon my appointment to the See of Peoria. It seems to me that the last thing a sensible man ought to desire is to be a bishop, at least in the United States. I hope there may be some right way of escaping this responsibility and that Some one more fit to build up a new diocese may be appointed.[96]

In spite of an apparent reluctance to shoulder the burdens of the episcopacy, Spalding was soon engaged with the many preparations that had to be attended to before his consecration. In March, relieved of parochial duties at St. Michael's, he wrote once again to Gibbons to say that Cardinal McCloskey had consented to consecrate him in St. Patrick's Cathedral and that Bishop Foley of Chicago was to be a co-consecrator. "If it is not presumptious [sic]," he continued, "I would beg you also to be an assistant consecrator. I am bold in asking this, but I know your great affection for my uncle and feel that this gives me a certain claim upon your kindness."[97] Several weeks later, however, Spalding remarked to Michael A. Corrigan, Bishop of Newark, just home from Rome and his *ad limina* visit: "Had I known you were to be home so soon, I should have asked you to do me the honor to act as assistant consecrator, but now I can only hope that you will at least be present at my consecration."[98] Although Corrigan may well have been Spalding's second choice, in the years ahead the Bishop of Peoria would frequently part company with his friend of Newark and ally himself with Gibbons in a number of the major matters that were to divide the future Archbishops of Baltimore and New York.

At length, the day arrived when John Lancaster Spalding was to be made a bishop. On Tuesday, May 1, 1877, the feast of Sts. Philip and James, shortly after ten o'clock, the procession of

[96] AANY, C–3, Spalding to Gibbons, Baltimore, January 1, 1877.

[97] AANY, C–3, Spalding to Gibbons, Baltimore, January 1, 1877.

[98] AANY, C–3, Spalding to Michael A. Corrigan, New York, April 23, 1877.

priests and prelates left the cathedral rectory and proceeded to old St. Patrick's Cathedral on Mott Street. Besides the cardinal and the co-consecrators, ten other bishops, two monsignori, and more than one hundred priests were in attendance at the ceremony: James A. Healy of Portland, Maine; Ramon Moreno y Castañeda, Vicar Apostolic of Lower California; Michael A. Corrigan of Newark; Joseph Dwenger, C.PP.S., of Fort Wayne; Thomas A. Becker of Wilmington; Jeremiah F. Shanahan of Harrisburg; Sylvester H. Rosecrans of Columbus; John J. Conroy of Albany; Patrick N. Lynch of Charleston; John Loughlin of Brooklyn; Monsignor Silas E. Chatard, rector of the American College in Rome; Monsignor Robert E. Seton, pastor of St. Joseph's Church in Jersey City. Cardinal McCloskey was the celebrant of the Pontifical Mass with William Quinn, his vicar general, as the assistant priest. Thomas J. Ducey, a curate with Spalding at St. Michael's, was deacon of the mass while Benedict J. Spalding, brother of the new bishop, was subdeacon. For chaplains, the Bishop-elect chose his pastor, Father Arthur Donnelly, and Michael Hurley, the first bishop-elect of Peoria. Preacher for the occasion was Sylvester H. Rosecrans, Bishop of Columbus, who knew Spalding well, having been president of Mount St. Mary's of the West when the new bishop studied there. Following his consecration, Bishop Spalding remained in New York for another two weeks. On May 3, Father Donnelly gave a banquet in honor of one whom he called his "coadjutor," since Lancaster had been his senior curate.[99] The Sunday following, the new Bishop preached at the dedication of St. Agnes,[100] and finally, on May 14, he set out for Chicago where he preached in the Cathedral of the Holy Name.[101] Then, in the company of Bishop Foley and a number of priests, he took the train for Peoria.

[99] AANY, Burtsell Diary, May 3, 1877.
[100] Ibid., May 6, 1877.
[101] Peoria *Daily National Democrat,* May 22, 1877.

3

Bishop of Peoria

PEORIA, the Pimiteoni of the Indians, was by the 1870s one of the chief cities of the Illinois Valley. Marquette had tarried in Peoria in 1675, and the Recollect Friar Louis Hennepin built a log cabin there. Not far from Peoria, Robert Cavelier Sieur de La Salle established Fort Crêvecoeur, and the Jesuit Jacques Gravier arrived in 1689. But only one hundred and fifty years later did a new era begin for the Catholic Church in Peoria, when the Lazarists, priests of the Congregation of the Mission, commonly called Vincentians, came to the Illinois Valley.

The outward circumstance that led to the settlement of north central Illinois in the nineteenth century was the construction of the Illinois and Michigan Canal, which was to connect the Great Lakes with the river system of the Mississippi Valley. The Illinois River was navigable from Ottawa in La Salle County to its mouth. In Indian times, the headwaters of the river and that of the Chicago River were connected by a road over which canoes could be carried. By connecting the two streams and deepening the channel by means of a canal, the Illinois would empty into Lake Michigan, and would be of incalculable value for trade and commerce. Work on the canal began on July 4, 1836, both in Chicago and in La Salle. Around Christmas of 1837, the contractor, William Byrne, visited Bishop Joseph Rosati of St. Louis and asked for missionaries, since construction of the proposed waterway had induced hundreds of Irish Catholics to come into the region. Rosati promised priests at once, with the village of La Salle chosen as center of the mission. The Vincentians John Blase Raho and Aloysius J. Parodi were charged with establishing the network of mission stations in northern Illinois, and Peoria, though without a church, was designated St. Philomena's Mission.[1] Not until 1842, however, was any notable progress made, when Peter Richard Kenrick, at that time the recently consecrated Coadjutor Bishop of St. Louis, announced an episcopal visitation of the La Salle Mission and its dependencies. Black Patridge in Woodford County, then Kickapoo, and finally Peoria were his subsequent stops, though at St. Philomena's only six Peorians were confirmed.[2] At the Bishop's urging, the Catholics of Peoria elected to build a church, and in 1846 the first St. Mary's Church was opened. St. Mary's was the original parish in what was later to be the See city in the Diocese of Peoria.[3]

One year after Kenrick's visit, the Fifth Provincial Council met in Baltimore and decided that the western half of Illinois should be withdrawn from the jurisdiction of St. Louis, and that a new diocese, one comprising the entire state, be erected.[4] The Diocese of Chicago came into being in November, 1843, and had a Catholic population of 136,900 in one hundred and twenty counties.[5] Ten years later, the diocese was divided for the first time, with the creation of the Diocese of Alton; and on February 12, 1875, it was divided a second time, and the new See of Peoria erected. The Diocese of Peoria embraced twenty-

[1] John Rothensteiner, "The Northeastern Part of the Diocese of St. Louis under Bishop Rosati," *Illinois Catholic Historical Review,* IV (October, 1921), p. 148.

[2] *Ibid.,* p. 151.

[3] *History of Peoria's Churches,* II, p. 372.

[4] *Acta Gregorii Papae XVI* (Rome, 1901–1904), III, p. 304.

[5] "Illinois," *American Cyclopedia* (New York, 1874), IX, p. 191d.

two counties in northern Illinois, and included much of the territory within the original mission of La Salle.[6]

The Peoria of the late 1870s was already a flourishing city when Bishop Spalding arrived. Second in size only to Chicago in Illinois, and sixty-seventh in the nation, it was a prospering trading center, the meeting terminal of nine railroads, the seat of a large grain traffic, and the site of a number of leading manufacturers of malt and distilled liquors. Regularly laid out, Peoria could boast of wide, well-graded streets which centered about a public square. Its population was 23,000.[7]

Spalding's first task was the organization of his missionary diocese, which had only fifty priests and seventy churches to care for the estimated 40,000 Catholics under his jurisdiction.[8] To assist him in this work, Bishop Spalding requested the help of his brother Ben, whereupon Benedict J. Spalding secured an *exeat* from the Diocese of Louisville and came to Peoria. Father Spalding became the first chancellor of the diocese and rector of the cathedral, posts that he held until his death.[9]

The Bishop's first major project, however, was the construction of St. Francis Hospital in his See city. In the Spring of 1876, Mother Xavier Termehr, O.S.F., foundress of the Sisters

---

[6] *Pii IX Pontificia Maximi Acta* (Romae, 1889), VII, pp. 23–25.

[7] "Peoria," *American Cyclopedia* (New York, 1874), XII, p. 277d.

[8] *Sadliers' Catholic Directory* (1878) (New York, 1878), p. 341.

[9] ADP. Benedict Joseph Flaget Spalding, brother of the Bishop of Peoria, was born in Lebanon, Kentucky, in 1851. He entered the College de Namur in Belgium on October 18, 1869. On March 27, 1871, he transferred to the College d'Evain, Les Bruins, Haute Savoire, in France and later entered the American College at Louvain, July 25, 1873. He was ordained a priest in Louisville in 1875. From September, 1877, until the Summer of 1887, he was pastor of St. Mary's Cathedral in Peoria, and it was he who built the new cathedral. Ill health forced him to return to Lebanon in the Summer of 1887, where he died on November 28, of that year. Cf. also, *The Record* (Louisville), December 10, 1887.

111

of St. Francis, who had come to Dubuque, Iowa, from Germany in the wake of the *Kulturkampf*, received a request to establish the hospital in Peoria, and accepted. Spalding, however, had a further request, that the community be diocesan in character and separate from the motherhouse in Dubuque. This also the sisters agreed to, and on July 16, 1877, they became the Sisters of the Third Order of St. Francis of Peoria. Property was soon purchased, contracts awarded, and on September 30 of that same year Spalding laid the cornerstone of St. Francis Hospital.[10]

In the way of acquiring more priests for his diocese, Spalding turned to the Franciscan Order. At his request, both the Order of Friars Minor and the Order of Friars Minor Capuchin agreed to come to Peoria. In September, 1878, Franciscans from the Province of St. John the Baptist in Cincinnati were assigned to Minonk, which until then had been a mission of El Paso, Illinois. Streator, Bloomington, Washington, Washburn, Pekin, and Metamora were likewise given to their care. The Capuchins were assigned to the new parish of the Sacred Heart in Peoria itself, and continued to work in the diocese until lack of priests forced their withdrawal in 1892. At that time, Sacred Heart and St. Boniface parishes were transferred to the Friars Minor, under whose care they still remain.[11]

Spalding's interest in social welfare also continued to grow, and in an address at the thirty-fourth annual commencement exercises in the University of Notre Dame in June, 1878, he devoted his thoughts to the rectification of social evils, calling for equal rights for women, the abolition of child labor, and broader educational facilities.[12]

In his inexorable absoluteness, however, Spalding revealed

[10] Florence Crane, *The Catholic History of Peoria* (Chicago, 1912), p. 38.

[11] Diomede Pohlkamp, O.F.M., "The Chronicle of Father Philip Rothmann," *Provincial Chronicle*, XVI (1943–1944), pp. 63–71.

[12] Spalding, *Education and the Higher Life*, pp. 24–25.

himself to be in many ways a child of his time. He believed in the nineteenth century doctrine of America's manifest destiny, and he saw the United States as "the divinely appointed leader" that would translate into action the principles of justice and love. This American remedy would not be proffered by businessmen and politicians, but by the common man who, through the use of reason and religion, would add to pure religion the best of intellectual culture. It was a highly idealistic goal, and one that Spalding would frequently repeat in the years to come.

Even as the Bishop of Peoria was speaking at Notre Dame, there were some of his fellow bishops who believed that the right moment had already arrived when John Lancaster Spalding, though consecrated only the year before, should be advanced to a more important diocese. It was a belief which, had it been translated into action, might well have lessened the tensions that were to harass the American Church in the years ahead. "No decade in the history of the Church in the United States," it has been written, "evidenced a more gradual yet relentless building-up of tension and emerging conflict than the years of the 1880s." Catholics, clerical and lay, were concerned during these years with "procedural and racial differences" which would broaden until in the 1890s they broke forth "in charges of countercharges of Americanism and Cahenslyism." Basic to these issues was the so-called German question, which became of paramount importance with the mounting German immigration within the "German triangle" of Cincinnati, St. Louis, and Milwaukee.[13]

Open manifestation of dissatisfaction with the German triangle first appeared in 1878. On May 7, 1878, Archbishop Gibbons of Baltimore received a letter from Father George L. Willard of Fond du Lac, Wisconsin, regarding the petition of John Martin Henni, the first Archbishop of Milwaukee, for a coadjutor with the right of succession. Archbishop Henni, feeling

[13] Colman J. Barry, O.S.B., *The Catholic Church and German Americans* (Milwaukee, 1953), p. 44.

the need of help in the administration of the Church in Wisconsin, had submitted to the Congregation de Propaganda Fide the names of Bishops Michael Heiss of La Crosse, Joseph Dwenger, C.PP.S., of Fort Wayne, and Francis Xavier Krautbauer of Green Bay as possible choices, and had circulated these names to various archbishops for their recommendations. Willard saw in this petition a serious threat to the welfare of the Archdiocese of Milwaukee, the principal object of which was, he believed, "to perpetuate a young Germany here."[14] A day later, Gibbons received a memorial from six priests of Milwaukee protesting against the German nationalism rampant in the archdiocese.[15] Gibbons, loath to disregard the names submitted by the Archbishop, and yet believing the letters from Milwaukee worthy of consideration, delayed his recommendation to the Holy See until he could consult John J. Williams, the Archbishop of Boston, on the Milwaukee succession. He told Williams of the memorial of the English-speaking priests, and mentioned Bishop Foley of Chicago as one who was favorable to the memorial, adding that Archbishop James F. Wood of Philadelphia was inclined toward Dwenger of Fort Wayne for the Milwaukee coadjutorship, since he was thoroughly familiar with both the German and the English language. Gibbons remarked, however, that Bishop Spalding of Peoria might, perhaps, very well be placed second or third on the *terna*, since he spoke German fluently.[16]

When the Propaganda received the original *terna* from Milwaukee, they informed Archbishop Henni that, according to the legislation of the Second Plenary Council of Baltimore, he must first consult his suffragan bishops. A meeting of the provincial bishops was therefore held in Milwaukee on September 4, 1878. Bishop Thomas L. Grace, O.P., of St. Paul later reported to

[14] AAB, 73-S-1, Willard to Gibbons, Fond du Lac, May 7, 1878.
[15] AAB, 73-S-2, P. F. Petit *et al.*, Gibbons, Milwaukee, May 8, 1878.
[16] Ellis, *Gibbons*, I, p. 337.

Gibbons on the meeting. He told the Archbishop that of the six bishops present, he was the only non-German, and that it was with the utmost difficulty that he obtained his colleagues' consent to nominate an American prelate as one of the candidates for coadjutor. Grace's choice was likewise Spalding of Peoria, who, he said, "created a most favorable impression in Milwaukee on the occasion of some lectures he delivered there."[17] Non-Catholics as well as Catholics, Germans as well as English-speaking Catholics, had expressed the highest esteem of Spalding. On the evening before the meeting, Grace continued, the venerable Martin Kundig, Vicar General of the Archdiocese of Milwaukee, had visited with him, and had urged him for the sake of religion to do all in his power to have Spalding's name on the list of candidates. He assured the Bishop of St. Paul that it was a false impression, indeed, if such existed, that the German people "would not be satisfied with any other than a German bishop for the succession."[18] There was a leaning toward Spalding, he maintained, among the intelligent and influential Catholics of Milwaukee, and the knowledge that he was thoroughly familiar with the German language was sufficient to remove any objections entertained by the people in general. But at the meeting, Grace had great difficulty in getting Spalding's name on the *terna,* since thereby one of the bishops already mentioned had to be dropped. On the final vote, Grace explained, Dwenger's name was eliminated by a vote of four against two, Krautbauer's name was advanced to the second place, and Spalding was chosen for third. Grace then gave Gibbons the tabulated vote:

1. Rt. Rev. Bishop Heiss of La Crosse, himself not voting—four favorable, one not favorable.
2. Rt. Rev. Bishop Krautbauer of Green Bay, himself not voting—four favorable, one not favorable.

[17] AAB, 73-W-3, Grace to Gibbons, St. Paul, September 8, 1878.
[18] *Ibid.*

115

3. Rt. Rev. Bishop Spalding of Peoria, three favorable, three not favorable.

"The opposition to Rt. Rev. Bishop Spalding on the part of the three Bishops," Grace hastened to add, "had no other ground than that the Bishop was not a German."[19]

Several weeks later, Father Kundig and a group of Milwaukee priests wrote to various members of the hierarchy with regard to the new *terna*. They begged John Cardinal McCloskey, for example, to use the influence "which your name and position give you to have Bishop Spalding chosen for in our opinion, he would be just the man for the place."[20] They were convinced of the necessity for an English-speaking bishop in Milwaukee, and they maintained that they were only expressing the desires of the priests and people when they urged and prayed for the appointment of Spalding. As they told the Cardinal of New York:

His thorough knowledge of German would make him acceptable by the German element, and from all accounts he is the first choice of all the English-speaking Catholics. His advent in Milwaukee would usher in a new era of prosperity for the Church in the North West which has so long been laboring under foreign rule. His well-known energy and ability would enable him to grasp and control all the conditions arising from the contact of the Church with the world. He would thereby make the Church attractive to Americans who are numerous and well-disposed—in fact many of them are already on the threshold of the faith—but hitherto they have been spurned—no effort being made for their conversion except in individual instances.[21]

Gibbons had received a similar letter, and since he had been the first to suggest the name of Spalding for Milwaukee, it is not surprising to note in his diary that he had written to Giovanni

[19] *Ibid.*

[20] AANY, A-30-a, Martin Kundig *et al.*, to John McCloskey, Milwaukee, September 22, 1878.

[21] *Ibid.*

Cardinal Simeoni, Prefect of the Propaganda, on the Milwaukee succession, and had recommended the Bishop of Peoria as "the most worthy in my estimation."[22]

All parties concerned anxiously awaited Rome's decision. In mid-May, 1879, Cardinal Simeoni informed Archbishop Henni that the cardinals of the Propaganda had held a meeting on the Milwaukee coadjutorship. It was on this occasion that Simeoni told the Archbishop that the cardinals preferred Spalding because of his obvious qualifications, American birth and fluency in German, and that they would have acted at once in recommending him for the appointment to Milwaukee, but that out of consideration for Henni's position, they had again postponed any action on the matter. If Spalding remained unacceptable, Simeoni had added, Henni was to forward another list from which a choice could be made.[23] Some months elapsed before a new *terna,* consisting of Heiss of La Crosse, Kilian C. Flasch, Rector of St. Francis Seminary, Milwaukee, and James O'Connor, Vicar Apostolic of Nebraska, was submitted to Propaganda, an action which was occasioned, as Gibbons wrote, "by the fact that the two P. [Krautbauer and Spalding] who were respectively second and third on the former list have declined."[24] At length, on April 9, 1880, Michael Heiss, Bishop of La Crosse, was chosen to succeed the aging Archbishop of Milwaukee, and thus "one of the earliest contests of this kind between the German element and their coreligionists resulted in a victory for the Germans."[25]

Milwaukee was to be only the first of a number of dioceses for which Spalding's name would be put forth during his lifetime. In

[22] AAB, Diary of Cardinal Gibbons, September 28, 1878, p. 118.

[23] Peter Leo Johnson, *Crosier on the Frontier* (Madison, 1959), p. 195.

[24] AAB, Diary of Cardinal Gibbons, October 25, 1879, p. 129.

[25] Ellis, *Gibbons,* I, p. 339

117

1890, he was again suggested for Milwaukee, but by then it was too late. Issues had since broadened and major controversies would be under way; by that time, too, Roman opposition would preclude any possibility that John Lancaster Spalding would ever rule the Church in Wisconsin.

While Spalding's friends were undoubtedly disappointed with the turn of events in Milwaukee, the Bishop of Peoria was personally less concerned with the German question just then than he was with the problem of the colonization of Irish-American Catholics. For some years prior to 1879, he had been interested in the colonization movement, but until then he had no opportunity to take an active part in the work. It was this fact, perhaps, that has led one historian to remark that "Spalding . . . as a young priest in New York had opposed the western settlement of Catholics."[26] Yet Spalding, who believed city life conducive to disease and vice, was later to be recognized as the champion of Irish colonization. Further, he saw it a sublime mission to "[preach] to the people the wisdom of leaving the overpopulated centers of population for the vast and fertile districts of the thinly populated West."[27]

Catholic colonization in the United States, even on an organized basis, was not new. Mathias Loras, the first Bishop of Dubuque, and Joseph Cretin, the first Bishop of St. Paul, were among the earliest prelates to recognize the necessity and possibility of systematic colonization of Irish Catholic immigrants; yet it was not before the 1850s that organization on a national scale was attempted. Motivated by a desire to promote western colonization among his countrymen, Thomas D'Arcy McGee planned and assembled in 1856 what has since been referred to as the Buffalo Convention "for the purpose of encouraging Irish Catholics in the seaboard cities of the United States to re-

[26] James P. Shannon, *Catholic Colonization on the Western Frontier* (New Haven, 1957), p. 257.

[27] Spalding, *The Life of the Most Rev. M. J. Spalding,* p. 357.

move to the western States and Canada."[28] Episcopal disapproval of McGee of Young Ireland fame, particularly that of John Hughes, Archbishop of New York, was sufficiently strong, however, to insure the failure of the convention and the prospect of an organized national movement. Subsequently, in October, 1869, two Catholic laymen, Dillion O'Brien of St. Paul and William J. Onahan of Chicago, succeeded in calling together a colonization convention which was held in St. Louis. "Of course, there were very many eloquent speeches," Onahan later reminisced, "and a string of resolutions. There was a banquet and a steamboat excursion, and everything was agreeable and harmonious down to the adjournment. And that was all. Nothing ever came of it. A committee had been named to carry out the design of the convention. The committee never met."[29] Onahan and O'Brien persisted, nevertheless, and ten years later, on the suggestion of John Ireland, Coadjutor Bishop of St. Paul, they called for a national colonization convention to be held in Chicago on the following St. Patrick's Day, 1879. This meeting eventually proved successful, and laid the foundations for the organization of the Irish Catholic Colonization Association of the United States.[30]

Bishop Spalding had not attended the Chicago convention, since he was in New York at the time preaching the Lenten discourses at St. Michael's Church. It was due primarily to Bishop Ireland that the Bishop of Peoria received an invitation to an organizational meeting of the I.C.C.A. Ireland had first suggested Spalding's name to Bishop O'Connor, Vicar Apostolic of Nebraska, because, as he put it, "living so near to Chicago and

[28] Sister Mary Evangela Henthorne, B.V.M., *The Career of the Right Reverend John Lancaster Spalding as President of the Irish Catholic Colonization Association of the United States, 1879–1892* (Urbana, 1932), p. 32.

[29] Sister Mary Sevina Pahorezki, O.S.F., *The Social and Political Activities of William James Onahan* (Washington, 1942), p. 86.

[30] *Ibid.*, p. 87.

119

being an energetic, enterprising prelate, he might think it strange that we did not invite his cooperation." Cooperation of the hierarchy, Ireland realized, was absolutely necessary to secure the success of the movement, and he told O'Connor that, "unless we have there five or six bishops, the movement will be a failure. The laymen will be discouraged and nothing will be done."[31]

The meeting on April 18 drew five bishops—Ireland, O'Connor, and Spalding, together with Louis M. Fink, O.S.B., of Leavenworth and John J. Hogan of Kansas City. At first, the difficulties seemed insurmountable, and just as "external pressure had killed the convention of '56, internal weakness had rendered that of '69 fruitless . . . now in '79 the paralyzing fear of failure seemed about to frustrate this last effort. . . ."[32] It was at this point, according to Patrick V. Hickey, editor of the Brooklyn *Catholic Review,* who was later a member of the Board of Directors of the I.C.C.A., that the Bishop of Peoria saved the day for Irish colonization. Hickey told his readers:

Had not one of the bishops, who with the position of a western prelate combines the experience of a missionary in one of the most thickly populated parishes of the East, at a critical moment cast, with his characteristic eloquence and vigor, the force of his influence on the side of active organization for Irish colonization, it is not impossible that the fear of difficulties would have seriously hampered the Board.[33]

In any case, on May 20, 1879, after several additional meetings, the Association was legally incorporated under the laws of the State of Illinois as a stock company with a capital of $100,000 in shares of $100 each. Though the project was essentially philanthropic, the members of the Association were determined that it should be established on a sound financial basis and that it should promise a return to its investors. On the same day, Spalding was elected President of the Board of Directors of the

[31] Henthorne, *op cit.,* p. 40.
[32] *Ibid.,* p. 43.
[33] *Catholic Review,* May 3, 1879.

120

I.C.C.A., a position which he held until the demise of the organization.[34]

Immediately after the colonization meeting, Spalding and Ireland set out for New York for the dedication of the new St. Patrick's Cathedral on Fifth Avenue.[35] Since there were many bishops in the city for the festive occasion, Spalding took advantage of the opportunity to summon an informal meeting of the Board of Directors at St. Stephen's Church to arrange to appear before a gathering of the lay Catholics of New York. Cardinal McCloskey approved, and the hall of the Young Men's Catholic Lyceum was made available. Ireland spoke of the successful colonies already established in Minnesota, while Spalding emphasized the safeguards that would insure success of the plan. Many in the audience apparently were convinced by the arguments of the western prelates. Father Arthur J. Donnelly subscribed $1,000, which was matched by Father Thomas Ducey in behalf of the Young Men's Catholic Lyceum.[36] Even James A. McMaster, noted for his opposition to all western colonization plans as cure-alls, seemed in favor of the movement.[37]

Several days later, Spalding delivered his first major address on Catholic colonization at Cooper Institute. His approach embodied the twin conviction that the Irish had a special mission of reviving Catholicism in the English-speaking world, and that they could best do this in the United States by leaving the cities and returning to the land. Spalding fully appreciated the economic necessity for the city and its important role as the focus of intellectual life, and he did not naïvely believe that the life of the farmer was ideal; yet he remained convinced that "the farmer is still the strongest and the healthiest member of the

[34] Henthorne, *op. cit.,* p. 46.
[35] New York *Freeman's Journal,* May 31, 1879.
[36] *Ibid.,* June 7, 1879.
[37] *Ibid.,* June 7, 1879.

social body . . . the most religious and the most moral."[38] As a curate at St. Michael's, he said, he had witnessed the harmful effects of city life on the Irish, who were unable to break away from the peonage of unskilled and domestic labor. It was against this somber analysis of urban society that Spalding voiced his plea for Catholic colonization, "the systematic and deliberate effort to take our people from the great cities and factory towns, from the mines and the railroads, from domestic service in hotels and private houses, and to place them upon the cheap and fertile lands of our country."[39] Colonization was at least a partial answer, he believed, to the problems of urban industrialism and its impact on American Catholicism.

To promote the I.C.C.A., Ireland and Spalding spent many months on begging tours in various dioceses along the eastern seaboard. Despite their efforts, however, they could only raise $83,000 of the $100,000 subscribed by the directors. With that sum, the Association established several small communities in Greeley County, Nebraska, and assisted colonies in Minnesota and Arkansas. Five years after its birth, its immediate purpose realized, the Association was dissolved. In a restricted sense, the I.C.C.A. could be called a success, for all the colonies flourished and the stockholders were fully reimbursed and with interest. Yet as an instrument for transferring Catholics in large numbers from the eastern cities, it failed. "No proponent of colonization," an historian has observed, "worked out so elaborate a rationale for it as Spalding. . . ."[40] But rural colonization never took hold among American Catholics, and in addition the necessary support of the eastern clergy was generally lacking. Undoubtedly,

[38] J. L. Spalding, *The Religious Mission of the Irish People and Catholic Colonization* (New York, 1880), pp. 75–80.

[39] *Ibid.*, p. 219.

[40] James E. Roohan, "American Catholics and the Social Question, 1865–1900," p. 219; this is an unpublished Ph.D dissertation at Yale University.

eastern bishops such as John Loughlin of Brooklyn, Corrigan of Newark, and Williams of Boston were sincere in granting permission for Ireland and Spalding to collect in their dioceses, but few did more than lend their names to the movement.

Bishop Spalding's interest in colonization, as we have said, arose from his conviction that the mission of the Irish was essentially a religious one. If the Catholic Church had in the previous century risen to new life in the whole English-speaking world, it would have to be admitted that the Irish were "the providential instrument through which God has wrought this marvelous revival. As in another age men spoke of the *gesta Dei per Francos,* so now," he contended, "may we speak of the *gesta Dei per Hibernos.*"[41] Were it not for Ireland, he believed, Catholicism would be a feeble force in the United States:

No other people could have done for the Catholic faith in the United States what the Irish people have done. Their unalterable attachment to their priests; their deep Catholic instincts, which no combination of circumstances has ever been able to bring into conflict with their love of country; the unworldly and spiritual temper of their national character; their indifference to ridicule and contempt, and their unfailing generosity, all fitted them for the work which was to be done, and enabled them in spite of strong prejudices against their race which Americans have inherited from England, to accomplish what would not have been accomplished by Italian, French or German Catholics.[42]

In light of this attachment to the Irish race, it was only natural that Spalding should have become aroused when he read in the *North American Review* a diatribe by James Anthony Froude entitled, "Romanism and the Irish Race in America."[43] The basis of the English historian's attack on the Irish Catholics of the United States stemmed, Spalding believed, from Froude's own definition of history. "It often seems to me," Froude had written,

[41] Spalding, *The Religious Mission of the Irish People,* p. 61.
[42] *Ibid.,* p. 62.
[43] James A. Froude, "Romanism and the Irish Race in the United States," *North American Review,* CXXX (January, 1880), pp. 31-50.

123

"as if history was like a child's box of letters, with which we can spell any word we please. We have only to pick out such letters as we want, arrange them as we like, and say nothing about those which do not suit our purpose."[44] Spalding did not let the attack go unchallenged. In a communication to the same journal, he contended that Froude's triple pseudo-historical process of falsification, invention, and arrangement was responsible for his absurd conclusions concerning the Irish character of the Church in the United States. He reminded Froude that there was a strong German element in the American Church, that thirteen of the bishops were Germans or of German descent, that the descendants of the Maryland colonists, together with converts, chiefly of English origin, were represented in the hierarchy in addition to a very respectable Franco-American and French Canadian Catholic population, all of which made it "ridiculous to speak of the Church in the United States as simply an Irish Church."[45]

Froude had likewise raised the question of Catholic separatism, claiming that Irish Catholics formed a body apart in America, segregated from the mainstream of the nation's life. For the most part, the Bishop disregarded the charge and simply labeled it absurd, since, as he said, "if an Irishman had no other reason for loving this country than our victorious rebellion against English tyranny, that of itself would suffice to make him loyal." On the contrary, Spalding believed, there was "a tendency to what I call ultra-Americanism in the children of Irish Catholics. They are so intensely American that they often fail to recognize the obvious defects of our country and the short-comings of the American character."[46] It was mere prejudice that blinded Froude when he implied Catholics formed a separate and distinct group

[44] J. L. Spalding, "Mr. Froude's Historical Method," *North American Review*, CXXX (March, 1880), p. 280.

[45] *Ibid.*, p. 286.

[46] *Ibid.*, p. 287.

in the American Republic. Spalding admitted that the Catholic Church here was a powerful and well-organized body, while Protestantism, broken up into warring sects, bewildered its adherents with what he called "its confusions and ineffectualities." But he failed to see what this had to do with government or politics in the American scene. "I have been brought up to believe," he said, "that this is a secular government, that there is here no union of Church and State, that the American citizen is neither Protestant, nor Catholic, neither Jew nor Gentile, that it is not within the competency of Congress 'to make laws respecting the establishment of religion or prohibiting the free exercise thereof.' " If, therefore, this church grew strong or that one died out, the American government had no more right to check the growth of one or revitalize the other than it had "to prescribe what should be the uniform of the French army."[47]

"It is only as long as they are a small minority," Froude had warned, "that Catholics can be loyal subjects under the American Constitution. Give them power and the Constitution will be gone. A Catholic majority under spiritual direction will forbid liberty of worship and will try to forbid liberty of conscience."[48] Spalding countered that such a statement was mere speculation divorced from reality. Political action by Catholics was as little controlled by the Church as that of Protestants or infidels. Bishops and priests, with rare exceptions, wholly abstained from intermeddling in politics, and were they to attempt to do so, the first to condemn them would be "the Catholic people themselves." He admitted that the great majority of Catholics voted with the Democratic Party, but said that the Catholic Church was in no way responsible for the preference, since "Catholics have as little to hope from the success of the Democratic party as they have to fear from that of the Republican." As for the attempt to predict what any body of men would do were abso-

[47] *Ibid.*, p. 295.
[48] *Ibid.*, p. 297.

125

lute power given to them, this was a kind of speculation in which wise men never indulged, for

the destinies of nations and of civilizations are God's secrets. No man can know with certainty what he would do in trying circumstances, when the path of duty seems to fade away from sight; much less can he know what vast bodies of men would do in imaginary contingencies; and when Mr. Froude undertakes to predict in mathematical accuracy what a Catholic majority in the United States would try to do, he takes his place among weather-prophets and soothsayers. The superstitious may believe him.[49]

To bolster his argument that a Catholic majority would eventually forbid liberty of conscience as well as liberty of worship, Froude had appealed to the example of the Middle Ages. Spalding showed how unreasonable it was for the historian to argue that Catholics in the nineteenth century must hold the political views of the twelfth century, just as it would be foolish to suppose that New Englanders of today must approve the burning of witches. Then, stating his philosophy on the relations of Church and state, an unvarying theme throughout his career, Spalding remarked:

We may not deny, as a principle, that the power of religion and the power of the State should work in harmony, but the relations of the Church and State which would best promote this end vary with the changing conditions of social life. The medieval connections of the Church were in no way ideal. They were the outcome of the accidents of time; and as the past does not return they will not return. That the Church survives the destruction of social forms which seemed to be part of her life, and develops new strength in surroundings which had been held to be very fatal to her very existence, is one of the evidences of her chronic vigor and indefectible power.[50]

Authority and liberty were both essential to the social order, but excesses had led both to tyranny and anarchy. Christianity was the great mean between these extremes. "Henceforth," he

[49] *Ibid.*, p. 298.
[50] *Ibid.*, p. 298.

said, "Church and State are forever distinct; and as the Church leans more to the side of authority, and the State more to liberty, so in proportion as man attains to greater freedom, he ought more and more to recognize the divine authority of religion." The highest representative of this authority was the Catholic Church, and hence, Spalding concluded, "It is surely not rash to think that she has a great and beneficent mission to fulfill in an age and a country in which the individual has attained to the possession of the fullest liberty."[51]

If the Catholic Church were to fulfill the mission that Spalding envisioned for it in the American Republic, there were few agencies that would prove more helpful than a Catholic university. As early as 1865, his uncle the Archbishop of Baltimore, anticipating a plenary council, had asked Bishop John Timon of Buffalo: "Why should we not have a Catholic university?"[52] At the Second Plenary Council in October, 1866, Archbishop Spalding had raised the question again, but for a variety of reasons the hierarchy did not go beyond the expression of a desire when they stated in one of the decrees:

> Would that in this region it were permissible to have a great college or university which would embrace the advantages and the usefulness of all these colleges, whether domestic or foreign; in which, namely, all the letters, both sacred and profane, could be taught. Whether or not the time for founding such a university has arrived, we leave it to the judgment of the Fathers, that they may examine the whole matter more maturely.[53]

John Lancaster Spalding had played a very minor role at the council of 1866, but it was he who one day would be the one most responsible for the founding of the Catholic University of America.

[51] *Ibid.*, p. 299.

[52] AAB, Letterbook, Spalding to Timon, Baltimore, August 23, 1865, p. 150.

[53] *Concilii Plenarii Baltimorensis II., in Ecclesias Metropolitana Baltimorensi . . . Decreta* (Baltimore, 1868), p. 228.

Spalding had first brought the university question into public view while he was serving as temporary editor of the *Catholic Advocate* in Louisville.[54] To his mind, he editorialized at that time, the chief defect in Catholic education in the United States was the fact that American Catholics had no university, no central seat of learning. It was true that there were certain "rudimentary Greek and Latin grammar schools, kept by the Jesuits and others, which, in sheer mockery of the name, are called universities." But these titles deceived no one, and if, on leaving one of these institutions, a graduate showed sufficient education to enable him "to construe words grammatically, we must be satisfied." Many candidates for the priesthood had been sent to seminaries in Europe, but whatever advantages a European education might offer, they were not a substitute for the great good which Catholics in this country would derive from a university of their own. Spalding was confident that

there can be no real obstacle to the founding of a Catholic university in the United States similar to that of Dublin or Louvain. We have perfect freedom and abundant wealth for the purpose, and we feel confident that the laity would eagerly engage in an enterprise, in which they have such great interests, both as Catholics and American citizens. It would be easier to raise two million dollars to endow an American university, than half a million to establish a foreign college. The existence of a first class university, by creating a demand for talent, would call it forth. What is there to prevent us from having a University? Surely local and personal prejudices are not sufficiently strong to prevent the realization of a project which is of such vital importance to the highest interests of the church in the United States.[55]

Spalding's forceful editorial of 1871 was without doubt the occasion for several unsigned articles in the *Catholic World*

[54] AAB, 39-Q-3, Ben J. Webb to Martin J. Spalding, Louisville, March 27, 1871.

[55] *Catholic Advocate,* January 28, 1871. There is no doubt that Spalding was the author of the unsigned editorial. Identical passages are to be found in other writings, as well as in Spalding's correspondence with Archbishop Elder of Cincinnati.

which gave further publicity to this important issue. While writing the biography of his uncle, Spalding had again stressed the great need for a university. "The idea of a university," he wrote, "is that of an institution whose soul-life is the inter-communion and mutual connection of all the sciences." The great intellectual work of the American Church, he was convinced, was to show that theology, as queen of the sciences, was not only not in contradiction with, but was essential to and the central point of all knowledge. Hence, the mission of a Catholic university was "to be the crown of all other institutions of learning." No general system of education could be complete which did not terminate in and receive its complement from the university, and since American Catholics had their own system of education it was necessary to crown the edifice with a university.[56]

Shortly after Spalding had become Bishop of Peoria, financial disaster overtook the Archdiocese of Cincinnati, and it quickened his hope that this failure might offer the occasion for beginning a university. Late in 1878, the private banking business of Father Edward Purcell, brother of Archbishop Purcell, brought on a financial crisis, and among the diocesan institutions that were forced to close was Spalding's alma mater, Mount St. Mary's Seminary of the West. Feeling a more than ordinary concern, he wrote to William H. Elder, formerly Bishop of Natchez and now Coadjutor Archbishop of Cincinnati:

I have been thinking of late that possibly the troubles in the finances of Cin. might offer an opportunity to make a beginning towards founding a Catholic University; and I hope you will pardon me for inquiring whether you will be forced to sell your Seminary property. If so, might not the Bishops of the U.S. buy it and start there a Theological High School for the best students who have already made the three years course of theology in the different seminaries of the country. In this high school they would go through what is called the profound course of theology. I see no other way by which we can hope to raise the standard of Clerical Education and you know better than I how difficult

56 Spalding, *Life of the Most Rev. M. J. Spalding,* p. 316.

129

it is to find priests who have the learning which bishops ought to have; and as our dioceses are becoming so numerous it seems to me to be necessary to set about doing something in earnest by which we may raise up a class of men in the priesthood who will become the ornament of our holy faith. If you think there is anything in this suggestion I should be glad to cooperate to help carry out some such plan.[57]

Although, as in so many areas of Spalding's life, there is little personal correspondence to go by, it is certain that Elder's answer was favorable to the suggestion, since the Coadjutor had the habit of jotting down brief replies on many of the letters he received, and on Spalding's communication he had noted. "Answered September 5, 1860, I will be glad. What Professors? Jesuits of Woodstock?"[58]

About a week later, feeling greatly encouraged, Spalding again wrote to Elder. All the bishops in the United States, he was sure, would admit the necessity of raising the standard of clerical education. Several had, in fact, urged him to take a special interest in the matter, and since no one else seemed at the moment to be taking the lead, he thought that there would be no harm to sound out some of the more prominent bishops and discover their real thought. As for Elder's question concerning professors in the proposed university, Spalding's answer was quite direct. "To begin, I should think it unwise," he wrote, "to entrust such an institution to a religious order. *Omne animal generat simile sibi,* and secular priests alone can efficiently train secular priests." This question, he felt sure, would be easily solved when the proper time came; the location of the university would be more difficult unless there were some preponderant reason for deciding on one particular site. This was why he had thought of Cincinnati, for, as he told Elder, "The diocese is in great trouble. The bishops sympathize with the archbishop and yourself; and by agreeing to locate the Theological University there they would add dignity to the See, inspire courage in Peo-

[57] AAC, 612-b, Spalding to Elder, Peoria, August 29, 1880.
[58] *Ibid.*

ple and by buying your Seminary property help in some slight measure to lighten your financial burden." If the Archdiocese of Cincinnati, however, intended to continue Mount St. Mary's as a diocesan institution, then, of course, Spalding understood that his suggestion need not be considered. If otherwise, he was confident that two or three bishops could be induced to canvass the country to raise funds to found and endow in Cincinnati "the Theological University of the U.S." As yet, he had not written to Cardinal McCloskey, nor to anyone except Elder, since he did not want to take further steps until he had the approval of Purcell and his Coadjutor.[59] On receipt of another favorable response, Spalding told Archbishop Elder:

> You are perfectly right in saying that if Cincinnati is to be chosen, the impulse and agitation should come from others, not from you. All that my plan contemplates is your consent and cooperation. The institution would have to be under the supreme direction of a Board chosen by the Bishops of the Country and representing their authority. I beg you therefore to mention the subject to the archbishop, as you suggest, and to any others whom you may care to consult. I should also like to get a rough estimate of what you think we ought to pay for the property, together with a statement of the amount of ground and some general description of the buildings. When I have a tangible proposition of this kind I shall try to enlist the Cardinal, the archbishop of Baltimore and others.[60]

He then mentioned that Bishop Grace of St. Paul had begged him to undertake this work, and since Grace was noted for his piety, he thought this might be an indication of the will of God; he was also confident that the Holy Father would be delighted with the project. Three weeks later, Spalding received the tangible proposition he was seeking when Elder answered: "All approve. Building cost about $110,000. 5 acres: $15,000. I will get the appraisement & send it to you."[61]

At this point, Spalding's plan encountered a setback. When he

[59] AAC, 612-c, Spalding to Elder, Peoria, September 7, 1880.
[60] AAC, 612-d, Same to same, Peoria, September 16, 1880.
[61] *Ibid.*

tried to enlist the aid of the Archbishop of New York in support of the university, as his uncle had done fourteen years before in anticipation of the Second Plenary Council, then as now,
Cardinal McCloskey was less than enthusiastic. In his letter the
Bishop of Peoria reviewed the situation to date and told him of
Cincinnati's approval, assuring McCloskey that if New York
sponsored the undertaking there was no doubt that several of the
younger bishops would offer their services to appeal for funds
throughout the country. As for himself, he remarked, "I should
be willing to devote my whole life to such a work, for I am
persuaded that in no other way shall we be able to meet the demands which the near future will make upon us." Whether or
not his plan was feasible, the cardinal would have to decide, and
he ended by saying: "If you do not think favorably of it, I shall
at once put it out of mind."[62]

Cardinal McCloskey's reply was evidently unfavorable, for on
November 6 Spalding informed Elder that he feared the project
could not be carried out and asked if he had any other suggestions. Perhaps, he said, Mr. Reuben Springer, a great benefactor
of the Church in Cincinnati, might be induced to buy the seminary property and present it to the hierarchy with the proviso
that they agree to establish a university there.[63] Elder's full reaction is unknown as he simply noted on Spalding's letter: "Answered November 10, 1880: I hope it is not conclusive."[64] It was
not, indeed, conclusive at least as far as Spalding was concerned
since, in spite of his promise to the cardinal, he took up this
matter again with Elder and sincerely hoped that something
might still be done, adding: "nothing that I can do shall be
omitted. I would be willing even for a few years, to become a
teacher in such an institution." If only the bishops had the will,
he knew a Catholic university could be founded. Unfortunately,

[62] AANY, A-35, Spalding to John McCloskey, Peoria, October 23,
1880.

[63] AAC, 612-e, Spalding to Elder, Peoria, November 6, 1880.

[64] *Ibid.*

132

the bishops who had urged him to undertake this work were like himself in new or small dioceses, and Spalding fully realized that the impulse for the university must come from those in more prominent positions. At one point he confessed to Cincinnati's coadjutor that he had almost lost heart. But recovering almost immediately, he urged Elder to sound out the Archbishop of Baltimore and others on their plan, repeating that he would be delighted to beg, work or do anything as the servant of the bishops if they would only unite and at least say that they would make the effort. To bring about the unified effort, Spalding suggested: "Would it not be well to have the Holy Father get the bishops to meet in some sort of Council?"[65]

Archbishop Elder went as far as to contact Gibbons of Baltimore and to outline Spalding's plan for the purchase of Mount St. Mary's as the nucleus for a Catholic university. Aside from the troubles besetting the Archdiocese of Cincinnati and the selection of the seminary for its location, the coadjutor was convinced that the project ought no longer to be delayed, and although His Eminence of New York seemed to think the time had not yet arrived, Elder for one believed it might be instituted within a year or two even on a small scale. Furthermore, he continued,

One chief factor of success is to have a person able & willing to work for it. This we have in Bp. Spalding himself, and another time such a person might be hard to find. He himself may be advanced to a position demanding all his attention. Please consider & consult & use your influence to push it without delay. I wd. very much like that our building be taken for it, but wherever it is, I wd. like to see it begun speedily.[66]

The Cincinnati Prelate must have been aware at the time he wrote to Gibbons that the Bishop of Peoria had already been proposed for promotion. In fact, when Michael Corrigan had been appointed in October, 1880, as Coadjutor Archbishop of

[65] AAC, 612-f, Same to same, Peoria, November 14, 1880.
[66] AAB, 75-M-9, Elder to Gibbons, Cincinnati, November 19, 1880.

New York, the name of Spalding was mentioned to fill the Newark vacancy. But again Spalding declined. According to his own words, he was willing to devote his whole life for the cause of a university and even to teach in it for several years; yet, oddly enough, he was unwilling to leave Peoria for a more important diocese when he must have known that this would afford him the opportunity to push his project with a much greater guarantee of success. When Spalding refused Newark, Corrigan passed the information on to Bernard J. McQuaid of Rochester, and told him: "Bp. Spalding has written absolutely to Card. Simeoni that he would *not* leave Peoria under any consideration; and this seems to have been accepted at headquarters."[67] Several weeks later, McQuaid remarked to Corrigan concerning the *terna* for Newark:

What is meant by Spaulding [*sic*] refusing to go to Newark? Perhaps Miss Edes is only repeating newspaper talk. Such a rumor went the rounds a short time ago. Is there anything to it? Can somebody else be thrusting himself into the management of the N.Y. Province? I do not think that any one Province has been playing a double game?[68]

In reply, Corrigan simply repeated what he had written before: "Bp. Spalding himself told me of his writing to Rome (more than once) of his absolute reluctance to leave Peoria for any other field of labor."[69] Corrigan, of course, was only reporting. Did this reluctance include the university? Was there a certain impetuosity in Spalding that more than once prompted him to give expression to statements that belied his true state of mind and forced him to reconsider on the sober second thought?

Shortly after Corrigan's advent to New York as coadjutor, Joseph Sadoc Alemany, O.P., the first Archbishop of San Francisco entered the picture. Alemany had been anxiously awaiting

[67] Frederick J. Zwierlein, *Letters of Archbishop Corrigan to Bishop McQuaid* (Rochester, 1946), p. 34.

[68] John Tracy Ellis, *The Formative Years of the Catholic University of America* (Washington, 1946), p. 76.

[69] *Ibid.*, p. 76.

a coadjutor since 1878 when he had believed William Elder, then Bishop of Natchez, would come to his assistance. In congratulating Corrigan on his translation to the See of New York, he remarked that on account of his advancing years, he also needed a coadjutor, and after much advice and reflection he expected to ask the Holy See to grant him one of the following bishops: John J. Keane of Richmond, John L. Spalding of Peoria, William H. Gross, C.SS.R., of Savannah or John J. Kain of Wheeling.[70] Alemany had also communicated with Gibbons on the subject, and after a lapse of a year the Archbishop of Baltimore noted that Alemany, "after consulting with me, had recommended Keane, Spalding and Gross to Rome in that order," to which he added: "I have written to Card. Simeoni strongly advising the confirmation of Dr. Keane or of Dr. Spalding."[71] Spalding, however, had no desire to leave Peoria for San Francisco, and a year after Gibbons had sent his recommendations to Rome the Archbishop of San Francisco was still patiently awaiting a coadjutor. At the same time, the See of Charleston was vacant since the death of Bishop Patrick N. Lynch, and Spalding had heard the rumor that his friend and confrere of Louvain days, Father Patrick W. Riordan of Chicago, had been nominated for that diocese. Thinking that this would be a great mistake, he informed Gibbons that Riordan was capable of filling a more important position. He then continued:

> There is an impression in Rome that I may be induced to accept the coadjutorship of San Francisco. This is a mistake. My present responsibility is greater than my ability and my conscience will not permit me to go to San Francisco. Now I have a wide acquaintance with the priests of the U.S. and I know no one so well suited to the position of coadjutor for San Francisco as the Rev. P. W. Riordan.

Riordan's appointment to Charleston, Spalding added, would shut out all hope of getting him into a position where he could

[70] AANY, A-30-a, Alemany to Corrigan, San Francisco, October 6, 1880.

[71] AAB, Diary of Cardinal Gibbons, February 3, 1881, p. 147.

do far more good, and though he was giving only his personal opinion on the subject, he sincerely believed that Riordan would refuse the Diocese of Charleston.[72] Whether or not Spalding's influence was the deciding factor, it is difficult to say. In any case, less than a year later Riordan was named coadjutor to Alemany with the right of succession.

If during these years the Bishop of Peoria refused several opportunities for advancement to a more prominent diocese, never for a moment did he relax in his efforts to establish a Catholic university. At the silver jubilee of St. Francis Seminary in Milwaukee on June 30, 1881, he was the preacher on the occasion, and he chose as his subject the Catholic priesthood, a topic which gave him an opportunity to speak on the higher education of the clergy and to further his plan for a university. The aim of the Catholic Church was, he told his audience, "to create a priesthood which to the highest culture will unite the most perfect discipline of life."[73] The American seminaries, he pointed out, had not been inferior to those of Europe and yet, he continued,

> You will not . . . misunderstand me when I affirm that it is not possible that seminaries such as these are and must remain here and elsewhere, should give the highest intellectual education. They are elementary schools of theology, and to deprive them of this character would not only be a departure from the end for which they were instituted, but would render them useless. . . .[74]

The seminaries were established to prepare priests for the ordinary work of the ministry to supply a general want, to give the education which the common run of students were capable of

[72] AAB, 76-C-9, Spalding to Gibbons, Peoria, August 30, 1882.
[73] J. L. Spalding, *Lectures and Discourses* (New York, 1882), p. 150. The Milwaukee sermon was published in this work under the title, "The Catholic Priesthood."
[74] *Ibid.*, p. 151.

receiving. "For more than this," he remarked, "we must not look, unless we think it worth while to cherish delusions."[75]

Since the ordinary seminary could not under any circumstances foster the highest intellectual culture which was so indispensable, where was the institution in the United States capable of this task? There was none. There were only elementary schools of theology, and in this category he likewise placed the American colleges at Louvain and Rome. The one exception was the Jesuit seminary at Woodstock, but this was the special work of a particular order, and, as he said "the secular priests of this country are not and cannot be brought under its influence." There was no institution where the secular clergy could receive this highest intellectual culture. What, then, was the remedy? Spalding believed he had the answer even though it involved a considerable scaling down from his original idea:

I am not speaking of a university, but of something far simpler, less expensive, and in my opinion, better fitted to supply the most pressing want of American Catholics. The institution of which I am thinking might be called a High School of Philosophy and Theology.[76]

To this higher school only the best students would come upon completion of their seminary course. One such school would be sufficient and its location would not be that important, though "Some secluded spot, hallowed by memories of true men who have departed, like the Old Mountain near Emmitsburg, would be more favorable to high thinking and undisturbed meditation than the suburbs of a great city."[77] It would be a college "which would teach theology, not like the seminary, with a view to practice, whether in the pulpit or the confessional but it would consider it as a subject of contemplation. It would seek to impart not pro-

[75] *Ibid.*, p. 152.
[76] *Ibid.*, p. 154.
[77] *Ibid.*, p. 153.

fessional skill but cultivation of mind."[78] Some might say that the time was not here, that it was impossible. To these he replied:

> . . . it is possible to try. There are things which ought to be done, and if men succeed in doing them it is their highest honor and reward; and if they fail, having tried with honest purpose and persevering effort, they are not less worthy of homage. Ambitious men may fear failure, but good men need not be subject to this weakness.[79]

For himself, Spalding concluded, "I can only put forward the feeble plea on an honest purpose, or, it may be, fall back upon the thought that, when the good and wise are silent, even an idle voice may serve to start the flow of reason." He had faith that in God's providence "a sublime destiny awaits this New World, and consequently the Church of Jesus Christ in America."[80]

"I am not speaking of a university," he had said. Had he purposely made his terminology vague, preferring an indirect approach rather than a frontal attack to reach the same end? Did he, perhaps, foresee that his "high-school" and/or "college" with the rallying cry about the higher education of the clergy would, indeed, be the beginning of a university? Spalding himself had been university trained, and he knew the general history of universities. Had not Louvain reopened in 1834 with a faculty of theology? So, too, the American Catholic university would begin. Later he would write:

> While we look, therefore, to the founding of a true university, we will begin, as the university of Paris began in the twelfth century, and as the present University of Louvain began fifty years ago, with a national school of philosophy and theology, which will form the central faculty of a complete educational organism. Around this, the other faculties will take their places, in due course of time, and so the begin-

[78] *Ibid.,* p. 156.
[79] *Ibid.,* p. 157.
[80] *Ibid.,* p. 159.

138

ning which we make will grow until like the seed planted in the earth, it shall wear the bloomy crown of its own development.[81]

Quite independent of the life and work of John Lancaster Spalding, the Milwaukee sermon, excluding, as it seemed, the idea of a university, was indeed odd. But if one remembers the youth at Louvain, afraid of a field engagement, one can perhaps understand the man, oblivious of terminology, yet ensuring the ultimate success of his battle for a university. The following year, Spalding published the Milwaukee sermon in his *Lectures and Discourses,* and he sent a copy to Gibbons, who commended him on his work. In turn, the Bishop told the Archbishop of Baltimore:

> It is very difficult to write anything worthwhile in the midst of the labors and cares in which a missionary bishop finds himself. If we could only begin a University college for the higher education of priests, it would be my greatest happiness to go into it, and devote the rest of my life to this work, which, I am convinced, is of all others the most important and the most urgent.[82]

For the next two years little progress was made to realize Spalding's plan; it would have to await the Third Plenary Council for effective action.

In September 1882, Spalding prepared for his first *ad limina* visit to Rome. Peoria had grown extensively in five years, and, in fact, was now the suffragan See of a new ecclesiastical province. After the death of Thomas Foley, Coadjutor Bishop of Chicago, in February 1879,[83] the Holy See had removed James Duggan, Ordinary of the See, on account of prolonged insanity. A year later, Rome had raised Chicago to the rank of a metropolitan

[81] J. L. Spalding, *University Education Considered in its Bearing on the Higher Education of Priests. A Discourse Delivered by the Right Reverend J. L. Spalding, D.D. . . .* at the Cathedral, Baltimore, Sunday, November 16, 1884 (Baltimore, 1884), p. 34.

[82] AAB, 76-A-8, Spalding to Gibbons, Peoria, July 18, 1882.

[83] James J. McGovern, *The Life and Writings of Rt. Rev. John McMullen, D.D.* (Chicago, 1888), p. 204.

See, with the dioceses of Alton and Peoria as suffragans, and had appointed Patrick Augustine Feehan, Bishop of Nashville, as first Archbishop of Chicago. At the same time, the new arch-diocese was further limited in boundary by detaching La Salle, Bureau, Putnam, Henry, and Rock Island counties and incorpo-rating them into the Peoria Diocese.[84] These changes added 3,433 square miles to Spalding's diocese, making him responsible for an area totaling 18,544 square miles.

[84] Cornelius J. Kirkfleet, *The Life of Patrick Augustine Feehan* (Chicago, 1922), pp. 376–378. Spalding was pleased with the new diocesan boundaries and asked Giovanni Cardinal Simeoni, the Prefect of the Propaganda, to convey his thanks to the Pope for his goodness. He promised to work with all his strength to establish the Catholic faith on a solid basis in the new territory and told the Prefect that he would order an annual collection to be taken up for the needs of the Holy Father, Cf. Archives of the Sacred Congregation de Propaganda Fide, Lettere et Decreti della Sagra Congregazione, vol. 34 (1800), Spalding to Simeoni, Peoria, December 13, 1880. Hereafter these ar-chives will be cited as ACPF; Lettere, etc., as Lett.

4

American Catholicism in Transition

"SPALDING will be in Rome in the fall," Bishop McCloskey told Abbot Bernard Smith, O.S.B., his Roman agent. "Watch him closely for I suspect that he is, in some way, in league with those soreheads."[1] Trouble had been brewing for some time in the Diocese of Louisville, and McCloskey was apprehensive. From the outset, the Spaldings had plagued him. He had begun his administration, he well knew, "under the shadow of Archbishop Spalding's disesteem," since the latter had characterized the former rector of Rome's American College as financially inept and a poor administrator.[2] The priests of the diocese, notwithstanding, as Father Lancaster Spalding could attest, had not been allowed to remain long in ignorance that it was Bishop McCloskey and not the Archbishop of Baltimore who was in authority in Louisville. Independent in spirit and scornful of local tradition, McCloskey had demonstrated from the beginning that he would be under obligation to no one. This had been his studied policy as rector, and it had been quite successful in his handling of Roman seminarians. But with the Louisville clergy it might take a longer time, for there were other difficulties. Constant appeals to Rome, questioning his policies and undermining his authority, had kept the diocese in

[1] AASPOW, McCloskey to Smith, Louisville, October 19, 1882.
[2] Robert F. McNamara, *The American College in Rome, 1855–1955* (Rochester, 1956), p. 160.

turmoil,[3] and McCloskey could not help but believe that his former secretary and chancellor, now the Bishop of Peoria, would support the malcontents or, as he characterized them, "the discontented clique." It was not surprising, therefore, to find him urging Smith to "report everything to me fully and promptly. I count on this."[4]

It is difficult to say whether or not John Spalding entered into the plans of the disgruntled priests in his former diocese, though later events would seem to indicate that he probably did not. In any case, it soon became obvious that the Bishop of Peoria had set out for Rome at a critical period for the American Church. Distrust and difficulties among the bishops, strained relations between bishops and their priests, and knotty entanglements with the laity all had provoked situations which bewildered the Holy See. Some priests had suggested the appointment of an apostolic delegate to the United States who would shield the lower clergy against the ambitious rule of some bishops;[5] most of the bishops, altogether unsympathetic to such an idea, sought rather the accrediting of an American agent at Rome who would represent the American hierarchy and would be able to give a true picture of the problems facing them in the United States; still others preferred to let matters rest as they were, lest an American agent might provide an opening wedge for the Holy See to send an Italian delegate to the country.[6]

[3] Catholic University of America, Ellis Papers, Samuel J. Boldrick to John Tracy Ellis, Louisville, February 21, 1944. The late Judge Boldrick wrote: "During McCloskey's term more than 40 appeals were carried to Rome and he lost all but one." Hereafter this collection will be cited as CUA, Ellis Papers. Cf. also AASPOW, McCloskey to Smith, Louisville, December 7, 1882.

[4] AASPOW, McCloskey to Smith, Louisville, October 19, 1882.

[5] Cf. William Mahoney, The Rights of the Clergy Vindicated; or, A Plea for Canon Law in the United States (New York, 1883), pp. 341–356.

[6] Ellis, Gibbons, I, p. 603.

Concerned to steer a middle course between the arbitrary exercise of episcopal power and the danger of clerical stratagems, Propaganda sought to remedy the situation when on July 20, 1878, it issued the instruction *Quamvis,* which provided for a commission of investigation in disciplinary and criminal cases affecting the clergy. Previously, the plenary council of 1866 had adopted the procedures of the First Provincial Council of St. Louis held in October 1855, and had made this the common law of the land. Rome realized, however, the inadequacy of this method, and was determined to protect innocent clerics from unjust punishments, as well as to prevent the escape of guilty ecclesiastics from needed discipline. Hence the *Quamvis,* with the subsequent *Responsa ad dubia* in 1879, were provisional decrees—stepping stones to a more stable condition of things when the full force of Canon Law might be applied to the United States.[7]

American reaction to the Roman decrees was varied, and in some instances in sharp contrast. Father Richard Lalor Burtsell, pastor of the Church of the Epiphany in New York, who was to play a leading role in the turbulent years ahead, was delighted, for after examining the principles and methods for the investigation, correction, and punishment of clerical abuses in other countries, he had come to the conclusion that in their attempt to devise a satisfactory method for this country, the bishops of the United States had been, to say the least, nonplused. Burtsell condoned Rome's action, and hoped that in its efforts in behalf of uniformity, one could look forward to the future when a single standard of justice would prevail for the welfare of the clergy.[8] On the other hand, a number of bishops were distressed when the instruction arrived in 1878, fearing that it had set aside the Baltimore conciliar legislation; they were

[7] "Ecclesiastical Jurisprudence," *The Pastor,* II (May, 1884), p. 194.
[8] Richard L. Burtsell, "Notes on the Istruzione L'Ordinario," *The Pastor,* II (July, 1884), pp. 278–279.

143

only reassured a year later, after the Holy See had responded to their doubts. Bishop McQuaid of Rochester, who believed himself responsible for this favorable interpretation of *Quamvis,* was greatly pleased, and he told Bishop Corrigan: "The Instruction as explained is not the great thing that some disaffected priests looked for. Fixity of tenure and immunity of discipline were what they wanted. Bishops and people were to have no rights against their claim."[9] Thus while both the hierarchy and the clergy claimed initial success, appeals from disgruntled priests continued to pour into Rome, convincing the cardinals of Propaganda that their decrees had been largely disregarded.

The question of an American agent at Rome, or a delegate resident in the United States, was an even more sensitive one, and McQuaid expressed himself quite freely to Bishop Richard Gilmour of Cleveland:

> We bishops, shunted off on sidetracks, can do little toward a settlement of the question of an Agent to Rome or from Rome to this country. We are not taken into account in the matter. Any interference on our part would be regarded as meddlesome impertinence. This condition of things will continue until Metropolitans hold stated meetings . . . for private consultation as a means to uniformity of action. At present the rule seems to be: every man for himself and the devil catch the hindmost.

As a result, there was diversity of action, conflicting opinions, weak and uncertain legislation, and, as McQuaid remarked, "discipline consequently going to the dogs by default." If all the metropolitans would protest against a Roman representative in the United States, the Holy See would not send one. "It will be a downright misfortune for the Church in the United States," he added, "should she do so."[10] Spalding had left for Rome on October 11, and McQuaid wondered how the Bishop of Peoria

[9] Frederick J. Zwierlein, *The Life and Letters of Bishop McQuaid* (Rochester, 1926), II, p. 191.

[10] *Ibid.,* II, pp. 289–290.

stood on the question of an agent. He knew that Spalding was well able to present his view and make it appear the right one, but since, as he told Gilmour, "his practical experience as a working priest has been nil," he was afraid that he would not advance their cause very much, being too much taken up with the university scheme. Just as he had written those words, there had arrived a letter from one of his students at Rome who told the Bishop of Rochester:

> Bp. Spalding has left for the East. He is to be absent three months in Palestine, etc. His pet work, the American University, has fallen through completely, it seems, *ut erat exspectandum*. I have heard many reasons why; but can say nothing for certain. Now, they say, he is working for a National Council. Moreover, they say, Rome would gladly see three or four American bishops delegated to Rome by the American bishops. They should stay here for a time, long enough to settle affairs or to prepare for a future National Council.

Although Bishop McQuaid's informant in Rome had been on the whole quite accurate in his report, time would prove that Spalding's "pet work" had not fallen through. Indeed, the American Catholic university would have many stumbling blocks along the way, none more obstructive perhaps than those placed in its path by the Bishop of Rochester himself. Spalding, it was true, was working for another plenary council. When Cardinal McCloskey had shown initial opposition to the university project in 1880, Spalding had suggested to Archbishop Elder that the Holy Father should have the bishops meet in plenary session.[11] And now that he was in Rome, he would stress the need for action.

On Sunday, January 14, 1883, Spalding, accompanied by Father Louis E. Hostlot, rector of the American College in Rome, was received by Pope Leo XIII in private audience.[12] A week later, Spalding wrote to his friend, John Ireland of St. Paul: "I

[11] Cf. Chapter 3, note 65.
[12] *Catholic Telegraph* (Cincinnati), February 22, 1883.

am trying to do all that I can, and must say that I find everybody, the Holy Father included, most anxious to hear about
America and willing to do anything that may seem reasona-
ble."[13] Leo XIII asked him to write out whatever he thought
might be useful for the Pope to know, and he was now engaged
in that task. The Propaganda officials, he thought, would call
three or four American bishops to Rome for consultation, and
then, unless there was a change for the better in the present state
of affairs in the American Church, they would summon another
plenary council. "There are as you know," he reminded Ireland,
"some old fogies in America who are opposed to this and their
opposition will have to be met." There was nothing within reason that Rome would not gladly do, he had been assured, if the
confusion among the bishops as to what ought to be done did
not keep the Roman authorities "in a kind of labyrinth from
which the way out is not easily discovered." If the bishops who
understood the situation would write freely to Propaganda, Spalding was convinced that much good might be accomplished. In
spite of Propaganda's instruction of 1878, appeals over the heads
of the American bishops were incessant, and Rome was growing
impatient. "I am thoroughly convinced," Spalding declared,
"that we can do nothing better for the present than to work for
a council."[14]

In Spalding's memoranda to Propaganda, there were many
other topics for the cardinals' consideration, but perhaps none
alarmed them more than his views on the pitiable plight of
Italians in the United States. "I have stirred them up considerably," he related to Ireland, "on the subject of colonizing the
Italian immigrants to America."[15] Only two years earlier, in
the staid pages of the *Dublin Review,* he had asked:

[13] Archives of the Archdiocese of St. Paul, Spalding to Ireland, Rome,
January 21, 1883. Hereafter these archives will be cited as AASP.

[14] *Ibid.*

[15] *Ibid.*

What is to become of the 12,000 Italian peasants who have come to the United States during the last twelve months? They have all settled down in the slums and the alleys of the cities, or have been hired as laborers by the contractors who build railways or undertake public works; and in either case their lot is hopeless. There are a few so-called Italian churches here and there in the great cities, but, when we come to examine into the matter, we generally find that the worshippers are Irish; and there can be little risk in affirming that the increasing multitudes who leave Italy for the United States will not add strength to the Catholic cause here, unless something is done in Italy itself to guide and control this emigration.[16]

The heart of a Catholic, he said, could be filled only with misgivings as he contemplated the situation of the Italian in America. And yet there were Texas and Arkansas with an abundance of cheap land, a climate less than severe, which beckoned for colonists, but unless Italians were directed there, they would sink into the aggregate masses and be lost. The same year that had seen 12,000 Italians immigrate to the United States had witnessed an influx of 19,000 Scandinavians, all Protestants, who had gone to the West to become farmers while the Catholics remained in the cities. The history of the American people, as Spalding maintained, had been the expansion westward, for the stream of population flowed from expensive to cheap land, from the East to the West. If Catholic immigration could be channelled into that current, the danger of leakage would be as improbable as in Ireland and the Tyrol. But if the preservation of the faith was to be thus accomplished, bishops and priests must bring the full weight of their authority to bear on their people, so many of whom set out each year for the new world. Only in that way could the American Church hold the multitudes; only then could it truly say: *"Quos dedisti mihi custodivi, et nemo ex eis periit. . . ."*[17] Propaganda had, indeed, reason to be startled.

[16] J. L. Spalding, "The Position of Catholics in the United States," *Dublin Review,* V (January, 1881), p. 118.
[17] *Ibid.*

At the close of his *ad limina* visit, Spalding departed for Palestine and the holy places where on Easter Sunday he said Mass at the Holy Sepulchre.[18] While he was in the Near East, the Holy See, despite opposition, addressed a letter to the ecclesiastical provinces in the United States inviting them to send representatives to Rome for preliminary conferences with the cardinals of Propaganda. A month later, Spalding arrived in New York on board the *Republic,* where at dockside the reporters were waiting. "I know nothing about a national council," Spalding parried in response to questioning. As for a university, it was desirable, but, he stated, "it will be a product of time and development rather than a creation of money and the first step is the agreement of the bishops on some plan for the higher education of the clergy." It was only in France that Spalding had found hatred for the Church. But this he realized was to a great extent a matter of politics, as it was in Italy. The French clergy were for the most part royalists, and the republicans persecuted the Church for its monarchical tendencies. He was confident, however, that "had there been a man, a real leader on either side, the Napoleonic or the Legitimist, France at this time would have had either an Emperor or a King."[19]

Several days later, Spalding called on Archbishop Corrigan, who soon after informed Bishop McQuaid that "the Bp. of Peoria had little news from Rome," except what they all knew, namely that the Holy See was annoyed with the continual bickering among bishops and priests. But Spalding had said that a "delegate, assisted by four or five canonists, will come over for the council and remain provisionally on trial." Then if the results warranted it, the delegate would definitely be appointed.[20]

On June 12, Bishop Spalding entrained for Chicago where he was to meet his brother Benedict. Rumors of discontent among

[18] *Catholic Telegraph* (Cincinnati), June 21, 1883.
[19] *Michigan Catholic,* June 16, 1883.
[20] Zwierlein, *Letters of Archbishop Corrigan,* p. 59.

148

the Irish Catholics of Peoria were rampant at the time, and it was reported that some societies might possibly not turn out to welcome Spalding home. The ill-feeling was not directed against the bishop, whom they had grown to like, but against Leo XIII, whom the Irish planned to boycott because of his condemnatory letter regarding Charles Steward Parnell, president of the Irish Land League and the new leader in the fight for Irish independence. By 1880, the land question was viewed as the stepping stone to national independence, and in that same year Parnell had visited the United States to raise money to meet the League's expenses and to assist the Irish farmers who were near the point of starvation. Spalding, of course, had on several occasions supported Irish independence,[21] and was in general sympathetic with Parnell.

Rome, however, had never looked with favor on the Land League agitation, and regarded it largely in terms of a revolt against legitimate authority.[22] It was not surprising, therefore, that on May 11, 1883, Cardinal Simeoni addressed a letter to the Irish hierarchy forbidding the bishops and priests to solicit funds for the so-called "Parnell Tribute."[23]

In the States, the Irish were furious and hurt that Leo XIII should have allowed himself to be deceived by English politicians. Spalding, who heard of the letter while in New York, confessed that he was somewhat perplexed as to the immediate motive of Simeoni's statement. But one thing was certain, he told reporters, in a masterpiece of understatement:

The Pope receives from the English Government as well as from the bishops a mass of secret information that the public never has command of. On these data legislation is often framed. There is no doubt at all

[21] J. L. Spalding, *The Religious Mission of the Irish People and Catholic Colonization* (New York, 1880), p. 338.

[22] R. Barry O'Brien, *The Life of Charles Stewart Parnell, 1846–1891* (New York, 1898), II, p. 25.

[23] New York *Freeman's Journal*, June 9, 1883.

that the English feeling against the Irish and the letter based on the facts presented to the Pope is likely enough his sense of the situation as laid before him. Everyone knows that the Pope condemns assassinations and the use of dynamite. There was no need to stress that.[24]

The newspapers, however, were confused by this vague comment, and the word spread to Peoria that boycotting the Pope was not to be extended to Bishop Spalding, for he had not said that Simeoni's letter was "framed."[25] Several thousand people, the *Western Catholic* narrated, gathered at the Rock Island Depot on the afternoon of June 14, to extend a welcome to their bishop that was "as harmonious, unanimous, and enthusiastic as any saint or sinner could desire."

Diocesan duties kept Spalding close to his desk during the first weeks after his return from Europe, but he did not hesitate to put them aside to preach the eulogy for his friend, John J. McMullen, first Bishop of Davenport, at whose consecration he had assisted only two years before, and who now, on July 6, 1883, was being buried from St. Marguerite's Cathedral.[26] The biennial retreat for the priests of the diocese was also scheduled for late August, but before the bishop joined his clergy at St. Viator College at Bourbonnais Grove for the spiritual exercises, he informed a young and distant cousin from Kentucky, Edward L. Spalding: "I have written to Monsigneur De Nève, the Rector of the College at Louvain, that I intend to send you to the college as a student of this diocese. . . . It will be sufficient to present this letter."[27] Over the years, Spalding had remained loyally attached to John De Nève, who now once again headed the American College at Louvain. From 1860 until 1871, De Nève had served as rector, when a mental breakdown compelled him

[24] *Michigan Catholic*, June 16, 1883.

[25] *Western Catholic*, June 16, 1883.

[26] McGovern, *Life and Writings of Rt. Reverend John McMullen*, p. 280.

[27] AAC-L, Spalding to Spalding, Peoria, August 14, 1883.

to relinquish his duties. Fully recovered some years later, alumni and friends of the institution urged De Nève to resume the management of the college. Rome was consulted and Cardinal Simeoni advised the former rector to visit the United States to confer with various prelates before a decision should be made. On his arrival, the monsignor was affectionately hailed by his former students who enthusiastically supported his candidacy for another term.[28] A number of the hierarchy, however, were more than reluctant in recommending him. Gibbons knew little of the Louvain College. Caspar Borgess, Bishop of Detroit, was convinced that the utility of the institution had passed, while McCloskey thought it better to leave the solution of the difficulty to the wisdom of the Holy See.[29] Spalding believed otherwise. After a grand reunion in Peoria in June 1880, there was no stronger advocate for De Nève's reinstatement than the Bishop of Peoria. De Nève had already called on Archbishop Elder in Cincinnati, and since the latter knew the details of the case, Spalding wrote:

I am persuaded that the best interests of religion would be furthered by having Father De Nève replaced in his old position of rector. The present incumbent whom I know well, is, in my opinion, altogether unsuited to the position. I have not given the college encouragement because I have no confidence whatever in the management of the present superior. Your word will have weight in Rome, and as my former connection with the college, and the fact that my brother studied there under the present rector, put me in a position to know something of the matter, I have no hesitation in respectfully stating to you that I am convinced that nothing will have so much power to put it on a new footing as the reinstatement of Fr. De Nève in his former office.[30]

Across the top of Bishop Spalding's letter, Elder jotted: "Answered 15th. On yr judgement I will advise the change provided the Card ascertains Mgr. De N's *permanent* restoration

[28] Van der Heyden, *The Louvain American College,* p. 170.
[29] Ellis, *Gibbons,* I, pp. 196–197.
[30] AAC-67, Spalding to Elder, Peoria, June 11, 1880.

of mind."[31] In 1881, De Nève resumed rectorship, much to Spalding's satisfaction.

Another event that revived Louvain memories was the announcement in the summer of 1883 that his Louvain schoolmate, Patrick W. Riordan, pastor of St. James Parish in Chicago, had been named coadjutor with the right of succession to Archbishop Alemany of San Francisco.[32] Spalding, rumored for the position himself, had been the first to suggest Riordan for the office of coadjutor.[33] Archbishop Riordan was consecrated on September 16, 1883, at St. James Church, with Spalding preaching the sermon. The occasion is worth noting for Spalding's bold and direct comments addressed to the assembled prelates. "Mitres are put on our heads," he then remarked, "for the poor as well as the rich, for the poor even more than the rich, for our followers are generally poor, even the poorest of the poor." Therefore, he continued, the American bishops had the duty to urge their people to leave the cities and take advantage of the benefits of the West. Only then, he said, could they be counted among the greatest benefactors of mankind.

The bishops had heard it all before, and there is no way of knowing their reaction to this particular invective, though Archbishop Elder of Cincinnati, for one, was more convinced than ever that had Spalding been chosen for San Francisco, he would just have been a "cause of trouble." Archbishop Riordan, however, was to remain steadfast in friendship to Spalding, and never more so than in later years when the shadow of serious trouble would begin to gather over the Illinois bishop.

Immediately after the ceremony, Spalding left for Minnesota

[31] *Ibid.*

[32] Chicago *Times,* July 12, 1883.

[33] Spalding had begged Simeoni "to leave me peaceful in my new diocese where there is so much to do." Cf. Archives of the Sacred Congregation de Propaganda Fide, Congregazione generale, 1010 (1879), foglio, 774rv, Spalding to Simeoni, Peoria, le 5 Mai 1879.

to confer with Bishop Ireland on the work of the I.C.C.A.[34] While he was in St. Paul, Richard M. Spalding, his father, passed away in Lebanon, Kentucky.[35] During the summer months, the bishop had heard frequently from his father, who with his characteristic generosity and family loyalty had been deeply concerned about his half-brother, Sam, then in financial straits. The late Archbishop Spalding and Father Benedict, the elder Spalding's brothers, had invested in the Franklin Bank of Louisville which had failed, and now after many years dividends were to be declared which would accrue to the Spalding estate.[36] Lancaster had referred his father to Archbishop Gibbons, who had been named executor of the will of Martin Spalding. Gibbons had been more than willing to surrender the fund, and Richard Spalding had written to thank him, adding that he had written directly at the suggestion of his son, the Bishop of Peoria, in order to save time for, as he said, "I feel anxious to close up this affair as soon as possible."[37] A month later he was dead. None of his children was with him at the moment of death. Kate was visiting her sister, Mamie, Mrs. Frank Slevin, in Peoria, and Leonard was out of town. When the news of their father's grave illness reached them, they hurried by train to Lebanon, but it was too late. No one could contact the bishop, and only after Benedict arrived from Peoria did John learn by telegram in Minnesota of his father's death. Several weeks went by before the Bishop of Peoria arrived in Lebanon to celebrate the month's mind for his father in St. Augustine's.[38]

During these years immediately prior to the Third Plenary Council, John Ireland and John Spalding, linked by their mutual

[34] New York *Freeman's Journal*, September 29, 1883.

[35] *Ibid.*, October 13, 1883.

[36] AAB, 75-I-5, Spalding to Spalding, Lebanon, July 14, 1883.

[37] AAB, 77-J-11, R. M. Spalding to Gibbons, Lebanon, August 27, 1883,

[38] New York *Freeman's Journal*, October 13, 1883.

interests in the American Church, had become affable colleagues. Totally different in personality, and with widely divergent views on many questions of the day, they would remain, in spite of long estrangements, friends through the years. On their collection tours for the I.C.C.A., the two bishops would visit at the home of William and Molly Onahan in Chicago with Father Daniel Riordan, pastor of St. Elizabeth's Parish and brother of Archbishop Riordan of San Francisco. Mary Onahan Gallery, a daughter of the Onahan's, remembered these visits very well and later reminisced:

> Rather small in stature with keen gleaming eyes and alert in all his movements, John Lancaster Spalding impressed one instantly as a live wire. . . . Indeed, Bishop Spalding would have abruptly disclaimed the charge that he was a dignitary of any sort. His own shafts of satire and ridicule were often merciless. Even his brother bishops did not always escape them. . . . He was a great tease and would often poke fun at Bishop Ireland and torment him ceaselessly. Bishop Ireland would just smile and rub his hands together, a favorite gesture of his, ignore his adversary completely until the shafts became too keen, when suddenly he would make a swift and telling retort and there would be general laughter. Bishop Spalding would subside for a while. Then he would begin again. And so the evening would pass.[39]

One day as they were driving about Chicago trying to raise money for the colonization project, as another Catholic layman, Clarence C. Copeland, was later to recall, Spalding proposed that they visit the breweries and distilleries in the area. Ireland objected strenuously, but changed his mind when the Bishop of Peoria got out of the carriage and said: "The breweries, Bishop, or I go home to Peoria."[40] The visit, however, was probably not for tasting purposes, as Ireland was at the time one of the foremost leaders of the temperance movement, and Spalding advo-

[39] Mary Onahan Gallery, "Monsignor Daniel Riordan," *Illinois Catholic Historical Review,* IV (January, 1922), pp. 328–329.

[40] ADP, Copeland to Spalding, Pittsburg, Kansas, January 18, 1898.

cated prohibitory legislation as a means of promoting temperance.[41]

The philosophy behind Spalding's views on temperance also gives a clue to his political views. When the fourteenth annual convention of the Catholic Total Abstinence Union met in Chicago on August 6, 1884, the Bishop of Peoria was there. During a lively session, Archbishop Patrick J. Ryan, recently named to succeed the late James F. Wood in the See of Philadelphia, advised the delegates by letter "to avoid the fanaticism of prohibition."[42] The Philadelphia contingent, the strongest at the convention, supported their ordinary in his belief that the Union should not go beyond moral suasion, the traditional view of the C.T.A.U. Ireland and Spalding both differed with Ryan's views, each wishing to bring about total abstinence by moral suasion and legislation. Spalding, however, opposed groups such as the C.T.A.U. "Take a stand in favor of prohibition," he later wrote William Onahan, who was organizing the first Catholic Lay Congress, "and let temperance societies gently slide down an indefinitely sloping plane."[43]

If the C.T.A.U. and the temperance movement were what their historian has termed "the incarnation of Archbishop Ireland's ideal of a prosperous, civic-minded, American Catholicism,"[44] for Spalding the movement was a more basic thing.

[41] Sister Joan Bland, *Hibernian Crusade, The Story of the Catholic Total Abstinence Union of America* (Washington, 1951), p. 116.

[42] *Ibid.* In April, 1884, Spalding had been mentioned to succeed Wood as Archbishop of Philadelphia. Cf. AANY, C-17, John J. Williams to Corrigan, Boston, April 21, 1884. "This morning I received a letter from the Propaganda asking if I thought Bishop Spalding or Bp. Chatard a good choice for Philadelphia. . . . I know Bp. Chatard pretty well, and think him scarcely large enough for the place . . . I know Bp. Spalding less, but he seems to me a strong man—you must know him well. . . ."

[43] UND, III-3-c, Onahan Papers, Spalding to Onahan, Peoria, May 22, 1889.

[44] Bland, *op. cit.*, p. 267.

With Ralph Waldo Emerson, Spalding urged that "the end of all political struggle is to establish morality as the basis of legislation," since it was manifest, as he wrote at the height of the presidential campaign of 1884, that "our politics have become essentially immoral."[45] In what was, perhaps, the most exciting presidential campaign since the Civil War, the administration of Chester A. Arthur came to an end, "although the only real issues between the parties was the possession of government."[46] Disappointed with Arthur, who had succeeded to the presidency on the death of James A. Garfield, the Republican Party turned to James G. Blaine, "the plumed knight" to the rank and file, but a "simple grafter" to upright and intelligent reformers. Disgusted with the corruption of the day, the reform element, the "Mugwumps," bolted the party and agreed to support any decent candidate that the Democratic Party might nominate. With victory at last in sight, the Democratic Party selected Grover Cleveland, reform Mayor of Buffalo and Governor of New York.[47] But for Spalding, there was little hope to be had in supporting either party. To his mind, neither dared to touch any question that was holier or higher than that of tariff or no tariff, while the eternal principles of justice and morality were ignored and electoral contests degenerated into mere struggles for office. Even to suggest that conscience should reassert itself in American politics was to make oneself ridiculous; and all the while, so Spalding, decadence stared Americans in the face.[48] Spalding was particularly unsympathetic toward newspapers,

[45] J. L. Spalding, *Socialism and Labor and Other Arguments* (Chicago, 1902), p. 44. Chapter II of this work originally appeared as "The Basis of Popular Government," *North American Review*, CXXXIX (September, 1884), pp. 199–208. It will be quoted only when in variance with the revised edition.

[46] Samuel Eliot Morison and Henry Steele Commager, *The Growth of the American Republic* (New York, 1942), II, p. 225.

[47] *Ibid.*

[48] Spalding, *op. cit.*, p. 45.

which exploited all forms of vice and sordidness in their columns. The reader, as he said, in a lavish of rhetoric, was constantly met with

. . . reckless assertion, crude generalization, special pleading, ignorant or dishonest statement of half-truths, insincere praise and lying abuse of public men, frivolous treatment of the highest and holiest subjects. . . . And this half-mental and half-bestial brothel-and-grog mixture, brought from the great cities by special trains to every household, falls like mildew upon the mind and conscience of the people . . .[49]

No one American institution, he thought, existed that was great enough to inspire love and enthusiasm, to be the soul of national unity. The nation's chief concern was money, and the significance of its political contests lay in the emoluments of office. So long as this condition of affairs lasted, the best men would have to remain aloof from political struggle. What America needed, he said, was a moral ideal, but, unfortunately, "our two great parties are the principal obstacle in the way of such a movement." His remedy: ". . . that one or other party cease to exist; that a new party, springing from the deep yearning of the people for purer and nobler national life, and upheld by the enthusiasm inspired by high moral aims and purposes, may take its place."

Preparations, meantime, were still going on for the Third Plenary Council under the direction of Gibbons, who in December 1883 had been named apostolic delegate. In a letter of March 19, 1884, to the American hierarchy, Gibbons formally convoked the council and set the date of opening for the following November 9.[50] In the Spring, Spalding asked Father John S. Foley, a secretary of the council, to be excused from accepting Gibbons' invitation to preach at the council on the higher education of the clergy and the need of an American Catholic university. Two weeks before the council was to open,

[49] *Ibid.*, p. 46.
[50] Ellis, *Gibbons,* I, p. 203.

however, he again wrote to Gibbons, informing him that a certain Miss Mary Gwendolen Caldwell of New York, a wealthy young heiress, was interested in the university project and was disposed to donate a large sum of money for this purpose.[51] He was anxious, he said, that Miss Caldwell have a good seat in the cathedral, interested as she was in the founding of what he termed the *Unum Seminarium Principale*. He added that his discourse on the higher education of the clergy would be quite long, and that therefore he hoped Gibbons would allow him an evening rather than the Solemn Mass as the occasion for the talk.[52]

The Third Plenary Council of Baltimore formally opened on Sunday, November 9, in the Cathedral of the Assumption. *The*

[51] AAB, 78-S-11, Spalding to Gibbons, Peoria, October 26, 1884. Miss Caldwell, "Mamie," and her sister, Mary Elizabeth, "Lina," were the daughters and sole heirs of William Shakespeare Caldwell, a native of Virginia who later moved to Louisville where he married Mary Eliza Breckenridge. After the death of his wife in childbirth, Mr. Caldwell had moved to New York City where he died in May, 1874. Spalding, then in residence at St. Michael's Church, had never met Caldwell, but he became acquainted with the girls when they were students at the Academy of the Sacred Heart on 17th Street through Mrs. Mary G. Andrews, who had been designated their guardian. Mary Gwendolen, "Mamie," was born in Louisville in 1863 and died on board ship outside New York harbor in 1909. In 1896 she had married the Marquis des Monstiers-Merinville. Mary Elizabeth, "Lina," had likewise been born in Louisville in 1865, married the Baron Moritz von Zedtwitz, and died in Frankfort, Germany in 1910. Interview of the writer with Waldemar Conrad von Zedtwitz, son of Lina, New York, February 27, 1957. It was by reason of her friendship with Spalding that "Mamie" became interested, as she later recalled, in the idea of "doing something to lift the church from the lowly position which it occupied in America and so I thought of a university or higher school, where its clergy could be educated, and if possible, refined. Of course in this I was merely influenced by Bishop Spalding of Peoria, who represented it to me as one of the greatest works of the day." Cf. New York *Times,* November 16, 1904.

[52] *Ibid.*

Chicago Tribune commented on the remarkable growth of the American Church and printed the names of the eleven archbishops, fifty-eight bishops, and six abbots who marched in procession, and recorded that 30,000 people had gathered at sunrise to await the glorious spectacle.

On the following day, the work of the Council began. Two public congregations were to be held each week, while private congregations of the bishops were to gather each day, except Sundays and Thursdays, in the *aula maxima* of St. Mary's Seminary to discuss the *Schema decretorum,* the subjects for debate in secret session which had been based on the document entitled *Capita proposita,* the legislation as originally suggested by Rome. Twelve committees of theologians were designated, each headed by an archbishop with several bishops and a select number of theologians entrusted with a particular section that was to be discussed. Following the method pursued in the Council of 1866, these sections were called titles; in the official *Acta et decreta* these titles were, in turn, subdivided into chapters and each chapter into decrees. The official *Acta* as later published, however, did not contain all the proceedings of the plenary Council, and only in the privately printed version are the roles played by the various bishops as they made their votes fully documented.[53] From these, it becomes evident that Spal-

[53] Ellis, *Gibbons,* I, p. 211 and *passim.* For a concise explanation of the various documents pertaining to the council as they developed chronologically: the *Capita praecipua, Capita proposita, Relatio collationum, Relationes, Schema decretorum, Acta et decreta* (private edition), official *Acta et decreta,* cf. Francis P. Cassidy, "Catholic Education in the Third Plenary Council of Baltimore," *Catholic Historical Review,* XXXIV (October, 1948), pp. 262–263. The *Capita proposita,* mentioned in the text, was the result of the joint action of the cardinals of Propaganda and the American prelates in their Roman meetings of November-December, 1883, a new draft of the *Capita praecipua* which contained the main topics for discussions and legislation at the council. Cassidy has given the full titles of these conciliar documents; cf. p. 262.

ding's role was no minor one during the month the prelates spent in Baltimore.

It was also a hectic one. One sore point among the gathered bishops was Spalding's opposition to the theory and practice of democracy, in this case democracy in the Church. As a young priest in Rome, he had speculated more than once in letters to his Uncle Martin on the "dedication of the vulgar many" and the fundamental fallacy of majority rule. "Even when a school boy," he had written at the time, "I never had much faith in what the spirit of the age calls liberty and I now have less. . . . People are the most gullible animals on earth and where they are King, fools inevitably rule." It was the few, he was convinced, who led the many in most things worthwhile, and, "if this were tyranny, it was better to be tyrannized by one man than by the vulgar crowd."[54] Spalding never forgot that he could trace his family back to another Lancaster, King Edward III of England.

This particular philosophy met with vociferous opposition at the Council, for among other things the prelates had met to discuss ways of introducing a more representative form of government in the American Church. Particular opposition was provided by Patrick Corrigan, pastor of Our Lady of Grace Parish in Hoboken, who a year before had issued a pamphlet—suppressed by his bishop, Winand Wigger of Newark—entitled *Episcopal Nominations: Do the Interests of the Church in the United States Require that the Priests Should have the Power of Nominating Bishops?* Suppression of the pamphlet had not discouraged Corrigan, who continued his agitation to the very eve of the council, when he published another treatise, *What the Catholic Church Most Needs in the United States, or the Voice of the Priests in the Election of the Bishops.* The Church, he demanded, needed representative men, and the clergy and laity alike should insist on getting them.

[54] AAB, 37-A-7, Spalding to Spalding, Rome, January 5, 1865.

160

The Holy See, cognizant of the inadequate method used in the selection of candidates for vacant American sees, had already determined on new legislation subject to debate in the council. Rome proposed that within thirty days after a vacancy, the diocesan consultors and irremovable rectors were to meet under the metropolitan or senior suffragan bishop and select three candidates whose names would then be submitted to the bishops of the province. Within ten days after the meeting, the bishops of the province, in turn, were to gather for discussion on the priests' candidates with the right to approve or disapprove any or all of the nominees and to propose others according to rules prescribed in an instruction of January 1861.[55] When the proposal was introduced in the private sessions of the Council, Peter Richard Kenrick offered a substitute resolution that would have made for more representative government. He suggested that on the day of a bishop's funeral, the remaining bishops of the ecclesiastical province should confer among themselves concerning a successor for the vacant see. Thirty days later, all the rectors of churches, including religious, who had exercised the ministry for ten years would convene and propose three names as candidates to the bishops. The metropolitan would thereupon call the suffragan bishops to a conference, where the qualifications of the nominees would be discussed and then would present one name to the Holy See for the vacant bishopric.[56]

Archbishop Elder of Cincinnati praised Kenrick's proposal, but he thought that more than one name should be offered for consideration, and he agreed with Archbishop Ryan of Philadelphia that all rectors of churches, even those not ten years ordained, should have a vote. McQuaid of Rochester wished to broaden the substitute resolution and to include chancellors,

[55] *Capita proposita*, pp. 4–5.

[56] *Acta et decreta concilii plenarii Baltimorensis tertii* (Baltimore, 1884), p. lii. This will be cited hereafter as *Acta et decreta*, private edition.

deans, rectors of cathedrals, and even superiors of seminaries. The bishop chosen would thus be all the more favored in proportion to the number of votes he has amassed. At this point, Spalding rose to dispel the aura of prevailing harmony. He informed his confreres that he not only disagreed with the proposal of Archbishop Kenrick, but also with the schema proposed by Propaganda. "If either of these be accepted here," he warned, "we shall walk a rough road from which there is no return." In Spalding's opinion, if priests were given the right to vote, the laity would soon expect the same. "I believe all should be kept from voting," he said, "except the diocesan consultors."[57] The debate reached an impasse, when Archbishop Gibbons, in one of the rare occasions when he intervened in the conciliar discussions, simply noted that he did not believe that the Congregation Propaganda Fide would easily revoke the instruction already given. It was enough to turn the tide, for on the vote both Kenrick's proposal and Spalding's objections were defeated,[58] and the decrees as finally approved limited the vote to consultors and irremovable rectors.[59]

The Holy See had also pressed for the appointment of diocesan consultors who would aid the American bishops in the administration of their dioceses, and who would serve for some of the functions performed by cathedral chapters in Europe.[60] In Europe, of course, the chapters, whose members were called canons or capitulars, served as one governing body with the bishop of a diocese and, as it were, constituted an episcopal senate. While in Rome, Gibbons had told the Propaganda that such chapters would not be expedient and that diocesan con-

[57] *Ibid.*

[58] *Ibid.*, p. liii.

[59] *Acta et decreta concilii plenarii Baltimorensis tertii* . . . (Baltimore, 1886), pp. 12–14. This will be cited hereafter as *Acta et decreta*, official edition.

[60] *Capita proposita*, p. 3.

sultors would suffice.[61] The cardinals conceded the point, but demanded that diocesan consultors be made mandatory. Rome also insisted on the creation of irremovable factors in every diocese within three years after the close of the council.[62]

Once the debate got under way, however, the main question in Baltimore reduced itself to determining to what extent a bishop was to be made dependent on his consultors. That is, would the bishop need his consultors' consent, or merely their counsel? Bishop Joseph Dwenger, C.PP.S., of Fort Wayne declared absolutely that Propaganda held for the word "consent," but after considerable debate "counsel" was inserted. Spalding had noted how much he abhorred the use of such words as "election," "vote," and "consent" when speaking of the rights of priests.[63] His opposition to Rome's insistence on the appointment of irremovable rectors was even more vehement. Until this time, all rectors of churches were removable at the will of the bishop: this right was not in accord with the general law of the Church, which held that rectors having the care of souls be irremovable. In 1883, Propaganda had suggested to the U.S. bishops that rectors of churches be made canonical parish priests and, as such, irremovable. When debate at the council opened on the qualifications needed for irremovable rectorships, Spalding demanded the floor. Again in opposition to Dwenger, he maintained that the "present discipline is more consonant with that of the ancient Church. . . . Here we have no benefices. Here we do not depend nor shall we ever depend on the state or any form of political regime." The Sacred Congregation, he continued, "desires to grant this privilege because it believes the Clergy demand it. This is not true. Good and pious priests do not wish this, but only the troublemakers, and the scandal-mongers, who charge that bishops are tyrants. The Sacred Congregation

[61] Ellis, *Gibbons,* I, p. 213.
[62] *Capita proposita,* p. 3.
[63] *Ibid.,* p. xxxiv.

has little knowledge of the affairs in the American Church. . . ."[64]
He added that, were the Holy See's wishes realized in the
United States, "zeal for souls will be extinguished in our priests
just as in Italy."

Closely related to the problem of irremovability of certain
rectors was the method of procedure to be used in disciplinary
and criminal cases of clerics. For some years before the Third
Plenary Council, the claims of malcontents for "fixity of tenure
and immunity of discipline" had been a bone of contention.
Bishop McQuaid had thought that in 1879 he had saved the day
on this point when the *Responsa ad dubia* of the Holy See had
temporarily eased the anxiety of many of the bishops frightened
by the instruction *Quamvis*. In 1884, a new instruction entitled
Cum magnopere had superseded the previous Roman communications with a demand for the creation in every diocese of ecclesiastical courts for the trial of clerics.[65] At the council, Kenrick
offered the suggestion that the form of the trial prescribed by
the Provincial Council of St. Louis in 1855—and later adopted
by the Plenary Council of 1866—be retained until it was explicitly abrogated. He made it clear that his proposal was not
intended as a substitute, for that would be irreverence to the
Holy See, but merely as an easier method for the consideration of the council within the framework of Propaganda's latest
instruction. At this point, Spalding inquired whether or not the
question had been discussed by the archbishops in their Roman
conferences with Propaganda in 1883, and, if so, what had been
agreed on.[66] Archbishop Ryan replied that the subject had not
been discussed, because they knew at that time that the new
method had been commanded by the Holy See itself. Ryan also
preferred the form used in St. Louis, but it had rarely if ever been
employed throughout the country; hence, after many appeals and
constant vexation, Propaganda had enjoined the new form.

[64] *Acta et decreta,* private edition, p. xlviii.
[65] *Acta et decreta,* official edition, p. 287.
[66] *Acta et decreta,* private edition, p. lxxxviii.

McQuaid then rose to say that he thought it was the right and duty of the Council to indicate to Rome the difficulties which the new method would encounter, one of which was that the guilty would never be punished. Dwenger expressed the contrary view, that the new method would be easier and simpler than the 1878 instruction; and then it was Spalding's turn to address the assembly. He objected to the new form, he said, because it "is filled with too many details and if these be omitted, the case might go to Rome." The bishops were intent, he continued, on fair trials for priests, but without the noisy fighting in which Protestant clergymen were often involved, and which always resulted in loss of good reputation. "I would rather renounce the episcopacy," he said, "than ever to prosecute a case against a priest at Rome."[67] At length, a committee was appointed by Gibbons to study the matter further, and in the meantime the bishops were to obey *Quamvis*. Eventually, Rome decided that the bishops were to erect episcopal courts within three years, and that during the interim they were to obey the instruction with its subsequent interpretation, that is, *Cum magnopere*.

In the closing days of the council, Spalding hammered away at what he believed to be the only adequate solution to another major problem. "Religious in charge of a mission," he told the bishops, "ought to possess property under the same title as are all other diocesan properties." Bishop Ryan of Buffalo interceded to inform Spalding that the matter had been debated at the Second Plenary Council, but that nothing had been settled, and that he thought it better, therefore, to refer it to the committee on new business.[68] But the next day, Spalding again introduced the subject, backed by Ireland and Gilmour. Spalding began by saying that he was not talking of hypothetical cases, but of actual occurrences he had himself witnessed. For example, he said, "a religious community, invited by the bishop, enters the

[67] *Ibid.,* p. lxxxix.
[68] *Ibid.,* p. xciii.

diocese, builds a school with parochial or diocesan funds; soon they quarrel with the bishop, sell the school, go into another diocese. . . . If there is no remedy for past evils, at least future mishaps can be prevented."[69]

The Council had encountered another impasse, so a special commission was appointed to solve the difficulty.[70] The commission eventually recommended possession of church property by religious, and in the last session of the Council the decree was passed by majority, but not unanimous, vote. On October 17, 1885, however, Propaganda informed the American hierarchy that the decree was to be deleted, since "the question has not been fully discussed." Simeoni added that it was the Pope's wish that the entire matter be fully reviewed at the next plenary council.[71]

The most important item on the Council's agenda, for Spalding, was the controversial question of an American Catholic university.[72] Several days after the beginning of the Council, Miss Caldwell, as Spalding had predicted, informed Gibbons that it was her intention to donate $300,000 to the bishops for the founding of a national Catholic school of philosophy and theology. But the proffered benefaction was to be given under certain conditions, which, if not written by Spalding, at least had his complete approval. These conditions stipulated that the school was to be a separate institution in the United States under the control of an episcopal committee representing the Ameri-

[69] *Ibid.*, p. xcvi.

[70] *Ibid.*, p. xcix.

[71] *Acta et decreta,* official edition, p. lxvii. "*S. C. de P. F. consultius esse duxit hoc decretum non esse retinendum cum haec qaestio plenius non fuerit examinata. . . .*" Epistola Card. Praefecti S. C. de P. F., 17 October, 1885.

[72] This subject, however, was not mentioned in the *Capita proposita* but evolved from Title V of the *Schema decretorum,* prepared by the corps of theologians for discussion at the Council.

can hierarchy. Since post-graduate studies were to form the curriculum, only ecclesiastics who had completed their elementary courses in philosophy and theology were to be admitted. The institution was never to be under the control of any religious order, and its chairs were to be filled preferably by professors chosen from the diocesan clergy and the laity. It was hoped that, in time, other faculties might affiliate with the national Catholic school of philosophy and theology with a view to forming a Catholic university. The fund was never to be diverted from the purposes for which it was given, and the site, once chosen, was not to be changed without the gravest reasons. Finally, in consideration of the donation, Mary Gwendolen Caldwell was to be considered the founder of the institution.[73] At the time, the heiress was twenty-one years old.

Three days after the Council had heard Miss Caldwell's offer, Spalding delivered his discourse on "University Education Considered in its Bearings on the Higher Education of Priests" on Sunday evening in the Cathedral of the Assumption. While in substance the sermon was an amplification of his Milwaukee jubilee oration of 1881, it was a more powerful plea that the Catholic Church in the United States face up to reality, "to learn to see things as they are."[74] According to Spalding, what the Catholic priest needed most after holiness was cultivation of the mind, a refinement, a culture. The education of priests, he said, had to be more than merely professional; it had to be given freedom of mental play. The ecclesiastical seminary, he noted, was simply a training school for the practical work of the ministry, not a center of intellectual culture. Textbooks, subjects, and professors therein were ill-equipped to offer the students with the opportunity to go beyond more than ordinary intellectual advancement.

[73] AAB, 78-T-6, Caldwell to Gibbons, Baltimore, November 13, 1884.

[74] Spalding, *University Education,* p. 20 and *passim.*

167

"If we are to be intellectually the equal of others," Spalding continued, "we must have with them equal advantages of education, and so long as we look rather to the multiplying of schools and seminaries than to the erection of a real university, our progress will be slow and uncertain." No place in the world was more inviting, he added, for a Catholic university than the United States, for here "almost for the first time in her history the Church is really free." Without a Catholic university, there was little hope that the American Church would prove to be a determining force in the controversies of the age; with forces scattered, bishops would continue to act in a vacuum, united in faith but going separate and random ways. Catholics of wealth would continue to send their sons to institutions where their faith might be undermined, and the struggle for many needed reforms would fail, since, as he maintained, "we shall lack the wisdom of the best counsel and the courage which only skillful leaders can inspire."

Whether an American Catholic University was desirable was not, Spalding declared, the question, for no longer could there be two opinions among enlightened men. But was it feasible? There were difficulties, not the least of them lack of money, but this, he was persuaded, could be obtained. As for students who would consent to continue their education after years of study for the priesthood, Spalding was convinced that they could be found, just as they were in other countries. In the United States, it was true, there was a tendency to rush with precipitancy and insufficient preparation into one's life work. But was this not a sign of immaturity? The American Church must learn that haste betrays a lack of maturity, that "he who is certain of himself and master of his tool, knows that he is able, and neither hurries nor worries, but works and waits." Ought not this lesson be taught to young priests who were to be the future leaders of Catholic thought? And where but in a university could this be learned?

168

Let there be, then [he concluded], an American Catholic university, where our young men, in the atmosphere of faith and purity, of high thinking and plain living, shall become more intimately conscious of the truth of their religion and of the genius of their country, where they shall learn repose and dignity which belong to their ancient Catholic descent, and yet not lose the fire which flows in the blood of a new people; to which from every part of the land our eyes may turn for guidance and encouragement, seeking light and self-confidence from men in whom intellectual power is not separate from more purpose; who look to God and his universe from bending knees of prayer . . .

Ten days after Spalding's appeal, the university question came before the council, where it met with fierce opposition. The twelve theologians who had been deputed to report on the matter, unable to agree, had finally stated simply that the entire subject matter be referred to a special committee. Bishop Tobias Mullen of Erie had heard enough, and thereupon made a motion that the entire chapter be expunged or at least referred to the next plenary council. Though seconded by Kenrick and accepted by Ryan of Philadelphia, who were joined by twenty other bishops, Mullen's motion was defeated, by a meager three votes, and the university question remained on the agenda. Gibbons then appointed the special committee suggested by the theologians, and named to it Alemany, Kenrick, Corrigan, Ryan of Philadelphia, and Spalding.[75] This action was later reported by Corrigan to Cardinal McCloskey, with the observation that the special committee "will report favorably, recommending the acceptance of Miss Caldwell's gift and the beginning of a nucleus of a future university."[76] On December 2, 1884, the special committee of bishops made its report, which proposed:

1. A seminary is to be erected like the Dunboyne in Ireland or Louvain in Belgium, from which as from a seed the University is to grow.
2. It is to be erected near a large and populous city.

[75] *Acta et decreta,* private edition, p. lx.
[76] AANY, A-22, Corrigan to McCloskey, Baltimore, November, 1884.

3. A very respectable lady has promised that she will give $300,000 for the erection and endowment of the Seminary.

4. A commission is to be formed of five or seven prelates and some laymen to whom is to be given the care of erecting and administering the Seminary.[77]

It was the most memorable action taken by the council for the future of the Catholic Church in the United States.

It is sometimes argued that the Fathers of the Third Plenary Council founded not a university, but only a higher seminary; yet, the seed that was planted in 1884 is today the university of which Spalding had dreamed, and he, in any case, was speaking of a university. Less precise at the Milwaukee jubilee, knowing perhaps that to be too clear is at times to be found out, Spalding now discarded his vague terminology of three years before and declared emphatically on Sunday, December 7, 1884, as the Third Plenary Council of Baltimore came to a close:

We have laid the foundation of an institution which, under God's providence, is destined to grow into an American Catholic university, the measure of whose usefulness, the grandeur of whose scope, and the fruitful blessings of which, cannot be forecast by the mind.[78]

The Third Plenary Council of Baltimore was itself an epoch in the history of American Catholicism, and likewise an important stage in Spalding's career. "No age seems wonderful to those who live in it," Spalding had remarked at the occasion. "No work seems great to him who does it; but in other centuries, men will look back not without gratitude to what has been accomplished here."[79]

If the Holy See had shown some apprehension before the

[77] *Acta et decreta,* private edition, p. lxxix.

[78] *Catholic Mirror,* December 13, 1884. Archbishop Riordan had been scheduled to preach but had taken ill. Spalding's sermon, "The Work of the Council," will be found in revised form in *The Memorial Volume, A History of the Third Plenary Council of Baltimore* (Baltimore, 1885), pp. 245–254.

[79] Spalding, "The Work of the Council," p. 253.

council, suspicious, as the Bishop of Richmond had expressed it, "that there was not a perfect disposition of accord and union on the part of the American hierarchy toward the Holy See,"[80] the officials of the Roman Curia apparently found Spalding's candor a bit unsettling. Some months before the close of the council, Father Denis J. O'Connell, then in Rome as an agent of Gibbons, reported that "Bp. Spalding is not considered strongly attached to Rome nor to Roman training. Someone asked me if Spalding and Ireland were not severe on the Regulars in the council."[81]

Doubtless, Spalding's type of candor was easily confused with imprudence, if not indiscretion. In his Council sermon on the university, he had remarked: "Only they who do nothing derive comfort from the mistakes of others, and the saying that a blunder is worse than a crime is doubtless true for those who have no other measure of worth and success than the conventional standards of superficial public opinion."[82] But public opinion, superficial or not, was a force to be reckoned with in both Church and State affairs. It was not difficult to foresee that John Spalding, indeed, would need watching.

[80] AAB, 77-I-1, John Keane to Gibbons, Florence, July 4, 1883.
[81] AAB, 79-F-9, O'Connell to Gibbons, Rome, March 8, 1885.
[82] Spalding, *University Education,* p. 34.

5

The Middle Years

THE years following the Third Plenary Council were to be difficult for American Catholics. Misunderstandings, conflicts, and contentions were to arouse angry and rancorous thoughts in the next decade, which has led one historian to remark that the decrees of the council "are historically more notable for the topics they avoided than for what they decided." Even when the Fathers of the council dealt with specific problems, they only stressed the ideal, "while the reality and the attempt to achieve the ideal—which were not really discussed—were to make those decrees a source of serious controversy."[1] It was an era when

. . . procedural and racial differences on a practical level, though seemingly unrelated, crystallized the basic issues which were to occupy Catholic leaders, both clerical and lay, in the years ahead. These issues broadened and intensified until by 1891 they broke forth in charges and countercharges of Americanism and Cahenslyism. When these procedural and racial differences of the 1880s were combined in the 1890s with supposed doctrinal errors related to the school question, Heckerism, liberalism, and minimism, a major controversy ensued which has been termed "Americanism."[2]

For the Bishop of Peoria, it was a period of disenchantment, and some four years after the close of the Baltimore Council he would write:

[1] Thomas T. McAvoy, C.S.C., *The Great Crisis in American Catholic History, 1895–1900* (Chicago, 1957), p. 34.

[2] Barry, *The Catholic Church and German Americans*, p. 44.

In looking back, we see that after much toil we have accomplished little. What we hoped to do, we have not; or having done, have ceased to care for . . . How shall we, . . . grown older, take up the old task with the old ardor? And surely the brave must lose heart when to these difficulties there is added the loss of mental composure which misunderstandings, conflicts, and contentions involve. . . .[3]

It was a time when even the normally buoyant Archbishop Ireland was to lose heart and exclaim: "The Ch. . . . humanly speaking is stuck fast in the grooves; & he loses his time who strives to move her out. Bp. Spalding is about right; each one to his own shanty & write poetry or—save his soul."[4]

In the lull before the gathering storms, Spalding returned to Peoria after the close of the Council, where his immediate concern was to expedite the publication of the proposed uniform

[3] Spalding, Introduction to James J. McGovern, *The Life and Writings of the Rt. Rev. John McMullen*, p. xxi.

[4] CUA, Keane Papers, Ireland to Keane, St. Paul, March 30, 1891. Spalding fancied himself a poet, but Maurice Francis Egan in *Recollections of a Happy Life* (New York, 1924), p. 169, wrote that Spalding's "prose was admirable; but he could never convince me that he could write poetry though he tried to often enough." *America and Other Poems* (New York, 1885), and *The Poet's Praise* (New York, 1887) were published by the Bishop under the pseudonym Henry Hamilton, a name derived from his paternal grandmother, Henrietta Hamilton Spalding. The New York *Freeman's Journal* on May 21, 1887, quoted the *London Athenaeum's* review of *The Poet's Praise:* " 'Mr. Hamilton' has gone to the trouble of devoting more than 150 pages to singing the poet's praise in a variety of metres. The subject, as might be expected, is tedious and monotonous to a degree—never enlivened as it were by even a gleam of that malicious wit which Shakespeare loves to irritate the mighty conceit of poets in general, as when he makes Hotspur say: 'I had rather be a kitten and cry mew, Than one of these same metre ballad mongers.' " Later poetical works were a translation, *Songs Chiefly from the German* (Chicago, 1895), and *God and the Soul* (New York, 1901). Spalding viewed the latter as "the best I have done . . . There are sonnets that will survive." Cf. UND, Hudson Papers, Spalding to Hudson, Peoria, April 7, 1907. Time has disproved the Bishop's prediction and confirmed Egan's judgment.

catechism. As early as August 25, 1884, he had been named to the committee of bishops who were to report at the Council on the expediency of adopting a uniform catechism, to name the catechism they preferred, and to consider whether non-English-speaking Catholics in the United States should have a translation of the catechism to be adopted.[5] Sebastian G. Messmer, a secretary of the Council, reminisced some years later as Bishop of Green Bay that, according to the *Schema decretorum,* the question of the catechism was to have been considered at a much later date; and yet, in the private congregation on November 11, the commission of bishops asked leave to report at once. Strong sentiment, they reported, urged the adoption of Butler's *Catechism,* which had been recently issued by the council held at Maynooth in Ireland, with changes for the United States.

Opinion in favor of a new catechism prevailed, however, and the question arose again on November 29 when the commission of bishops reported several changes in the schema which were adopted as they now read in the decrees of the Council. From the minutes, it would appear that a new commission of bishops was appointed to report once more to the Council. This was done in the last private congregation when a draft of the new catechism, hurriedly compiled by Monsignor Januarius De Concilio, pastor of St. Michael's Parish, Jersey City, and printed on galley sheets, was distributed to the assembled bishops for suggestions and changes. Time was too short, Messmer recalled, and the bishops were therefore requested to forward their suggestions as soon as possible to the Bishop of Peoria.[6] Early in the new year,

[5] AAB, 78-L-11, Gibbons to Alemany, August 25, 1884, copy.

[6] Sebastian G. Messmer, D.D., to John K. Sharp, Milwaukee, December 3, 1928, in John K. Sharp, "How the Baltimore Catechism Originated," *American Ecclesiastical Review,* LXXXI (December, 1929), pp. 575–576. The review will henceforth be quoted as *AER.* Monsignor Januarius De Concilio was born in Naples, Italy, and came to America in 1860. In 1865, he was appointed the first pastor of St. Michael's Parish,

Spalding wrote to Archbishop Gibbons that he had examined all the suggestions with regard to the catechism, and telling the archbishop that "Mr. Kehow [*sic*] will, in a day or so, send you copies for the final amendments of the archbishops." He hoped the latter would send their observations as soon as possible that he might, as he wrote, "get the work off my hands."[7]

While it is a tribute to the bishops of the commission, and especially to Bishop Spalding, that within six months after the end of the Council there appeared the first edition of the *Baltimore Catechism*,[8] the Bishop of Peoria was undoubtedly relieved,

---

Jersey City. At the Third Plenary Council he served as a theologian to Bishop James O'Connor, Vicar Apostolic of Nebraska. In 1888, De Concilio was reported to have told Father Mark Moesslein, C.P., the facts about the authorship of the Baltimore Catechism, namely that one of the bishops appointed to prepare the catechism came to him to discuss the matter and asked him to draw up a catechism for submission to the episcopal committee. De Concilio thought it not worthwhile to take great pains about the matter because "the bishops would dump it in the wastebasket anyhow." He acted accordingly and the result was the Baltimore Catechism. When he finished it, he sent it to the Bishop but heard no more of it. He was greatly surprised to see it in print at the Council, and greater was his chagrin that the committee of bishops did not allow him to revise it and make it worthwhile. Cf. *AER* XCIII (December, 1935), pp. 613–614. Sharp later confirmed the fact that "the Baltimore Catechism was prepared hurriedly by Monsignor De Concilio," but there was still doubt as to its sources. Cf. *AER* LXXXIII (December, 1930), pp. 62–64. The decrees of the Council on the catechism will be found in Titulus VII, Caput II, nn. 217–219, in *Acta et Decreta Concilii Plenarii Baltimorensis Tertii*, pp. 118–120.

[7] AAB, 79-A-1, Spalding to Gibbons, Peoria, January 2, 1885. Lawrence Kehoe (1832–1890) was at the time editor of the Catholic Publication Society founded by Isaac Hecker in 1866.

[8] Francis Connell, C.SS.R., "Is the Baltimore Catechism Outmoded?" in *AER*, CLXXI (January, 1960). The abridged as distinct from the complete catechism is dated April 11, 1885, while the latter bears the date of September 8, 1885. One might understand De Concilio's surprise at seeing his compilation already in galley proofs at the Council,

as he said, to get the work off his hands so that he might devote his time and energies to what would prove to be a more difficult task, namely the making of a Catholic university a reality. When Spalding thanked Archbishop Corrigan of New York for "the prompt and useful suggestions regarding the catechism," he added: "I am glad you are to have a meeting of the Committee on the university. I have notified Bishop Ireland but I beg you to have your secretary notify the others as it would look awkward for me to do it."[9] It would, perhaps, have been awkward for Spalding to initiate the project at this stage, for despite her promise made at the council, Miss Caldwell had not turned over the money, since, as she told Gibbons, she felt that "as long as there is nothing definitely settled, I prefer to allow the investments to remain as they are." But, she added, as soon as the money for the foundation of the university was needed, it would be forthcoming.[10] It was this promise that prompted Gibbons' remark to Corrigan: "You might show the letter to Bp. Spalding on the occasion of the dedication on the 25th & perhaps another appeal might be made to her with more success. We can take no steps till we have her money."[11]

The dedication of the Church of St. Paul the Apostle, adjacent to the Paulist mother house on Fifty-ninth Street in New York, was the occasion for the university committee to hold its initial meeting on January 26, 1885, at Cardinal McCloskey's residence. After a formal resolution whereby the Caldwell offer

and yet his Italian translation of the same work appeared in March, 1886, just six months after the English edition appeared. Cf. Francis Augustine Walsh, O.S.B., "More About the Catechism of the Council of Baltimore," *AER,* XCV (September, 1936), pp. 274–279.

[9] AANY, C-3, Spalding to Corrigan, Peoria, January 15, 1885.

[10] AANY, C-7, M. G. Caldwell to James Gibbons, New York, January 9, 1885. The treatment of the early years of the University is based in part on John Tracy Ellis, *The Formative Years of the Catholic University of America* (Washington, 1946). Cf. Chapters II and III, pp. 87–198.

[11] AANY, C-7, Gibbons to Corrigan, Baltimore, January 11, 1885.

of $300,000 was accepted under certain conditions—which would cause serious difficulties in the years ahead—one of the first matters for consideration was the question of a site for the proposed university. Seton Hall College at South Orange, New Jersey, was suggested, and while Ireland preferred Washington, D.C., the motion for Seton Hall was carried with the amendment that Miss Caldwell should first be consulted.[12] Spalding reported back the next day that Miss Caldwell consented to give $180,000 for the buildings at South Orange. But then a letter was read into the minutes from Bishop Winand Wigger of Newark, who declared that he had not been the one to propose the sale of Seton Hall, but that the proposal had come from "Rt. Rev. Bp. Spaulding [sic], who had spoken to him about the matter during the sessions of the Baltimore Council." Wigger told the committee that he was still willing to sell, however, but he set May 1, 1885, as the deadline, after which the offer would be withdrawn. Spalding then countered with a proposal to examine some property in Washington, D.C. at Miss Caldwell's suggestion; and since, as he reminded the committee, Miss Caldwell had been conceded the privilege of deciding the site, he thought it best to visit the property in Washington before any further action be taken.[13] A little more than a week later, Spalding reported his findings to Archbishop Ryan of Philadelphia:

The place I went to Washington to inspect, seems to me a little too far from the city. My visit, however, makes me think that Washington is beyond doubt the proper site for the university . . . Washington is neither a Northern nor a Southern nor a Western city, but common ground upon which we can all meet to establish a National Institution.

[12] CUA, minutes of the meetings of the University committee, Monday, January 26, 1885. These minutes, strictly speaking, are not the minutes of the subsequent board of trustees, and hence will not be quoted as in Ellis, op. cit., where these minutes are cited as MMBt; rather, the designation MMuc will be used.

[13] Ibid., January 27, 1885.

. . . Unless it is absolutely necessary, it seems to me a mistake to buy a college like Seton Hall to start an absolutely new institution.[14]

It was soon evident that Miss Caldwell believed, as did Spalding, that Washington was "the common ground upon which we all can meet." About ten days after the New York meeting, she informed Gibbons that she was interested in locating the university somewhere near Washington, since the archbishop already knew how much opposed she was to its being established in the North, and she trusted, therefore, that he would give the project his "very kind consideration and approval."[15] The question of the university site, however, was to be settled only after a very lengthy process; and although the nation's capital was finally selected, it was not without misgivings that some members of the hierarchy viewed the role that Miss Caldwell had assumed in the proceedings. Bishop Gilmour believed that the young lady should not be permitted "to direct either location or management of the university,"[16] and while Corrigan thought the project should not be abandoned, he declared that the "bishops cannot be the mere obedient servants of any Lady Bountiful."[17] Gibbons wholeheartedly agreed, and related to Corrigan an account of an interview he had had with the young heiress. He told the New York archbishop: "It would be of great advantage if sufficient money could be obtained without her aid to purchase the site."[18]

Another difficulty in the university matter was the question of a rector. At a meeting in Baltimore on May 12, 1886, Ryan, Corrigan, Williams of Boston, and Gibbons were constituted by the committee to choose the man for that all-important post.[19]

[14] *Ibid.*, Spalding to Ryan, Peoria, February 8, 1885. This letter was included in the minutes.

[15] AAB, 76-D-6, Caldwell to Gibbons, New York, February 6, 1885.

[16] AAC, Gilmour to Elder, Cleveland, March 26, 1885.

[17] AAB, unindexed, Corrigan to Gibbons, New York, March 25, 1885.

[18] AANY, C-2, Gibbons to Corrigan, Baltimore, April 1, 1885.

[19] CUA, MMuc, Baltimore, May 12, 1886.

Obviously, Spalding seemed the logical choice. Two years before the plenary Council, he had told Gibbons: "If we could only begin a university . . . for the higher education of priests, it would be my greatest happiness to go into it, and devote the rest of my life to this work, which, I am convinced, is of all others the most important and the most urgent."[20] Father Denis J. O'Connell, soon to be nominated Rector of the American College in Rome, fully agreed that Spalding was the man, and he wrote to Gibbons from Rome:

I hope . . . that you can secure the resignation of Peoria to take control of it. It may be objected that he is to [sic] ardent for the office of presidency, but it will be some time yet before the place will be ready for the services of a calm presiding officer and the ardor of Peoria is required to build it. I have reason to suspect the choice of the location will do nothing to increase the assistance to be expected from other Sees, but if Peoria resigned he wd be committed to it and he would put forth all his energy to carry the plan through.[21]

The final selection of Washington as the site of the university alienated a segment of the hierarchy, and O'Connell voiced his concern some weeks later when he told the Archbishop of Baltimore: "I am very much afraid the University at Washington will be a failure, considering the feeling in N.Y. and Philad., unless you can make sure of the undivided energy of Bp. Spalding. If he were to drop from the scene now I do not know who there would be to take his place in carrying the plan through."[22] There was, indeed, feeling in New York and Philadelphia, and O'Connell had argued it precisely; some three weeks before he had written to Gibbons, Ryan had remarked to Corrigan: "As I foresaw, the next move is to have Bp. Spalding appointed Rector. This is a matter for grave consideration."[23]

[20] AAB, 76-A-8, Spalding to Gibbons, Peoria, July 18, 1882.

[21] AAB, 79-K-1, O'Connell to Gibbons, American College, Rome, May 28, 1885.

[22] AAB, 79-N-13, Same to Same, American College, Rome, June 28, 1885.

[23] AANY, C-3, Ryan to Corrigan, Philadelphia, June 4, 1885.

The choice of the nominating committee, not without surprise, was Spalding, of whom Gibbons would write many years later:

> All great works have their inception in the brain of some great thinker. God gave such a brain, such a man, in Bishop Spalding. With his wonderful intuitionary power, he took in all the meaning of the present and future of the Church in America. If the Catholic University is today an accomplished fact, we are indebted for its existence, in no small measure, to the persuasive eloquence and convincing arguments of the Bishop of Peoria.[24]

But more surprising, and to the relief of many, Spalding refused the post, and the burden of leading the infant university fell to John Keane, Bishop of Richmond. Keane later reminisced:

> . . . the Most Rev. Chairman came to tell me that their choice had fallen on me. I was utterly astonished, for I had always considered it a matter of course that, as the establishment of the University was mainly owing to the eloquent appeal of Bishop Spalding and to the generousity [sic] of his protégée Miss Caldwell, it would naturally be that he would have charge of it. . . . Gibbons answered: the committee had first offered the post to Bishop Spalding and that he had refused it most positively, and that he was as earnest as they in urging that I should accept. This Bishop Spalding repeated to me, adding that, for years to come, the post would practically be that of the President of a Seminary, a post which he could in no way be induced to fill.[25]

Though Spalding may have declined the rectorship because he felt himself ill-equipped for the presidency of a higher seminary, there may have been and most likely were other, more telling reasons. However, since much of Spalding's correspondence has been lost or destroyed, it is impossible fully to determine these reasons. In this case, it is easier to eliminate reasons for his refusal of the post. Eight years after Keane's appointment, for instance, the *Catholic Citizen* of Milwaukee reported that Spal-

---

[24] James Cardinal Gibbons, *A Retrospect of Fifty Years* (Baltimore, 1916), II, 195. The occasion was the celebration of the University's silver jubilee, April 15, 1915.

[25] CUA, Keane Papers, "Keane Memorial," pp. 4–5, May 12, 1886.

ding had expected to be appointed the university's first rector, and had attributed his failure to receive the post to Archbishop Ireland. By the time of the report, Spalding and Ireland were no longer close friends and Spalding replied to the *Citizen:*

> There is not even a shred of truth in this assertion. When Cardinal Gibbons informed me that my name had been suggested for the position, I assured him that under no circumstance would I accept the offer should it be made. I have never blamed Archbishop Ireland, have never known that I have reason to blame him for this or anything else in which I am personally concerned. It is not and never has been in the power of any man or body of men to keep me from a coveted position or office, for I have coveted or covet none.[26]

A subsequent attempt to explain Spalding's *volte-face* occurred when, just four months before his death, the Abbé Alphonse L. Magnien, S.S., retired as rector of St. Mary's Seminary in Baltimore. Magnien, in the minds of many, had played *éminence grise* to the Cardinal Archbishop of Baltimore; and, in fact, on Magnien's death Gibbons himself had noted: "I had been so accustomed to consult the Venerable Abbé on important questions, and to lean upon him in every emergency . . ."[27] The Hartford *Catholic-Transcript,* reporting the Abbé's retirement, spoke of his great influence at the Third Plenary Council, and, in doing so, recalled a rumor, said to be common at the time, that Magnien "met, in one of the corridors of the seminary, the Right Rev. John Lancaster Spalding, after listening to the latter's eloquent, but somewhat egregious discourse on university education, and incidentally dropped a few words of disapproval which His Lordship was presumably human enough to disrelish." It was worthy of note, the *Transcript* continued, that before the sermon was delivered, the most prominent name mentioned for the rectorship was the name of the same eloquent and accomplished prelate, but "ere the sessions of the council ceased, it was known that Peoria was not to lose its learned Bishop, and

---

[26] *Catholic Herald Citizen* (Milwaukee), December 19, 1894.
[27] Ellis, *Life of Gibbons,* II, p. 475.

that someone more according to the heart of the Superior of St. Mary's was to be set over the new institution."[28] Perhaps this note offers a clue to John Keane's surprise when he told O'Connell about his own selection as Rector, and added that Gibbons "was authorized to negotiate with the Asst. Superior of St. Sulpice . . . to obtain the Sulpitians [*sic*] to have charge of the discipline—a most important point settled and without a dissenting voice, Bp. Spalding approving as earnestly as any."[29] Though it cannot be said for certain whether Magnien did or did not have any part in transferring the rectorship to Keane, incurring thereby Spalding's resentment, it is certain that Spalding had not great liking for Gibbons' adviser. A year before the Abbé's death, Spalding had informed the Archbishop that "the Abbé Magnien is bitterly hated by many priests in the West as a meddler and intriguer."[30]

Though Spalding refused the rectorship, he did not hesitate to expend his eloquence and energy to insure the success of the university by canvassing diocese after diocese for the needed funds to get the institution under way.[31] He was the obvious choice, therefore, to give the inaugural address at the ceremony of the laying of the cornerstone on May 24, 1888, which was attended by President Grover Cleveland, several members of his cabinet, and some thirty bishops.[32] The address was to prove a turning point in Spalding's career. In it, he reviewed the progress of the Catholic Church in the United States, and he attempted an analysis of the American pluralistic consensus. Spalding recognized the essence of that consensus—a nation under God conceived in the natural-law tradition, a government by

[28] *The Review* IX (September 25, 1902), 602. Arthur Preuss, the editor, quoted the Hartford *Catholic Transcript.*

[29] ADR, Keane to O'Connell, Richmond, May 20, 1886.

[30] AAB, 99-C-5, Spalding to Gibbons, Peoria, October 11, 1901.

[31] Ellis, *Formative Years,* pp. 167, 170–71, 173.

[32] AAB, Episcopal Register, May 24, 1886.

the people, and a free people who understood that freedom was not the power of doing what one likes, but the right of being able to do what one ought.[33] He thus could urge that it was not to numbers or wealth that the American Republic owed its significance among the nations, but to the fact that:

> ... we have shown that respect for law is compatible with civil and religious liberty; that a free people can become prosperous and strong ...; that the State and the Church can move in separate orbits and still cooperate for the common welfare; that men of different races and beliefs may live together in peace ... that the government of the majority where men put their trust in God and in knowledge, is in the end the government of the good and the wise.[34]

The significance of American Catholic history, in like manner, lay not in mere externals of growth—a common theme for declamation, but rather in the fact that "our example proves that the Church can thrive where it is neither protected nor persecuted, but is simply left to manage its own affairs and to do its work."[35] It was a unique experiment, yet its success was of such world-wide importance that he was sure that it would be "the position toward the Church which all the nations will sooner or later assume; just as they will be forced finally to accept popular rule, since the underlying principle of democracy—that all men are brothers and have equal rights ... is a truth taught by Christ, is a truth proclaimed by the Church."[36]

[33] John Courtney Murray, S.J., *We Hold These Truths, Catholic Reflections on the American Proposition* (New York, 1960), p. 36.

[34] J. L. Spalding, "University Education," Chapter VIII in *Education and the Higher Life* (Chicago, 1890), p. 176. This speech is to be distinguished from the discourse that Spalding delivered at the Baltimore cathedral during the sessions of the Third Plenary Council and which was entitled "University Education Considered in its Bearings on the Higher Education of Priests."

[35] *Ibid.*, p. 177.

[36] *Ibid.*, pp. 178–179.

Spalding also pleaded with the Catholic community to make itself intellectually aware of the conditions for its own co-existence within the American pluralistic scene. Ignorance, he said, was the chief source of misery, and since the nineteenth century was an age of science "in which natural knowledge has placed in the hands of the wise forces which angels may not wield," and since the prosperity of the Church was left subject to human influences, "shall the Son of Man find faith on earth when he comes," he asked, "if the most potent instrument God has given man is abandoned to those who know not Christ?"[37] If in the past it were to the glory of the Church to have labored to civilize the barbarian world, was it not part of her mission now to encourage scientific research? To be Catholic was to be drawn not only to the love of whatever was good and beautiful, but also to whatever was true, and to be effective and productive "the Catholic Church must fit herself to a constantly changing environment, to the character of every people, and to the wants of every age."[38] While like the old the Church could look to the past, like the young she could look to the future, and if there were Catholics who lingered amid glories that had vanished, there were also those who in the midst of their work felt a confidence which left no place for regret, who well understood that the earthly environment in which the Church lived was subject to change and decay, and that new surroundings implied new tasks and imposed new duties.[39]

Since science, Spalding continued, with its new views of the physical universe which the modern world was forced to take, brought the Catholic Church face to face with new problems in religion and morals, in politics and society, it was imperative that

[37] *Ibid.*, p. 183 and *passim*.
[38] *Ibid.*, p. 184.
[39] *Ibid.*, p. 185.

whatever we may think of the past, whatever we may fear or hope for the future, if we would make an impression on the world around us, we must understand the thoughts, the purposes, and the methods of those with whom we live; and we must at the same time recognize that though the truth of religion be unchangeable, the mind of man is not so, and that the point of view varies not only from people to people, and from age to age, but from year to year in the growing thought of the individual and of the world.[40]

Opinions and manners of men grew different, and they who observed from widely separated positions did not see the same things or did not see them in the same light. To strive to attain truth under whatever form, therefore, was to seek to know God, for a faith which ignorance alone could keep alive was little better than superstition. Catholics must, accordingly, teach themselves to see things as they are, without preoccupation or misgivings, "lest what is should ever make it impossible for us to believe and hope in the better yet to be."[41] It was a privilege, Spalding believed, to live at a time when knowledge was increasing more rapidly even than population and wealth; hence, it was necessary for American Catholics, if they hoped to stand in the front ranks of those who know how to keep pace with the onward movement of the mind, not to turn away and not to look back, for to do so was to love darkness more than light. Therefore, Spalding said, there was a need in America for a Catholic university which:

. . . will teach the best that is known and encourage research; it will be at once a scientific institute, a school of culture, and a training ground for the business of life; it will educate the minds that give direction to the age; it will be a nursery of ideas.[42]

Spalding then proceeded to indict the ages past in hyperboles that must have seemed in contradiction to literal fact. In his

40 *Ibid.*, p. 189.
41 *Ibid.*, p. 190.
42 *Ibid.*, p. 197.

opinion, the learning of former times had become the ignorance of his own. Classical literature, he cited by way of example, had ceased to be the treasure house of knowledge, since Greek and Latin were accomplishments chiefly, and a classical scholar, unacquainted with modern science and literature was, he believed, hopelessly ignorant. The Germans in philosophy, the English in poetry, and the French in prose, in wealth of thought and knowledge had so far excelled the Greeks and Latins as to preclude comparison. He continued:

> Aristotle is a great mind, but his learning is crude and his ideas of Nature are frequently grotesque. Saint Thomas is a powerful intellect; but his point of view in all that concerns natural knowledge has long since vanished from sight. What a poverty of learning does but the early medieval scheme of education reveal; and when in the twelfth century the idea of a university rises in the best minds, how incomplete and vague it is.[43]

Amid ruins of castles and cathedrals one might be tempted to grow humble, to think oneself inferior to men who thus could build, and yet, he reminded his listeners, "they were not as strong as we, and they led a more ignorant and a blinder life; and so when we read of great names of the past, the mists of illusions fill the skies, and our eyes are dimmed by the glory of clouds tinged with the splendors of a sun that has set."[44]

The address was carried in full or in extracts in most of the leading Catholic and daily papers in the East. The *Catholic*

[43] *Ibid.*, p. 196.

[44] *Ibid.*, p. 197. Despite the misgivings that several members of the hierarchy entertained as to the part that Miss Caldwell was to play at the cornerstone laying, Spalding did not hesitate to conclude his oration with the words: "And now, how shall I more fittingly conclude than with the name of her whose generous heart and enlightened mind were the impulse which has given to what had long been hope deferred and a dream-like vision—existence and a dwelling place—Mary Gwendolin [sic] Caldwell." *Ibid.*, p. 210.

Mirror spoke of it as a "masterly oration," and remarked that Spalding's words would not soon be forgotten "by those who were fortunate enough to be present to hear them."[45] Nor were they soon forgotten by those who later read them. ". . . Did you read Bp. Spalding's Inaugural?" asked Thomas Preston, pastor of St. Ann's Parish in New York City and one of the vicars general of the archdiocese, of Abbot Bernard Smith, O.S.B. "One thing is certain," he continued, "this clique does not understand philosophy, ethics & sociology."[46] Later, apparently, the contents of the address were reported to the Congregation of the Propaganda, and the prefect, Cardinal Simeoni, wrote to Archbishop Corrigan that he had been informed that Spalding's address contained *"idee singolare, e poco sane"*—unusual and not very sound ideas. The Cardinal said he understood there were copies of the talk available and he would appreciate having one sent to him.[47] Though the Propaganda archives do not contain Corrigan's reply to Simeoni, it is nonetheless possible that Spalding also heard from Rome, and had been taken to task for his *"idee singolare"*; the supposition would at least supply a tentative explanation for Spalding's attitude in the years ahead, when he described "middle age" as "an epoch when there comes to many a period of discouragement. . . . In looking back we see that after much toil we have accomplished little. What we hoped to do, we have not; or having done, have ceased to care for...."[48]

It might also explain why the Bishop of Peoria was not present at the formal opening of the Catholic University of America set for November 13, 1889, in conjunction with the centennial

[45] Ellis, *Formative Years,* p. 290.

[46] ASStPOW, Preston to Smith, New York, December 18, 1888.

[47] AANY, L-42, Giovanni Cardinal Simeoni to M. A. Corrigan, Rome, April 8, 1889

[48] Spalding, Introduction to James J. McGovern, *Life of the Rt. Rev. John McMullen,* p. xvi.

of the American hierarchy. It had been announced that he would again be the principal speaker for the occasion, but early in October John Keane wrote to Corrigan:

About two weeks ago I learned to my great distress that Bishop Spalding was commanded by his physicians to desist temporarily from all work, and therefore he could not give the inaugural on Nov. 13th as announced. I instantly wrote, begging him in view of the strait in which this would leave us, to make the effort—but I learn that he cannot possibly be with us on that day.[49]

In connection with the hierarchy's centennial and the formal inauguration of the university, a congress of the Catholic laity was also planned whose object was

A closer union of all the members of the Catholic body in the country, increased activity of the laity in aid of the clergy in religious work, and the declaration of the views on the important questions of the hour and the assistance and relief of the poorer classes of society.[50]

Ever since his attendance at the German Catholics' *Generalversammlung* as a seminarian and young priest, Spalding had envisioned a lay congress as the one means that would most certainly and effectively bring about the intelligent cooperation of the clergy and the laity for the furtherance of Catholic interests. The difficulties arising from lay trusteeism had tended to make laymen more or less indifferent to the wants of American Catholicism, precisely, as Spalding expressed it, because "of the concentration of the whole management of the affairs of the Church in the hands of ecclesiastics."[51] The opportunities for laymen in the work of the Church were in some respects greater than those of priests, since in their manifold relations with one another more opportunities arose than in clerical life for effec-

[49] AANY, C-16, Keane to Corrigan, Washington, D.C., October 28, 1889.

[50] *Souvenir Volume of the Centennial Celebration and the Catholic Congress* (Chicago, 1893), p. vii.

[51] Spalding, "The Work of the Church in the United States," p. 141.

188

tive Christian social action. There was, nevertheless, work for every man and woman, and if, Spalding said, opportunity was denied to anyone, it was not because the Church was not wide and great and rich enough, and "endowed as she is with the treasures of the mind and heart of Christ, but because those who happen to shape her course and policy at the moment are narrow and unintelligent." A more living participation of all Catholics in the work of the Church was, he believed, a most urgent need, and therefore, "whoever might have power to awaken in them a longing for this larger and higher life and open a way for them in the Church to exercise an influence in the things which concern man's permanent and most essential interests" was, he said, "the leader whom we should all hail with delight and follow with enthusiasm."[52]

The idea of a Catholic congress at this time is said to have originated with Major Henry F. Brownson of Detroit, son of the convert layman and author, Orestes A. Brownson. Brownson soon enlisted the aid of William Onahan of Chicago, who was still actively engaged with Ireland and Spalding in the colonization movement.[53] Onahan informed Brownson in the spring of 1889 that he expected to meet Bishop Spalding to discuss the subject, since the latter should be "one of the active movers in the Congress,"[54] which he had so earnestly advocated. But the illness that precluded Spalding's presence at the opening of the university likewise prevented him from attending the Catholic Congress. In the months preceding the convocation of the Catholic laity, Spalding proved, however, to be an interested if not dis-

[52] J. L. Spalding, "The Mystery of Pain," in *Socialism and Labor and Other Arguments* (Chicago, 1902), pp. 177–178. All evidence points to the fact that "The Mystery of Pain" was written during this period of the middle years and was later incorporated into the above work.

[53] Pahorezki, *The Social and Political Activities of William James Onahan,* p. 109.

[54] UND, III-3-c, Brownson Papers, Onahan to Brownson, Chicago, April 28, 1889.

illusioned observer. When Onahan asked for advice on the agenda to be discussed at the congress, Spalding replied that it would be wise in his opinion to take up two or three points rather than many and to present a practical and business-like method of dealing with the interests concerned, since, as he said,

Talk is cheap and nearly all our gatherings begin and end in words. Take for instance lay cooperation and devise some means by which laymen may really take part in Church work. And you need say nothing about Indians and niggers and colonization. Take a stand in favor of prohibition and let temperance societies gently slide down an indefinitely sloping plane. It was not my intention, however, to make any suggestions further than to say that phrases are no longer needed. Let us cease to pretend to wish to do what we really have no intention of doing.[55]

Illness, personal pique at Roman reaction to the inaugural address, wounded vanity, all these separately or in combination may possibly account for Spalding's withdrawal from the national scene, a withdrawal that on the surface, at least, appears quite alien to the generous and resolute spirit of a man who in a more philosophical mood would write: "If today I see that what I have held to be truth is not truth, it follows that I have grown wiser and so I take courage, fresh courage and sail for new worlds. Life is full enough of disenchantments and the lessons they teach are not hard to learn."[56]

Though Spalding was, in the years that followed the Council, concerned with problems that beset the present and the future of the American Church as a whole, the Diocese of Peoria had not meanwhile been neglected. In June 1885, the cornerstone of the new St. Mary's Cathedral was laid. During the ceremony, a paper reviewing the progress of the diocese was read:

On the 28th day of June, A.D. 1885, John Lancaster Spalding, first bishop of the diocese of Peoria laid this cornerstone of St. Mary's Ca-

[55] UND, Onahan Papers, Spalding to Onahan, Peoria, May 22, 1889.
[56] J. L. Spalding, *Thoughts and Theories of Life and Education* (Chicago, 1897), p. 131.

thedral. The diocese of Peoria was erected in A.D. 1876 [sic] by Pope Pius IX. . . . There were then thirty-three priests in the new diocese, some seventy churches, five religious institutions, three academies, twelve parochial schools and a Catholic population of about fifty thousand. . . . In the eight years which have elapsed . . . the church's development in spiritual and temporal affairs has been rapid. There are now 160 churches, seventy of which have been built in the last eight years, one hundred priests, sixteen religious institutions, eight academies, forty-one parochial schools, one orphan asylum and a Catholic population of nearly one hundred thousand. . . .[57]

At the ceremony, Spalding's words were few. "We have built not only for the diocese of Peoria," he remarked, "but for the Church. The building is, perhaps, too pretentious for the size of our diocese, but it will stand as a monument for the sacrifices of both the clergy and the laity of the diocese working for the salvation of souls."[58] St. Mary's would also stand as a monument to the untiring energy of his brother, Benedict, the rector of the cathedral, who was destined to see neither its completion nor its dedication. Always in poor health, he returned to Lebanon in the Summer of 1887, where on November 28 he died of consumption.[59] At the month's mind in old St. Mary's, Father James Ryan, pastor of St. Columba's Church in Ottawa, preached the eulogy for his fellow Kentuckian.[60] Some two months later, through the efforts of Bishop Spalding, Ryan was named third Bishop of Alton and was consecrated in his See city on May 1, 1888, by his former ordinary.[61] When, many years later, sorrows

[57] Peoria *Journal,* June 29, 1885.

[58] *Ibid.*

[59] New York *Freeman's Journal,* December 10, 1887.

[60] Joseph J. Thompson, *Diocese of Springfield in Illinois, Diamond Jubilee History* (Springfield, 1928), p. 456. Originally the Diocese of Quincy, the title and See city was changed to Alton in 1857, to Springfield in Illinois in 1923.

[61] According to Monsignor Francis A. Cleary, the late pastor of St. Columba's Church in Ottawa, Illinois, on the death of Bishop Peter Baltes of Alton, February 15, 1886, the See was vacant for two years.

had engulfed the Bishop of Peoria, Ryan would stand by him with a loyalty that prompted the by then older and wiser prelate to exclaim, "You are the best and most generous of friends and I shall never cease to thank God for having brought you to my side."[62]

Another great concern of Spalding during these years was the care of the various national groups in the Diocese of Peoria, especially the German Catholics. Catholics comprised more than 35 per cent of the total German immigration to the United States after the Civil War, and in the 1880s German Catholic immigration reached a new high with 400,000 Catholics from Germany and 134,000 from Austria-Hungary.[63] From the very beginning, Illinois had attracted many German immigrants, and, as one historian has noted, "all the cities that rose up and gave

---

Archbishop Feehan of Chicago favored his vicar general, Patrick J. Conway, while Spalding's choice to succeed Baltes was the Reverend Daniel J. Riordan, pastor of St. Elizabeth's Parish in Chicago. Ryan was the compromise candidate, a *persona grata* to both prelates, and suggested by Bishop Spalding. Interview of the author with Monsignor Cleary, Peoria Public Library, Peoria, April 23, 1953. James Ryan was born June 17, 1848, near Thurles, County Tipperary, Ireland and came to America in 1855 with his parents, who settled in Louisville, Kentucky. Ordained by Bishop McCloskey of Louisville in the cathedral on December 24, 1871, he engaged in pastoral work until 1874, when on his own request he was appointed to St. Joseph's College, Bardstown, where he taught for several years. When Spalding was appointed to the See of Peoria, Ryan was soon permitted to join him. He first completed the church at Wataga in Knox County, then he was transferred to Danville, where he erected a new church. In 1881, he became pastor of St. Columba's Parish in Ottawa and built a new church which Spalding dedicated in 1884. On February 27, 1888, Ryan was nominated third Bishop of Alton and was consecrated there by Spalding, with McCloskey of Louisville and Bishop John Janssen of Belleville, as co-consecrators. Feehan of Chicago preached on the occasion. Bishop Ryan died July 2, 1923, in his seventy-eighth year. Cf. ADP.

[62] ADP, Spalding to Ryan, December 28, 1905.

[63] Barry, *op. cit.,* pp. 3–4.

promise of a great future received a good contingent of German immigrants at the very beginning of their hopeful career. Such were Vandalia, Peoria, Quincy, Springfield, Peru and Chicago."[64] Until 1852, Peoria's German Catholics worshipped at St. Mary's Church. In that year, a committee of Germans called upon Bishop James Van de Velde of Chicago on the occasion of his dedication of the new St. Mary's in Peoria, and requested the use of the church at 8 o'clock for themselves on Sunday morning. However, Father Alphonsus Montuori, the pastor, refused and instead offered the Germans the exclusive use of old St. Mary's.[65] Thus St. Joseph's Church, renamed, distinctively German in character, became the nucleus also for both Sacred Heart and St. Boniface's for the care of German Catholics, who were later entrusted to the charge of the Franciscans.[66]

Benedictine Fathers from Chicago also continued to visit the German congregations in the Diocese of Peoria when they had ceased to be under Chicago's jurisdiction, and since Spalding needed German-speaking priests he welcomed their assistance. He had many times expressed his thanks to Abbot Boniface Wimmer, O.S.B., of St. Vincent's Archabbey in Latrobe, Pennsylvania, and on April 27, 1887, he asked the abbot to assume the direction of St. Anthony's Church in Streator. This request was refused, but shortly after Father Alexius Grass, O.S.B., was sent to St. Joseph's in Peoria to help as an assistant.[67] Spalding kept up his contact with the Benedictines, and where he heard of their desire to establish a college, he encouraged them to plan the institution for his See city. With Spalding's support, the

[64] Albert Bernhardt Faust, *The German Element in the United States* (New York, 1927), I, p. 460.

[65] Crane, *Catholic History of Peoria,* p. 27.

[66] Cf. Chapter 3, note 11.

[67] Theodore Fuertges, O.S.B., "The History of Saint Bede College and Abbey, Peru, Illinois, 1889–1941," pp. 24–25. This is an unpublished master's dissertation at the Catholic University of America (June, 1941).

Chicago Benedictines addressed a signed petition to the chapter at St. Vincent's in the latter part of 1888, together with an appeal from Spalding asking St. Vincent's to establish a college within his diocese and promising financial assistance. The offer was accepted, and on June 5, 1889, Spalding concluded an agreement with the Benedictines which led to the establishment of St. Bede's Abbey in Peru, Illinois.[68]

In the meantime, Archbishop Heiss of Milwaukee had died, and the question of his successor, as had been the case in 1878 when he had succeeded Archbishop Henni, aroused bitter feeling between warring factions of Germans and Irish. Once again, the English-speaking consultors of the archdiocese addressed the archbishops of the country, asking them to use their influence in having an English-speaking ordinary appointed to the See. But on April 18, 1890, after a meeting of the bishops of the province, Bishop Katzer of Green Bay sent the *terna* to Cardinal Gibbons and told him that the choice of Katzer of Green Bay, Flasch of La Crosse, and Henry J. Richter of Grand Rapids in that order was identical with the *terna* proposed by the majority of the consultors.[69] No one, perhaps, was more concerned with the Milwaukee succession than the Archbishop of St. Paul. "The German consultors chose Bp. Katzer *pro primo loco*," Ireland wrote to Gibbons, "a man thoroughly German and thoroughly unfit to be an archbishop."[70] Ireland had already written to several other archbishops asking them to delay in writing to Rome until he had the leisure to inform them in full. "The Milwaukee question," he told Archbishop Elder of Cincinnati on the same day, "is a most important one for the American Church and I will greatly rely on your enlightened cooperation in solving it."[71]

Gibbons likewise favored a delay until the archbishops could

[68] *Ibid.*
[69] AAB, 87-J-2, Katzer to Gibbons, Green Bay, April 18, 1890.
[70] AAB, 87-J-5, Ireland to Gibbons, St. Paul, April 21, 1890.
[71] AAC, Same to Elder, St. Paul, April 21, 1890.

convene in Boston the following day in what was to be the first
of the annual meetings of the metropolitans of the country.
There, he felt, they would be afforded ample opportunity for
discussion of the Milwaukee succession.[72] In the interim, Ireland
kept busy. "Spalding is the only man for Milwaukee," he told
Denis O'Connell. "We may as well decide that at once and work
up to it," and he knew that Bishop John Vertin, the senior suffragan of the province, would favor the Bishop of Peoria.[73] "I
am very pleased with what you say of Bishop Spaulding [*sic*],"
he told John Keane, and "I am more than satisfied that he is
the one, and the prospects of our succeeding are daily brighten-
ing."[74] To Archbishop Elder, however, Ireland confessed that his
early choice for Milwaukee had been Bishop Camillus Maes of
Covington, and that Gibbons had also favored him, but when they
learned of Maes' inability to preach in German, they had changed
their minds. He thought the health of Bishop Dwenger of Fort
Wayne might be some argument against his candidacy, though
he was sure that if Dwenger were chosen, he would be sufficiently American and would likewise satisfy the Germans. "Some
archbishops talk of Bp. Spalding," he continued, since "he speaks
German well & is looked upon by Germans as rather their
friend." But of Katzer he noted that "at the last meeting of
German societies he has said such bitter things and has shown
such violence of temper that the American people have conceived a great dislike for him—the daily papers speaking most
harshly of him."[75]

When the archbishops convened in Boston on July 23–24,
1890, the first item to be discussed was the question of a successor to the See of Milwaukee. Following a discussion of the
candidates, the name of Katzer was set aside, and as in 1880

[72] AAB, 87-J-3, Gibbons to Simeoni, May 13, 1890, Latin copy.
[73] ADR, Ireland to O'Connell, St. Paul, May 28, 1890.
[74] CUA, Keane Papers, Ireland to Keane, May 29, 1890.
[75] AAC, Same to Elder, St. Paul, June 3, 1890.

they chose John Lancaster Spalding "for the sake of peace and the advancement of religion," as the most suitable to govern the Church of Milwaukee. Gibbons sent off the results to Cardinal Simeoni with a strong recommendation of Spalding, and what was described as "an approving nod for Bishop Martin Marty, O.S.B., of Sioux Falls, and the expression of a doubt that Richter of Grand Rapids would prove a suitable candidate due to the peculiar circumstances of the Church in Milwaukee."[76] Yet the archbishops had not been unanimous in their choice of Spalding, for a little more than a week after the Boston meeting, Archbishop Francis Janssens of New Orleans made known his displeasure when he confided to Elder of Cincinnati:

Somehow or other I do not like the choice of having the name of Bp. Spalding first on the list for Milwaukee, and I regret that the name of Bp. Flasch was not retained. We have made almost a total disregard of the list offered, by consultors & Bps. We have placed as first, one who is not a German by birth or descent, though that seemed to be agreed upon in the beginning of the discussion and then the more I have seen of Bp. Spalding the less I like the choice. It seems to me he is not only cynical but sometimes queer in his remarks. Well, I hope and trust Rome will appoint for the best. . . .

To this, Elder jotted down the summary of his response: "Answered Aug. 5, 1890: The difficulty was made for us. I do not think we could have done better."[77]

While all interested parties awaited an announcement from the Holy See, Denis O'Connell informed Ireland in August that Richter, whose name had appeared on the three lists, seemed to be gaining in Rome, since "they don't trust Spalding," he said, "and Katzer goes very probably as the recognized head of a party."[78] Three weeks later, O'Connell told Keane, "It seems Richter will go to Milwaukee, since his name is found on three

---

[76] Ellis, *Gibbons,* I, p. 365.
[77] AAC, Janssens to Elder, Brooklyn, August 2, 1890.
[78] AASP, O'Connell to Ireland, Rome, August 18, 1890.

lists. Then Spalding did not have a heavy vote in Boston. I think his small vote gave them relief."[79] A month later, O'Connell again reported to Ireland that he had a very strong letter from Father James J. Keogh, one of the English-speaking consultors in Milwaukee, against Richter, and that he thought a petition could be procured in favor of Spalding against Richter. O'Connell then asked.

> What, then, shall we unite on Spalding? They don't want Marty. If so, write Keogh to prepare his petition. You only want a few Abps. more and get them, even if necessary, visit them. In the province Vertin's vote makes Spalding as strong as any of them. This thing of submitting the school question to the Abbps. [*sic*] gives the nomination grave importance . . . If you say Spalding then "war to the hilt" for Spalding agitation in Milwaukee against Richter will help greatly. Strengthen the Cardinal. It is either Richter or Spalding. You might as well come out bravely. They can't hate you more. Only a few more names and you have Spalding.[80]

The Milwaukee appointment was to come up in December, O'Connell later wrote, and no one seemed to favor Marty but Ireland himself, and while "Jacobini wheeled round a little in favor of Spalding, Simeoni is down on him. 'He is traveling about all the time lecturing etc.' I said something about his being a neutral man and a good German scholar and he answered: '*si ma costi ci vuole un buon vescovo*'."[81] Evidently, Simeon had not forgotten the "*idee singolare, e poco sane*," and was opposed to Spalding ever ruling the Church in Wisconsin. Shortly before Christmas, it was announced that Francis Xavier Katzer, first on the original *terna*, had been chosen as the new Archbishop of Milwaukee.

Archbishop Ireland was undoubtedly chagrined by the choice

[79] CUA, Keane Papers, O'Connell to Keane, Rome, September 7, 1890.

[80] AASP, O'Connell to Ireland, Rome, October 1, 1890.

[81] AASP, Same to Same, November 15, 1890. Simeoni's remark in English: "Yes, but in that place a good bishop is needed."

of Katzer, but his judgment that Spalding was the man for Milwaukee would probably have been very much qualified had he known of Spalding's views on two questions, namely nationalism in the American Church and the school question. These, in Ireland's view, made the Milwaukee appointment one of grave importance. It was true that Spalding was looked on by many Germans as their friend; what Ireland failed to realize was the reason which, when it became known, would hardly make the Bishop of Peoria the "neutral man" O'Connell believed him to be. It was the latter who first grew suspicious, and in the Autumn of 1891, when writing to Ireland on the school question, he added in a postscript: "We are trying to discover for what Spalding's hand enters."[82] During the next two years, as nationalism and the school question seemed to fuse into one problem—"uniting the cause of the Cahenslyites with other non-Germans"[83]—both Ireland and O'Connell were to discover the true views of the man whom they had at one time hoped to see as Archbishop of Milwaukee.

The cause of the Cahenslyites, or Cahenslyism as it came to be called, was defined by Father John Conway, editor of the *Northwestern Chronicle,* Ireland's diocesan newspaper, as "a combined effort of ecclesiastics and journalists, mostly German, with the representatives of foreign powers for the purpose of promoting foreignism in this country and for using the Roman Catholic Church to that end."[84] Those who accepted Conway's definition saw the strenuous efforts made by some Germans during the 1880s to persuade Rome to choose more German bishops for the American Church as a mere prelude to the more tumultuous struggles against the conspiracy which they labeled as "Cahenslyism." There was, for example, the affair of the so-

[82] AASP, O'Connell to Ireland, Grottaferrata, October 20, 1891.
[83] Barry, *op. cit.,* p. 184.
[84] John Conway, "Cahenslyism versus Americanism," *Review of Reviews* VI (August, 1892), p. 47.

called Abbelen Memorial, the petition of Father Peter Abbelen, Vicar General of the Archdiocese of Milwaukee, to Propaganda in November 1886, which was said, in general, to contain accusations of the unfair treatment and persecution of the German minority by the Irish majority. The Abbelen document urged, in particular, that all immigrants from Europe be assigned to a church of their own language group, that efforts "to root out the language, manners, customs and devotional practices of the German" cease and that bishops be admonished, especially in dioceses of mixed ethnic backgrounds, to appoint a German vicar general in addition to the Irish counterpart, or at least one who had a knowledge and ready use of the German tongue.[85]

When Ireland and Keane heard of the Abbelen Memorial, they were already headed for Rome to secure the Holy See's approval of the University; Ireland rushed to Rome from London, and soon both he and Keane prepared their own memorial which answered the charges made against the American bishops. Early in the new year of 1887, Gibbons arrived in Rome and succeeded in obtaining a rejection of the German demands, which, in the words of Keane, were "of the most ruinous character," and which would have meant "the introduction of Germanism and nationalism in general . . . disastrous to the unity of the Church in the United States."[86] The protests against the Bennett Law, the German Catholic congresses, and the Deutschers-Priester Vereine were all viewed as calculated conspiracies to perpetuate an element of foreignism in the American Church. During the same month that the German Catholic congress met in Pittsburgh, an international conference of Catholics at Liège in Belgium was igniting a fuse that was to explode at Lucerne, Switzerland, the following December. According to one historian of that movement, "it was then that so-called Cahenslyism

85 Barry, *op. cit.*, p. 295.
86 *Ibid.*, p. 64.

became the center of truly grave discord among American Catholics."[87]

Cahenslyism took its name from Peter Paul Cahensly, a German merchant whose concern for the protection of the religious and social interests of German immigrants was instrumental in 1883 in the establishment of the American branch of the St. Raphaelsverein, a society under the patronage of St. Raphael, patron of travelers. It had a three-point program: "to help the emigrant in every possible way before he sailed, during his voyage, and at the ports of debarkation."[88] The American branch endeavored to achieve the third aim of the society by caring for the German immigrants when they reached this country. By 1890, branches of the St. Raphael Society were established in Germany, Austria, Belgium, and Italy, as well as in the United States, and in an effort to discuss their common problems it was determined that the board of directors of the European branches should meet in Lucerne on December 9–10, 1890.[89] As a result of this conference, a memorandum presented to the congress by the Marchese Battista Volpe-Landi of the Italian society to suggest means of safeguarding emigrants of various nationalities in the practice of their faith after their settlement in the United States was accepted by the delegates, and Volpe-Landi and Cahensly were deputed to bear the memorial to Pope Leo XIII. The Lucerne Memorial, as it was later called, set forth eight recommendations which in general called for the establishment of separate churches for each nationality, with priests to be of the same nationality as the faithful; for parochial schools to be set up everywhere and separated as far as possible into each ethnic group, with the language of the country of origin of each group included as a subject in the curriculum; and for bishops in the American hierarchy to represent the various national groups.[90]

[87] *Ibid.*, p. 125.
[88] *Ibid.*, p. 30.
[89] *Ibid.*, p. 134.
[90] *Ibid.*

The reaction to the Lucerne Memorial, along with the story of the explosive cables manufactured by Denis O'Connell in Europe associating the name of Cahensly with an international conspiracy, has been well documented by the historian of German nationalism in its American Catholic setting,[91] and his conclusions are worth repeating:

> To attack Cahensly without checking or at least giving an ear to his clear denials of having arranged a plot; to release manufactured cables in which his name was associated with a conspiracy; to coin a phrase playing upon the name of a man who had struck out under hierarchical direction, as a pioneer in social work for emigrants . . . before any American bishops or societies had inaugurated such activity; to associate political intrigue of a Pan-German character with a man who had been at odds with his own government over emigrant care—all this was . . . unjust.[92]

To Spalding, the affair was more than unjust; it was simply laughable to see a kind of treason against American liberty in the Lucerne Memorial. Actually, Cahensly's plan did not entail any major changes in America, and, as Spalding saw it, it was a prudent proposal to place the care of souls in the hands of priests who spoke their parishioners' language.[93] "Cahenslyism, as commonly presented to the public, is simply a bugaboo," Spalding wrote, "this and nothing more," since, as he continued:

> There never has been and there never could be any serious thought of introducing into the United States national extra-territorial bishops. No sane man, I suppose, imagines that the Catholic Church in this country is seeking an opportunity to commit suicide or that those who have the power to select and appoint bishops are anxious to ruin the Church in America. Cahenslyism, as thus understood, is simply a bugbear which is made use of to throw suspicion on the loyalty of Germans, and more especially German Catholics. If by Cahenslyism you mean Mr. Cahensly's efforts to do what he can for the spiritual interests of his countrymen

[91] *Ibid.,* pp. 141 ff.
[92] *Ibid.,* p. 177.
[93] *St. Raphael's Blatt,* VI (August–October, 1891), p. 63.

in America, I affirm that such efforts are worthy of the approval of wise and good men, for the more faithful the immigrants remain to their conscientious convictions the more surely will they become useful and desirable citizens of the Republic.[94]

Moreover, the attempt to throw suspicion on the loyalty of Germans, whether Protestant or Catholic, was to Spalding's mind unjust, since, he said, the Germans were loyal citizens, industrious and law-abiding, not only upholders of political and religious freedom but also "foremost defenders of a national social liberty, without which life becomes dreary and burdensome."[95]

Cahenslyism might, in Spalding's opinion, be a mere bugaboo, but the Archbishop of St. Paul thought otherwise. Ireland associated German nationalism with the school question,[96] and in so doing he felt that it had simply prolonged and exacerbated that issue within the American Church. The root of the school question, of course, was the public or the common school versus the parochial school.

In a famous address before the National Education Association at St. Paul in July, 1890, on "State Schools and Parish Schools," Archbishop Ireland had attempted to come to terms with the public schools by investigating the possibility of union between the two educational systems. "The free school of America!" he exclaimed, "Withered be the hand raised in sign of its destruction." He regretted the necessity of the denominational or parish school, and in behalf of the state school he called upon his fellow Americans "to aid in the removal of this necessity." State schools tended to eliminate religion from the minds and hearts of the young, and to remedy the difficulty Ireland suggested that the religion of the majority, "be this religion as Protestant as Protestantism can be," should permeate the state schools, while denominational schools for minority groups should receive tax

[94] Peoria *Journal*, October 19, 1892.
[95] *Ibid.*
[96] Barry, *op. cit.*, p. 200.

funds equal to the cost of tuition for a pupil in a state school. Another plan he would suggest was the extension of the so-called Irish Plan, variously termed the Poughkeepsie Plan, or the Georgia Plan, whereby the parish school would be rented by the state with the tacit understanding that so long as the teachers, Catholic in faith, passed their qualifying examinations under the supervision of the local school boards, they would not be replaced by teachers of another faith. Religion would be taught outside the regular school hours and nothing would be paid by the state for this religious instruction. In such a way, therefore, Catholics would add to the splendor and majesty of the public schools, Ireland concluded, "by putting side by side religious and secular instruction, neither of them interfering with each other, each of them borrowing from the other aid and dignity."

When the contents of Ireland's suggestion became known, however, shocked Catholic editors, especially in the German Catholic newspapers, took the Archbishop to task for what they considered his lighthearted abandonment of the parish school, built up so laboriously and successfully in the aftermath of the Third Plenary Council, and his advocacy of the state schools long branded by many bishops and priests as Godless.[97]

Three months before in the *Catholic World,* Spalding had also given his views on the impending school question. He maintained that Americans, whether Catholic or Protestant, would act in a wiser and broader spirit if "besides keeping up a controversy in which, after all, there is nothing new to be said, and which is irritating, they set themselves resolutely to work to improve educational methods." What was called the school question would be settled, he believed, if it were settled at all, by facts rather than by arguments, and the fact of the matter was that "the Catholics of the United States have an educational system of their own," and he referred to the pastoral letter of the

[97] John Ireland, "State Schools and Parish Schools," in *The Church and Modern Society* (St. Paul, 1905), I, pp. 220–232, *passim.*

Third Plenary Council where the purpose of the bishops in education was designated as twofold: "to multiply our schools and to perfect them." He realized that in the United States, at least, multiplication was infinitely easier than perfection; consequently, he said, "if it is really our purpose to make our schools excellent, it will be necessary to devote to this end far more thought and labor than will suffice to increase their number." As for those who accused Catholics of sinister designs against the public schools, "they are bigots or politicians," he said, "and need not be taken seriously."[98]

But bigots and politicians were taken seriously, and while there was, perhaps, nothing new to be said, there was the Archbishop of St. Paul, and he was a man to be reckoned with. No mere theorist, Ireland soon implemented the ideas of his NEA speech in the Summer and Fall of 1891 in what came to be called the Faribault-Stillwater agreements. It was an attempt at compromise, and while similar attempts to combine public and parochial schools within a single institution had been tried, for example, at Poughkeepsie, New York, the most publicized attempt in the nineteenth century was that in the towns of Faribault and Stillwater, Minnesota. The essential features of these plans in general, and of the Faribault-Stillwater project in particular, were that an existing parochial school was leased to the public-school district whose board operated the public school in a parish building, paid maintenance and salary costs, with religious instruction scheduled before or after regular school hours. Likewise, the school board, with the approval of the pastor, appointed teachers, furnished textbooks, and had full control over examinations, promotions, and general school policies.[99] It was a makeshift arrangement and then and now such

[98] J. L. Spalding, "Normal Schools for Catholics," *Catholic World,* LI (April, 1890), pp. 89–90.

[99] Neil McCluskey, S.J., *Catholic Viewpoint on Education* (New York, 1959), pp. 19–39, *passim.*

arrangements, a recent commentator has argued, are doomed to fail since; "A single dissenting voice will invariably rise to challenge the arrangement since ensuing litigation divides the community and shatters harmony."[100] American public opinion was greatly disturbed in the 1890s over the agreements entered into with the approval of Archbishop Ireland. Members of the American Protective Association, a nativist society founded in Iowa in 1887, saw in Ireland's plan a plot whereby "the public school system is to be wrecked by the scheme of Romanization." "Do you understand?" asked one Minneapolis writer. "We mean that the public schools will be used by Rome. For Rome and against the American people. They will be Romanized in every possible way."[101]

There was likewise a Catholic opposition which began to crystallize with the publication of Father Thomas Bouquillon's pamphlet, *Education, To Whom Does it Belong?*, viewed by Ireland's opponents as an apologia for the Faribault-Stillwater plans. The controversy intensified when Father René Holaind, S.J., replied to Bouquillon in his pamphlet, *The Parent First!*, compiled at the instigation, so Ireland believed, of Archbishop Corrigan of New York. Newspapers, both Catholic and secular, made much of the furor, especially when Ireland, interviewed at the Fifth Avenue Hotel in New York, criticized Holaind's pamphlet as unfair, castigated the German Catholic newspapers for attacking his plan, and maintained that their motives could be apprehended without much difficulty. On this occasion, the Archbishop was said to have thrown down the gauntlet "that earned the undying opposition from German Americans, Jesuits, both American and Italian, and Michael A. Corrigan, the Archbishop of New York."[102]

[100] *Ibid.*, pp. 33–34.
[101] Burton Ames Huntington, *The Coming American Civil War* (Minneapolis, 1893), p. 122.
[102] Reilly, *The School Controversy* (*1891–1893*), Washington, 1943, p. 257.

After Archbishop Ireland had sailed for Rome to explain his views to the cardinals of the Propaganda, the heated controversy was temporarily resolved on April 21, 1892, when a committee of five cardinals approved the Faribault agreement with the famous words *"tolerari potest,"* while at the same time they declared that the decrees of the Third Plenary Council on the schools were to remain firmly in force.[103] The decision was interpreted by Ireland and his followers as a victory, but the opposition saw in it only the approval of a local arrangement and nothing more. "The so-called Faribault plan is now formally allowed," Ireland wrote jubilantly to Father James C. Byrne, pastor of the Immaculate Conception Church, Minneapolis, "in spite of Germans and Jesuits."[104] Ireland's letter was quoted in the St. Paul *Dispatch* on May 9, and two days later the New York *World* "scooped" its rivals when it published the *tolerari potest* decision in English translation.[105] The Bishop of Peoria, an interested spectator amidst the clamor of the controversy, but hardly non-partisan, confided to his friend Bishop Ryan of Alton on the day after the publication of the decision: "Archbishop Ireland has evidently lost his case, though he will attempt to make it out a victory." To this he added: "The publication of his letter to Father Byrne is a stupidity. Under his own signature he thus publicly forces the Germans and the Jesuits into the same camp. Is it not amazing what an infinite ado is made about nothing?"[106]

With the *tolerari potest* decision, however, the storm over the school question hardly abated during the Summer months of 1892, and as Cardinal Gibbons began to lay plans for the third annual meeting of the archbishops scheduled to open in New

---

[103] *Ibid.,* p. 170.

[104] AASP, Ireland to James Byrne, Rome, April 27, 1892, copy.

[105] Reilly, *op. cit.,* p. 171.

[106] ADP, Spalding to Ryan, Peoria, May 12, 1892.

York on November 16, he received a request from Propaganda that they consult with their suffragans on the question of parochial schools before they met with Archbishop Francesco Satolli, who would attend the meeting since the latter was coming to America to represent Pope Leo XIII at the Columbian Exposition.[107] The World's Columbian Exposition was to be held in Chicago from May to October, 1893, to mark the four-hundredth anniversary of the discovery of America. Anxious that the world's fair illustrate more than the mere "mechanical and material triumph of mankind, an auxiliary was created to arrange a series of world congresses at which humanity's major problems would be discussed—to promote the unity and prosperity, peace and happiness of the world." The subjects for discussion were to be education, religion, social reforms, labor problems, the substitution of arbitration for war, and the establishment of a world court to adjudicate international disputes.[108] Included in the general scheme and programming of world congresses was the Columbian Catholic Congress which was to be held at the world's fair from September 4 to 9. As in 1889, William Onahan of Chicago was the driving force and secretary-manager of this second Catholic lay congress. When the plan and the scope of the gathering became more definite, the Christian Brothers, led by Brother Maurelian, F.S.C., president of the Christian Brothers' College in Memphis, Tennessee, suggested that the Catholic schools participate in an education exhibit. This suggestion won the approval of the archbishops at their Boston meeting in 1890, where a special committee of prelates was appointed to carry out the project. Spalding was named chairman and Brother Maurelian was to act in the capacity of secretary-manager.[109]

[107] Ellis, *Gibbons*, I, pp. 622–623.

[108] Jessie Heckman Hirschl, "The Great White City," *American Heritage*, XI (October, 1960), p. 10.

[109] Pahorezki, *op. cit.*, p. 154.

For the next three years, Spalding worked closely with Onahan and Brother Maurelian and their committees as they prepared for the Catholic contribution to the Columbian Exposition. In an effort to stimulate interest in the proposed educational exhibit, he published an article in the *Catholic World* in July 1892, some three months after the publication of the *tolerari potest* decision. Spalding opened with this note: "The writer of this article has considered the question of religious education from a general point of view, and its bearings on the Catholic Educational Exhibit, without any thought of recent controversies, or any desire to offer an expression of opinion on recent utterances of the Propaganda on the subject. —J.L.S."[110] The phrase "*tolerari potest*," or the Faribault-Stillwater Plan, were, therefore, not even hinted at; yet a partisan could easily read into the bishop's words a lack of sympathy for Ireland's plan when he wrote:

. . . the church does not and cannot consent to the exclusion of religion from any educational process. When our common school system was finally organized as exclusively secular, nothing was left for Catholics to do but to build and maintain schools of their own, in which will, the heart, and the conscience as well as the intellect, should be educated. If Catholic children have a right to Catholic education it follows that the duty devolves upon Catholics to provide the means whereby it may be received; and the Catholics of the United States have accepted the task thus imposed with a spirit of self-sacrifice which is above all praise.[111]

The parochial school system was and is, he continued, an organic part of the Church's constitution, and, therefore, "we cannot if we would, we would not if we could, recede from the position we have taken." Catholics, he maintained, held the common or public school system to be radically defective, though they had no disposition to interfere with those to whom the system com-

[110] J. L. Spalding, "The Catholic Educational Exhibit in the Columbian Exposition," *Catholic World*, LV (July, 1892), p. 580.
[111] *Ibid.*, p. 581.

mended itself. They conceded to others, as they demanded for themselves, religious and educational freedom. Catholic conviction on this point was unalterable, and since there was a question of vital temporal and eternal interests, there could be no compromise which conflicted with the principle of religious education, because "the Catholic Church is irrevocably committed," Spalding remarked "to the doctrine that education is essentially religious, that purely secular schools give instruction, but do not properly educate . . ."[112] Since the Catholic Educational Exhibit would be the only distinctively Catholic feature in the Columbian Exposition, Spalding urged Catholics to leave nothing undone to make it worthy of the event to be commemorated, and worthy, too, of their own zeal in the cause of Catholic education. Especially was this important in an age in which the tendency was to take the school from the control of the Church and to place it under the state in such a way as to weaken the school's religious character.[113]

Meanwhile, on the other side of the Atlantic, the Columbian Exposition was also in the mind of the Holy See. Leo XIII had been invited to send a representative, and his choice fell upon Francesco Satolli, titular Archbishop of Lepanto. Satolli arrived in New York on October 12, 1892, in company with Monsignor Denis O'Connell. After a hurried trip to Baltimore, the Delegate, accompanied by Cardinal Gibbons, visited the Secretary of State John W. Foster in Washington. On October 18, Gibbons, Satolli, Ireland, and O'Connell left for Chicago, where the Cardinal gave the invocation at the ceremonies dedicating the buildings for the Columbian Exposition. From Chicago Satolli journeyed on to St. Paul, where he was the house guest of John Ireland until it was time for the scheduled meeting of the archbishops in New York.[114] As November 16 drew near, Spalding grew apprehensive about how the metropolitans would handle

[112] *Ibid.*, p. 583.
[113] *Ibid.*, p. 584.
[114] Ellis, *Gibbons*, I, pp. 624–625.

the school question. He expressed himself to Archbishop Corrigan with his customary candor when he wrote:

> It is our plain duty to stand by our Catholic Schools with more courage and firmness than ever before. It is to me simply incredible, incomprehensible how prelates of the Church should imagine that they have found a better way to solve our educational problem than that which commended itself to all the Bishops of the country in the Second and Third Plenary Councils, and which received the Pope's approval. I deplore this tendency to try to unsettle things of the most vital importance upon which hitherto we have all agreed and this disturbance is raised just when we were building more schools than ever before, and making more earnest and successful efforts to improve them.[115]

If faith could be put in the newspapers, he understood that the Pope had sent instructions to consider in the New York meeting the question what could be done for Catholic children who did not attend parochial schools. He believed that the number of these children had been deliberately exaggerated, and he told Corrigan that the only thing to do was to arouse greater enthusiasm for parish schools and to build more of them, and where it was impossible, to enjoin upon pastors and parents the urgent need of providing for the religious instruction of children at home and in the church.[116]

When the third annual meeting of the archbishops convened at Archbishop Corrigan's residence, Archbishop Satolli, introduced to the metropolitans by Gibbons, laid before them ostensibly for their consideration a pamphlet which contained fourteen propositions designed to compose the difficulties over parochial schools. At the outset, the propositions seemed to espouse the further erection of parochial schools, but toward the end of the document the proposals favored Archbishop Ireland's stand on the question. On December 8, the New York *Herald* carried the full text of Satolli's address,[117] and once again the opposition swung into action. Spalding was in New York at the time to

[115] AANY, C-44, Spalding to Corrigan, Peoria, October 25, 1892.
[116] *Ibid.*
[117] Ellis, *Gibbons,* I, pp. 695–696.

address the metropolitans at the third session on the plans for the forthcoming Catholic Educational Exhibit.[118] When he learned the details of the Satolli proposals, he publicly made known his opposition to what he called Faribaultism. Considering the general conception of the plan, he told a reporter, he believed the majority of the bishops were opposed to it, and that

[118] *The Third Annual Conference of the Most Reverend Archbishops of the United States, An Abstract of the Minutes* (Baltimore, 1892), pp. 7–8. At the third session, Spalding "was allowed to introduce a Greek priest who, notwithstanding a late ruling of the Sacred Congregation of Propaganda Fide, asked that married priests of his rite might be allowed to care for the souls of many thousands of united Greeks who have migrated to the United States. He contended that unless this was granted there was great danger of these people falling into schism; and he argued that on account of the difference or rite, language and peculiar customs, the fact that some of their priests were married would not give scandal to the people of other nationalities. However, after mature deliberation it was agreed, that the rule laid down by the Propaganda should be insisted on, and that every effort should be made to induce the Basilian monks to take charge of the united Greeks in this country. . . ." *Ibid.,* p. 8. Bishop Edward Fitzgerald of Little Rock, Arkansas, objected to Spalding's presence at the archbishops' meeting and in identical letters to several of the metropolitans wrote: "I desire to enter my protest against the action of the Archbishop admitting Bp. Spalding to their counsels. I have no objections to Bp. Spalding but if one of the Bishops be permitted to ride his hobby I insist that every bishop in the country shall have the same privilege." Elder of Cincinnati who had the happy habit of jotting down summaries of his answers to his correspondence, wrote: "Answered Jan. 6, 1893, Bp. Spalding took no part. Asked to speak about Educational Exhibit. Any other Bp. wd have received the same attention." Cf. AAC, Fitzgerald to Elder, Little Rock, December 14, 1892. Business matters concerning the Caldwell estate were also the occasion for Spalding's trip to New York. Cf. AANY, C-44, Spalding to Corrigan, Fifth Avenue Hotel, New York, November 20, 1892. With the resignation of Eugene Kelly, the first treasurer of the University committee, as trustee of the Caldwell estate on May 26, 1893, Spalding and the United States Trust Company of New York were appointed co-trustees of said estate. Cf. Files of the United States Trust Company of New York.

Archbishop Ireland had conceded too much to the state in permitting religious emblems to be removed from the schools. While Rome had tolerated the Faribault and Stillwater agreements, he said, it did not follow that the plan had ever been recommended to the rest of the bishops. He wanted it made perfectly clear that so far as the Diocese of Peoria was concerned, he would not permit it. In this mid-December account of the Spalding interview, he was quoted as having said: "I think Archbishop Ireland's desire was to force his plan, whatever it is, upon the rest of the country, and that was a mistake on his part. That may be the cause of the continued strife. It would have been better if the New York Conference had never taken place. It only created mischief."[119]

But the New York conference was taking place, and on November 17 Satolli informed the archbishops of the Holy Father's great desire to establish a permanent apostolic delegation in the United States. All of the metropolitans, with the exception of Ireland, stated that they did not feel warranted in taking action on so important a matter without an opportunity to consult with their suffragans; and there the matter for the moment seemed to rest.[120] As soon as Spalding heard of the proposal, once more he publicly declared that the establishment of a permanent delegation would be a disaster, that the very idea was mischievous and full of evil to the American Church.[121] When Ireland's *Northwestern Chronicle* in a formal editorial

[119] St. Louis *Chronicle,* December 16, 1892; on the day previous, the Bishop of the Province of St. Louis placed Spalding's name first on the *terna* for the office of coadjutor to the aged Peter R. Kenrick, Archbishop of St. Louis, but on December 27, 1892, Gibbons wrote to Propaganda and informed them that, "*Ipse Rmus. Spalding jam manifestavit se ita esse disponitur ut onus illud accipere non posset.*" Cf. AAB, 90-W-7, Gibbons to Ledochowski, Baltimore, December 27, 1892, Latin copy.

[120] Ellis, *Gibbons,* I, p. 626.

[121] St. Louis *Chronicle,* December 16, 1892.

advocated Satolli's appointment as first delegate, the Bishop of Peoria was quick to reply. The editorial would be a surprise to no one, Spalding conceded, were it not for the generally known fact that the archbishops, with a single exception, in their recent conference, had refused their assent to such an appointment. If it were doubtful whether Leo XIII, in spite of this protest, was still uncertain what had best be done, would it not be wiser and more in accord with Catholic usage to get the views of all the bishops of the country than to seek to manufacture a public opinion by newspaper discussion. Since priests and laity had hitherto been willing to be guided in religious matters by their bishops, was it not altogether probable, he asked, that they were perfectly satisfied to leave this delegate business in their hands with whom alone, after all, the pope could directly deal? The bishops were the normal channel through which the pope received information concerning the needs and peculiar surroundings of the American Church; was it not incredible, therefore, that in a disciplinary matter of such far-reaching import, he would refuse to be guided by their advice, since, as Spalding continued,

There is, and has been for years, in the Catholic Church of the United States a deep feeling of opposition to the appointment of a permanent Delegate for this country. This opposition arises in part from the fixed and strongly-rooted desire, which exists throughout the whole English speaking world to manage as far as possible one's own affairs. The firm determination of the American people to permit no needless foreign interference is shown in the Monroe Doctrine, and it was more practically demonstrated by the overthrow and death of Maximilian. Catholics who live here, and who, wherever they were born, are true American citizens, feel the impulse of this desire and wish to manage as far as possible their own affairs. They are devoted to the Church; they recognize in the Pope Christ's Vicar, and gladly received from him the doctrines of faith and morals; but for the rest, they ask him to interfere as little as may be.[122]

[122] *New World* (Chicago), December 21, 1892.

In this sentiment, he said, Catholics in the United States were simply brothers of the English and Irish Catholics, and it was well known that the Holy Father would not think of appointing a permanent delegate for England or Ireland because he knew from the bishops of those countries that it would be injudicious to do so. For far stronger reasons, Spalding believed, it would be injudicious to appoint a permanent delegate for the United States, since "whoever he might be and whatever he might do, public opinion would make use of him to foster the belief that American Catholics are under the direct influence and control of a foreign power . . . the most deadly weapon the Pope could put in the hands of the enemies of the Church."[123]

In its coverage of this episode, the *Northwestern Chronicle* had informed its readers that an apostolic delegate had also been appointed for India and had accomplished much good there. This, Spalding replied, was not meant as an insult to American Catholics, but simply an attempt at humor, and what good the Indian delegate might have done would remain a matter of doubt since the *Chronicle* writer had assured his readers that Satolli had already wrought wonders for the American Church. This was a view that the *Chronicle* writer was free to take; but Spalding could not believe that it was the one that was generally accepted when, he said, it was well known that "Archbishops, Bishops and priests, with comparatively few exceptions, hold that his so-called Address, if it means anything other than what the Baltimore Council teaches, must be interpreted as a sort of apology for schools other than parochial, and that if it is so to be taken, the harm it will do would not be compensated for the settlement of whatever number of quarrels between Bishops and priests."[124]

The three plans suggested by Archbishop Satolli at the New

[123] *Ibid.*

[124] *Ibid.* On December 23, 1892, Satolli absolved Dr. Edward McGlynn from his ecclesiastical censures.

214

York meeting for Catholic children in non-parochial schools were, as far as the Bishop of Peoria was concerned, either not practicable or, so far as they were feasible, they had already been adopted. Agreements such as the Faribault-Stillwater between bishops and public school boards could so rarely be made in a way at all compatible with the principles of religious education that the recommendations needed no serious consideration. To advise the teaching of catechism outside the public school building was easy; to reduce the advice to practice would be found most difficult. Satolli's third recommendation, "that parents ceaselessly be taught their duties toward their children and that catechism classes be established where parochial schools do not exist," was one which did not need emphasizing in the United States, for this had been the practice of the American Church from the beginning. It was thus simply impossible, Spalding argued, "for an Italian to enter by an inner line of thought into American character or into the vital principles which underlie and mould American institutions," and it was already a well known fact that "Msgr. Satolli has failed to do this."[125]

Three weeks later, on January 14, 1893, notwithstanding the protests of the Bishop of Peoria and many of his fellow bishops, the Holy See created the Apostolic Delegation at Washington and appointed Archbishop Satolli the first permanent delegate.[126] In the ensuing months, as opposition mounted to Satolli's defense of Ireland's position on the school question, Cardinal Gibbons anxiously awaited an answer to his plea that Leo XIII bestow a formal blessing on the delegate's fourteen propositions. Gibbons' hopes were answered on May 31 when Pope Leo XIII sustained his delegate and at the same time took great pains to emphasize that the school legislation of the Baltimore council of 1884 had not been abrogated. In mid-June, the Pope's letter

[125] *Ibid.*
[126] AAB, 91-B-4, O'Connell to Gibbons, Rome, January 14, 1893, cablegram in Latin.

had been printed and distributed to the bishops of the country, "and even the strongest opponents in the hierarchy," Gibbons' biographer has noted, "now subsided and insofar as the bishops were concerned the debate was over." Thus the Cardinal of Baltimore could write in July to Mariano Cardinal Rampolla, Secretary of State, to express his thanks for the papal brief and his gratitude "that the Holy Father had put an end to the school controversy and brought a longed-for peace to the American Church."[127]

But the debate was not over so far as the Bishop of Peoria was concerned, even if the attempted sequel proved to be abortive and merely anticlimactic. Only a week after Gibbons had written to Rampolla, Spalding completed an introduction to a biography of Mother Caroline Freiss, Commissary General of the School Sisters of Notre Dame, which had been written by Father Peter Abbelen, author of the 1886 memorial about the Germans that had so infuriated Archbishop Ireland. Brief but pointed, the introduction was one last word on nationalism in the American Church and the school question. Mother Caroline's services in behalf of Catholic schools, Spalding stated, had been of inestimable value, and "*without parish schools,*" he emphasized, "*there is no hope that the Church will be able to maintain itself in America.*" The parish school system was now a permanent fact, growing from year to year with teachers who were becoming more and more efficient; new schools were being founded, and he was certain that "opposition unites all true Catholics in a more invincible determination to maintain at whatever cost the cause of religious education." From the German Catholic sisterhoods, American Catholics had already learned "what miracles of labor, economy and perseverance make possible."[128] There were those who urged a hasty, narrow Americanism, he con-

[127] Ellis, *op. cit.,* I, p. 702.

[128] Spalding, Introduction to Peter M. Abbelen, *Venerable Mother M. Caroline Freiss . . . A Sketch of Her Life,* p. 15.

tinued, but they simply had failed to remember that the growth of the Church in the United States, as that of the country itself, was due to the cooperation of many races; and if this commingling of heterogeneous elements had disadvantages, it was on the other hand productive of much good. The presence of many races would teach Americans a broader tolerance, a wider sympathy, and in America "for the first time the selfishness, the hardness and the narrowness of nationalism," he optimistically believed, "shall cease to exist." Since it was part of the American creed to give to each individual the largest liberty compatible with the rights of others, Spalding insisted that immigrants from whatever part of the world had the right to maintain their customs, languages, and religious practices when to be a true American citizen it was only necessary to be a good man, a lover of liberty, and a foe of injustice. The best were always the slowest to abandon their old ways, "and they who are most faithful to the memories and lessons of early life," he concluded, "will be found most faithful also to the duties imposed upon them by new surroundings."[129]

Faribaultism had also been the occasion, Spalding said, for the establishment of the apostolic delegation, and although by the end of 1893 "the worst of the storm within the American Church over the apostolic delegation was over," since the bishops of the country "were by this time in the main reconciled to his presence,"[130] the Bishop of Peoria nevertheless seemed to grow more determined in his opposition. In a series of letters to Bishop Ryan of Alton, who had already been reprimanded by the Holy See for his indiscreet cablegrams to Rome in opposition to the delegation,[131] Spalding revealed his plan. "I have taken it into my head to draw up a *Memorial*," he told Ryan, "setting forth my views of Satollicism and Faribaultism and our recent trou-

[129] *Ibid.*, p. 16.
[130] Ellis, *Gibbons,* I, p. 646.
[131] *Ibid.*, I, pp. 633–634.

217

bles." While he had not as yet decided whether to present the memorial to the Roman authorities, to write it, he thought, would do no harm, and so he needed help to make the document as strong as possible.[132] Four days later, as Archbishop Satolli and a good part of the hierarchy gathered in Baltimore to celebrate Gibbons' silver episcopal jubilee,[133] the Bishop of Peoria was not there, for on the very day he again wrote to Ryan in seeming impatience and said:

It matters not how desultory your notes and reflections may be: put down things as they appear to you. I have no documents—you have them all. Look through those clippings and pick out what may be to the point. Some of the *Sun* articles had good points, especially the Satollicism versus Catholicism one. Ireland wrote to his suffragans urging them to go to the Balt. celebration. It is all intrigue and lying. I think I shall go to Rome at the end of Nov. It is eleven years since I went and I may be able to make myself interesting.[134]

He had no illusions about the difficulty of his proposed task, and "if I do not succeed," he wrote, "it shall not be for lack of courage." Buoyed up momentarily by a report from Father Joseph McMahon of St. Patrick's Cathedral in New York that "things are looking favorable," that "the Pope himself, it seems, is beginning to get disgusted with the cabal," Spalding urged the Bishop of Alton to "work hard and come up with plenty of ammunition on Monday, November 8th,"[135] as he intended to leave for New York about the middle of the month. But his buoyancy was short-lived, for when he read of Corrigan's sermon on the occasion of Gibbons' jubilee, he confided to Ryan that in his judgment it was one of the worst, and he added, "I am not looking forward with any pleasure to my visit to Rome."[136]

132 ADP, Spalding to Ryan, Peoria, October 14, 1893.

133 Ellis, *Gibbons,* I, p. 645.

134 ADP, Spalding to Ryan, Peoria, October 18, 1893.

135 ADP, Same to Same, Peoria, October 29, 1893.

136 ADP, Same to Same, Peoria, November 14, 1893. Gibbons had invited Archbishop Corrigan to preach at his jubilee as a further step

Meanwhile, Archbishop Ireland had become quite aware of the sentiments of the Bishop of Peoria, and he soon informed Denis O'Connell: "Spalding is going to Rome. I am sorry to have to say that he is bitter against you and me. . . . It is comical to hear him *pose* in the name of Catholic Schools."[137] The Archbishop was undoubtedly displeased, but he was hardly concerned, and Keane of the Catholic University of America probably voiced his feelings when he also told O'Connell that "the embassy of Bishop Spalding, about starting to Rome . . . could not excite apprehension in any mind."[138] The rector of the American College, already characterized by Spalding as "a little Machiavelli,"[139] was quick to reassure Keane that in Rome "Bishop Spalding . . . won't count for much,"[140] just as he had been able to write three years before that "they don't trust Spalding."[141]

---

toward a *rapprochement* between Satolli and Corrigan. In his sermon, the latter referred to the presence of the "venerated representative of the Holy Father." Cf. Ellis, *op. cit.,* I, p. 646.

[137] ADR, Ireland to O'Connell, St. Paul, November 12, 1893.

[138] ADR, Keane to O'Connell, Washington, D.C., November 16, 1893

[139] CUA, O'Connell Papers, John Moore to O'Connell, Chicago, Sept. 20, 1893. Bishop Moore of St. Augustine had written to O'Connell: "I am inclined to believe you are something of what Spalding called you—a little Macchiavelli." (Macchiavelli is a variant spelling of Machiavelli.)

[140] ACUA, Keane Papers, O'Connell to Keane, Rome, December 4, 1893.

[141] AASP, O'Connell to Ireland, Rome, August 18, 1890.

6

The American Way

"SPALDING in Rome & other prelates in America continue to talk against Mgr. Satolli," Archbishop Ireland lamented early in 1894 to Denis O'Connell. Attacks on the delegate had begun again in the New York *Sun*, Ireland reported, and Satolli had become discouraged, well aware as he was of the hostile attitude of certain American bishops, as well as of the opposition of several Roman cardinals of the Congregation de Propaganda Fide.[1] While there is no evidence that Spalding presented his views on the Faribault school plan or on Archbishop Satolli to the Holy See during his Roman visit, he did submit to Propaganda an account of the progress in the Diocese of Peoria, which since his last *ad limina* visit had grown considerably. Nothing in the report even hinted at the controversies over nationalism and the schools on which he and Ireland had parted company, and only near the report's conclusion did the Bishop depart from a statistical narration to inform Cardinal Miecislaus Ledochowski, Prefect of the Congregation de Propaganda Fide, of the revival in 1893 of an anti-Catholic nativism which had spread throughout the United States, "the causes of which," said Spalding, "are not unknown."[2]

[1] ADR, Ireland to O'Connell, St. Paul, February 16, 1894.

[2] ACPF, Lett., Folder, 153/94, no. 6089, Diocesis Peoriensis, Relatio ad S. Congreg. de Propaganda Fide, Fevrier 8, 1894, p. 4. In the report, Spalding regretted that among the five or six hundred Italians in Spring Valley, Illinois, he had been unable to do much for their spiritual wel-

One of the oldest of the antiforeign traditions in America was the antipapal, anti-Catholic prejudice which saw in the Catholic Church a dangerous foreign undermining force in national life. In one sense, therefore, the arrival of Archbishop Satolli was ill-timed, and his appointment as delegate in January 1893 struck a number of Protestants as good reason for strengthening the American Protective Association, organized just five years previously with the avowed purpose of fighting the advance of Catholicism.[3]

Under the leadership of Henry F. Bowers, its principal founder, the A.P.A. took on characteristics of a secret fraternal order, borrowing heavily from Free Masonry in its black and yellow regalia and elaborate initiation; more important, a large source of its membership was the Orange lodges, tinged as they were with anti-Catholic sentiments. Until 1893, the organization had grown steadily though with little fanfare; with the new leadership of William "Whiskey Bill" Traynor of Michigan, however, it sprang abruptly into prominence. Fear of a long-range papal scheme to overthrow American institutions had bothered a good many Protestants during the early nineteenth century, but only in 1893 did they gird themselves to meet an

---

fare, that he had placed a good Italian priest there but that the father had found his fellow countrymen impossible. The Bishop wrote: "*C'est la seul portion de la population Catholique du diocese pour laquelle je ne puis rien de faire.*" *Ibid.*, p. 3. Cardinal Ledochowski succeeded the late Cardinal Simeoni on February 3, 1892, as Prefect of the congregation.

[3] Cf. Bowers to Humphrey J. Desmond, Clinton, Iowa, March 1, 1899, quoted in Desmond, *The A.P.A. Movement, A Sketch* (Washington, D.C., 1912), p. 15. Bowers wrote: "We looked upon Satolli as a representative of the Propaganda at Rome to direct and influence legislation in this country, more especially his settling down in the city of Washington, and several moves which were made . . . which gave rise to an opinion at least that he was interfering with the public institutions of this country." Cf. also, Ellis, *op. cit.*, I, p. 625.

imminent Catholic uprising when Traynor's newspaper, the Detroit *Patriotic American*, gave wide circulation to a bogus encyclical letter addressed to American Catholics by Pope Leo XIII which allegedly absolved them from any oath of loyalty to the United States and instructed them to exterminate all heretics on a certain date in September.[4] Burton Ames Huntington in *The Coming American Civil War* improved on the story with the allegation that 700,000 papal soldiers, organized in all large American cities, were ready to spring into rebellion at a moment's notice. The *Tri-City Blade* of Rock Island, Illinois, was quoted by Huntington in a way which, he said, spoke for itself:

A short time ago Bishop Spaulding [sic] of Peoria received a consignment of supposed wine. The officials, however, suspected that all was not quite right and seized the wine and upon opening the cases, found therein a large number of Winchester rifles. Deny this, O Rome, if you can. All unbelievers can write to the Custom House authorities at Peoria and prove the authenticity of this assertion. . . . In Moline, Illinois, a member of the local Romish church . . . made public the fact, while intoxicated, that local priests have received rifles and ammunition in large quantities. . . . And so it is throughout the country. In accordance with the order of the Pope, the priesthood of the Romish church are preparing for the coming struggles.[5]

Bishop Spalding, interviewed by reporters shortly after the appearance of Huntington's book, dismissed as "simply insane" the idea that Catholic churches in his diocese had been converted into arsenals. This very reason was given on Bloody Mon-

[4] J. Higham, *Strangers in the Land. Patterns of American Nativism, 1860–1925*, New Jersey, 1955, pp. 84–85.

[5] Huntington, *The Coming American Civil War*, p. 41. The author noted that the sentence beginning "All believers . . ." was misleading and, therefore, unfortunate, but he added: "The rifles were not received through the Customs House, and so the authorities there have no *official* knowledge about them. The fact, however, that they were received and exposed to the eyes of 'heretics' is established beyond doubt" (p. 178).

day of 1855, he recalled, when, at the height of the Know-Nothing bigotry in Louisville, arson was attempted on St. Martin's Church and the Cathedral of the Assumption. In the aftermath of that day of terror, Spalding said, "there was no market for real estate; no new enterprises were started; grass grew in the streets and hogs sunned themselves in the filth of the gutters; and this stagnation did not pass away until the awful storm of civil war had passed over it and purified the air."[6] He acknowledged that in the Diocese of Peoria this new Know-Nothingism had shown a certain vigor in Peoria, Rock Island, Bloomington, Danville, Streator, Ottawa, and other larger towns. He knew, he said, the names of the Peoria members of the A.P.A. and the oaths that they had taken. For the most part, they were Republicans, since "as the Whig party, when ruin threatened, sought to save itself by making an alliance with the Native American Party, so the Republicans, here in Illinois at least, seem to have some sort of understanding with the A.P.Aists." Certain railroads, the Rock Island for instance, seemed to give encouragement to this form of bigotry, and this was done, he was certain, "not from hatred of the Church, to which, being soulless, they are indifferent, but," he continued, "from a desire to weaken and cripple the labor unions." From one of the more respectable of the A.P.Aists, Spalding concluded, "I hear their great grievance is the presence of the apostolic delegate."[7]

[6] *Catholic Citizen* (Milwaukee), April 8, 1893.

[7] *Ibid.* Cf. ADP, A song especially composed for the A.P.A. by a Mrs. Ida J. Tibbens read as follows:

> ON! ON! WE WILL NOT FALTER
> The A.P.A. grows fast
> And Satolli stands aghast;
> For he knows that they will overthrow his plan.
>
> Chorus:—

Archbishop Satolli's presence in the United States was but a minor incident, however, in the general expansion of bigotry since, as it has been argued, "only the depression of 1893 can adequately explain the surge of Protestant nativism that year."[8] A.P.A. organizers, nevertheless, did not fail to exploit the climate of economic disaster.

Several months after his return from Rome, Spalding answered the charges of un-Americanism leveled against his coreligionists in the *North American Review*, where he discussed the problem of "Catholicism and A.P.Aism."[9] Facts were stronger than arguments, and it was little better than a waste of words, he said, to trace the loyalty and devotion of American Catholics who from the earliest colonial period had taken part in every phase of private and public life, and who had founded a colony, "the first in the New World, the first, indeed, in all the world," he maintained, "to make freedom of conscience an organic part of the constitution of the State." None more generously than Catholics had enlisted in the service of their country in the American Revolution, and if long tenure, fidelity, and honorable deeds had any efficacy, then Catholics had the right to be Americans; nor had this right ever become forfeited by any act or attempt of the Catholic Church in the United States.[10]

If, Spalding continued, most Catholics were Democrats rather than Republicans, this was not due to the influence or interference of priests and bishops, who, he said, "seldom know or care

---

> On, on, we will not falter,
> Cheer up, our cause is right,
> With the ballot in our hand,
> We will soon redeem our land,
> And will put Leo and Satolli to flight. . . .

"The music to the above," Mrs. Tibbens noted, "is grand and stirring . . . and should be in every A.P.A. council."

[8] Higham, *op. cit.*, p. 81.

[9] J. L. Spalding, "Catholicism and A.P.Aism," *NAR*, CLIV (September, 1894), pp. 278–287.

[10] *Ibid.*, p. 278.

to what political party the members of their congregations belong."[11] There were a great number of Catholics, he added, though generally Catholic only in name, who had often been too busy with municipal politics, but this was a common right of all American citizens. In some urban areas, Catholics were undoubtedly implicated in the hypocrisy, trickery, and fraud by which the whole political picture was tainted, but a bad Catholic, Spalding replied, was no better than any other bad man. Since the Catholic Church, in spite of whatever those ignorant of her spirit might think, was broad and tolerant, she was slow to expel anyone from the fold, loath to pluck up the cockle lest the wheat also be uprooted. And while thousands of the poorest and most ignorant laborers of Europe, many of them Catholics, induced by the reckless greed of American money-getters to come to the New World, had in some instances supplanted more intelligent and costly workers, the Church was not responsible, since, far from desiring this kind of immigration, "the American bishops and priests," he wrote, "would be glad to have it cease."[12]

Toward their fellow citizens who were not of their faith, American Catholics had always been above reproach. They had never sought to excite prejudice or to persecute any man for conscience's sake. No body of Catholics, not under the condemnation of the Church, had ever banded together in secret oath-bound societies for good or evil ends. If here and there, Spalding said, cowardly attacks on American Catholics had led to violence and riots, the employers of these agitators whose only arguments had consisted in outrageous insult were responsible, for Catholic bishops and priests had always advised their flocks to keep away

[11] *Ibid.*, p. 279.

[12] *Ibid.* Spalding was not, of course, an official spokesman for the American bishops and priests. Gibbons for one regarded restrictions on immigration as unwise. Cf. Ellis, *op. cit.*, II, p. 533. The Bishop of Peoria was guilty, in a sense, of fostering a species of racism.

from these men and the places in which they had held their meetings. Bishops and priests had no hidden policy, no deep laid schemes. Catholic life was undisguised; churches were open to all; Catholic literature was available for all; and whoever desired information about the Church did not have to look for long. What, then, was the cause of the abuse heaped on American Catholics, Spalding asked, of the distrust of which they seemed to be the object, and why had it been thought necessary to organize secret societies to oppose and hurt Catholics?[13]

At the root of all such outbreaks and movements there was, Spalding believed, the traditional Protestant view of the Catholic Church which still held sway not over enlightened minds, but over those who were too busy or too ignorant to be able to react against inherited prejudice. The latter still believed that the Church was the Scarlet Woman, the Pope the Man of Sin; that Jesuits were cunning hypocrites who were never happy unless they were up to mischief; that nunneries were prisons, or worse; that priests sold permission to commit sin and were ever ready to betray any country they might belong to at the dictate of the pope. All this and more the true victims of the Protestant tradition were ready to believe, and though such retarded minds were few, they were still numerous enough, he felt, to form a nucleus around which might gather all those who, whether honestly or from motives of self-interest, were glad to enter on an anti-Catholic crusade. The Orange lodges, or the Masons, constituted a center of this kind for the A.P.A., as a force ready at hand, in English-speaking countries, for those who wished to stir up religious strife—no more bitter, blind, or fanatical religious spirit existed than theirs, and, Spalding added, "its hatred is as genuine as it is unreasoning and unrelenting when like a wind-fanned flame it leaps forth with mad glee whenever there is opportunity to do harm to Catholics."[14]

[13] *Ibid.*, p. 280.
[14] *Ibid.*, p. 281.

What, he asked, were the causes which had led so many Americans who had no sympathy with Masonry to form an alliance with bigots of this sect for the purpose of attacking Catholics? The rapid and vigorous growth of the Church in the United States had, Spalding supposed, excited apprehensions in many Protestant minds, and the Church's success, largely due to immigration, might have also aroused jealousy as well as fear, since it was well known that the envious rivalry of Protestant denominations among themselves was a chief source of their own weakness. Another factor was a certain spirit of boastfulness among Catholics, who—though losses of the faith were, as he viewed it, greater than the accessions from Europe—had begun to proclaim that at no distant day was America destined to become Catholic. These utterances were merely the expression of zeal and the outburst of a fervid temper, he knew, but they had also aroused unkind thoughts in many whose dislike of Catholics was more genuine than their love of toleration.[15]

To make matters worse, Spalding continued, Catholics then began to quarrel among themselves, and national differences of thought, sentiment, and custom threatened to prove stronger than the harmonizing forces of a common religious faith. The controversial spirit was let loose, and the real issue came to be not truth and justice, but victory. Wild words were spoken, overbearing deeds were done, and reporters, scenting scandal, had rushed in filling the country with sound and fury. The loyalty of German Catholics was called into question, and they were accused of conspiring with a certain Cahensly, a citizen of Prussia, against the interests of the country, and yet, Spalding insisted, Cahensly

. . . was as powerless as he was unknown, and if harm he could do, he could do it only by influencing the Pope to do wrong; and the Catholics who made such an outcry seemed really to dread lest the Pope should be induced to do a foolish or wicked thing. Their temper was controversial, but the bigots took them seriously. Intelligent people among us

[15] *Ibid.*

227

know that the Pope would not if he could, could not if he would, hurt America; but to the multitudes the cry of danger from the Papist is as effective as Dalila's shout to Samson that the Philistines were upon him.[16]

Cahenslyism had unwittingly been entangled with the school question, and thus the Faribault school compromise had been another cause of alarm. The incident was neither novel nor important, he believed, and it would doubtless have escaped notice had not the impression been created that it was a scheme whereby Catholics hoped to get a share of the school funds. Though, in fact, it was a local affair, "unacceptable from the Catholic point of view," and simply tolerated by Rome, word had gone forth that it was a jesuitical plot to undermine the public schools; and while the charge was as false as it was ridiculous, "when public opinion is aroused," Spalding declared, "assertion is as effective as proof."[17]

The Faribault episode, insignificant in itself, had also been the occasion, Spalding was certain, for the establishment of the apostolic delegation, and he thereupon proceeded to review this "affair of grave moment." From the very beginning, he said, the American bishops, whenever consulted, had strongly opposed the project, and when the question had been put to the archbishops at their annual meeting in New York in the Fall of 1892, it had been their almost unanimous opinion that it would be unwise to appoint a delegate for the United States. The question of a delegation was, of course, in his view, "not a question of faith or morals, or discipline, or rule, affecting the whole church but one of ecclesiastical policy," and those whose knowledge of the country was most accurate believed that the establishment of the apostolic delegation would be bad policy. Whether this opposition had been justified so far as the internal affairs of the Church had been concerned, he believed

16 *Ibid.*, p. 282.
17 *Ibid.*

228

it unnecessary to inquire, but, he said, "that the Delegate has been and is a source of strength to the A.P.Aists there can be no doubt."[18] Anti-Catholic prejudice was largely anti-papal, and when newspapers had filled their pages with the sayings and the doings of the "American Pope, who though a foreigner, with no intention of becoming a citizen, ignorant alike of our language and our traditions, was supposed to have supreme authority in the church in America," it was then, Spalding insisted, that "fresh fuel was thrown upon the fires of bigotry." The fact that Archbishop Satolli's authority was merely ecclesiastical was lost sight of by many who were persuaded that the papacy was a political power eager to extend its control wherever opportunity might offer. It was this feeling, he recalled, that had led John Carroll, the first American bishop, to make an official declaration in 1797 that the obedience Catholics owed the Pope was "in things purely spiritual," for such had been the uniform belief and teaching from the beginning of the American Church.[19]

From the statement of the causes that had led to the rise and spread of the new Know-Nothingism, Spalding proceeded to consider some of the charges which the leaders of the anti-Catholic crusade had advanced as justification for their attacks on American Catholics. There was, first of all, the time-honored contention that Catholics, since they owed obedience to the Pope, could not, therefore, be loyal American citizens. Deeds rather than words, he maintained, had proven Catholic patriotism, and it was not necessary "to hold the flag in our hands when we walk the streets, to wave it when we speak," nor, as he continued, "to fan ourselves with it when we are warm, and to wrap it about us when we are cold."[20] The objection of a divided and incompatible allegiance among American Catholics had, likewise, an obvious answer, since, as he wrote,

[18] *Ibid.*, p. 283.
[19] *Ibid.*
[20] *Ibid.*, p. 285.

Our obedience to the Pope is confined to the domain of religious faith, morals, and discipline; and since the state, with us at least, claims no jurisdiction over such matters, there can be no question of conflict. We have, and none are more thankful for this than Catholics, a separation of the Church from the State. If it is urged that to draw the line of demarcation is difficult, I reply that in the general course of things this difficulty presents itself hardly at all. That it may arise, all confess, but it arises just as easily for Protestants as for Catholics. All men in our age . . . hold a double allegiance and are prepared, if needs be, to appeal from men to God, from laws to conscience, from authority to reason, from numbers to justice . . .[21]

The Pope had never attempted to intervene in the civil or political affairs of the American Republic, "and were he to attempt to do so," Spalding warned, "his action would be resented by Catholics more quickly than by others." The Pope was simply a religious, not a civil or political superior, and that was one reason why "our representative men have always opposed the appointment of a papal delegate for the United States," since Spalding knew that they were unwilling "to give our enemies even a pretext for accusing us, as citizens, of being under foreign influence."[22]

Another complaint, "which like the brook with its senseless prattle goes on forever," was that Catholics were the foes of the common schools, or, "as the amiable Episcopal Bishop Doane of Albany puts it," Spalding wrote, "that 'they do not love the public school system nor the theory of universal education'."[23] Were it not that most men became victims of oft-repeated assertions, he continued, it would be difficult to explain the persistence of this accusation, since the Catholic position on the question of education was at once as simple as it was authoritatively proclaimed:

[21] *Ibid.*, p. 284.
[22] *Ibid.*, p. 285.
[23] *Ibid.* William Croswell Doane (1832–1913) was the first Protestant Episcopal Bishop of Albany, New York. Cf. Doane, "The Roman Catholic Church and the School Fund," *NAR,* CLVIII (January, 1894), pp. 30–40.

We believe that religion is an essential element of human nature, and, therefore, of right education; and where it is possible to do so, we found and maintain schools, in which along with other things, we teach also what we believe to be religion. Inasmuch as this is not done in the common schools, we find the system defective, but we do not condemn it; for in a country such as ours no other system of state schools seems to be possible, and we are openly and without reservation in favor of free schools, and consequently, in favor of a school tax.[24]

For himself, and he believed that he expressed the general Catholic view, "I not only would not, had I the power to destroy the public school system," he asserted, "but would leave nothing undone to develop and perfect it," since he believed in free schools, in universal education, and, wherever public opinion was sufficiently enlightened, in compulsory school attendance. If here and there individuals had made efforts to get public moneys for parochial schools, the Catholic body, he insisted, was not to be held responsible for their acts.[25]

The attempt, moreover, to commit American Catholics of the nineteenth century to all the deeds and utterances of Catholics in the Middle Ages was, Spalding concluded, futile. Intelligent Catholics did not hold that the popes had never been wrong, nor were they bound to defend the policy or the acts of particular popes whether they reigned before or after the Reformation. If the public law of Europe in the eleventh or twelfth century had allowed the pontiffs "to declare forfeit the authority of tyrannical princes and emperors," it did not follow that they were permitted to do so in the nineteenth century. "We are Catholics, but we are also men," he wrote, "and though the essential tenets of the faith are immutable, we ourselves, change with a changing world." Thus, American Catholics accepted with frank sincerity, with cheerful acquiescence, the principles involved in the rule of the people, by the people, and for the people.[26]

[24] *Ibid.*
[25] *Ibid.*, p. 286.
[26] *Ibid*

Since all Americans agreed that freedom of conscience and liberty of worship were inalienable rights, why, Spalding inquired, were secret oath-bound societies allowed to exist when their one great aim was to subvert this primary article of the American creed? No American Catholic could object to the free discussion of his religious beliefs; but the abuse, lies, and forgeries of the A.P.Aists could not advance the cause of truth. In face of all this, Spalding wondered, how could Bishop Doane ask American Catholics to take a more conciliatory tone, since this was asking the lamb to conciliate the wolf, "for which the only possible conciliation," Spalding said, "is having the lamb in its maw." A.P.Aism would, of course, pass away, since the American people loved justice and fair play. "They live and they let live," he wrote, and "their very genius is good will to men." But meanwhile, A.P.Aism was detrimental to the best interests of the country inasmuch that "it separates friend from friend . . . sows the seeds of suspicion and distrust . . . makes innocent victims, and is doing all that it is possible to do to verify the saying of a well-known Englishman that the only civilized country in which it is less pleasant to live than in the United States is Russia."[27]

Word of Spalding's views on the latest recurrence of the anti-Catholic crusade soon became known, and there was consternation in certain quarters where some seemed convinced that the Bishop of Peoria was doing his utmost to persuade Archbishop Satolli that Matthew Arnold's criticism of the United States was not completely untrue. "Have you read Bp. Spalding's article in the *North American Review* . . . ?" Monsignor John M. Farley, pastor of St. Gabriel's Church in New York City, asked Denis O'Connell. "Get it if not," he added. "I fear he will get into

[27] *Ibid.*, p. 287. Matthew Arnold, quoting a Sir Lepel Griffin, had written: "Yet we find an acute and experienced Englishman saying that there is no country, calling itself civilized, where one would not rather live than in the United States except Russia." Cf. Allan Nevins (ed.), *American Social History as Recorded by British Travellers* (New York, 1923), p. 503

trouble. It seems that we are never to get out of trouble; 'breakers ahead,' seems to be the feelings of all of us now."[28] Father David S. Phelan, editor of the St. Louis *Western Watchman*, thought Spalding had made an egregious fool of himself, for whether or not the delegate intended to become an American citizen was a matter that concerned him personally, and Spalding had no right to decide the matter for him in advance.[29] John Keane told reporters that the article was unfortunate and untimely;[30] but Spalding replied that the important question was whether what he had said was true inasmuch as a thing might be unfortunately true, which, he felt, was doubtless Bishop Keane's meaning when he termed the article unfortunate. That it was untimely, he also failed to see, since in his opinion it was an honest and dispassionate discussion of a subject which attracted general attention and was not without importance. If his very moderate views on a question which was actually before the public and of great concern to both Church and state were to be condemned as unfortunate and ill-timed, then "rational discussion among Catholics," he believed, "is no longer to be thought of and Catholic universality is but a pretense. . . ."[31] Keane had likewise intimated in the newspaper interview that Cardinal Gibbons had thought it necessary to express regret to Pope Leo XIII. "The least I can do, I suppose," Spalding responded, "is to regret that he should have to regret to express his regrets to the pope." Moreover, regrets were idle, "and the only manly and American thing is to confront me with arguments, and not attempt to frighten me with groanings."[32]

[28] ADR, Farley to O'Connell, New York, September 28, 1894.

[29] *Western Watchman* (St. Louis), September 27, 1894.

[30] *The Review*, I (October 3, 1894), p. 17. Arthur Preuss, the editor, quoted Keane and Spalding's reply.

[31] *Ibid.*

[32] *Ibid.* When Gibbons wrote to deny that he had expressed regrets to the Pope, Spalding thanked him and added: "It was not said that you had been interviewed on the subject, but that Bishop Keane . . . had

233

Meanwhile, Archbishop Satolli had written to Spalding, not to confront him with arguments—since the delegation, already a *fait-accompli,* was not a question for public debate—but to admonish him for his continued and bitter opposition not only to the delegation itself, but also to Satolli's appointment as the first delegate, since, as he said,

Time and again, from its very inception, you have been so bold in speech, not only here, but even at Rome, as to overstep the limits of prudent moderation which a Bishop, above all, ought to have in matters pertaining to the decrees and decisions of the Holy See. Your personal reproach upon me for my ignorance of the idiom and customs of this land was easy enough to bear, but your direct attack upon the action of the Supreme Pastor . . . Leo XIII . . . appears to me to be absolutely intolerable, and coming from a Bishop, a great and monstrous scandal. Not content with your past efforts, you have now written an article . . . in which (Omitting whatever would be in seeming contradiction to a more sound kind of theology) you re-echo those same critical observations. These are untimely, harmful, not consistent with the truth; they also smack of a brashness towards the Roman Pontiff to the extent that you take it upon yourself to repeat that from the time the Apostolic Delegation was founded, the A.P.A. has launched a more vigorous attack against the Catholic Church.[33]

It was wise, occasionally, to be sensible, Satolli warned, as it was fitting for those invested with dignity and authority to lead their subjects by example, in a spirit of humility, charity, and whole-hearted obedience toward their own superiors rather than by mere words. In all sincerity and fraternal charity, the delegate said, he felt that he must mention this matter, and at the same time he wished the Bishop of Peoria to know that he would immediately inform the Holy Father, who would be

affirmed that you had expressed regret to the Pope. How the Bishop could have made this statement, I cannot understand. . . ." Cf. AAB, 93-L-2, Spalding to Gibbons, Peoria, October 6, 1894.

[33] ACPF, Lett., Folder 153/94, no. 9458, Satolli to Spalding, Washington, September 7, 1894, Latin copy.

greatly pained, he was certain, when he learned the nature of this offensive attack on the apostolic delegation.[34]

True to his word, Archbishop Satolli wrote at once to Cardinal Rampolla, the Secretary of State, and enclosed the September issue of the *North American Review* together with a copy of the letter he had addressed to Spalding.[35] Rampolla, thereupon, instructed Cardinal Ledochowski that it was the wish of the Pope that Propaganda give a suitable admonition to the Bishop of Peoria for the article in question and to reprimand him for his hostile attitude toward the apostolic delegation.[36] Pope Leo's wish was executed, for on New Year's Eve, 1894, Spalding confided to Bishop Ryan of Alton, "I wrote to the Pope, some six weeks ago or more. Simply said, in a single phrase, I regretted having given him pain, and then went on to do my best to persuade him that everything is going to the devil here, and appealing to him to call some representative men, as those who most loudly proclaim themselves the possessors of his confidence, have not that of the clergy or people." His letter, he told Ryan, might do some good, but it would do no harm.[37]

One week later, on January 6, 1895, Leo XIII addressed the encyclical letter *Longinqua oceani* to the American hierarchy, in which he took great pains to emphasize the functions of the recently established Apostolic Delegation in the life of the American Church.

Disagreements within the hierarchy, however, over the solution of many problems facing the Church continued to thwart, to a degree, the Pontiff's hope that the presence of Archbishop Satolli would lead to a "mutual esteem" among the bishops. Men of the stamp of Ireland, Gibbons, and Keane, "those who

[34] *Ibid.*

[35] ACPF, Lett., Folder 153/94, no. 9458, Satolli to Rampolla, Washington, September 7, 1894.

[36] ACPF, Lett., Folder 153/94, no. 9458, Rampolla to Ledochowski, Rome, September 20, 1894.

[37] ADP, Spalding to Ryan, December 31, 1894.

loudly proclaimed," as Spalding believed, "that they were possessors of the pope's confidence," were soon to learn that Leo XIII was also inclined to include other prelates who in the first two years of Satolli's American stay had been less voluble in claiming his confidence.

The first indication of a possible break between the Delegate, the interpreter of the Holy Father's wishes, and the liberal wing of the American hierarchy arose over the problem of secret societies.[38] The growth of these societies in the late nineteenth century had been phenomenal, and by the year 1900 secret fraternal groups had the names of more than six million Americans on their rosters. These societies offered a means whereby social contacts could be more easily fostered, the need for recognition satisfied through parades, pageantry, elaborate rituals and lavish regalias, and in the more practical order an agency by means of which sickness and death benefits might accrue to members and their families. In the last two decades of the century, some four hundred and ninety such societies were established in the United States, and, like their fellow citizens, American Catholics had the same instinct for "joining" that made men flock into the secret lodges, with the consequence that there was a weakening, if not a positive loss, of faith.[39]

At the Third Plenary Council, there had been a wide divergence among the bishops as to the nature of certain societies and the method of procedure to be taken in their regard. Bishop Francis Chatard of Vincennes, for example, suggested the condemnation of the Ancient Order of Hibernians, while Patrick Feehan, Archbishop of Chicago, defended it.[40] Early in the debate, the apparently wide divergence of views had led Spal-

[38] Ellis, *Gibbons*, I, pp. 439–485. These pages will be used in part for background material. For a detailed treatment of the problem down to 1895; cf. Fergus Macdonald C.P., *The Catholic Church and the Secret Societies in the United States* (New York, 1946)

[39] *Ibid.*, I, p. 439.

[40] *Acta et decreta*, private edition, p. lxxvi.

ding to suggest that for the sake of uniformity a commission of five or more archbishops should be set up who would "prudently and accurately deliberate on these things and finally decide in the name of the Council." Archbishop Alemany of San Francisco, thereupon, expressed a preference for making all the archbishops members of this commission, and with this amendment the fathers agreed to the Spalding proposal.[41] Later, when Bishop McQuaid suggested that a committee be designated to investigate the Ancient Order of Hibernians, Spalding afterward reminded the assembly of what had already been decided on and the necessity for what was termed the "permanent commission of all the Archbishops who would inquire into societies about which a doubt had arisen and make a judgment about them."[42] The process was to begin with the individual bishops, who were to examine personally or through others the nature of suspected organizations in their dioceses to see if they merited condemnation. The case was then to be referred to the commission of archbishops, who, when they could not reach a unanimous decision about a society in question, would then refer the matter to the Holy See for judgment.

In the time after the Council, however, it became evident that the mechanism suggested by Spalding for the solution of the problem of secret societies had failed. Gibbons' fear of alienating large groups from the Church had impelled him to believe that more good would result "from a vigilant, masterly inactivity than by any hasty legislation,"[43] while Ireland, "the pleader of the cause of secret societies,"[44] followed the theory that as much liberty as was consistent with principle should be allowed Catholics, and on this basis Ireland sought to secure toleration for those organizations which in his opinion were not

[41] *Ibid.*
[42] *Ibid.*, p. lxxviii.
[43] AAC, Gibbons to Elder, Baltimore, July 20, 1886.
[44] Moynihan, *Life of John Ireland,* p. 214.

hostile to the Church. Lines were drawn, consequently, when other members of the hierarchy, Archbishops Katzer, Elder, and Corrigan, for example, disagreed with the so-called liberal position and regarded some of the societies in doubt as worthy of condemnation. At the first annual meeting of the metropolitans in Boston, in the summer of 1890, secret societies had been discussed, but the minutes merely laid down the principle that, with the exception of the Masons, Catholics should simply be dissuaded from joining them. But since there seemed to be no absolute certainty of any positive evil in them, no general mandate could be issued forbidding them.[45] "Precisely who and what lay behind this surprisingly moderate judgment within the meeting it is impossible to say," John Tracy Ellis has remarked, but Archbishop Ireland had been the secretary of the meeting, and his account of the proceedings "created the impression that societies like the Odd Fellows, the Sons of Temperance, and the Knights of Pythias were now tolerated by the Church."[46]

Some two years later, for instance, Spalding still entertained the notion that the Boston conference had given permission to Catholics to become Odd Fellows, which seemed to him, he told Archbishop Corrigan, "to have been a fatal blunder." Priests and people, along with many bishops, Spalding maintained, were in doubt on the subject, and many laymen, "acting on the principle *in dubio libertas*' had become Odd Fellows," and would be weaned away from the Church, since "the difference between Odd Fellows and Masons," he asserted, "is chiefly one of name." He realized that the problem rested in the hands of those archbishops who were more fully informed on the subject of the societies, but there could be little doubt, he thought, that "the present state of doubt and uncertainty is the worst possible and

[45] AAB, 87-R-4, Minutes of the Meeting of the Archbishops, Boston, July 23–24, 1890
[46] Ellis, *Gibbons,* I, p. 457

ought to cease even if a direct appeal to the Pope be required."[47]

Yet, the doubt and uncertainty increased, and subsequent meetings of the metropolitans in New York and Chicago witnessed only the reënactment of scenes marked by the lack of unanimity, until finally it was acknowledged that the conciliar mechanism worked out in 1884 had failed.[48] An appeal was made, therefore, to the Holy See, and on August 24, 1894, Raffaele Cardinal Monaco of the Congregation of the Holy Office forwarded an instruction to Archbishop Satolli which obliged all the ordinaries in the United States to do their utmost to restrain the laity from joining the Odd Fellows, the Knights of Pythias, and the Sons of Temperance. They were to inform the faithful of the condemnation and to warn them that if they persisted in their attachment to these societies and were unwilling to sever their actual connection with them, they would not be admitted to the reception of the sacraments.[49] The Delegate communicated the decree to the archbishops assembled in Philadelphia in the Fall of 1894, but the metropolitans, conservative and liberal, now unanimously agreed that, in the light of the current anti-Catholic crusade, it was inopportune to publish the condemnations. Moreover, they agreed not to transmit the decree even to their suffragans, and resolved finally that "no individual Archbishop or Bishop should promulgate it, unless its promul-

[47] AANY, C-44, Spalding to Corrigan, Peoria, October 25, 1892. Spalding was unaware of the fact, obviously, that at the St. Louis meeting in November, 1891, the metropolitans had agreed that the wording of the Boston resolution was somewhat inexact and had changed it to read that the question of membership in a given society should be decided "by the conscience of each individual under the direction of his confessor." Cf. AAB, 89-D-5/1, Minutes of the Meeting of the Archbishops, St. Louis, November 29, 1891.

[48] Ellis, *Gibbons,* I, pp. 462–464 and *passim.*

[49] "Decretum C.S.O. De Societatibus," in *AER,* XIII (July, 1895), pp. 67–68.

gation was expressly ordered by the Holy See or by the Archbishops in convention assembled."[50]

Early in December, however, Satolli notified Gibbons that it
was the Holy Father's wish that the decree be explicitly promulgated.[51] This directive troubled the Cardinal, as it angered the
Archbishop of St. Paul. "Ireland has been badly bruised and
battered," Spalding told Bishop Ryan of Alton, but he admitted
that the St. Paul Prelate would not easily concede, since, as
he expressed it, "he is a chameleon and will take any color at
all from APAism to Byzantinism."[52] Ireland did not readily retreat, however, and when Gibbons prepared to go to Rome in
the Spring of 1895, where he hoped, among other things, to
secure a nullification of the decree, Ireland urged him on, saying, "You are needed there. Go to conquer, and return, having
conquered." But Gibbons' visit to Rome was an unhappy one,
for shortly after his arrival Denis O'Connell submitted his resignation as Rector of the American College[53] at the request of
Cardinal Ledochowski of the Congregation of the Propaganda,
and soon thereafter Gibbons suffered one of the first major re-
verses in his ecclesiastical career, over the question of the secret
societies.

The opposition had, meanwhile, been hard at work, and
among them Spalding had hastened to inform Ledochowski that
conscience prompted him to speak his mind about the decree
condemning the secret societies. The condemnation, remarked
Spalding, was precisely what ought to be made known, since
Catholic societies would soon have to disband for lack of members, and in the end, he said, "we will have only women in our

[50] AAB, 93-L-4, Minutes of the Meeting of the Archbishops, Philadelphia, October 10, 1894.

[51] Ellis, *Gibbons,* I, p. 467.

[52] ADP, Spalding to Ryan, Peoria, December 31, 1894.

[53] Ellis, *Gibbons,* I, p. 467; II, pp. 31–32. Opponents of the so-called
liberals alleged that O'Connell's resignation had been demanded because of his "partisanship for Gibbons and his friends . . ."

churches," if Catholics continued to be allowed to enter the prohibited lodges. Gibbons and Ireland opposed the condemnation, he told the Cardinal Prefect, because they were timid and feared the effect of the decree on public opinion. Moreover, several archbishops had permitted Catholics to enter these groups, and in some instances the laity now refused to quit them. It was better, however, to lose, perhaps, several thousand men, Spalding felt, than to see the Church destroy herself in the United States. "I know my own country and I am persuaded that it is necessary to insist that the decree be published by all the bishops," he declared, "since her authority here will suffer immensely" if Rome withdrew the decree. Spalding had not as yet promulgated the decree in his own diocese, since he was well aware, he explained, of the agitation to prevent its execution.[54] Cardinal Ledochowski thereupon forwarded the Bishop's letter as "*un altro documento*," he noted, "concerning the publication of the decree condemning secret societies," to the Congregation of the Holy Office,[55] where the fears of Gibbons and Ireland about the effect of the decree on public opinion would shortly be shown to be of no avail.

Just four days prior to his departure from Europe, Gibbons had regretfully admitted in a letter to Bishop Keane that on the subject of secret societies he could only report failure. He informed the Rector that the Holy Office had been inflexible, and that a few days before he had arrived in Rome a letter had been forwarded to Satolli ordering a more explicit promulgation binding on all the bishops. "Interested parties were working with the H. Office," Gibbons commented, ". . . representing some prelates as neglectful in this regard."[56] Early in the year,

[54] ACPF, Lett., Folder 16, no. 13388, Spalding to Ledochowski, Peoria, May 25, 1895

[55] ACPF, Lett., Folder 16, no. 13388, Propaganda to Tancredi Fausti, Rome, June 16, 1895. Monsignor Fausti was the assessor of the Sacred Congregation of the Holy Office.

[56] CUA, Keane Papers, Gibbons to Keane, Rome, June 29, 1895.

241

Gibbons' initial reluctance to publish the decree had provoked a startled Delegate to acquaint Cardinal Rampolla with the fact that, for the first time, he had to face an attitude on the part of Baltimore's Cardinal which he could interpret in no other way but as insubordination.[57] On June 11, 1895, Satolli notified Ireland of the latest directive from the Holy Office, and advised Ireland that if he knew of any diocese in his province where it had not been published, he was to see to it that it was done.[58] It was evident that, in Satolli's view, Gibbons and Ireland had been "neglectful in this regard," and this may very well have been the reason why the Delegate wondered if, perhaps, his confidence in the progressive wing of the hierarchy had been misplaced.

The clearest manifestation of Satolli's "sudden definite and public turning" from his friends of the first two years of his residence in the United States took place, most likely,[59] in April, 1895, at Pottsville, Pennsylvania, on the occasion of the laying of the cornerstone of the new St. John the Baptist School. There, for the first time, the Delegate ostensibly championed the position that German Catholics had been defending through all the previous controversies, and, as it has been said, "put his stamp of approval on all the German activities," some of which, it was

[57] Satolli to Rampolla, Washington, January 5, 1895, in UND, Soderini notes, quoted in Patrick H. Ahern, *The Life of John J. Keane* (Milwaukee, 1955), p. 167.

[58] AASP, Satolli to Ireland, Washington, June 11, 1895.

[59] Barry, *The Catholic Church and German Americans*, p. 223. Barry wrote that Pottsville was the occasion for Satolli's "sudden, definite . . . and public turning." Cf. Ellis, *Gibbons*, I, pp. 648–649. Ellis described the scene at Pottsville "as the clearest manifestation," while Ahern, *op. cit.*, p. 167, wrote of it as "the first public occasion, so far as the present writer could determine. . . ." Cf. also, McAvoy, *The Great Crisis in American Catholic History*, p. 126, who observes that Pottsville was "the first notable manifestation of Satolli's friendship for the Germans."

added, "had been the subject of false charges and accusations."[60] The Pottsville ceremony might very well have been the occasion chosen by the Delegate for a public disclosure of his subsequent policy; yet, in light of a less dramatic but nonetheless interesting prelude, his "public turning" was hardly sudden. Six months before, shortly after the publication of Spalding's analysis of the anti-Catholic crusade, the German Roman Catholic Verein held its annual convention in New York. The Apostolic Delegate, invited but unable to attend, addressed a letter to the delegates through Conrad Strassburger, the secretary of the Verein, which Monsignor Joseph Schroeder translated into German and read at the final session.[61]

The letter of Archbishop Satolli was a simple congratulatory message, and yet he took the opportunity to trace the origins and the purposes of the German Catholic congresses, which, he believed, were a forceful response to the enemies of the Church. Less definite, perhaps, than the Pottsville declaration wherein the Delegate had praised German Catholics as good American citizens who stood second to none and who rightly defended their usages and customs, their language and their schools,[62] the Satolli letter to the New York convention at least foreshadowed the increasing *rapprochement* with German Catholics and a

[60] Ahern, *op. cit.*, p. 168.

[61] Satolli to Conrad Strassburger, Secretary, Washington, September 14, 1894, quoted in the New York *Times,* September 18, 1894.

[62] Ellis, *Gibbons,* I, p. 649. Three months after the Pottsville declaration Satolli asked Rome for instructions concerning future participation in meetings similar to the Chicago Parliament of Religions at which Gibbons, Keane, and Ireland had given addresses. On September 18, 1895, Leo XIII addressed a letter to Satolli in which he ordered a discontinuance of future participation. Cf. ". . . De Coetibus Vulgo Dictus, 'Parliaments of Religion,'" in *AER,* XIII (November, 1895), p. 395. Rome's answer was also regarded as a significant blow to the liberal cause. The Bishop of Peoria had played no part in the Parliament of Religions.

growing disenchantment, it was believed, with the so-called Americanizers in the Church of the United States.

The complete explanation of Satolli's *volte-face* remains, nevertheless, something of a mystery, and it is of interest here only so far as the break between the Delegate and the liberal wing in the hierarchy tended to accent Spalding's discontent with the general state of affairs in the American Church. His intransigence on "home rule" had already precluded the possibility of any real *rapport* between Spalding and Satolli; the Germans' New York meeting merely aggravated the less than cordial relationship. It was there Spalding later told his close friend, Bishop Ryan of Alton, that "Satolli tried to get Schroeder to denounce me . . . but the Dr. did not have the grit."[63] The latter's lack of courage was readily understandable at the time, however, for it would have been foolhardy even for Schroeder publicly to arraign the bishop who from the outset, though indisputably American in background and sympathy, had advocated so cogently the cause of the German Catholics in the United States.

In any case, the Apostolic Delegate's remarks at New York and Pottsville boded ill for the liberals in the American Church, and possibly colored Satolli's views on the condemnation of the secret societies and on other controversial matters in the years ahead. Created a cardinal by Leo XIII in the November consistory of 1895,[64] the pro-delegate, as he was thereafter called, delayed his departure for Rome until the following October when Archbishop Sebastiano Martinelli, O.S.A., his successor,

[63] ADP, Spalding to Ryan, Peoria, December 1, 1894.

[64] "Allocutio SSDN Leonis XIII Occasione Creationis Cardinalium in Consistorio. Die XXIX, Nov. An. MDCCCXCV," *AER*, XIV (January, 1896), pp. 74–76. Gibbons conferred the red biretta on Satolli on January 5, 1896, in the cathedral at Baltimore. The day before, Spalding remarked to Father Hudson: "I found it impossible to get away for Satolli's hat. I regret it, but there was no help for it." Cf. UND, Hudson Papers, Spalding to Hudson, Peoria, January 4, 1896.

arrived in the United States.[65] Only the month before, Keane, Ireland, and Gibbons met with fresh evidence that Cardinal Satolli had, indeed, been won over to the conservative cause when, on September 28, a saddened Gibbons handed to Keane a letter from the Pope dismissing him from the office of Rector of the University.[66] The removal, inspired by Satolli, it was whispered, was interpreted as "a victory for the conservative and anti-American party in the Church, another blow at 'home rule' in American affairs."[67] Some conservatives were jubilant. "What collapses on every side," exclaimed the ever candid McQuaid to Corrigan. "Gibbons, Ireland and Keane!!!" he crowed. "They were the cocks of the walk for a while and dictated to the country and thought to run our dioceses for us. They may change their policy and repent. They can never repair the harm done in the past."[68]

But for the Bishop of Peoria the dismissal of John J. Keane was not an occasion for good cheer. Two years before, perhaps annoyed by the University's support of Ireland's stand on Cahenslyism and the school question, Spalding had not hesitated while in Rome to proclaim everywhere that the University was a failure,[69] but now he was seemingly nettled by the rumor abroad that the Pope, "in slapping Bp. Keane in the face," had given a death blow to the Washington institution.[70] A more disgusting state of affairs than the ecclesiastical situation in the United States, he told Father Daniel Hudson, C.S.C, editor of

[65] New York *Times,* October 16, 1896.

[66] Ahern, *op. cit.,* p. 178.

[67] Barry, *op. cit.,* p. 227. And yet it was Archbishop Ireland who at the New York meeting in 1892 had alone favored the establishment of the apostolic delegation while the so-called conservative archbishops opposed it and thus, in the main, favored "home rule."

[68] AANY, McQuaid to Corrigan, Rochester, October 3, 1896.

[69] AAB, 93-B-3, O'Connell to Gibbons, Rome, January 17, 1894.

[70] UND, Hudson Papers, Spalding to Hudson, Peoria, December 6, 1896.

Ave Maria, was hardly conceivable,[71] and for which he held John Ireland primarily responsible. The Archbishop of St. Paul was, in Spalding's opinion, the "perpetual storm center," the "Big Drum,"[72] banging away throughout the American Church where the only important question seemed to be whether he was falling or rising in favor with Rome. "If we could only hear nothing more of him," he lamented, "it matters little whether he fall or rise." He had also lost all patience with Bishop Keane. "If the Pope had him down on all fours kicking him," remarked Spalding, "each time he lifted his foot, the enthusiastic bishop would shout: See how the Holy Father honors me."[73] Later, when Keane took up residence in Rome as a Canon of St. John Lateran, Spalding grew even more querulous. "Abp. Keane, I see," he complained to Hudson, "is to get eighty dollars a month . . . and with that I suppose, he has to hire his apartment and live. Abp. Ireland, I think, is a hoodoo—whatever he touches seems to go wrong."[74]

With Keane's dismissal from the rectorship, rumors were plentiful as to his successor, and again it was thought that the probable choice of the University's Board of Trustees would be Spalding. Only a year previously, the Chicago *Inter Ocean* had announced in March 1895 the contemplated appointment of Bishop Spalding to the See of Boston as coadjutor-archbishop with the right of succession,[75] and the Boston *Congregationalist* had rejoiced in the prospect of having near at hand the bishop who was "fearless enough to criticize Leo XIII and Monsignor Satolli and will not hesitate to challenge and puncture the mis-

[71] *Ibid.*

[72] ADP, Spalding to Ryan, December 31, 1894.

[73] UND, Hudson Papers, Spalding to Hudson, Peoria, December 6, 1894.

[74] UND, Hudson Papers, Same to Same, Peoria, February 7, 1897. The apostolic brief which promoted Keane to the rank of titular Archbishop of Damascus was sent on January 9, 1897. Cf. Ahern, *op. cit.,* p. 212

[75] Chicago *Inter Ocean,* March 13, 1895.

statements of those who are disposed to vilify Rome."[76] There
was no foundation for the newspaper rumors, Spalding told reporters, nor was he in the least on the hunt for a new diocese.[77]
But the talk persisted, and even greater credibility was given to
mere hearsay when the Reverend Edward R. Knowles, Protestant
Episcopalian minister in Worcester, Massachusetts, recently returned from abroad, was quoted in the Worcester *Telegram* as
saying that the first question that he had heard discussed while
in Rome was the possibility of redeeming the unfortunate reputation of the Archdiocese of Boston by the appointment of
Bishop Spalding as coadjutor-archbishop, "so as to make it possible for Catholicity to make real progress among New Englanders
independently of immigration." Spalding's courtesy, refinement,
and spirituality, Knowles observed, would be a charming contrast "to the scurrilous, ignorant and arrogant controversial style
of the pseudo-American clergy so plentiful in New England and
to their exuberant materialism and blindness to the spiritual
side of existence."[78] But the Protestant divine was to be disappointed, for when Spalding read the Knowles' statement he
simply sent it on to Bishop Ryan of Alton with the note that,
although there may very well have been some talk in Rome, he
was sure that the rumors originated with those who were un-
friendly to Archbishop Williams, and that it did not concern
him in the least.[79]

Regarding his candidacy for the rectorship, the *Catholic Citizen* had spoken of Spalding as "the only prelate who can succeed Bishop Keane with a popular impression engendered that
an improvement had been made,"[80] while the Washington correspondent of the St. Louis *Globe-Democrat* claimed that the
Germans, in the majority on the University's Board of Trustees,

[76] *The Congregationalist* (Boston), March 28, 1895.
[77] Chicago *Times-Herald,* April 6, 1895.
[78] Worcester *Telegram,* April 28, 1895.
[79] ADP, Spalding to Ryan, Peoria, May 5, 1895.
[80] *Catholic Citizen* (Milwaukee), October 10, 1896.

would select Spalding as the new rector.[81] Father Herman J. Heuser, editor of the *American Ecclesiastical Review,* had also thought Spalding to be "the most probable candidate."[82] But the speculation proved to be altogether idle, and on January 19, 1897, Father Thomas J. Conaty, pastor of Sacred Heart Church in Worcester, was installed as the second Rector of the Catholic University of America.[83] Spalding, meanwhile, remained in Peoria, where, in addition to his diocesan duties, he could keep abreast of contemporary currents of thought and where he was, as he put it, pleasantly situated.[84]

The American people had, in the meantime, elected their twenty-fifth president, William McKinley of Ohio. The defeated candidate was William Jennings Bryan, advocate of "Free Silver." Americans were soon to be distracted, however, from the domestic issue of gold or silver, for the spirit of Manifest Destiny was once more abroad in the land. In Europe, as British Colonial Secretary Joseph Chamberlain had remarked, the day of small nations had long since passed away, and the day of empires

[81] *Globe-Democrat* (St. Louis), cited by *Amerika* (St. Louis), October 13, 1896, quoted in Ahern, *op. cit.,* p. 190.

[82] UND, Hudson Papers, Heuser to Hudson, Overbrook, October 18, 1896.

[83] Peter E. Hogan, S.S.J., *The Catholic University of America, 1896–1903, The Rectorship of Thomas J. Conaty* (Washington, 1949), pp. 28–29. Father Philip J. Garrigan, Vice Rector of the University, had asked Spalding to attend the installation, but the latter told Hudson: "I could not think of going," and he added that Father Stone had written to his sister, Mrs. Richard Slevin, "that he went to Washington for the installation . . . and was thoroughly disgusted. Dr. Conaty himself, it seems, was a great disappointment to him . . ." Cf. UND, Hudson Papers, Spalding to Hudson, Peoria, February 7, 1897. Father James Kent Stone, known in religion as Father Fidelis, C.P., a convert from Episcopalianism, was ordained a priest in 1872 and shortly after became a Passionist, authored several works, and served for a time as a missionary in South America.

[84] Chicago *Times-Herald,* April 28, 1895.

had arrived.[85] While in America the path taken by Manifest Destiny differed from that of European imperialism, the ideology was fundamentally the same. Yellow journalism also fed the flames of American chauvinism, and on the eve of the Spanish-American War, the Washington *Post* wrote, "The taste of Empire is in the mouth of the people even as the taste of blood in the jungle. It means an Imperial policy, the Republic nascent, taking her place with the armed nations."[86]

The Cuban revolution of 1895 brought American chauvinism to a head, and gave rise to the demand that the entire Caribbean area be under American control. From the very beginning, the United States had been inextricably involved in the Cuban revolution, and in the three-year period, 1895–1898, a campaign of anti-Spanish propaganda ensued until finally, in behalf of humanity, America was forced to intervene. On April 25, 1898, Congress declared war.

Five days after the resolution, Spalding, vacationing in France, sailed from Le Havre,[87] and on May 8 he arrived in New York.[88] It would be a short war, Spalding told reporters on reaching Peoria, certainly ending by November, when the Republican Party would again be victorious at the polls. At that time, he said, Spain would be willing to come to terms.

At the time of his departure for Europe, however, Spalding would have thought a man foolish who insisted that before his return his country would be at war with Spain. The prospects at that time, he said, seemed to indicate that an amicable settlement between the two countries over the question of Cuba was still

[85] Geoffrey Bruun, *Nineteenth-Century European Civilization, 1815–1914* (New York, 1960), pp. 171–172. Joseph Chamberlain (1836–1914), a British statesman, was Colonial Secretary in the third Salisbury cabinet; he was the father of Sir Neville Chamberlain, Prime Minister, 1937–1940.

[86] Samuel Eliot Morison and Henry Steele Commager, *The Growth of the American Republic* (New York, 1942), II, p. 324.

[87] Quoted in *New World* (Chicago), April 30, 1898.

[88] New York *Times,* May 9, 1898.

249

possible, and there probably would not have been further trouble, he felt, had the *Maine* disaster not occurred. In any case, he continued, it was most unlikely that the Spanish were involved in the incident, since it was hardly in their interest to show spite for the Americans. In fact, the Cubans, fully aware of the war spirit in the United States, might very well have blown up the *Maine,* sensing that the blame would be placed on the mother country. This view was not his alone, Spalding remarked. Stewart L. Woodford, American Minister to Spain, and the attachés of the United States delegation in Madrid had also sailed on the *Touraine* for New York, and, he said, "they think as I do, that the Spanish had no hand in the blowing up of the *Maine,*" and were of the opinion that this was the work of Cubans. France likewise believed that Spain was not responsible for the loss of the American battleship, Spalding said, and had taken the position that "there were no grounds for war."[89]

Spalding's prediction on the length of the war was correct, for the "splendid little war," as John Hay wrote to his friend Theodore Roosevelt, lasted only one hundred and fifteen days. But for Spalding, the war was "a miserable thing." "God grant that no serious complications may arise," he wrote to Father Hudson.[90] He had already expressed the hope, in his Peoria interview, that the United States would not attempt to hold any of the possessions acquired during the war, especially Cuba and The Philippines, mainly because, as he said, "we could not pro-

[89] *New World* (Chicago), May 21, 1898. Stewart L. Woodford (1835–1913), Lieutenant Governor of New York, 1868–1870, member of Congress, 1872–1874, was Minister to Spain, 1897–1898. On arrival in New York, the Bishop was quoted as saying: "The feeling of the French towards Americans was intensely hostile . . . that the reason for this was that 8/10 of the public debt of Spain was held by the French people and that nearly all the railroads operated in Spain are owned by Frenchmen." Cf. New York *Times,* May 9, 1898.

[90] UND, Hudson Papers, Spalding to Hudson, Peoria, May 19, 1898.

tect them and also because it would complicate our politics and our form of government."[91]

This hope was not to be realized, however. By the treaty of peace signed in Paris on December 10, 1898, Spain relinquished all claim and title to Cuba, and ceded The Philippines, Guam, and Puerto Rico to the United States. An American empire was, in a sense, under way, for the treaty marked the first time that the United States, in acquiring new possessions, gave no promise of citizenship.[92]

A great number of Americans were, of course, opposed to the idea of an American empire. Less than a month before the peace treaty was signed, the Anti-Imperialist League had been organized in the Boston office of Edward Atkinson, retired textile manufacturer, with a view to preventing, "by every legitimate means, the acquisition of The Philippine Islands, or of any colonies away from our shores, by the United States." The hard core of what has been called "the first great national propaganda organization of the twentieth century" was composed of Boston bankers and lawyers, but there soon gathered about them "a nation-wide galaxy of literary lights, college presidents, leaders of industry and labor, editors, and politicians,"[93] and from the ranks of the Catholic hierarchy, John Lancaster Spalding. At its peak in 1899, the League claimed 30,000 members located in a dozen large cities from Boston to Portland, Oregon. The first political battle it fought, the only one in which the anti-imperialist came close to victory, was the heated debate over the ratification of the peace treaty with Spain in January and February 1899, and in particular over the controversial article which provided for the cession of The Philippine Islands to the United States. For the anti-imperialists, this was a simple matter of

[91] *New World* (Chicago), May 21, 1898.

[92] Julius W. Pratt, *A History of American Foreign Policy* (New York, 1956), pp. 388–389.

[93] Harold A. Larrabee, "The Enemies of Empire," *American Heritage*, XI (June, 1960), p. 77.

political morality, and though the Senate had ratified the treaty on February 6, 1899, they hoped to administer, by their continued agitation, "such a shock to sensitive American consciences that the burden of guilt could not be lifted."[94]

At the Creve Coeur Club banquet held in Peoria on Washington's birthday, 1899, Spalding spoke on true Americanism and the love of country.[95] He told an audience, said to be overwhelmingly imperialistic in sentiment, that there was a higher love than love of country, namely love of truth, for which the true patriot was willing to suffer, since only then could he rightly serve his country.[96] Americans were so accustomed, he said, to bow to the will of majorities that they easily forgot that votes counted for nothing when there was a question of truth, and where there was every likelihood that the minority was right and the majority wrong. They were dominated by the present, unwilling to wait, selfish, and very little influenced by large ideas and generous aims.[97] Men of this kind allowed themselves to be hypnotized "by glaring type and loud shouting," as was shown, Spalding remarked, "in the silver campaign when the bimetallists would have won had it not been for Hanna's millions and the terrorism exercised by the employers of labor . . ."[98] Little able to think for themselves, they resented independence of thought precisely in those matters where such thought was

[94] *Ibid.*, p. 80.

[95] J. L. Spalding, "The Patriot," in *Opportunity and Other Essays and Addresses* (Chicago, 1900), pp. 190–212. This address appeared first in the Peoria *Journal*, February 24, 1899. The newspaper version will be cited only when it is at variance with the revised text.

[96] *Ibid.*, p. 193.

[97] *Ibid.*, p. 202.

[98] Peoria *Journal*, February 24, 1899. Marcus [known as Mark] Alonzo Hanna (1837–1904) was known as an American businessman and politician and was reputed to have been McKinley's political mentor. Bimetallism was the doctrine that two metals should form the basis of the currency. The advocates of bimetallism were popularly known as "free silverites" since they favored the free coinage of silver at a ratio of sixteen to one.

most needed. The voices that expressed the ideas of the most serious minds were not only not heeded, they were drowned in the clamor of those who knew little, and who had at heart their own popularity and profit. Thus a public opinion was created, and the American people were commanded to accept it without question as the will of the nation. The highest government officials, when they yielded to the outcry of the mob, were commended for their wisdom and their patriotism, whereas, in fact, "our best minds do not guide us," the Bishop lamented, "our best men do not govern us."[99]

By faithful adherence to the principles upon which the nation had been founded, Americans had grown to be a prosperous and mighty people, and if success was an argument for continuing in a given line of policy and conduct, no people had so good a reason for following the old way. Though the country's material progress had been great, Spalding warned, love of principle and strength of moral conviction seemed to have grown feebler. With America comprising territory sufficient to support three hundred or more millions of human beings, why, Spalding asked,

should we go to the ends of the earth to take forcible possession of islands lying in remote oceans under tropical skies, inhabited by barbarous or savage tribes where both race and climate preclude the hope of ever attaining to any high degree of culture. Why should we own Cuba? We do not need it, its population is undesirable, and to hold it we must increase our army and navy and gradually drift into a militarism which must threaten our most cherished institutions. What can imperialism bring us except the menace of ruin and military rule?[100]

"It is not too late . . . it is still possible, probable even," Spalding later urged at the Chicago mass meeting of the Anti-Imperialist League in the Spring of 1899, "that the American people will reconsider the whole question of the complications

[99] Spalding, *op. cit.*, p. 203.
[100] *Ibid.*, p. 205.

in which our victories over Spain have involved us."[101] Spalding reminded his audience that the United States had not gone to war to become an empire, but to help others throw off the yoke of a tyrannical rule. Americans had never looked upon themselves as predestined to subdue the earth, to compel other nations to accept the American way of life. "We have always believed in human rights, in freedom and opportunity, in education and religion and we have invited all men to come to enjoy these blessings. . . ." But the people of this country had never dreamed, he warned, "that they were articles to be exported and thrust down unwilling throats at the point of a bayonet."[102] If no man was good enough to govern another without the other's consent, he remarked in a paraphrase of Lincoln's words, to say that the Filipino people were unfit for freedom was to put forth the plea of the tyrant in all ages and everywhere. Even if the inhabitants of The Philippine Islands came gladly and threw themselves into American arms, the United States should refuse to do more than to "counsel, guide and protect them until they form themselves into a stable and independent government." Yet he was aware there were those who seemed resolved to rule or to exterminate the Filipino people "believing probably that the only good Filipino is a dead Filipino."[103]

Some of the American imperialists he knew had argued that the policy of the United States had always been one of expansion, but the expansionists' plea had no place in the discussion of the present crisis. Manifest Destiny had purchased land, not human beings—land that was, in Spalding's view, part of the American inheritance—but now the United States was ready to buy in one stroke ten million human beings.[104] "If it is our

[101] J. L. Spalding, "Empire or Republic," in *Opportunity*, p. 214. This address was delivered at the Central Club in Chicago on April 30, 1899.

[102] *Ibid.*, p. 215.

[103] *Ibid.*, p. 216.

[104] *Ibid.*, p. 218

destiny to become an empire," he insisted, "it is not our destiny to endure as a republic." Imperialism may have proved a blessing to Great Britain, but in this matter there was no parity between England and the United States. Britain's widely scattered dominions, though possibly necessary for her existence as a first-class power, were also a cause of weakness, for "let her colonies but become dissatisfied," Spalding predicted, "and they will fall from her as easily as the ripe fruit falls from the bough." Britain governed her colonies wisely, he added, "because only in this way can she govern them at all."[105]

While Spalding granted that it was hardly possible for any American to speak of England and not to be grateful to that country for the liberties and language bequeathed by it to the American continent, nevertheless he urged the United States to remain aloof from Great Britain, since it

. . . has not an ally in the world, and there is probably not a nation in the world which would trust her as an ally. She has never loved us from the days in which she oppressed the colonies to the dark days when, by aiding the Confederacy, she sought to make the disruption of the Union permanent. She does not love us now. We are the most dreaded rival she has, because we threaten her supremacy in what is nearest and dearest to her—her finances.[106]

When the American people resolved not to hold what they had never intended to take possession of, Spalding concluded, there would be no difficulty in finding a solution to the Philippine dilemma. "Let them not hearken to the siren voice of English flattery; let them not stop to think what other nations will say," but rather let them remember that the true work of the American people lies at home and not ten thousand miles away, for in the success of the American experiment the hopes for a higher life were centered. "If we fail, the world fails," Spalding cautioned, "if we succeed, we shall do more for the good of all

[105] *Ibid.*, p. 224.
[106] Spalding, "Empire or Republic," pp. 224–225.

men than if we conquered all the islands and continents," for in Spalding's judgment it was the mission of the Americans to show that popular government was compatible with the best culture, the purest religion, the highest justice, and "that it can permanently endure."[107]

Reaction to Bishop Spalding's stirring address was widespread but varied. The Washington *Post,* which played courtier to the McKinley administration, alluded to the Bishop's views as "a good man's mistakes," and singled out the statement that, to emancipate the slave, the United States had gladly sacrificed the lives of thousands of its soldiers, but now "the American soldier, who should never shoulder a gun in an unrighteous cause, is sent 10,000 miles across the ocean to shoot men whose real crime is that they wish to be free, wish to govern themselves." The *Post* dismissed Spalding's "dash into history" as anti-expansionist zeal which clouded his recollection of historical facts and distorted his views of current events. This was true inasmuch as the war for the Union had not been "an abolition war," the *Post* declared, "and slavery was abolished, not as an object, but as an incident of the war."[108] In a "Letter from the South" to the *Catholic Mirror* of Baltimore, a special correspondent replied to the Washington paper that, of course, slavery was abolished as an incident of war, but it was one of the incidents that had made the war inevitable. "The Bishop of Peoria is not in the habit of making historical mistakes," the correspondent said, "and if he should deem it worthwhile he may easily run the *Post* to cover." The squealing of the imperialists, he concluded, simply indicated that Bishop Spalding had touched them on the raw when he had convicted them of their horrible paradox.[109] The *Catholic Times* of London congratulated Spalding for his

107 *Ibid.,* p. 228.

108 ADP, Spalding clippings, Washington *Post,* May 6, 1899.

109 ADP, Spalding clippings, *Catholic Mirror* (Baltimore), May 13, 1899.

"plain, unvarnished truth" and expressed the hope that Americans would take to heart the lessons taught by the eloquent prelate.[110] But when William Henry Thorne, convert-editor of the *Globe,* reviewed the speech, he moaned, "It came too late . . . Why in God's name did he not speak in time? It is too late my dear Bishop Spalding. We have committed the irretraceable blunder of a great nation when we went into this war with Spain . . ."[111]

While Spalding was thus decrying what he considered a distortion of the American way of life, there was a growing fear in some European circles that the adolescent irresponsibility of the American people had had an ecclesiastical parallel, and counter-forces had already arisen which sought to halt what some looked upon as a basic aberration in the development of American Catholicism. From the outset, the war with Spain had not been one, Spalding had remarked, in which religion was to play any role, and although Leo XIII had attempted to intervene to prevent the war, his efforts, Spalding believed, had been in vain because he was too late.[112] Cardinal Rampolla had, indeed, contacted Archbishop Ireland through Archbishop Keane, requesting him to do all in his power to prevent the impending hostilities, since "the danger of a conflict between the United States and Spain," the Secretary of State told Keane, "has caused His Holiness as well as all Catholics great anxiety."[113] But Pope Leo's attempts for peace, as a saddened Ireland informed O'Connell, had not been started soon enough.[114] And, in fact, religion had played its part in the sense that to many Europeans,

[110] ADP, Spalding clippings, *Catholic Times* (London), n.d., quoted in Ave Maria, n.v. (June 17, 1899), n.p.

[111] *The Globe* (St. Louis), IX (June 10, 1899), p. 130.

[112] *New World* (Chicago), May 21, 1898.

[113] Rampolla to Keane, Rome, March 27, 1898, quoted in McAvoy, *op. cit.,* p. 205.

[114] ADR, Ireland to O'Connell, May 2, 1898. Cf. Moynihan, *op. cit.,* pp. 162–176, for Ireland's role in attempting to avoid war.

American aggression against Catholic Spain had simply accentuated their fears concerning the so-called Americanizing tendencies of some "liberal" Catholic leaders in the United States.

For Monsignor O'Connell, however, his country's war with Spain was but a symbol of the future of the importance of the Anglo-Saxon world. "Force upon the Curia by the great triumph of Americanism," he urged Ireland, "that recognition of English-speaking people that you know is needed." It was not simply a question of Cuba, but a matter of much greater moment, the question of two civilizations. "It is," O'Connell believed, "the question of all that is old and vile & mean & rotten & cruel & false in Europe against all this [*sic*] is free & noble & open & true & humane in America." When Spain was swept off the sea, he was confident, much of the meanness of Europe would be replaced by the freedom and openness of America. It was a war against Europe itself, "and that is why they are all against us and Rome more than all," he insisted, because when the prestige of Spain and Italy will have passed, the pivot of the world's political action will no longer be confined within the limits of the continent, and "then the nonsense of trying to govern the universal church from a European standpoint . . . according to exclusively Spanish and Italian methods" would be evident. Neither Italy nor Spain would ever furnish the principles of the civilization of the future. God had now passed the banner to the hands of the United States to bear it in the cause of humanity, "and it is your office," he told the Archbishop of St. Paul, "to make its destiny known to America. . . ." O'Connell would have John Ireland become its grand chaplain, "God's Apostle in modern times to Church and Society."[115]

In the opinion of many European Catholics, it might well be but a brief jump from an unduly enthusiastic O'Connell to an Emile Zola, who less than two years before had been quoted in the Paris *Figaro* as saying, "Out there in America what a virgin

[115] AASP, O'Connell to Ireland, Rome, May 24, 1898.

and fruitful soil for a triumphant heresy! How easily can one imagine Mgr. Ireland some fine morning raising the standard of revolt, making himself the apostle of a new religion, freed from Dogma, more human, the religion that our democracies are awaiting."[116] It was an unwarranted fear, perhaps, a ridiculous conclusion, but as the United States prepared to embark on the adventurous path of imperialism, Pope Leo XIII dispatched to Cardinal Gibbons and the American Church, on January 22, 1899, the apostolic letter *Testem benevolentiae*. While it was nominally sent as a token of the Pontiff's affection, it warned of certain views "which some comprise under the head of Americanism," and which raised "the suspicion that there are some among you who conceive of and desire a church in America different from that which is in the rest of the world."[117] Thus, as the nineteenth century came to a close, the American bishops received a reminder that, while they should, indeed, glory like the Fathers in council in Baltimore some fifteen years before, they should bear in mind that they were "not the American Church, nor the Church in the United States nor a Church in any other sense exclusive or limited, but an integral part of the one, holy, catholic and apostolic Church . . ."[118]

[116] *The Review,* III (January 2, 1896), p. 2. Arthur Preuss quoted the Paris *Figaro.* Emile Zola (1840–1902) was the French novelist and propagandist whose work on *Lourdes* in the series called the *Trilogy of Three Cities* had been upon publication in 1894 listed in the Index of Prohibited Books. It was about the same time that Zola wrote: "The Catholic movement in the United States interests me greatly, I confess, and if I cross the ocean, it is one of the questions that I shall investigate." Cf. New York *Times,* November 4, 1894.

[117] Ellis, *Documents,* pp. 561–562.

[118] *A History of the Third Plenary Council of Baltimore, op. cit.*

7

At the Crossroads

BISHOP Spalding's immediate reaction to *Testem benevolentiae* was brief. It had again been announced in the New York *Sun*, he wrote to Father Hudson, that Archbishop Ireland was to be made a cardinal. "I should be glad to see him made anything," Spalding commented irritably, "that would keep him silent"; to which he added, "I feel very sorry for poor Father Elliott."[1] For the question had been asked whether Father Isaac Hecker was a saint, and in the course of the discussion the term "Americanism" had rallied both defenders and opponents of a policy that Ireland, among others, had ostensibly championed as a portent of the increased importance of the American way in the life of the universal Church.

Occasion for the question was the French translation and adaptation of *The Life of Father Hecker* by Father Walter Elliott, C.S.P., with an introduction by Archbishop Ireland and a preface by the Abbé Félix Klein, a professor in the Catholic Institute of Paris.[2] In the compressed French version introduced by Klein's enthusiastic preface, both the aims and the methods

[1] UND, Hudson Papers, Spalding to Hudson, Peoria, March 1, 1899.

[2] *Le Père Hecker, Fondateur des "Paulists" Américains, 1819–1888 par Le Père W. Elliott de la même Compagnie. Traduit et adapté de l'anglais avec autorisation de l'auteur. Introduction par Mgr. Ireland. Preface par l'Abbé Félix Klein* (Paris, 1897). Klein had already translated some of Archbishop Ireland's discourses into French. Cf. *L'Eglise et le Siècle, conferences et discours de Mgr. Ireland, publ. avec une preface par l'Abbé Klein* (Paris, 1894).

of the Paulists' founder had been exaggerated and in some details carelessly expressed. But with its European publication in 1897, the biography of the Yankee convert who had achieved great success as a *convertisseur* in Protestant America became extremely popular among the younger French clergy. Heckerism, or the "Anglo-Saxon mystique," was spoken of as a kind of muscular Christianity which centered on the exaltation of the natural over the supernatural virtues. Sharp criticism had soon appeared in the pages of *Vérité française* by the Abbé Georges Peries, formerly Professor of Canon Law in the Catholic University of America, and by the Abbé Charles Maignen of the Congregation of the Brothers of St. Vincent de Paul. Maignen's denunciations, published in book form with a Roman *imprimatur* under the title, *Etudes sur l'Américanisme, le Pére Hecker, est-il un saint?*, had served as catalyst and precipitated a crisis in American Catholic circles.[3]

[3] The literature on Americanism is voluminous, but is to a great extent synthesized in McAvoy, *The Great Crisis,* which is the best general account to date. Both terms, "Americanism" and "phantom heresy," were in a sense unfortunate. McAvoy felt compelled to distinguish at least three types of Americanism. The first was that political Americanism which was a byword in the United States for patriotism and devotion to the political and social ideals of the country. It was the tacit approval of Ireland, Keane, and O'Connell for the French Hecker that led to a second type of Americanism labeled the "phantom heresy" garnered from Klein's preface and the compressed translation and which was reprobated by Pope Leo XIII in *Testem benevolentiae*. In the mind of the so-called Americanists, the ideas which the French liberal press culled from the biography were, however, but a caricature of the real ideals of Hecker and the so-called Americanists. Finally, there were certain tendencies which had divided the American hierarchy into disparate camps and which European liberals took out of context and rationalized into the principles condemned by Pope Leo. According to McAvoy, the bitterness of the controversy grew out of the effort of certain writers and ecclesiastics to make the first and third types of Americanism as well as the second come under the condemnation of the

Hecker, thought to be a forerunner of Americanism, if not its founder, believed that American Catholicism had to take on the behavior patterns of its environment, that the Gospel was to be preached in circumstances never quite tested before, that, in short, American Catholicism was and had to be structurally different, not in beliefs, but socially and politically, from continental Catholicism. His attempt, however, to initiate a closer understanding between the Church and the society wherein it existed as a prelude to their integration was aborted in the circumstances terminating in *Testem benevolentiae.*

For Spalding, the external aspects of the controversy were but an invitation to the Church in the United States to ask itself what it really was, since Americanism, he thought, represented both a moral and an intellectual crisis that demanded a rethinking, a reappraisal of how the Church was to organize itself to fulfill its purpose more fully by a deepening self-knowledge, and by a logical development of the old to suit the new. This, at any rate, was his theme some eight months after the apostolic letter was issued, when, on October 13, 1899, he gave the principal address at the dedication of Holy Cross College, a house of studies for the members of the Congregation of Holy Cross adjacent to the campus of the Catholic University of America. In a mood of self-examination and self-criticism, he spoke on "The University: A Nursery of the Higher Life," in words which, as

Pope's letter. Cf. McAvoy, "Americanism, Fact and Fiction," *Catholic Historical Review,* XXXI (July, 1945), pp. 133–135. According to one theologian, the *Testem benevolentiae* stigmatized neither any individual opinion of which it disapproved nor the sum total of these repudiated teachings with the note of heresy, since neither the term "heretical" nor its definition was to be found anywhere in the documents. On this point alone, the author concluded, "the designation 'phantom heresy' cannot be applied accurately to the teaching rejected in the *Testem benevolentiae* . . ." Cf. Joseph Clifford Fenton, "The Teaching of the *Testem benevolentiae,*" *AER,* CXXIX (August, 1953), p. 126.

Alfred Lilley has remarked, "only an American could have spoken, which at least only an American had any right to speak."[4] The lesson had become plain long before the crisis over Americanism had arisen; the way to profit was equally as plain, for the task remained the same: how was the Church to grow?

Since much spiritual activity was to be found outside of the Church, the Catholic religion, Spalding warned, will cease to be a power in the world unless Catholics themselves became morally and intellectually alive. They must learn to understand that it was more important that they do good than that they should do it in a particular way, more necessary that they should think than that they should think alike. Catholics seemed to have grown timid as though they feared human opinion might prevail over divine truth, but they must learn to walk without fear in the midst of a world of ever-widening knowledge since, he insisted, there was nothing in the Catholic faith that should impede advance in any department of learning.[5]

If ever men of exceptional intellectual and moral strength were needed, Spalding continued, they were needed by American Catholics, thrown as a minority[6] burdened with disadvantages into the midst of the eager, self-confident, and all-prevailing democracy of the new world. Here the Church lived and acted in virtue of its own power, neither having nor desiring the support of the state, content to lack the privileges which in other ages resulted from social conditions unlike those of the American milieu. "We could not have these privileges if we would and could we have them," Spalding warned his audience, "they would hurt, not help us."[7] It was enough that American Catholics had the rights which in a free country belonged to all alike—free-

[4] Alfred Leslie Lilley, *Modernism, A Record and Review* (New York, 1908), p. 109.

[5] Spalding, *op. cit.*, pp. 73–74.

[6] *Ibid.*, p. 87

[7] *Ibid.*, p. 88.

dom to teach, to publish, to organize, to worship where the Church was free, "free in the only way in which it is now possible to be free," he believed, and that was "free in the midst of the general liberty of a free people." That liberty had its dangers, he granted, but to lament that Catholics had fallen on evil days would indicate both a lack of knowledge and a lack of faith. "Things have never been right in this world," he said. "God made it, not we. Let us take it and do the best we can."[8]

There was, Spalding believed, a twofold task to perform. American Catholics had to upbuild and establish the Church firmly in the new world of universal opportunity and tumultuous passions; they must also do their part in purifying, uplifting, and civilizing the masses to which they belonged in American society. Knowledge alone would not suffice, and mere philosophic morality had no significance for the multitude because the moral dynamics of a people lay in its religion just as society rested on conscience and not on science. Since the Catholic view of education was the result of genuine insight into man's true nature, the vital question which American Catholics must ask themselves was, he said, how to make Catholic schools centers of moral influence.[9]

If Catholics in the United States were to have good primary and secondary schools, good academies and colleges, Spalding declared, they must first have genuine universities. It was a happy omen, he noted, when Notre Dame of the West came to open Holy Cross College to affirm, as it were, that the American Church should have not only a Catholic university, but a "school of schools, a mother of universities," a center about which the teaching orders could gather, just as Trinity College was then rising under the shadow of the university to be "a monumental witness to our faith in the right of woman to upbuild her being to its full stature, to learn whatever may be known, to do what-

[8] *Ibid.*
[9] *Ibid.,* p. 98.

ever right things she may find herself able to do."[10] There were, he acknowledged, some American Catholics who stood with averted faces ever looking backward to Europe, but he for one was not impressed:

What sacredness is there in Europe more than in America? Is not the history of Europe largely a history of wars, tyrannies, oppressions, massacres, and persecutions? . . . Has not its people long stood face to face, arms in hand, ready to butcher one another? Why should Europe be an object of awe or admiration for Catholics? Half its population has revolted from the church, and in the so-called Catholic nations, which are largely governed by atheists, what vital manifestation of religious life and power can we behold?[11]

Reaction to Spalding's address was mixed. While the Bishop of Peoria was still speaking, Archbishop Martinelli, the Apostolic Delegate, listened, an eyewitness reported,[12] in apparent discomfort, staring stiffly ahead while a mischievous Archbishop Ireland from time to time slyly glanced to the rear where Archbishop Corrigan sat seemingly annoyed. Father Charles F. Grannan, Professor of Scripture in the Catholic University of America, wrote to Denis O'Connell shortly after the affair that there "was hardly anything worth mentioning" except for "John Lancaster's sarcasm and his cuts and slashes . . . at the dedication of Zahm's college." He added that, while all regarded it as "bold and some did not like it," Americanism was hardly mentioned except when the press continued "to pitch into Katzer and his crowd."[13] Soon printed in pamphlet form, the discourse was praised by William Henry Thorne, the erratic editor

[10] *Ibid.*, pp. 106–107.

[11] *Ibid.*, p. 107.

[12] Interview of the author with the late Rev. Joseph McSorley, C.S.P., New York, October 16, 1960.

[13] ADR, Grannan to O'Connell, Hartford, October, 1899. The day was not specified. Zahm was Father John A. Zahm, C.S.C., the newly appointed Provincial of the Congregation of Holy Cross and a friend of the Americanists.

of the *Globe,* who saw in it "a new voice of God speaking to the bewildered . . . a new and inspired gospel for the hide-bound ecclesiasticism of the day."[14] Thus Spalding contributed his share, as John Tracy Ellis has written, "in helping to lay the ghost of what was called by some the 'phantom heresy'. . . ."[15]

In February 1900, the Spalding address would momentarily resurrect that ghost in European circles, when the *Revue du Clergé Française* published it in translation under the title "Mission Vitale de L'Université."[16] Its translator, the Abbé Klein, was said to have "discovered" the Peoria Bishop while executing his work, so that one no longer read of Hecker, or of Ireland, in the Americanism controversy, the Abbé later recalled, but of one whose name was new for an old world, Spalding, "a man of faith, intelligence and character the like of which one rarely sees in any country."[17]

About two months after the dedication of Holy Cross College, Spalding sailed for Rome,[18] where, on February 2, 1900, Leo XIII granted him an audience.[19] As Spalding later recounted to

[14] *The Globe,* XXXIX–XL (September–December, 1960), p. 243. Thorne added: "Long live the Bishop of Peoria. Let him hang all his so-called poetry on a sour apple tree, and utter and reutter such prose. . . ."

[15] John Tracy Ellis, *John Lancaster Spalding, First Bishop of Peoria: American Educator* (Washington, 1962), p. 73.

[16] J. L. Spalding, "Mission Vitale de L'Université," in *Revue du Clergé Français,* XXI (February 15, 1900), pp. 597–619.

[17] Félix Klein, *La Route du Petit Morvandiau, Souvenirs de L'Abbé Félix Klein. Sans Arrêt* (Paris, 1949), V, pp. 39–40. Hereafter these memoirs will be cited as Klein, *Sans Arrêt.*

[18] Cf. ADR, Mamie G. Caldwell des Monstiers-Mérinville to D. J. O'Connell, Paris, November 29, 1899. The Marquise wrote: "The Bishop has consented at last to come over this winter and will sail on Jan. 10th." Cf. also, *New World* (Chicago), January 6, 1900. Six weeks or more after the dedication of Holy Cross College, the Bishop spoke on "Opportunity" at the opening of Spalding Institute in Peoria, December 6, 1899. Cf. Spalding, *Opportunity,* pp. 7–44.

[19] Cf. "Chronology," in *AER,* XXIII (July, 1900), p. 56.

Father Elliott, the Pope asked him about Americanism, and he replied that no such errors were taught or believed in the United States. "That is what many American Bishops have written to me," the Pope was quoted as saying, "but there was that poor Hecker, he taught the guidance of the Holy Spirit without the Sacraments." To this Spalding responded, "Holy Father, I knew Father Hecker well and intimately, and he was a holy, disinterested, zealous and enlightened priest. I am certain that he never believed or taught what they accuse him of."[20] Spalding further confided to Monsignor O'Connell that he had told the Pope that the Americanism he condemned did not exist in America, and that the faith of the American Catholics was the same as the Pontiff's own. "Oh, it was that Hecker," Leo XIII reportedly retorted, but Spalding asked, "Holy Father, did you know Hecker?" When the Pope answered in the negative, Spalding replied, "Well then, I did and a better Catholic we never had."[21] It was a view that undoubtedly pleased the former Rector of the American College, who had already informed Archbishop Ireland, "I see a good deal of Riordan and Spalding. I may get the latter to come out soon. He is taking in things well—things he never took in before."[22]

The Bishop of Peoria did, indeed, "come out," when on March 21, 1900, in the Church of the Gesù at Rome, Spalding spoke on the subject of "Education and the Future of Religion,"[23] in what

[20] APF, Americanism File, "Reflections of Father Walter Elliott, St. Bede College. Peru, Ill., Ill., June 26, 1900." In a characteristic gesture after his return from Europe, Spalding had invited the Paulist to give the annual retreat for the diocesan clergy.

[21] AASP, O'Connell to Ireland, Rome, March 23, 1900.

[22] AASP, Same to Same, Rome, February 28, 1900.

[23] The Gesù discourse, as it was called, was first published in pamphlet form and was later included as Chapter V in J. L. Spalding, *Religion, Agnosticism and Education* (Chicago, 1902), pp. 147–192. The latter work will be cited.

has been described as his "most notable pulpit performance."[24] It was a sermon that contained, in the opinion of a friendly reporter, "the pure essence of Americanist ideas,"[25] a clear presentation of the attitude of those churchmen who believed that the teacher of religion must live in the current century, must fit the garb of faith to the latest truth discovered and must be a leader in the world about him. After stating his position on the question of higher education for women,[26] Spalding proceeded with the main theme, the relation of the Church to science and developing truth. He assured his audience that while he held fast to the principle of authority, the health of the Church depended on the ability of Catholics to acknowledge this authority without sinking into a deadening uniformity. Man's mind was free and had the right to inquire into and learn whatever might be investigated and known. If the Church was to live and prosper in the modern world, Catholicism, too, must have freedom not only to learn, but also to teach. Philosophic, scientific, and historical problems could be solved only by human research, and if Catholics hoped to present their supernatural beliefs to an age of civilization and culture, they must not neglect the chief means to put to good use their God-given talents. Nothing must be left undone, therefore, to provide Catholics with schools equal to the best, for if they isolated themselves from the highest intellectual and moral life of the world around them, he warned, they would

[24] Ellis, *Spalding*, p. 78.

[25] Monsignor Eugène Boeglin, the Roman agent of the Associated Press for Catholic news, whose articles in praise of Archbishop Ireland and the Americanizers were published in the New York *Sun* under the pen name "Innominato," had written in the *Journal de Génève*, May 31, 1900, that the Gesù discourse contained "*la pure moelle des idées américanistes.*" Quoted in Emile Barbier, *Histoire du Catholicisme libéral et social* (Bordeaux, 1924), III, p. 309.

[26] Spalding, *Religion, Agnosticism and Education*, pp. 152–153.

drift into a position of inferiority and lose the power to make themselves heard and understood.[27]

In her past, Spalding noted, the Church had always been able to take to herself what was true and good in pagan philosophy and culture, and if an Augustine and an Aquinas had known how to compel Plato and Aristotle to become helpers in the cause of Christ, why should Catholics now lose heart? The Church had not lost the faculty of assimilation, he insisted, and could always adapt herself to the demands of an ever-evolving environment. Human error could never prevail against God's truth which did not need the defense of concealment, of sophistical apology, or of lies. True, there was always danger of error and mistake, but they who dared must take risks since danger could be overcome only by encountering danger. The new times, he believed, demanded new men, and the ancient faith, if it were to be held vitally, must be commended with fresh vigor and defended with all the arguments which the best philosophy, science, and literature might suggest.[28] As a spiritual power, the Church must bring forth new things or the old would fall into discredit. It was imperative, therefore, that Catholics be prepared to meet all adversaries, to make reply to all objections if they would spread the faith. "We must think before we can think alike," he urged, "we must strive to understand those who differ from us for agreement is possible only when we understand one another."[29] To forbid men to think along different lines would only hinder the possibility of their meeting other minds, and would place Catholics in opposition to the deepest and most invincible tendency of the civilized world. Were it possible to compel obedience from Catholics in matters of this kind, they would "more and more drift away from the vital movements of

[27] *Ibid.,* pp. 154–158 and *passim.*
[28] *Ibid.,* pp. 159–165 and *passim.*
[29] *Ibid.,* p. 172.

the age," he warned, and in the end they would find themselves "immured in a spiritual ghetto."[30]

Many men, Spalding maintained, were already confused amid problems which the new sciences had raised, and they had begun to wonder whether human life would not be emptied of its spiritual content. If Catholics hoped to commend and enforce revealed truth efficaciously, they must be prepared to do so in the full blaze of the light which research and discovery afforded, and if in consequence, he insisted,

we find it necessary to abandon positions which are no longer defensible, to assume new attitudes in the face of new conditions, we must remember that though the Church is a divine institution, it is none the less subject to the law which makes human things mutable, that though truth must remain the same it is capable of receiving fresh illustration, and that if it is to be life giving, it must be wrought anew into the constitution of each individual and of each age.[31]

Since there was nothing, Spalding believed, that was not to be investigated and discussed, nothing that was not to be called into question and to be considered from every point of view, there was no need of "new devotions and new shrines," but rather a "new spirit, newness of life, a revivification of faith, hope and love, fresh courage and will to lay hold on the source of power,"[32] that Catholics might compel all knowledge and science to do homage to Christ. There was a need, therefore, for self-criticism, for Catholics to see not only things as "they are but themselves also" lest decay and degeneracy set it. They must be ever watchful that a genuine and wholesome development of life and doctrine did not give way to a false and morbid evolution; yet ceaseless vigilance was not the price of liberty alone, but the price all must pay for spiritual good, since "how shall we ever be vigilant," he asked, "if we are forbidden to criticize

30 *Ibid.*, p. 175.
31 *Ibid.*, p. 177
32 *Ibid.*, p. 182.

ourselves and the environment by which Catholic life is nourished and protected?"[33]

If the education which once might have sufficed for the Catholic was no longer sufficient, Spalding continued, how much more so for Christ's priests? The priest must be prepared to show himself as Christ's minister not only at the altar, in the pulpit, or in the confessional; he needed the breeding and culture to make him a leader in all spiritual movements, cognizant on whatever subjects of vital import to human welfare. Thus the priest must best commend his sacramental power, Spalding believed, not by emphasizing it, not by calling attention to it, but by leaving nothing undone whereby he might make himself a true and helpful man. He must not confine himself within monastic walls, not rest content with a culture and discipline merely theological and ascetical; rather he must go forth into the world as a guide and leader—into a world controlled by opinion, dominated by aims and ideals which more and more must be brought into harmony with the truth and love revealed in Christ. To win men for Christ, the priest must have sympathy with them; to gain their good will and confidence, he must make them understand that he is able and eager to help them. Only then would it come to pass, he said, that laymen would take an active interest in the welfare and progress of the Church, and find it possible again to cooperate with the priesthood in the cause of religion and civilization.[34]

Bishop Spalding assured his Roman audience that he spoke from the point of view of an American Catholic which seemed to him to be the only view which was or should be taken in the English-speaking Catholic world, since

In the ever-widening domain of the British Empire, in the ever-growing territory of the American Republic, democracy is triumphant; and in all these vast regions with the exception of the Anglican . . . and

[33] *Ibid.*, p. 183
[34] *Ibid.*, pp. 186–188 and *passim.*

271

Scottish Establishment, there is a separation of Church and State; a separation which those who are competent to judge recognize as permanent. There is everywhere freedom to write, to publish, to discuss, to organize; and there is no subject of thought, no sphere of action, no interest which it is possible to fence about and shut in from the all-searching breath of liberty.[35]

It was a condition of things which existed; every influence maintained and strengthened it, and as far as he was able to see, it did not appear that any earthly power could change or destroy it. It was a state of things that English-speaking Catholics accepted without mental reservations, without misgivings, without regrets which were always idle. Since the Catholic revival had begun in the English-speaking world, twenty million or more Catholics, he estimated, had built in fifty years probably as many churches, schools, convents, and institutions of charity as the rest of the more than 200,000,000 Catholics. There had, indeed, been losses to the faith in the United States, but they were to be traced, he stressed, largely to the indifference or ignorance of many who had come from countries that were called Catholic. Thus the root of the evil lay elsewhere than in the English-speaking world where the progress of Catholicism was real, where Catholics felt that the Church must be a school as well as a house of prayer, that God was in the world ever ready to help those who were willing to help themselves, where Catholics lived with the old truths, while they walked unafraid in the midst of the new and recognized that the Catholic religion was a life to be lived, more even than a doctrine to be taught and believed, "for only they who seek life in life, whose faith is action, whose hope is joy and strength, whose love is fruitful," Spalding concluded, "can rightly understand and hold the divine truth which Christ came into the world to make known."[36]

[35] *Ibid.*, pp. 188–189.
[36] *Ibid.*, p. 192

Hardly had Bishop Spalding descended from the pulpit than his discourse became the latest Roman sensation, for never before, the Abbé Albert Houtin later wrote, had the walls of the Gesù resounded with such trenchant tones as on that Spring day, when the Bishop gave his answer to *Testem benevolentiae.*[37] "My how Spalding has sounded the bugle!" O'Connell informed Archbishop Ireland. To O'Connell, Spalding was now "fully enlisted for the war," and he favored "a moral union of English-speaking Catholics throughout the world."[38] Still ruminating on the subject a week later, the Monsignor reported to Ireland that things had been "agitated ever since," and that "one half would crown" Spalding for the honesty with which he spoke "the faith that is in him," while the other half "would burn him" when at every point in the sermon "he hit up against something, and hit hard." Spalding, he believed, was in the field to stay.[39] For O'Connell, this was an exciting prospect. For Archbishop Ireland, however, it was to prove to be a matter of great concern.

In early April, accompanied by Mamie Caldwell, the Marquise des Monstiers-Merinville, Spalding left for Florence, where he visited with the Church historian, Father Franz Xaver

[37] Albért Houtin, *L'Américanisme* (Paris, 1904), p. 435. Albért Houtin (1867–1927), ordained a priest in 1891, became an assistant preacher at Saint-Sulpice in Paris, but lost the post after his book, *La Question Biblique chez les Catholiques de France au XIXme Siècle,* was put on the Index. One of the leaders of French modernism, Houtin later apostatized from the faith. According to McAvoy, *The Great Crisis,* p. 367, most studies of Americanism have begun with Houtin's documented study since he "wrote soon enough after the events to have personal knowledge of many of the participants and to have access to a wealth of printed materials, especially the newspapers and magazines in which most of the discussion was conducted."

[38] AASP, O'Connell to Ireland, Rome, March 23, 1900.

[39] Same to Same, Rome, April 1, 1900. "Achilles" was O'Connell's nickname for Spalding.

Kraus.[40] An able scholar, friendly to the Americanist cause, Kraus was also the author of the sensational "Spectator Letters" in the *Beilage zur Allgemeinem Zeitung,* in which he had attacked the integralists' position with great severity.[41] O'Connell had already written to Kraus about Spalding's Gesù sermon, and on the eve of the Bishop's visit the historian noted in his diary that Spalding had often read the "Spectator," and that someone had quipped that, with his sermon, the "Spectator" had gone up into the Gesù's pulpit.[42] For three days, Kraus and Spalding exchanged views on the Jesuits, papal power, and the lack of freedom and "ecumenicity" in the Church since the Vatican Council, and discovered, said Kraus, that their views of the ecclesiastical situation were "wholly identical." Delighted with Spalding, Kraus characterized him as "ingenious, richer in learning, freer and nobler in spirit . . . the most sensible, upright character that I have come to know among the bishops of the world, my man entirely, and *all* man."[43] It was a generous appraisal after so short a visit, over-enthusiastic perhaps, and one hardly calculated to endear the Bishop of Peoria to those who considered integralism and Catholicism one and the same thing.[44]

[40] Hubert Schiel (ed.), *Franz Xaver Kraus Tagebücher* (Koln, 1957), p. 734. On April 4, 1900, Kraus wrote: "I shall wait for the bishop's visit here on the day after tomorrow. . . ." Hereafter this work will be cited as *Kraus Tagebücher.*

[41] Friedrich Lauchert, "Kraus, Franz Xaver," in *CE,* VIII, pp. 699–700. Kraus (1840–1901) succeeded Johann Alzog in 1878 as professor of Church History in the University of Freiburg im Breisgau.

[42] *Kraus Tagebücher,* p. 734.

[43] *Ibid.,* pp. 734–735.

[44] Cf. Umberto Benigni, "Ultramontanism," in *CE,* XV, p. 125. According to Benigni, Ultramontanism denoted integral and active Catholicism, that is, "papal, anti-liberal and counter-revolutionary Catholicism." He censured Kraus for his "Spectator Letter II" in which the historian had defined an Ultramontane as "one who sets the idea of the Church above that of religion; who substitutes the Pope for the Church; who believes that the kingdom of God is of this world and

From Florence, Spalding traveled on to Milan,[45] where he met, among others, the Countess Sabina di Parravicino di Revel,[46] the Italian translator of several of Archbishop Ireland's lectures and an important contributor to *Rassegna Nazionale,* Milan's liberal journal. Soon to translate the Gesù discourse into Italian, the Countess noted the contrast between the two American prelates. As she told Denis O'Connell, "Ireland is a volcano . . . ; Spalding will be a great man, but he is an icicle in comparison to that eruption."[47] Meanwhile, O'Connell had informed the Abbé Klein of Spalding's impending visit to Paris, and asked him to send the Bishop a hundred copies of "Mission Vitale de L'Université." The irrepressible Monsignor was warm in praise of Spalding, whom he described as "most cultured and very courageous." He added that the Bishop, a great admirer of Hecker whom he had known personally, had not been in the least concerned with politics while in Rome, and had met only with the better type minds who had interested him for their personal

that, as medieval curialism asserted, the power of the keys, given to Peter, included temporal jurisdiction . . . ; who believes that religious conviction can be imposed or broken with material force; who is ever ready to sacrifice to an extraneous authority the plain teaching of his own conscience." Integralism and Ultramontanism were interchangeable terms, and Benigni insisted that "for Catholics it would be superfluous to ask whether Ultramontanism and Catholicism are the same thing: assuredly those who combat Ultramontanism are in fact combating Catholicism, even when they disclaim the desire to oppose it." If Kraus and Spalding were in complete agreement, *ganz identisch,* the Bishop, it would seem, would have fallen under the same censure. On Benigni, cf. W. Peters, *The Life of Benedict XV,* Milwaukee, 1959, pp. 46–52.

[45] ADR, Spalding to O'Connell, Paris, May 3, 1900. Spalding wrote: "My visit to Milan was delightful but I got the grip [sic] there and have been ill since."

[46] Sabina di Parravicino di Revel (1865–1944) was the daughter of General Thaon di Revel and the wife of Count Emiliano Parravicino (1864–1931)

[47] ADR, Sabina di Parravicino to O'Connell, Milan, n.d.

value.[48] Later, in still more extravagant tones, the "little Machiavelli," as Spalding once characterized him, told Klein that he believed that the Bishop of Peoria was destined to play a great role in the future, and he hoped that the Abbé would go to great lengths, therefore, to make Spalding *au courant* of the situation and to have him meet those whom O'Connell characterized as "our men." "Treat him, then," he wrote, "as the man of the future, and make him understand that if he wishes to be the leader of the movement, the others will follow."[49]

Shortly after Spalding's arrival in Paris, the young Abbé paid him a visit at 104 Avenue Champs-Elysees, the home of the Marquise, and several days later Klein gave a reception for the American Prelate at his own home in Bellevue near Paris, which was attended by friends of Klein from the Institut Catholique and from the staffs of *L'Univers, Le Correspondant, La Quinzaine,* and *Le Temps.* Years later, the Abbé wrote that he could not guarantee that Spalding had not spoken of Americanism on the occasion of his visit, but he was certain that there had been no plot to conspire secretly against the Church and to justify the fears of *La Verité* and the Abbé Charles Maignen, who, in a postscript to an article which he entitled "Nouvelle Campagne Américaniste," had written that "Monsignor Spalding, more American, if possible, than Monsignor Ireland himself, is actually at Bellevue near Paris with the Abbé Félix Klein." Spalding had already been visited by several Parisian newspapermen, Maignen asserted, whose help he had sought for the coming press campaign that would coincide with Ireland's arrival in Paris. But by May 23, 1900, when this meeting was supposed to have taken place, the Abbé recalled, Spalding had already returned to Peoria, "thousands of miles from Europe and its vain disputes."[50]

[48] Klein, *Sans Arrêt,* p. 44.
[49] *Ibid.,* pp. 44–45.
[50] *Ibid.,* pp. 46–47.

There was a growing fear, nonetheless, among the French integrists that the translation of Spalding's lectures was a harbinger of a new Americanist campaign.[51] "Mission Vitale de L'Université" had met with immediate success, and Père Lucien Laberthonnière,[51a] for one, had congratulated Klein for his discovery of Spalding. Greatly encouraged, and urged on by the Marquise, Klein proceeded to publish the Gesù sermon in the *Annales de Philosophie Chrétienne,* and Spalding's "Women and Higher Education" in the collection, *Science et Religion.* Moreover, he announced the forthcoming publication of several of the Bishop's lectures in a volume to be entitled *Opportunité.* With this announcement, the integrist opposition was further abetted, the Abbé later stated, by pressure from the United States to discontinue the translation of Spalding's works into French, this being "less than trustworthy." This tack had apparently originated with Thomas O'Gorman, Bishop of Sioux Falls, a suffragan of the Archbishop of St. Paul, and was passed on to Klein through de Foville, the eminent Sulpician at the Paris seminary, via a letter from Marie François-Xavier Herzog, the Sulpician procurator in Rome. According to Klein, Ireland and O'Gorman had, perhaps, feared "a supposition not without foundation," namely that the influence and prestige of Ireland were gradually being eclipsed by that of Spalding, whose reputation was steadily growing. The Abbé responded to the pressure, however, by telling de Foville that he would desist in his plans only if Spalding formally asked him to do so. Whether this answer was relayed to Sioux Falls, to St. Paul, to the Sulpician procure in Rome, or still higher, Klein did not know, but he was greatly relieved when Spalding wrote from Peoria saying that he

[51] Houtin, *L'Américanisme,* p. 435.

[51a] Klein, *op. cit.,* p. 43. Lucien Labérthonnière (1860–1932), French philosopher, whose *Essai de Philosophie Religieuse* (1903) developed the doctrine of immanence and was placed on the Index.

277

had perfect confidence in the Abbé, and authorizing him to place at the head of the volume whatever statement he deemed necessary to show his consent and approval.[52] On the following day, the Abbé received fresh support when Franz Xaver Kraus wrote of his delight in Klein's plan to publish the work of Spalding. He likewise told Klein that he had already sent on an article from the *Allgemeinen Zeitung* of Munich, in which he had given *"un primo gusto"* to the sermon at the Gesù.[53]

By the end of March 1901, Klein had completed the translations and had sent the preface in manuscript to Peoria.[54] Two months later, *Le Correspondant* gave advance to *Opportunité* when it published Klein's "Un évêque Américain: Mgr. Spalding, l'homme et l'oeuvre."[55] In the next few months, *Opportunité*[56] went through four printings, and with its success, Klein

[52] *Ibid.*, pp. 62–64.

[53] *Ibid.*, p. 65.

[54] *Ibid.*, p. 71.

[55] *Ibid.*, p. 97.

[56] *Opportunité* was not a simple reproduction of Spalding's *Opportunity and Other Essays and Addresses* which McClurg published in 1900. The English version contained the following essays:

I.   Opportunity
II.   Woman and the Higher Education
III.   The University: A Nursery of the Higher Life
IV.   The University and the Teacher
V.   Goethe as Educator
VI.   Goethe as Educator (continued)
VII.   The Patriot
VIII. Empire or Republic.

The French *Opportunité,* in addition to a twenty-six page biographical "notice," included:

I.   Opportunité
II.   L'Education et L'Avenir Religieux (the Gesù discourse)
III.   Mission Vitale de L'Université
IV.   L'Éducation Supérieure du Prêtre
V.   Le Faux Patriotisme et Le Véritable
VI.   Dieu et Le Christ.

recalled, Spalding's name acquired a certain amount of fame in European society.[57]

The reception accorded *Opportunité* by Maignen and *La Verité* was expectedly unfavorable, although an unsigned article in *L'Italie* thought that the new Catholicism merited serious consideration, if "by Americanism we mean *not a doctrine, but a method.*"[58] Maignen, however, liked neither the method nor the principles underlying Spalding's book. Under a new title, he said, the book was representative of the same idea, the same thesis, minus the enthusiasm, of Archbishop Ireland, and minus the

There was also a German edition of *Opportunity,* however, which was published in Munich in 1903, under the title *Gelegenheit.* For a criticism of the German edition by Alexander Baumgartner, S.J., cf., *The Review* (St. Louis), X (September 17, 1903), pp. 552–553. Briefly, Father Baumgartner called it "a serious mistake that these essays and addresses have been turned into German. By their haziness, their mixing of Catholic and 'modern' ideas, of the truth with falsehood and inaccuracy, they can do only harm." *Ibid.,* p. 553.

[57] Klein, *op. cit.,* p. 103. Klein gave extracts from the various reviews. In the *Revue Bibliographique Belge,* August 13, 1901, V.D.B. attacked the book as "full of worn-out axioms and advice known to all the world," and the Bishop was described as "one of those astonishing American thinkers" who when his thoughts were not commonplace, were "terribly false and perfidious." Possibly there was a truth specially reserved for the Americans, the critic continued, to which he added: "How I envy the Cubans who are now in a special way to learn it." *Ibid.,* p. 108. *The Catholic World,* LXXIV (December, 1901), p. 412, quoted this review. Père Laberthonnière in the *Annales de Philosophie Chrétienne,* XLV (October, 1901), pp. 92–96, wrote more favorably and said: "Each of the chapters is a meditation and a song; it is a living stream, which, welling from an inexhaustible spring, is broad, abundant, ever new, and yet calm, deep, impetuous, and strong. The soul revealed there is at once zealous and serene, uniting the tranquility of faith to the effort of investigation. To him everything is an occasion, an opportunity to drink in goodness . . . One is reminded of the 'Imitation,' and at the same time one feels that this book belongs to another period of the universal Christian life. . . ."

[58] "Un Evêque américaniste," in *L'Italie, Journal Politique Quotidien,* Rome, June 25, 1901.

naive originality of Father Hecker. Maignen maintained that Spalding, even in French dress, was but "a cold philosopher, sententious and obscure." Pressing further, he said that the "fundamental error of Americanism is found here in its extremity: confidence in one's self, exaltation of the human personality, the adaptation of the Church to the age, the worship of the future and contempt for the past."[59]

Klein sent copies of the various reviews to Spalding, though the latter had no intention of responding to criticism, since, as he told Klein, his only interest had been to spread the ideas which he had believed to be progressive and true.[60]

One of the more interesting, and somewhat puzzling, reactions to Spalding's thought was that of Friedrich von Hügel, theologian, Baron of the Holy Roman Empire, and founder of the modernist London Society for the Study of Religion. Having confessed that he had been much struck with "the keen insight of our Bishop Spalding," he still recalled three years after he had met Spalding in Rome that

. . . he developed before me with astonishing eloquence the contention, that history had conclusively manifested and established two things: the impossibility, for a society that would live and grow, of the Spanish, physical force, sheer authority and blind obedience type of Catholicism; and the incapacity of pure Protestantism, e.g., the Free Churches of America to produce the very deepest and largest saints. Hence the future seemed to him and to myself to demand that the legitimate aspirations and the undoubted benefits of Protestantism should be realized and should remain, and that corresponding changes should occur from within in the attitude and practice of Catholicism; but not that it should simply go or that . . . it should simply give place to its rival.[61]

[59] *The Review* (St. Louis), IX (May, 1902), pp. 273–276. Maignen's criticism of *Opportunité* first appeared in *La Vérité française* (Paris), August 1, 1901, and was then incorporated into Maignen's *Nouveau Catholicisme et Nouveau Clergé* (Paris, 1902), pp. 163–165. It is Preuss' translation in *The Review* that is quoted here.

[60] Klein, *op. cit.*, pp. 110–111.

[61] Von Hügel to Percy Gardner, London, April 25, 1903, in *Baron Friedrich von Hügel, 1852–1925, Selected Letters, 1896–1924* (Lon-

If the Baron's account of the conversation was accurate, it was not unlike the bishop. True, many years before the young Father Spalding had written to his uncle, the Archbishop of Baltimore, that there was nothing so sad as "this prurient eagerness for finding heresy in every Catholic writer of talent and originality who does not happen to think on every point as our own little selves."[62] Nevertheless, at times impulsive and thoughtless of the uses that might be made of his utterances, Bishop Spalding was himself responsible for the rumor that he was indeed "the prelate who embarked on the Roman vessel because it seemed to him that best equipped for the attainment of the complete ideal of humanity,"[63] only to become despondent

don, 1927), pp. 120–121. Baron Friedrich von Hügel (1852–1925) was born in Florence, the son of an Austrian diplomat and his Scottish wife. Married into English aristocracy, the Baron spent his mature years in London. He was devoted to the study of the philosophy and psychology of religion in addition to biblical studies. A life-long Roman Catholic, von Hügel was a confidant of many of the modernist group; "such slight cohesion as the modernist movement had," it has been said, "was largely derived from his co-ordinating activity." Cf. Alexander R. Vidler, *The Modernist Movement in the Roman Church* (Cambridge, 1934), p. 206. Percy Gardner (1846–1937), English archaeologist, was a professor at Cambridge (1880–1887) and at Oxford (1887–1925).

[62] AAB, 37-A-7, Spalding to Spalding, Belgian College, Rome, January 5, 1865.

[63] Albert Houtin, *The Life of a Priest, My Own Experience, 1867–1912* (London, 1927), p. 187. Houtin believed Americanism was the religious evolution that was drawing "all the sects alike in the direction of what we call in Europe 'Liberal Protestantism.'" In commenting on this statement, Lilley wrote that it was not, perhaps, exactly how even the most advanced Americanist would wish it expressed, but, he added: ". . . if a movement is to be judged by the tendencies of its greatest minds, then those who are acquainted with the writings of Bishop Spalding will recognize, if not the perfect adequacy, at least the general truth, of M. Houtin's estimate of the share of Americanism in the common trend of American religion. . . ." Lilley, *Modernism, A Record and Review*, p. 111. It was this tendency that must have gained the

and well-nigh mutinous when he failed in his attempt to guide the vessel to port.

Klein's "new Americanism," however, proved to be a short-lived affair in Europe, overshadowed as it was, even before *Testem benevolentiae,* by continental modernism, to which Americanism has been considered something of a preface.[64] Alfred Loisy, perhaps the most important figure in the modernist movement, recalled in his memoirs that, after Spalding had visited him at his residence in Bellevue, he had come to the conclusion that the Bishop of Peoria and Archbishop Ireland had precise and fixed ideas only on social and political matters, a disappointment to the author of *L'Evangile et l'Eglise,* for they had been preceded by the reputation of being "revolutionary innovators." "On these points alone," Loisy wrote, "are they in opposition to the Roman curia, but as far as our questions are

dubious honor of being the subject of a sermon at the Lenox Avenue Unitarian Church, New York, when Merle St. C. Wright told his parishioners: "If all Catholics are as Catholic as Bishop Spalding, then it is Catholic I wish to make you," and he then added that the Bishop was an exemplar of the universal religion since in his opinion Spalding was a "Catholic in the broadest sense of the term and the surprise was that he should not only rise in the Church in which he labored but that he should remain a Catholic in the narrowest sense. . . ." Cf. *New York Tribune,* December 15, 1902. Small wonder that the editor of the *Courrier de Génève* in reviewing *Opportunité* feared that "Bishop Spalding and his friends propose to make us Protestants so that there will be no Protestants." Cf. Klein, *op. cit.,* p. 108. Canon William Barry, a friend of the Americanists, recalled meeting Spalding in Rome where, he said, they held "full and frank conversations on the dangers and prospects of the Church." The American, as a rule, Barry continued, "is sanguine but the Bishop was rather despondent" and "with . . . not a few others, he held the Great Apostasy was drawing nigh." Cf. William Barry, *Memories and Opinions* (New York, 1926), pp. 220–221 and *passim.*

[64] Cf. McAvoy, *The Great Crisis,* pp. 346–348, for a brief discussion of this point.

concerned, they know little."[65] Another modernist reaction to Spalding's Americanism was that of English Jesuit George Tyrrell, who had read *Opportunité* and had found it difficult to believe that "it is by a Roman Catholic bishop, so full as it is of palpitating sympathy with all that is best and most Catholic in modern thought."[66] Amidst what he called the "catch-penny spasms of ecclesiastical vitality," he felt, Spalding was "waking up."[67]

Spalding, in the meantime, had returned to Peoria. He had spoken of matters of vital importance from the pulpit of the Gesù, so he believed, but, as he remarked to Father Hudson, "with us everyone is drawn to what is external that I doubt there will be many who will see the real meaning of the sermon."[68]

[65] Alfred Loisy, *Memoires pour servir a l'histoire religieuse de notre temps* (Paris, 1930), I, p. 547. Alfred Firmin Loisy (1857–1940), French Roman Catholic priest, was the Scripture scholar who was condemned as a modernist. He left the Church and taught in the Collège de France from 1911 to 1927. When Houtin in *The Life of a Priest,* p. 187, characterized Ireland and Spalding as "pure Rationalists," Loisy commented: "These bishops were hardly theologians but their mentality was not rationalistic, and I came to agree with the reservations von Hügel expressed on Spalding's scientific background, although he was the better educated of the two." *Memoires,* I, p. 547. Spalding had visited Loisy, who also lived at Bellevue, on May 8, 1900. *Ibid.,* p. 500.

[66] Tyrrell to von Hügel, Catholic Church, Richmond, Yorks, June 16, 1900, in George Tyrrell's Letters (New York, 1920), p. 78. Tyrrell (1861–1909) was a member of the Society of Jesus whose published works revealed his modernism and caused his dismissal from the Society and excommunication from the Church.

[67] Tyrrell to Henri Bremond, Richmond, Yorks, November 13, 1900. *Ibid.,* p. 5. The Abbé Henri Bremond (1865–1933) was the author of an unfinished *Literary History of Religious Thought in France.* Ordained in 1892, he left the Jesuits in 1904; he was later made a member of the French Academy.

[68] UND, Hudson Papers, Spalding to Hudson, St. Bede College, Peru, June 25, 1900. The Gesù discourse was hailed, however, by the New York *Independent,* a leading Protestant weekly, for "the intelligence, courage and sound Americanism of this admirable sermon." Cf. *The*

Though Spalding, too, was necessarily embroiled in externals on his return to Peoria, where, as he wrote the Marquise, he found "a thousand annoyances & everything generally going to the devil." Though he longed for "the green pastures and refreshing breezes of European life,"[69] he was now at home, and after an absence of four months, there was work to be done.

During his audience with Leo XIII, Spalding had asked for an auxiliary bishop to help him in the work of the diocese. The Holy Father had agreed to the request, and Spalding had thereupon written out his formal petition. "My health and the territorial extent of the diocese," he said, "has made it long impossible for me to fulfill the duties of my office alone." Since frequent attacks of rheumatism made it difficult for him to walk, he proposed, therefore, that Father Peter Joseph O'Reilly, his Irish-born Vicar General and pastor of St. Patrick's Church in Peoria, be nominated. The request was granted, and on July 10, 1900, the Sacred Congregation de Propaganda Fide forwarded to Archbishop Martinelli, the Apostolic Delegate, and to Bishop Spalding the brief which appointed O'Reilly auxiliary to the Bishop of Peoria.[70]

Independent, September 20, 1900, p. 287. Spalding was pleased. "I saw the article in the *Independent*," he wrote to Hudson, "it was very complimentary." Cf. UND, Hudson Papers, Spalding to Hudson, Peoria, October 8, 1900.

[69] ADR, Caldwell des Merinville to D. J. O'Connell, Paris, June 18, 1900. The Marquise stated that Spalding realized perhaps, that Mamie C. was not so much a burden as she seemed to be. "How sad it is that we all learn wisdom too late in life," she remarked, "to do us any good in this world—at least." In the Autumn of 1900, she suffered an attack of paralysis which completely crippled her side, Kraus noted in his diary, and added that Spalding and the Marquise were completely estranged. "She sent O'Connell Spalding's portrait," he wrote, "with the remark that she has no more room for it in her house." Cf. *Kraus Tagebücher*, p. 749.

[70] ACPF, Lett., Folder 153, no. 38675, Sacra Congregazione di Propaganda Fide to Mons. Giovanni L. Spalding, Vescovo di Peoria, di U.S.A., Rome, 10 Luglio, 1900.

8

"A Blessing, Pure and Simple"

"MY auxiliary is beloved by everyone," Spalding told Denis O'Connell on New Year's Day 1901, and, he added, "I expect to have more leisure than in the past."[1] But Spalding, now in his sixty-first year, soon discovered, as he informed Father Hudson, that he was still "hard at work."[2] Furthermore, there was trouble in the Archdiocese of Chicago, and storm warnings had already reached Peoria. "Abp. Feehan is in feeble health," Spalding had remarked to O'Connell shortly after his return from Rome, and he noted that "his auxiliary is unable to do anything."[3] Seventy

[1] ADR, Spalding to O'Connell, Peoria, January 1, 1901.

[2] UND, Hudson Papers, Spalding to Hudson, January 21, 1901. Bishop O'Reilly, as auxiliary, had undoubtedly relieved his ordinary of many routine tasks, such as confirmation tours, and had thereby provided Spalding with the time to pursue his extra-diocesan activities. Busy with the manuscript of *God and the Soul* [cf. Chapter 5, n. 4], the Bishop had another book in the planning stage at this time. He told Hudson: "I have attacked the tin box and can make a respectable volume which I think of entitling—'Aphorisms and Reflections on Life, Religion, Conduct and Culture.'" *Ibid.* The latter was published in 1901 with the title: *Aphorisms and Reflections. Conduct, Culture and Religion.* On January 27, Spalding preached at the dedication of St. Mary's Cathedral, in Covington, Kentucky, and on Washington's birthday he lectured at the Union League Club in Chicago. Cf. UND, Hudson Papers, Same to Same, Peoria, February 26, 1901.

[3] ADR, Spalding to O'Connell, Peoria, June 9, 1900.

years of age and his health shattered, Patrick Feehan had chosen
Father Alexander J. McGavick, one of his Chicago pastors, as an
episcopal assistant. But soon after his consecration on May 1,
1899,[4] the auxiliary had likewise become ill and incapacitated,
and the Archbishop had then proposed the name of his Ameri-
can-born chancellor, Peter James Muldoon, as a candidate for
the office, only to find that he had aroused the bitter opposition of a score of Irish-born priests. These, early in January
1901, had sent a delegation to Washington, D.C., where they
lodged a protest with Archbishop Martinelli against Muldoon's
elevation to the episcopacy.

Charges of priestly irregularities, followed by counter-charges
of defamation of character, soon divided the Chicago Archdiocese into two warring camps. "The candidate for auxiliaryship
is in full control," complained Father Hugh P. Smyth, pastor of
St. Mary's Church in Evanston, Illinois, to Monsignor O'Connell,
"and men are promoted in spite of their records." One such individual, the Evanston priest lamented, who had been hunted
from his parish by what he called "an indignant and outraged
people," had been brought into the city to build up a new
parish, and when his former parishioners had been refused a
hearing at the Chicago chancery, they had called upon Bishop
Spalding and had given him sworn affidavits with alleged proofs
of their accusations. There was need, said Smyth, for a coadjutor archbishop with the right of succession to Archbishop Feehan, and it was becoming more and more evident, he reported,
that Spalding would be the choice of the Chicago priests, as well
as of the bishops of the province. Archbishops Ireland and
Keane, he felt certain, would favor the Bishop of Peoria. However, there was one obstacle, wrote Smyth, since "it is generally

[4] Kirkfleet, *Life of Patrick Augustine Feehan,* p. 299. Spalding had
preached at McGavick's consecration as titular Bishop of Marcopolis
and auxiliary to the Archbishop of Chicago. In 1922, McGavick was
named Bishop of LaCrosse, Wisconsin.

believed here that Archbishop Riordan is anxious to come to Chicago and it is understood Bp. Spalding is aware of this."[5]

Despite the contentions aroused by his candidacy, and notwithstanding Smyth's speculations, Peter Muldoon was appointed auxiliary to the Archbishop of Chicago on July 10, 1901,[6] and two weeks later Sebastiano Martinelli, now a cardinal-designate and the pro-delegate,[7] came to Chicago to consecrate the new bishop in what has been described as "an effort to demonstrate

[5] ADR, Smyth to O'Connell, Evanston, Illinois, March 19, 1901. In the months that followed the death of John Hennessy, the first Archbishop of Dubuque, Spalding's name had been suggested as a successor for that metropolitan See. When interviewed on the possibility, however, the Bishop had replied:

In the first place, I would not leave Peoria. I have lived here twenty-three years, This has been my home. Here are my friends. Here I have done my work, and here I want to remain. In Dubuque or anywhere else it would be beginning all over again and I cannot see why, at my age, I should do such a thing. Furthermore, I would not feel that going to Dubuque and the archbishopic would be a step upward. The diocese [sic] is smaller than Peoria and the work offered is of no greater scope. No, I will not leave Peoria. Nothing could entice me away. I can think of no place I would rather live in and call my home.

Cf. Peoria *Herald-Transcript,* June 15, 1900. Keane had been appointed the second Archbishop of Dubuque on September, 12, 1900. He was installed and invested with the pallium on April 17, 1901, at which the Bishop of Peoria was present. Cf. John J. Toomey and M. C. Sullivan (eds.), *Souvenir of the Installation and the Investiture of the Most Rev. John J. Keane, D.D. as Archbishop of Dubuque* (Dubuque, 1901), p. 75.

[6] Owen B. Corrigan, "Chronology of the American Hierarchy," *CHR,* III (July, 1917), 154.

[7] Martinelli was created cardinal on April 15, 1901, and received the biretta from Gibbons on May 9, 1901. He sailed for Rome in May, 1902. Cf. Ellis, *Gibbons,* I, p. 651. Archbishop Diomede Falconio, O.F.M., formerly Apostolic Delegate to Canada, was appointed to succeed Martinelli on September 30, 1902. Cf. Bonaventure Cerretti, "Legate," *Catholic Encyclopedia,* IX, 120.

to all that Muldoon had the strong support of the authorities of the Church."[8] In the months that followed, however, the antagonism toward Muldoon did not abate. One of the leaders of the revolt, Father Jeremiah Crowley,[9] who had been ousted by Feehan from his pastorate at St. Mary's Church in Oregon, Illinois, because of his intransigence, was warned on October 13, 1901, by Martinelli to submit to the archbishop, to make public reparation for the scandal he had given, to desist from pressing his complaints in the civil courts, and to stop publication of a book wherein, it was contended, he intended to give "a full and authentic history of the sad condition of the Catholic Church in the Archdiocese of Chicago."[10] With his refusal to submit, Crowley was excommunicated on October 26, 1901.[11] Newspaper coverage of the incident was widespread, and in some instances the press carried both Martinelli's warning and the decree of excommunication together with the dissident priest's replies.

Two weeks before Crowley's excommunication, Spalding requested Gibbons to intervene in what appeared to be a small-scale eccesiastical war in Chicago. All his life, he said, he had tried to keep aloof from clerical factions and intrigues, and only in obedience to conscience and with extreme reluctance, he insisted, had he stepped into the fray. He enclosed a letter which he characterized as "a confidential document," and spoke of its

[8] Ellis, *Gibbons*, II, p. 416.

[9] Jeremiah J. Crowley, *Romanism a Menace to the Nation* (Cincinnati, 1912), p. 40. Born on November 20, 1861, in County Cork, Ireland, Crowley was ordained a priest in June, 1886, and left for the United States where he first served as a curate at St. Anne's Church in Manchester, New Hampshire. Sixteen months later, he returned to Ireland where he remained until 1896, when he again came to America, this time to Chicago. For three years he was curate at the Church of the Nativity when Archbishop Feehan appointed him pastor of St. Mary's Parish, Oregon, Illinois.

[10] Kirkfleet, *op. cit.*, pp. 378–379.

[11] *Ibid.*, pp. 380–381.

writer, Father Smyth, as "one of the best and wisest and most respected priests of Chicago." Unless action was taken, and quickly, Spalding warned, "a blow will be struck which will inflict irreparable harm on the whole Church in America."[12] Whether or not Gibbons attempted to play the role of peacemaker is not known; what is certain is that Spalding soon afterward appealed to Rome. He described the situation for Cardinal Ledochowski, Prefect of the Propaganda, as follows:

As the oldest suffragan of the Province of Chicago, it is my duty to inform you of the deplorable state of ecclesiastical affairs in the diocese of Chicago. The archbishop is no longer capable of governing. No one knows in what state the finances are. Good priests are quite discouraged, Catholic people are scandalized and the harm that has been done to religion is incalculable . . . and will grow day by day if a remedy is not found. It is absolutely necessary the Propaganda send some archbishop or American bishop to Chicago to make an investigation. It is the conviction of those who are the most capable of judging the actual condition of the church in this diocese. I have spoken of it to his Eminence the Apostolic Delegate but found him hesitant and timid and he did not understand, so it seems to me, the gravity of the situation. For myself I am close to the center of the trouble and know more than I wish to write. At any rate my only desire is to be useful to the Church and to prevent an enormous scandal.[13]

Roman reaction was immediate. The Cardinal Prefect sent a copy of Spalding's letter to the Pro-Delegate, ordering Martinelli to investigate the charges and to give an opinion as to whether or not an apostolic administrator should be given to the Archdiocese of Chicago, as had been the case in St. Louis, where, in his last years, Archbishop Kenrick had been given a coadjutor, John J. Kain, to whom had been given over the actual government of that See.[14]

[12] AAB, 95-C-5, Spalding to Gibbons, Peoria, October 11, 1901.
[13] ACPF, Lett. Folder 153, no. 47281, Spalding to Ledochowski, Peoria, November 24, 1901.
[14] ACPF, Lett. Folder 153, no. 47281. Sacra Congregazione de P.F. a Sua Eminenza Card. Sebastiano Martinelli, Pro Deleg . . . Roma, Dicembre 11, 1901.

Cardinal Martinelli filed his report on the archdiocese on February 4, 1902.[15] The rumors regarding the deplorable state of affairs in Chicago began, he noted, only when Father Muldoon became a candidate for the auxiliary bishopric. Prior to that, nothing untoward had been heard at the delegation. On the contrary, though he had had occasion to talk about Archbishop Feehan both in Chicago and elsewhere, no one had made unfavorable observations regarding his person or his administration, "not even those," he added, "who are now criticizing him severely and crying scandal."[16] To be sure, two factions existed within the Chicago clergy, one favorable, the other opposed to the archbishop. Each group endeavored to have its own adherents promoted to the better parishes, and on occasion they had recourse to reprehensible methods, especially to newspaper publicity which praised the virtues of some candidates and exaggerated the defects of others. It was this, Martinelli believed, that accounted for a large part of the rumors.[17]

In accordance with his instructions from Rome, the Pro-Delegate then informed Cardinal Ledochowski that he had asked others whom he considered "both conscientious and well informed on the truth or falsity of these rumors" for their opinions. And since Bishop Spalding had shown himself to be so very interested, he had deemed it advisable to write to him also, but he had requested Spalding not to limit himself to "general statements or to vague rumors but to get down to the facts and to specific evidence."[18] The Bishop of Peoria had replied in a con-

---

[15] ACPF, Acta di Propaganda Fide [hereafter cited as Acta], no. 53, Protocol no. 52583, Dicembre, 1902, num. XIII, L'Emo. Card. Martinelli, Pro-Deleg. Ap. degli Stati Uniti informa la S.C. circa lo stato attuale dell'Arcidiocesi di Chicago, Washington, D.C., 4 Febbraio, 1902, pp. 24–29.

[16] Ibid., p. 24.

[17] Ibid.

[18] Ibid., pp. 24–25.

fidential written report, but it was described as "more or less that which he had told me in person several months before, and which, as he writes to your Eminence, I was reluctant to believe."[19] Specifically, Spalding had charged that there was an increasing deviation from priestly standards of decorum among the Chicago clergy; that Archbishop Feehan was known to be at times intemperate; and that all diocesan property was registered exclusively in his own name, a system that could lead to abuse. Yet one looked in vain in Spalding's report, the Pro-Delegate asserted, for definite proof and for specific, verified cases, since all his evidence reduced itself to what was called, "In my opinion," "judging from the rumor," "as one says," "as they say." Perhaps it was prudence that had counselled Bishop Spalding to speak and write so circumspectly, Martinelli added, for, as he continued, "it seems that the accused are awaiting specific evidence to lodge the complaint of defamation against their defamers."[20]

Among those whose help the Pro-Delegate had sought in making a judgment, Bishop John Janssen of Belleville, also a suffragan of the Province of Chicago, had written that two factions did, indeed, exist within the archdiocesan clergy, "and it seems," Martinelli noted for Propaganda, "that one of these governs the Archbishop, who is not always well informed, and that the bad, instead of being corrected, are sometimes promoted."[21] Janssen acknowledged, however, that he had not heard about the sad state of affairs until July 1901, when Father Crowley began to make use of the public press. Father M. J. Fitzsimmons, one of Chicago's vicars general, had reported that the three hundred and sixty priests who comprised the archdiocesan clergy were no better or worse than those of any other diocese in the

[19] *Ibid.*, p. 25.
[20] *Ibid.*
[21] *Ibid.*

United States, and, whatever their hidden failings, there was no foundation for the rumors and insinuations spread about concerning the moral character of some of the priests.[22]

Another whose testimony figured in the case was that of Edward Joseph Dunne, Bishop of Dallas, a former Chicago diocesan, who wrote that his twenty-two years of experience in the Chicago clergy forced him to reject the accusations. His only regret, he said, was that Archbishop Feehan had followed the example of his predecessors in omitting clerical conferences and the examination for the junior clergy. The latter, he believed, would keep young priests out of many dangerous situations "by forcing them to prepare for examinations." Dunne also rejected the accusation of intemperance against Archbishop Feehan, as had Cardinal Gibbons, Archbishop Ryan of Philadelphia, and Archbishop Corrigan of New York, with each of whom Martinelli had had occasion to speak of the matter. "And the same is true," added the Pro-Delegate, "of the Bishop of Peoria, who was the first to refer the matter to the Delegation and who now repeats in writing that he does not know whether it be true or false."[23]

On the question of the archdiocesan properties, Martinelli then sought to distinguish for Propaganda between the legality and security of the title "from the prudent and conscientious administration of the property."[24] The Third Plenary Council of Baltimore had done no more, he affirmed, than to recommend one of three titles of property which varied in different states of the Union whereby property was recognized to secure its legal effects.[25] No one of these titles rendered property absolutely

[22] *Ibid.*, p. 26.

[23] *Ibid.*, p. 27.

[24] *Ibid.*

[25] *Ibid.* The three titles of property were: corporation sole, in trust, and in fee simple. Cf. *Acta et decreta Concilii Plenarii Baltimorensis Tertii,* Titulus IX, Caput II, n. 267, p. 153.

secure, since each carried with it dangers of greater or lesser degree, depending on circumstances, but the American Church had no other choice. If Bishop Spalding had meant to allude to the property title, what else, the Pro-Delegate asked, could Archbishop Feehan have done? On the other hand, if Spalding had meant to speak of the administration of the property, it seemed, so Martinelli believed, that "the proofs which he adduces are only insinuations."[26] It was true that Archbishop Feehan had built two houses for himself, one in the city, the other in the country, and it might likewise well be true that they cost a million dollars. Chicago was, however, "a vast and rich archdiocese," and it was mere supposition that the two buildings were not held as archdiocesan property. As for the alleged expenditure of a million dollars, Spalding had failed to indicate, he added, "that there is included an institution for poor and abandoned children built in the vicinity of the country house or 'villa' as Mgr. Spalding calls it."[27]

Martinelli concluded that, after studying the reports that had reached the Apostolic Delegation, he was convinced that the charges of great waste and corruption in the Archdiocese of Chicago were unjustified. Much could be accomplished, he was sure, if the Cardinal Prefect of the Propaganda would write to Archbishop Feehan, calling his attention to various points of discipline. But if, on the other hand, Ledochowski cared to give weight to Spalding's assertions, then he might ask the Archbishop for a financial report of the archdiocese. And as to the advisability of a coadjutor archbishop and apostolic administrator, he believed such action to be inexpedient and inopportune.

The Pro-Delegate's report, however, was not to be the last word on the Chicago controversy, for many doubts remained unresolved. Spalding, in fact, just one month after Martinelli

26 *Ibid.*, p. 28.
27 *Ibid*

293

filed his report with Rome, wrote to Gibbons, warning, "The Chicago scandals are a blight to the Church and God alone knows how the unfortunate affair will end."[28] As it happened, the "unfortunate affair" would end tragically for Spalding, and signal the demise of his ecclesiastical career.

In the meantime, however, in the interval of calm before the storm, the priests of the Peoria Diocese, under the direction of Bishop O'Reilly and Father Francis J. O'Reilly, Chancellor and rector of St. Mary's Cathedral, prepared for lighter, happier things. May 1, 1902, would mark the golden jubilee of St. Mary's as a parish and its consecration as a cathedral, and the silver jubilee of their Bishop's consecration,[29] and a triple commemoration was being planned.

No more ideal day could have been wished for, the Peoria *Journal* reported, than that May day when some two hundred and fifty priests, an abbot, sixteen bishops, four archbishops, and James Cardinal Gibbons walked in procession from Spalding Institute to the cathedral where Bishop Spalding celebrated Solemn Pontifical Mass. Following the chanting of the gospel, Gibbons, "robed in the brilliant scarlet of his office," was escorted to the pulpit, where, in a "voice not strong but clear," he spoke on the expansion and the glory of the Church.[30] In a personal note near the end of his sermon, Gibbons recalled how twenty-five years before he had been privileged to assist at Spalding's consecration, and how he had watched the growth of the See of Peoria "with profound interest and gratification" not only because of his friendship with the jubilarian, but also because of his affection for the jubilarian's uncle, "illustrious Archbishop Spalding of Baltimore," whom he "loved and revered as my

---

[28] AAB, 99-M-6, Spalding to Gibbons, Peoria, March 14, 1902.

[29] *Souvenir of the Episcopal Silver Jubilee of the Rt. Rev. J. L. Spalding,* pp. [7–8]. Hereafter this brochure will be cited as *Souvenir.*

[30] Peoria *Journal,* May 1, 1902. Cf. Peoria *Star,* May 1, 1902, for complete list of the members of the hierarchy in attendance.

father in God." Not only for the growth of his own diocese had Bishop Spalding employed his talents, the preacher continued, but also for the enlightenment of his fellow citizens throughout the land. Seconded in this "by a loyal and devoted clergy," upon whom he had impressed his own zeal, the Bishop of Peoria had likewise been sustained by the generous cooperation of an enlightened laity, "a triple alliance, more formidable than the triple alliance of Germany, Austria and Italy," since it was an alliance, the Cardinal concluded, "upheld by the cohesive and enduring power of divine love."[31]

After the Mass, the jubilee banquet was held at Spalding Institute.[32] Toasts and speeches were given by Gibbons ("Our Holy Father"), Riordan ("Our Country"), and Keane ("The Church in Our Own Country"), the last, the first rector of the Catholic University, declaring Spalding to have been "the first and strongest influence" in its founding. Father Thomas Keating, Pastor of St. Columba's Parish in Ottawa, later recounted the history of the diocese, recalling how, in 1877, "three or four schools had a sickly existence, and the churches, with scarcely an exception, were make-shifts . . ." Now, he said, the diocese could count a population of 120,000 Catholics, one hundred and eighty-one priests, two hundred and fourteen churches, three academies for boys, nine academies for girls, sixty-one parochial schools, two orphan asylums, seven hospitals, a home for the aged, and one industrial and reform school. Among the diocesan clergy, he added, there was good feeling and a brotherly spirit. Thus, he said, it was "the pride . . . of his devoted clergy to anticipate his every wish, believing implicitly in the soundness of his judgment and the absolute disinterestedness of his motives."[33]

[31] *Souvenir,* pp. 25–26.
[32] *Ibid.,* p. 28.
[33] *Ibid.,* p. 39.

As for himself, Spalding said when his turn had come, referring to the day when the episcopal office had been offered him, "If I hesitated to accept the burden and the honor, it was largely, if my memory deceives me not, from a dread lest my opinion of man's high estate, as revealed in the lives of priests and nuns, should be lowered by the more intimate knowledge of them which necessarily comes to those who are placed in authority over them.

"A personal experience of twenty-five years," Spalding continued, "is a broad basis for the judgment of an individual, and it is a source of inner strength and freedom, that though priests and nuns be not exempt from the infirmities which inhere in all that is human, I have found them to be the kindliest, the most unselfish, the most loyal . . . the most devoted of men and women."[34]

That evening, at the close of Vespers, Archbishop Ireland preached in St. Mary's Cathedral, wherein, seconding Keane, he affirmed that Spalding "is the founder of the university, and since its beginnings he has been its vigilant guardian and its sturdy defender. As it grows in strength and usefulness, so will the glory of the name of Bishop Spalding and the debt of gratitude which America owes him."[35]

Several days after the festivities, Spalding wrote to Canon de Becker, rector of the American College in Louvain, to thank him for his jubilee greetings. "The celebration," he simply noted, "was all that could be desired," and he added that he had already written Monsignor Adolphe Hebbelynck, rector of the Catholic University of Louvain, thanking him for the honorary degree which his alma mater had bestowed on him.[36] The Bishop was soon to be the recipient of a like honor from Columbia

[34] *Ibid.*, p. 59.
[35] *Ibid.*, pp. 76–77.
[36] AAC-L, Spalding to De Becker, Peoria, May 7, 1902.

University, for the university's trustees had voted unanimously to confer the degree Doctor of Laws, *honoris causa,* on the Bishop of Peoria "in recognition," Dr. Nicholas Murray Butler, the President, informed him, "of your eminence and service as Christian priest and bishop, as scholar and man of letters, as educator and as citizen."[37] Since it was the rule of the University that honorary degrees were conferred only on those candidates who were present to receive them, Spalding attended the commencement exercises on June 11, 1902, at Morningside Heights.[38] While in the city, he took the opportunity to dismiss still another rumor, that "the morning of a new career," as Archbishop Ireland had phrased it, had arrived, and that he was soon to be named the next Archbishop of New York.

Michael Augustine Corrigan, third Archbishop of New York, had died on May 5,[39] and the inevitable speculation as to his successor had been taken up by the press.[40] Father Richard Lalor Burtsell,[41] pastor at Roundout, New York, the canonist who had

[37] Archives of Columbia University, Butler to Spalding, New York, May 6, 1902.

[38] New York *Tribune,* June 12, 1902. Spalding was presented by the Dean of the University, Professor John Howard Van Amrings. *Ibid.* The citation read:

Right Rev. John Lancaster Spalding, LL.D., Bishop of Peoria, Descendant of a house honored among two peoples; Christian priest and prelate, man of letters, orator, educator and patriotic citizen.

Cf. *Columbia University, Honorary Degrees Awarded in the Years, 1902–1945. Appreciations by Nicholas Murray Butler, Twelfth President of Columbia University* (New York, 1946), p. 2.

[39] Peoria *Journal,* May 6, 1902.

[40] Peoria *Star,* May 12, 1902. The *Star* quoted the Decatur *Review* and the Kewanee *Star* which had carried the news item that the Bishop of Peoria might succeed the late Archbishop of New York. Cf. also, Peoria *Star,* May 17, 1902

[41] Cf. Chapter 4, note 8.

297

often been in open conflict with the late Archbishop, had met with several of the irremovable rectors in an informal caucus at Father Patrick McSweeney's rectory attached to St. Brigid's Parish, where they had considered the question of succession. Burtsell noted in his diary that they had discussed Bishop Spalding as a possible candidate, but some were strongly opposed to him. "I admitted their reasons, viz., his opposition to the trial of priests and his rejection of Apost. Delegate," but, added Burtsell, "I thought his past sins would be condoned in view of his frankness, honesty and ability." After they had taken an informal ballot and the results had been tabulated, it was announced that John M. Farley, the Auxiliary Bishop and Vicar General, had received seven votes, Joseph Mooney, the second Vicar General, six votes, and a scattering of votes for Bishop James Quigley of Buffalo, as well as for McSweeney and Burtsell. While only two ballots had been cast for Spalding, Burtsell concluded the day's entry, "I had tried to persuade all that New York belonged to the whole country and that we should look anywhere for the best man but the majority said 'home rule.' "[42]

When the diocesan consultors and irremovable rectors later met at St. Patrick's Cathedral rectory, Farley was overwhelmingly elected first choice; Spalding, almost predictably, received only one vote. Three months later, Farley was named fourth Archbishop of New York.[43]

[42] AANY, Burtsell diary, May 13, 1902. Years later, the cry of "home rule" would be heard again as the Archdiocese of New York awaited a successor to the late Patrick Cardinal Hayes, but it would be in vain. Robert I. Gannon, S.J., has noted: "The local clergy were not critical of outside talent, while it remained outside, but they always had a small-town feeling with regard to foreigners. It had once been remarked that Archbishop Corrigan's principal difficulty was the fact that he was a foreigner. He came from Newark, New Jersey." Cf. *The Cardinal Spellman Story* (New York, 1962), p. 128.

[43] Owen Corrigan, "Episcopal Succession in the United States," *CHR* II (July, 1961), p. 140.

Meanwhile, Archbishop Feehan of Chicago had died, on July 12,[44] and two days later, as senior suffragan of the ecclesiastical province, Spalding appointed Bishop Muldoon the administrator of the archdiocese, *sede vacante*.[45] Spalding also celebrated the Solemn Pontifical Requiem Mass for the first Chicago Archbishop, on July 17, at Holy Name Cathedral, and then summoned by letter the irremovable rectors and diocesan consultors to meet in the cathedral rectory on the following Thursday, the 24th.[46] The bishops of the province, James Ryan of Alton and John Janssen of Belleville, were also requested to meet later in the day to propose their own candidates for the vacant See.[47] After the two sessions, both of which Spalding presided at, he forwarded the results to Monsignor Francesco Marchetti, who as auditor was in charge of the apostolic delegation until a successor to Cardinal Martinelli should be named. At the priests' meeting, Spalding received nine votes out of sixteen cast, Muldoon seven votes; thus the Bishop of Peoria was named *dignissimus*. On the first ballot for *dignior*, Muldoon had eight votes, one short of the majority needed, but he was named on the subsequent ballot as the priests' second choice. For the third position on the *terna*, there were five ballots before Bishop James Quigley of Buffalo finally received a majority of nine, while Archbishop

[44] Corrigan, *op. cit.*, p. 152; or Chicago *Evening Post*, July 12, 1902.

[45] Archives of the Diocese of Rockford, Muldoon diary, Spalding to Muldoon, Peoria, July 14, 1902, telegram: "I appoint you administrator until I hear from Rome." Hereafter these archives will be cited as ADRoc. Cf. ADRoc, Muldoon diary, Same to Same, Peoria, July 21, 1902, telegram: "This is to certify that I as Senior Bishop of the Catholic Ecclesiastical Province of Chicago have appointed the Rt. Rev. Muldoon administrator of the Archdiocese of Chicago, Ill."

[46] ACPF, Scritture originali riferite nelle Congregazione generali, Allegatio A, n. 1, no. 51287, Spalding to Marchetti, Chicago, July 24, 1902. Hereafter Scritture, etc., will be cited as Scr. orig., Alleg.

[47] ACPF, Scr. orig., Alleg. A, n. 2, no. 51287, Spalding to Marchetti, Chicago, July 24, 1902.

Riordan finished with six votes, with one for Bishop Dunne of Dallas. In the afternoon, the bishops examined the priests' *terna* and discussed the qualifications of the names proposed. Ryan and Janssen then voted for Spalding as *dignissimus,* and, as Spalding noted, "as they constituted a majority, I had nothing to do but submit." But, he added, "my own preference was for Abp. Riordan." The bishops excluded the second and third names on the priests' *terna,* and chose instead Bishop George Montgomery of Monterey and Los Angeles as *dignior,* even though he had already been proposed as a candidate for the co-adjutorship to the Archbishop of San Francisco. For *dignus* they named Father Daniel J. Riordan, brother of the Archbishop of San Francisco, and Pastor of St. Elizabeth's Parish in Chicago, against whom there was only one objection, his health.[48]

On his return to Alton, Bishop Ryan informed Marchetti that in the selection of the administrator for the archdiocese, Spalding had been placed between two evils. If he had appointed the proper man, Father Riordan, his action would have brought into full public view serious matters which Ryan termed "absolutely needful to conceal." Thus Spalding had been constrained to appoint Bishop Muldoon and to allow things to pursue their previous course under the control of the men with whom Feehan had been surrounded in his last years.[49] The auxiliary, Ryan hastened to say, was not so objectionable himself, but he was victimized by a group whose actions, he declared, "were a stench in the nostrils of the better class of people and clergy" in Chicago, and who had spared no effort to strengthen their positions. Moreover, Muldoon was blindly ambitious, according to Ryan, and disposed to use power to form factions and "to push himself." The Bishop of Alton had assisted at Muldoon's consecra-

[48] ACPF, Scr. orig., Alleg. A, n. 3, no. 51287, Spalding to Marchetti, Peoria, July 25, 1902.

[49] ACPF, Scr. orig., Alleg. A, n. 4, no. 51287, Ryan to Marchetti, Alton, July 25, 1902.

tion, and thus, as he told Marchetti, he felt free to write to him to say "that it would be a graceful thing not to push or allow himself to be pushed forward untimely and unduly," and that, in the first place, Muldoon and his friends should vote "for one so much his elder, so obviously fit and so renowned as the senior suffragan."

As an irremovable rector, Father Hugh Smyth of St. Mary's in Evanston had also been present at the morning balloting, and almost immediately after, he likewise took pen in hand. It had been, he told Denis O'Connell, "an exceedingly well managed affair" in the interests of Bishop Muldoon, and the auxiliary had been made *dignior* because there had been some who thought the auxiliary should receive "a complimentary vote though they would not want to see him Archbishop." Riordan of San Francisco had five votes for *dignior* and six *dignus* and would have had more, Smyth added, "but some of those present feared him as a disciplinarian." Muldoon's strength had arisen from the fact, he believed, that four of the voters owed their positions to the auxiliary, four more had received honors from him in the past year, while two were in dread of anyone who would enforce the law. The archbishops would be almost unanimously for Spalding, he maintained, but it was feared, as he expressed it, "that Satolli may remember the past."[50]

One week later, the Evanston Pastor again wrote to Monsignor O'Connell, and enclosed an editorial from the Chicago *Evening Post* which was entitled, "IT POINTS TO BISHOP SPALDING." Smyth believed the editorial expressed the wishes of everybody, since "the laity, it would appear, to a man are wishing and praying for Spalding."[51]

More the realist, Spalding summed up his own view of the situation when he told a reporter of the Chicago *Evening Post* that there was no man in the United States who could say with

[50] ADR, Smyth to O'Connell, Evanston, July 24, 1902.
[51] ADR, Same to Same, Evanston, July 30, 1902.

any certainty on whom the choice of the Pope would fall. "Personally, I do not think I shall be named," he said, and he preferred "to remain in Peoria where my work has been chiefly done and where my friends are." Subject to the will of the Church in every particular, however, he would not, he said, allow any personal preference to affect his action.[52] If named the next Archbishop of Chicago, he seemed to say, he would not refuse it.

Bishop Montgomery was not, however, of the same mind, and when he heard the rumor that the bishops of the Province of Chicago had designated him as *dignior* on their *terna,* he informed Propaganda that it would be impossible for him to accept "this office and honor" should he be named Archbishop of Chicago. After his many years in California with its temperate climate, he stated, "it would be impossible for me to live and to work efficiently in a region so hot in the summer and so cold in winter. . . ." On the other hand, the Bishop of Peoria not only appertained to the province, but he was *persona grata* to the priests of the Archdiocese of Chicago, to the bishops of the province, and to the archbishops of the American Church. For these reasons, Montgomery prayed "that for the good of the Church and Religion, that Bishop John Lancaster Spalding be nominated Archbishop of Chicago."[53]

Needless to say, the energetic Archbishop of St. Paul agreed, and on that same day Ireland had also written to Propaganda to call the cardinals' attention to the importance of the Chicago succession. While there was no need to speak of the importance of this archiepiscopal See, he believed it imperative to state that

[52] Chicago *Evening Post,* July 24, 1902.

[53] ACPF, Acta, no. 53, Prot. no. 52583, Dicembre, 1902, num. VII, Montgomery to Eminentissime Princeps, Los Angeles, August 5, 1902, p. 16. Montgomery was appointed titular Archbishop of Osimo and coadjutor with the right of succession to Archbishop Riordan of San Francisco on March 27, 1903. He died on January 10, 1907.

he would regard the selection of Bishop Muldoon to succeed the old archbishop "a grave disaster for religion." Muldoon was, to say the least, said Ireland, "young, inexperienced, with very ordinary talents, with little public esteem among Catholics, no influence among Protestants." To place such a man at the head of such a large archdiocese, whose affairs were so vast and complicated and where a powerful influence could radiate throughout the United States, was he believed, to condemn Chicago to mediocrity.[54] For some years, the archdiocese had been practically without a head since Archbishop Feehan, described as "always timid and inactive," had been for five years incapable of work due to declining health. Consequently, there had been a terrible decline in the moral condition of the clergy, documents and proofs of which could be found in the Propaganda archives. Sad to say, he continued, Muldoon was supported by the guiltiest faction, while the priests who were opposed to him were the most respected of the clergy. He repeated his conviction, therefore, that the promotion of the auxiliary would prove to be disastrous to the cause of religion in Chicago.[55]

Archbishop Ireland likewise declared that while the other candidates were fine ecclesiastics, there was only one who had what he called the "*hauteur intellectuelle*" demanded by the position, namely the Bishop of Peoria, who would make, he was convinced, an excellent Archbishop of Chicago. "He is *au courant* of the affairs of the diocese [*sic*]," he stated, "and is very highly esteemed by all the people . . . is capable, intelligent, zealous." True, he said, Spalding was known to have spoken too frankly at times, and, he admitted, he had spoken against the establishment of the Apostolic Delegation, but he noted that Spalding had "revised his old views on that subject." In brief, there was no better candidate, and Propaganda could count on

[54] ACPE, Acta, no. 53, Prot. no. 52583, Dicembre, 1902, num. IV, Ireland to Eminentissime Seigneur, St. Paul, le 5 Aout, 1902, p. 11.

[55] *Ibid.*, pp. 11–12.

the fact that the good Bishop of Peoria would also be a good Archbishop of Chicago.[56]

Meanwhile, Monsignor Marchetti had gathered opinions on the qualifications of the candidates proposed from varied sources, and, on August 22, 1902, he summarized his findings for Girolamo Maria Cardinal Gotti, the new Prefect of the Propaganda.[57] Bishop M. Burke, of St. Joseph, had written that Father Daniel Riordan's health militated against his selection, that Bishop Montgomery, not known in Chicago, would not have sufficient prestige for the office, and that Spalding was the best candidate of those proposed.[58] Father Thomas Fitzgerald, S.J., on the other hand, maintained that Father Riordan, despite his health, was "before God" the man most worthy of the office, and in this judgment he was seconded by Abbot Jaeger of St. Procopius Abbey, who had objected strongly to Muldoon's candidacy.[59] There was no mention of Quigley, the third man on the priests' *terna*. The archbishops had likewise been canvassed for their views on the candidates, and in the main, as had been predicted, they favored the Bishop of Peoria.[60] Marchetti forwarded this

[56] *Ibid.*, pp. 12–13.

[57] ACPF, Acta, no. 53, Prot. no. 52583, Dicembre, 1902, num. III, Marchetti to Eminenza Rῆa, Washington, 22 Agosto, 1902, pp. 7–10.

[58] *Ibid.*, pp. 8–9.

[59] *Ibid.*, p. 9.

[60] *Ibid.*, pp. 9–10. Archbishop Elder of Cincinnati substituted Muldoon's name for Riordan's on the bishops' *terna*, but recommended Spalding's selection. Ryan of Philadelphia spoke well of all the candidates and did not single out a particular name. Ireland protested vehemently against Muldoon's candidacy, and while he regarded all the other candidates as excellent ecclesiastics, he preferred Spalding for the archbishopric. Placide Chapelle of New Orleans favored the Bishop of Peoria because he was first on both lists, while Pierre Bourgade of Santa Fe excluded Muldoon as too young, Montgomery as an excellent candidate for the coadjutorship to Riordan of San Francisco, Father Riordan for his health, and thus endorsed Spalding. Riordan of San Francisco thought that his brother's health precluded his selection; he wanted

information to Rome, and the period of suspenseful waiting then set in.

Among the American archbishops, there was none, perhaps, who had a more vital interest in the Chicago succession than Archbishop Riordan of San Francisco. A Chicago priest, he had been pastor of St. James Parish in that city in 1883, when he had been named coadjutor with the right of succession to Archbishop Alemany. Spalding had preached at Riordan's consecration, and he had been the first to suggest his Louvain schoolmate for the coadjutorship which he himself had declined.[61] There were ties of interest that could not be disregarded when both Riordan's brother, pastor of St. Elizabeth's Parish and a former chancellor, and Spalding, friend and Louvain confrere, were both proposed to head the archdiocese in which he had labored as teacher and pastor. In August 1902, Riordan sailed for Europe, specifically

---

Montgomery as a coadjutor and believed, therefore, that Spalding was the only eligible candidate. Keane of Dubuque also suggested Spalding while Alexander Christie of Oregon City simply substituted Muldoon's name for that of Montgomery's on the bishops' *terna*. Gibbons barred Muldoon's candidacy since the Auxiliary, he believed, was incapable at the moment of restoring peace in the archdiocese, Quigley from the New York province did not have the necessary experience and Spalding was the prelate needed under the circumstances. Williams of Boston thought Muldoon too young and that Quigley was needed in Buffalo. Archbishop Kain of St. Louis had failed to answer Marchetti's request for information on the two *ternae* and Katzer of Milwaukee was traveling in Europe. Katzer wrote to the Cardinal Prefect from Lins, in Austria, and told Gotti that Muldoon should not be nominated, Father Riordan in bad health was also a priest of an archdiocese divided into factions and was hardly suitable, Quigley and Montgomery he hardly knew, and he believed, therefore, that the Bishop of Peoria was the most worthy candidate and would prove a most capable successor to Feehan. Cf. APF, Acta, no. 53, Prot. no. 52583, Dicembre, 1902, num. V, Katzer to Eminentissime . . . D.D. Cardinalis S.R.E. Dignissime Praefecte . . . Lincii, die 16, Aug., 1902, p. 13.

[61] Cf. Chapter 4, note 33.

in the interest of the California Pious Fund Case which was to come before the new Permanent Court of Arbitration, called the Hague Tribunal.[62] Shortly after his arrival, the Archbishop told Monsignor O'Connell that he intended to visit Rome after the case was settled. He had no business in Rome except, he said, "to push the case of my coadjutor and to press the appointment of Bishop Spalding for Chicago." Riordan insisted that it was absolutely necessary that a first-class man should be sent to Chicago, since, he declared, "affairs there are in a most deplorable condition and I know no one who is able to remedy this except Bishop Spalding."[63]

Anxious as he was to see Spalding named the next archbishop of Chicago, on reaching Rome Riordan felt compelled to give Cardinal Gotti his views "on the deplorable state of that immense diocese."[64] First of all, one had to bear in mind, he said,

---

[62] The Pious Fund Case was concerned with the private benefactions to the Jesuits for their colonial missions in California. After the Jesuits were expelled in 1767, the fund was taken over by the Spanish government and upon the erection in April, 1840, of the Diocese of California, the income from the fund was assigned to it. When for some time after Mexican independence no support was forthcoming, a commission was created for the adjudication of claims under a convention signed by the United States and Mexico. When initial attempts failed, in 1875 Sir Edward Thornton, British Ambassador to Washington, was chosen as umpire and decided in favor of the Church's claims. Mexico paid the award but refused to pay the interest that had accumulated, and thus the dispute dragged on until 1902, when on October 14 the justices of the new Permanent Court of International Arbitration ruled that Mexico should pay $1,420,682.57 in accumulated interest and an annual sum of $43,650. These payments were made up to and including the year, 1913. Cf. Ellis, *Documents*, pp. 409–410.

[63] ADR, Riordan to O'Connell, Hotel des Indies [no place], August 31, 1902. Riordan had succeeded Archbishop Alemany in 1884 and now some eighteen years later had asked for a coadjutor to aid in the administration of the vast archdiocese.

[64] ACPF, Acta, no. 53, Prot. no. 52583, Dicembre, 1902, num. XII, Riordan to Eminenza Reverendissima, Roma, li 29 Ottobre, 1902, pp. 21–23.

that for twenty years there had been no ecclesiastical government to speak of in Chicago, since Archbishop Feehan, "physically infirm, mentally weak and often incapable of doing anything at all," had been content with total retirement, had allowed the archdiocese to run itself, and had adopted, asserted Riordan, with regard to the clergy "the norm: Live and Let Live." Consequently, ecclesiastical discipline had disappeared and scandals of all kinds had taken its place. Riordan described these scandals in detail for the Cardinal Prefect, and warned that it was no longer a mark of distinction in Chicago to be a Catholic. Loyal Catholics were consumed with shame while some of the weaker brethren had already abandoned the Church. Protestants, he said, regarded the Archdiocese of Chicago as "a bilge of corruption," and believed "that their forebears were right in calling the Catholic Church the whore of Babylon."[65]

Furthermore, Riordan continued, Muldoon's selection as auxiliary bishop had only made matters worse, since he was concerned with but one purpose, namely to strengthen his own position and to weaken that of the opposition. To accomplish this end, questionable characters had been promoted to important positions while "good, old, saintly priests, who are still struggling in circumstances marked by foul shamefulness in order to save the name of the Church," he declared, "have been divested of position which they had held for years, and have been publicly humiliated." He implored Cardinal Gotti, therefore, "for the love of the Church of Christ, for the love of all our good Catholics in the rest of the American nation," to put an end to the horrible scandal in the city where he had spent the greater part of his life. ". . . there I labored and sweated," Riordan concluded, "and now I beg you with all fervor of soul to help by nominating a worthy bishop to such an afflicted part of the Church of God."[66] No worthier candidate could be found, he believed, than Bishop Spalding.

[65] *Ibid.*, pp. 21–22.
[66] *Ibid.*, p. 23.

Within a few days, however, the Archbishop of San Francisco learned to his dismay that both Cardinals Gotti and Satolli had received letters[67] from the Baroness von Zedtwitz, the former Elizabeth Caldwell,[68] in which she had impugned Spalding's integrity and had leveled serious accusations against the Bishop of Peoria. Before he left Rome, therefore, Riordan promised Satolli that he would go to see the Baroness in Geneva concerning these startling charges. The latter, Riordan informed the cardinals from Paris in early November 1902, had reaffirmed her denunciation of the Bishop, and if their eminences so desired, she would come to Rome with witnesses who could swear to the truth of her assertions. But, in Riordan's judgment, these assertions were too vague, hardly supported by incontestable evidence, and they ought not, therefore, to be admitted. Moreover, he had known Spalding for over forty-two years, and never once had he heard the slightest insinuation against his good name. "I believe," Riordan insisted, that "he is a man of irreproachable character and without stain."[69]

[67] Cf. ACPF, Scr. orig., Folder 153/1903, no. 51081. La Baronne de Zedtwitz, née Caldwell, à Son Eminence le Cardinal Préfet de la Propagande à Rome, Paris, le 17 Août, 1902. Cf. also ACPF, Scr. orig., Folder 153/1903, no. 52375, Same à Son Eminence le Cardinal Satolli, Paris, le 17 Août, 1902.

[68] Cf. Chapter 4, n. 51. In June, 1890, "Lina" had married Baron Moritz Curt von Zedwitz, then German Minister to Mexico, in the chapel at Caldwell Hall, for which she had donated $50,000. Bishop Spalding performed the ceremony in the presence of Cardinal Gibbons, Bishop Keane, and about one hundred guests. Cf. Baltimore *Sun*, June 18, 1890.

[69] ACPF, Scr. orig., Folder 153/1903, no. 52375, Riordan à Son Eminence Cardinal Gotti, Paris, le 9 Novembre, 1902. Cf. also ACPF, Scr. orig., Folder 153/1903, no. 52375, Same à Son Eminence Cardinal Satolli, Paris, le 9 Novembre, 1902. On the same day, the Baroness repeated her charges in reply to a letter from Satolli, dated October 27, 1902. Cf. ACPF, Scr. orig., Folder 153/1903, no.

Six days later, in a thoroughly perplexed mood, the Archbishop of San Francisco advised Satolli from St. Patrick's College, Maynooth, that in the light of new evidence that he had uncovered in London, he was now convinced that Spalding had, indeed, been guilty of the charges in the Baroness' bill of indictment, and, he sadly wrote, "though it is most painful, I feel bound in conscience to prevent his promotion to the See of Chicago." If he were to be named archbishop, the Baroness' threat to make her arraignment of Spalding public would create scandal, "the greatest scandal," warned Riordan, "that ever occurred in the American Church."[70] Though the allegations thus appeared incontrovertible, the complete truth in this episode will perhaps never be known. If the Bishop of Peoria had, in fact, been found in contradiction, he might very well have replied in those words, so seemingly autobiographical, which he had written only a year before: "His best wisdom he has learned from his own faults and failures . . . and if he be discovered in contradiction with himself, it is because he, like all men, is made of contradictions."[71] Many years before, as he penned the preface to his uncle's biography, the young Father Spalding had confessed that "no life with which we are perfectly familiar can be wholly beautiful," since even then he knew that "time the approver, which destroys false and factitious reputations, is alone able to bring out in all their worth and loveliness those which are founded in merit."[72]

Speculation about the next Archbishop of Chicago, in the meantime, had continued. Father Charles Grannan, who had

52375, La Baronne de Zedwitz à Son Eminence le Cardinal Satolli, La Chartreuse, Suisse, le 9 Novembre, 1902.

[70] ACPF, Scr. orig., Folder 153/1903, no. 52375, Riordan to Satolli, Maynooth, Ireland, November 15, 1902.

[71] J. L. Spalding *Aphorisms and Reflections. Conduct, Culture and Religion* (Chicago, 1901), p. 9.

[72] Spalding, *Life of the Most Rev. M. J. Spalding,* p. iv.

309

arrived in New York from Europe in early October, was aston-
ished, he told Denis O'Connell, at the number of articles that
had appeared in American newspapers about Spalding and the
Chicago succession.[73] Two days before, the Catholic University of
America professor had relayed the latest rumors to the American
Monsignor in Rome. The *Western Watchman* had published a
report which declared that Propaganda had postponed discussion
of the Chicago appointment due to various objections the congregation had received about Spalding's "doctrines." This was
ridiculous, insisted Father David S. Phelan, editor of the *Watchman,* since there was no question at all of the Bishop's teachings.
After Archbishop Satolli had been appointed the first apostolic
delegate in 1893, many American bishops had strenuously objected, Phelan recalled, "but Bishop Spalding put the objections
in writing and Cardinal Satolli did not forgive his doing it."[74]
Apparently finding it good copy, the press kept the question of
the succession alive in the weeks that followed. There were two
reasons, the *Northwest Chronicle* asserted, that precluded the
possibility of Spalding's appointment to Chicago, for in addition
to Satolli's bitter opposition, some of the Bishop's writings, it was
said, could not bear the rigid scrutiny of orthodoxy, since "his
philosophical views were considered to be not quite sound."[75]
Added zest to the guessing game of the press came in the often
not inaccurate cables from their Roman correspondents. The
cardinals had divided into two camps, the New York *Tribune*
claimed, one that favored Spalding, the other advocating the
appointment of someone outside the Chicago area.[76] Finally, as
the cardinals gathered in general congregation to discuss the
Chicago appointment, the wires of the Associated Press carried

[73] ADR, "Jeshurun" [Grannan] to O'Connell, Washington, D.C.,
October 9, 1902.

[74] *Western Watchman* (St. Louis), October 7, 1902.

[75] *Northwest Chronicle,* December 6, 1902.

[76] New York *Tribune,* December 12, 1902

the news flash on the morning of December 15, 1902, that: "Satolli leads the minority in fight against Peoria Prelate."[77]

As the cardinals met in plenary session, it was, indeed, Cardinal Satolli who led the discussion, for he had been named *relator,* the cardinal deputed to study and to report on the day's agenda, namely the question of the nomination of a new archbishop of Chicago.[78] In his report, based mainly on letters received by Propaganda, Satolli presented the two *terna* with a brief biographical sketch of each candidate and summarized the information that Marchetti had forwarded from the Apostolic Delegation in Washington. For twenty-five years, Bishop Spalding had governed his diocese well, he admitted, and while Cardinal Gibbons and the majority of the archbishops had considered the Bishop of Peoria to be the best of the candidates who had been proposed, he directed the cardinals' attention to the grave implications of the von Zedtwitz and Riordan correspondence.[79] Against Muldoon's candidacy, there had been many letters and a few in his defense, he noted, but whether or not the allegations against the Bishop were true or false, many had believed them to be true, while those who had sought to defend Muldoon were neither the majority nor the better type of priest in the archdiocese.[80] From the data submitted by Cardinal Martinelli and by Archbishop Riordan, there had emerged a picture of weak government, scandals, and factions among the clergy that had reduced the Church there to a most deplorable condition. There was a need for a strong archbishop in Chicago, a man, Satolli maintained, "who with ability and energy can rule the various

[77] Chicago *Tribune,* December 15, 1902.

[78] ACPF, no. 53, Prot. no. 52583, Dicembre, 1902, Sacra Congregazione de Propagande Fide. Ponente Eminentissimo . . . Signor Cardinale Francesco Satolli, Relazione con sommario *Sulla nomina del nuovo Arcivescovo de Chicago* p. 1.

[79] *Ibid.,* pp. 2–3.

[80] *Ibid.,* p. 4.

311

factions and apply efficacious remedies to the festering evils that
have afflicted that diocese [*sic*]." Since Bishop Montgomery had
asked that his name be withdrawn and since Father Riordan's
health excluded him from consideration, Satolli asked his colleagues to take notice of the third candidate on the *terna* of the
consultors and irremovable rectors, namely Bishop Quigley of
Buffalo, who had been proposed by the bishops of the Province
of New York as the *dignior* candidate for that metropolitan see
and who had been deemed suitable, by all who had been questioned, to govern the important Archdiocese of New York.[81]
Finally, the *ponente* concluded the *ponenza* with questions or
dubia which were then put to a vote. To the question, "Whether
anyone of the candidates should be recommended to the Holy
Father for the vacant metropolitan see of Chicago?" the cardinals agreed, Satolli simply noted, to ask Pope Leo XIII to con-
firm their nomination of James Edward Quigley, Bishop of
Buffalo, as the new Archbishop of Chicago.[82] The meeting was
thereupon adjourned.

Within a few hours, American Catholics knew the name of
the new archbishop.[83] "Received word through the press of the
selection of Bp. Quigley as the next Archbishop of Chicago,"
remarked Muldoon in his diary, "Deo Gratias."[84] Some days
later, after several weeks spent in Scranton, Pennsylvania, Spalding returned to Peoria, where a young priest from the cathedral
greeted him at the train with the words, "Well Bishop, it looks

[81] *Ibid.*

[82] ACPF, Acta, no. 53, Prot. no. 52583, 15 Dicembre, 1902. The
decision of the general congregation of the Sacred Congregation de
Propaganda Fide is in Satolli's writing and simply reads: "*Affirmative
et supplicandum SSmo pro promotione Jacobi Quigley, Ep. Buf-
falensis.*"

[83] Cf. for example, the *Peoria Star*, December 15, 1902, "Bishop
Quigley new Archbishop."

[84] ADRoc, Muldoon Diary, December 15, 1902.

as though we're keeping you after all." "Yes, Father, and I knew it would be that way," replied the Bishop, "and it is well that it is so. This is my home. Why, at my age, should I start over again somewhere else? I am glad to stay here."[85] If hardly glad at the strange *denouement,* Archbishop Riordan was relieved, momentarily, at least, with the news that the Chicago affair had been settled. "He [Spalding] has no chance for a promotion," he informed Denis O'Connell, "let him remain where he is until God calls him."[86] Archbishop Ireland was disappointed with Quigley's appointment, but Ireland told Cardinal Gibbons that Satolli had written to say that Spalding's promotion had been an impossibility. "Poor Spalding! I have not yet ceased sorrowing," he lamented, "but I do not forgive Spalding," he added quickly, "for not having put on the list the name of Archbp. Riordan as he promised me to do."[87] Later, as he ruminated on the subject, Ireland observed that Spalding was the one American that Rome seemed not to have forgiven, "but then, he had gone far," he remarked to the Countess di Parravicino di Revel, "attacking directly the apostolic delegation of Washington."[88]

In Paris, the Abbé Klein, exasperated by the word from Rome, was convinced that the Propaganda's decision was but "a new proof of the stupidity of those who govern us," and, he told Spalding, he feared it would harm the interests of American Catholicism, "especially among those who know and appreciate

[85] Interview of Sister Mary Evangela Henthorne, B.V.M., in 1929 with Monsignor Maurice P. Sammon, late pastor of St. Bernard's Parish, Peoria, reportedly, the "young priest" in question. The young Father Sammon was at the time attached to St. Mary's Cathedral in Peoria. Cf. Henthorne, "The Life and Career of Bishop John Lancaster Spalding," p. 329, microfilm copy

[86] ADR, Riordan to O'Connell, San Francisco, December 30, 1902.

[87] AAB, 100-J-1, Ireland to Gibbons, St. Paul, March 2, 1903.

[88] UND, di Revel correspondence, Ireland to Sabina di Parravicino di Revel, St. Paul, March 9, 1903.

you."[89] Proposed by Monaco's Prince Albert I for the vacant bishopric in that 370-acre principality,[90] Klein's name had also been rejected by the Holy See, with the result that many newspapers, French and Italian in particular, saw more than a chronological coincidence in Rome's refusal to name the hero of the Gesù discourse to Chicago and the leader of "Americanism" in France to Monaco. Conservative journals, such as *La Verité française* and *L'Unita Cattolica* of Florence, Klein recalled, were spiteful, but no better analysis could be found, he believed, than in the Paris *L'Eclair's* discussion of "Americanism: The Case of Bishop Spalding and the Abbé Klein."[91] Of especial interest, it declared, was the case of the professor from the Institut Catholique in Paris, since four archbishops and two cardinals had supported his candidacy for Monaco and had offered the Vatican guarantees of his orthodoxy. Nonetheless, there were others who had predicted, and accurately so, that Rome would never sanction the episcopal elevation of the "Americanist" who had championed the cause of Father Hecker's *Life,* and who had thereby raised the specter "of a vast conspiracy in the United States, with accomplices in France, England and America," which, *L'Eclair* noted, had alarmed the Holy See, since it had sought, so it had been supposed, "to change the religion, to destroy the authority of the Pope, and to transfer to America supreme control of whatever would remain of the Church."[92] Against this "Americanism" that had never existed, Rome had used its heaviest artillery, and it yet feared the tendency "which more and more . . . inclines Catholics of Europe to look to the United States and to prefer the

[89] ADP, Klein to Spalding, Bellevue prés Paris, January 30, 1903.

[90] Felix Klein, *La Route du Petit Morvandiau, Souvenirs, VI: Au Debut du Siècle* (Paris, 1905), pp. 100–103 and *passim.* Charles F. B. Theuret (1887–1901) had been the first Bishop of Monaco. Cf. *Enciclopedia Cattolica,* VIII, p. 1259.

[91] *Ibid.,* pp. 100–101.

[92] *L'Eclair* (Paris), January 7, 1903, copy

314

way of doing things which succeed over there to those which fail here."

This anti-American attitude, which, *L'Eclair* was certain, had prevented the Abbé's nomination as bishop of Monaco, had been even more emphatic in the Pope's refusal to make Spalding Archbishop of Chicago. Rome had discovered that Spalding was "inactive" and too old to administer so important a see as Chicago. Neither Spalding nor Klein could be less suspected of Italianism than of Americanism, concluded the Paris journal, since they were hardly partisans of the Pope's temporal power, a concern which was really the least of their worries.[93]

Americanism, Italianism, and papal temporal power were, to be sure, the least of Spalding's concerns, when Klein's letter and the excerpt from *L'Eclair* reached him in Washington. "I regret that you were not appointed to Monaco," he replied briefly, "but failure to get Chicago is a blessing pure and simple for me."[94] In the painful years ahead, Bishop Spalding would yearn for many more such blessings pure and simple.

[93] *Ibid.* It was true to say that the Bishop of Peoria was hardly a partisan in the involved question of the pope's temporal sovereignty. When Archbishop Ireland reviewed the question in a sermon preached at St. Patrick's Church, Washington, on December 10, 1900, Spalding remarked to the Countess di Parravicino di Revel: "What in the world could have induced Abp. Ireland to come out at this time in favor of the temporal power! No one here seems to believe in his sincerity and the opinion grows that he is above all a politician." Cf. ADR, Spalding to Sabina di Parravicino di Revel, Peoria, undated. The countess had, undoubtedly, forwarded Spalding's letter to O'Connell. Cf. also ADR. Sabina di Parravicino di Revel to O'Connell, Lentate Sub Seveso, October, 1901: The Countess told O'Connell that Spalding had written that Ireland's "agitation in favor of the temporal power has not awakened an echo. No one here seems to think the question has any actuality."

[94] ADP, Spalding to Klein, Washington, March 11, 1903, copy.

9

The Gathering Storm

SPALDING'S stay in Washington had been a busy one, and, as he told the Abbé Klein, he was "still detained by the work of the coal commission."[1] Five months before, as interested parties continued to speculate on Rome's delay in the appointment of a successor to Archbishop Feehan of Chicago, the Bishop of Peoria had been both "surprised and honored"[2] when on October 16, 1902, the morning newspapers had carried a White House press release to the effect that he had been named by President Roosevelt to the arbitration commission appointed to settle the anthracite coal strike.[3] The strike had been called by John Mitchell, President of the United Mine Workers of America, after the mine operators had rejected the union's demands, and on May 12, 1902, 147,000 workers walked off the job.[4] It was

[1] ADP, Spalding to Klein, Washington, March 11, 1903, copy.

[2] Peoria *Evening Journal,* October 16, 1902.

[3] Peoria *Journal,* October 16, 1902. It was this morning edition that carried the White House press release.

[4] Robert L. Reynolds, "The Coal Kings Come to Judgement," in *American Heritage,* XI (April, 1960), p. 94. Mitchell was characterized as "a shy, introspective man," who "by sticking to the United Mine Workers in their earliest, most difficult days, by hard work, a talent for conciliation and a quiet maturity that inspired confidence . . . rose through the union's ranks to become national president in 1898 when he was only twenty-eight years old" (*Ibid.,* p. 56). Among

316

the first time that the laborers in an entire American industry had combined to strike, the first time that the entire public was affected; thus it was considered at the time as the greatest industrial crisis in American history. By October, industry had become frightened, railroad schedules had been cut to a minimum, and the *Times* of London predicted that coal riots would ensue in American cities as soon as the winter had set in. The people had become aroused, and in order to avert public, if not political, disaster in the November congressional elections, the President had found it imperative to intervene.[5]

Less than a month before his appointment to the arbitration board, Spalding had described the condition of the Pennsylvania coal miners as "a national disgrace," and he sincerely hoped that the strike might prove to be "the beginning of a better state of things for these, our overburdened and oppressed brothers."[6] The press could only guess at the reason for Spalding's appointment. The New York *Tribune* spoke of Roosevelt's esteem for the Bishop, but, the writer believed, "the suggestion of Bishop Spalding's appointment came from President Mitchell who holds the Bishop in the highest admiration as do all labor leaders." In the bituminous coal strike of 1900, asserted the *Tribune,* it was Spalding, through Father John Power, pastor of Immaculate Conception Parish in Spring Valley, Illinois, who had exerted a powerful influence in the preservation of order among the miners and in the final settlement of the strike.[7]

---

the union's demands were: 1) recognition of the United Mine Workers as a bargaining agent with the operators; 2) a minimum wage scale, and 3) an eight-hour day.

[5] Irving Stone, *Clarence Darrow for the Defense* (New York, 1941), p. 127. Mitchell chose the Chicago attorney to represent the United Mine Workers before the anthracite coal commission.

[6] Bloomington *Plantagraph* (Illinois), September 22, 1902, quoted in R. J. Cornell, *The Anthracite Coal Strike of 1902,* Washington, 1957, p. 231.

[7] New York *Tribune,* October 17, 1902.

No evidence has been discovered to support this claim. But it was true that Mitchell's objections to the original composition of the board of arbitrators as stipulated by the mine operators had prompted Roosevelt to promise to add a labor man as well as some "high Catholic ecclesiastic" to the commission, Mitchell having suggested the latter since so many of the anthracite coal miners were Catholics.[8] "I added to the Arbitration Commission on my own authority, a sixth member," Roosevelt later wrote, "in the person of Bishop Spalding of Peoria, a Catholic bishop, one of the very best men to be found in the entire country."[9]

While the tribunal's personnel met with the general approval of the press,[10] no one was more enthusiastic about the choice

[8] Cornell, *op. cit.*, p. 226. When the operators objected vehemently to the appointment of a "labor" man, Roosevelt resolved the difficulty by appointing the "labor" man as an "eminent sociologist," the fourth of the five-man commission as stipulated by the mine operators.

[9] Theodore Roosevelt, *An Autobiography* (New York, 1926), p. 460.

[10] Cornell, *op. cit.*, p. 231. At 2 A.M., October 16, 1902, the White House issued the following statement:

After a conference with Mr. Mitchell and some further conferences with the representatives of the coal operators, the President has appointed the members of the commission . . .

Brigadier General John M. Wilson, U.S. Army, retired . . . an officer of the engineer corps. . . .

Mr. E. W. Parker, Washington, D.C., as an expert mining engineer. . . .

Hon. George Gray, Wilmington, Delaware, as a judge of the United States Court.

Mr. E. E. Clark, Cedar Rapids, Iowa, Grand Chief of the order of Railway Conductors—as a sociologist—the President assuming that for the purpose of such a commission the term sociologist means a man who has thought and studied deeply on social questions and has practically applied his knowledge.

Mr. Thomas H. Watkins, Scranton, Pa., as a man practically acquainted with the mining and selling of coal.

of Spalding than the man who had been the first, perhaps, to bring the name of the Bishop to the President's attention. "I am especially delighted," Nicholas Murray Butler told Roosevelt, "that my dear friend, Bishop Spalding, is on the Commission. There is no better American under the flag than he, and few who see more clearly and more sympathetically into the social problems of the day."[11] Many years later, Butler recalled that early in Roosevelt's administration, he had offered the President a series of suggestions concerning men whom he described as "of the highest competence and disinterestedness" who might from time to time be called on for counsel and administrative assistance. Among the names was that of Spalding, who, he said, "might well be called upon . . . in anything that related to the consideration and solution of social problems quite apart from politics." The Columbia University President remembered distinctly that Roosevelt had discussed the composition of the arbitration commission with him, and, he added, "on my suggesting Bishop Spalding for membership upon it," the nation's chief executive exclaimed, " 'What you have said to me about that man interests me greatly. I believe he is just the man we want.' "[12]

Upon receipt of official word of his appointment, Spalding immediately thanked Roosevelt for the honor, and assured the President that he would do "whatever may lie in my power to

---

Bishop John L. Spalding, of Peoria, Illinois. The President has added Bishop Spalding's name to the commission.

Hon. Carroll D. Wright has been appointed recorder of the commission.

Ibid., pp. 229–230.

[11] Library of Congress, Roosevelt Papers, Butler to Roosevelt, New York, October 17, 1902.

[12] Butler to Sister Mary Evangela Henthorne, B.V.M. New York, December 19, 1928. This letter is in the writer's possession. Cf. also, Sister Mary Evangela, "Bishop Spalding's Work on the Anthracite Coal Commission," *CHR* XXVIII (July, 1942), p. 188.

further your patriotic and philanthropic purpose in appointing the commission."[13] Spalding arrived in Washington on October 23, 1902, and on the following morning in the company of his fellow commissioners he met with the President at his office in the temporary White House. After the President submitted the published statement of the mine operators, the commission members retired to the offices of Carroll D. Wright, Commissioner of Labor, where they elected Judge George Gray chairman of the arbitration commission.[14]

Immediately after the meeting, Spalding was interviewed by the waiting reporters. He expressed some delicacy about speaking for publication just at the moment about the work of the commission; nonetheless, he stated that in his opinion "the accumulation of capital in the hands of the few, the endeavor to procure labor at a minimum wage, and the organization of labor to protect its rights, were the natural corollaries of the commercial spirit of the age." These factors had not only produced bitter struggles between capital and labor, but, he felt convinced, they had also contributed to an intensification of international competition for the markets of the world. As a consequence, there seemed to be a growing tendency toward state socialism, with a resultant loss of individuality so indigenous to the American way of life. Indicative of the movement, he believed, were state inspection of food products and governmental enforcement of sanitary laws. Even the gradual unification of the public school system appeared to be intrinsically essential and salutary in the complex conditions of modern society; yet he maintained, they were "certainly far from the individualism

[13] Library of Congress, Roosevelt Papers, Spalding to Roosevelt, Peoria, October 18, 1902.

[14] Cornell, *op. cit.,* p. 236. At this meeting, Carroll D. Wright was also named to the commission to avoid the possibility of a tie vote during the hearings.

of the founders of the republic." Just before his appointment to the commission, Spalding continued, he had sent to press the manuscript of a book entitled, *Socialism and Labor and Other Arguments,* which further elaborated these views. Asked if he believed that a large number of the miners were anarchists, Spalding replied that that was impossible, for the simple reason that a majority of the miners were Catholics, and no Catholic could be an anarchist.[15]

At the commission's session on October 27, it was decided that formal hearings would begin on November 14, in Scranton.[16] To acquaint themselves with the actual operation of the mines and the working conditions of the miners, the commissioners made a week's tour of the anthracite coal regions, where they all donned miner's clothing and descended into the mines. *Harper's Weekly* was troubled, however, because The New York *Times* had reported Judge Gray and Bishop Spalding as having "distributed an unrecorded number of small coins among the boys working in those grimy edifices." Shocked by this action, *Harper's* had labeled it "a betrayal of sympathy for the miners" and an unwonted bias. With tongue in cheek, the *Times* wrote that it sincerely hoped that public confidence would not be withdrawn either from the Judge or the Bishop, since in the things that really mattered, the *Times* said, Spalding and Gray had shown themselves careful "to preserve the shadow as well as the substance of perfect impartiality." That two or all of the commissioners had given pennies to the breaker boys had, indeed, proved sympathy, but it had only been a sympathy for the "unfortunate little fellows," and, therefore, no harm had been done.[17]

Until the Christmas recess, the commission's hearings con-

[15] New York *Tribune,* October 25, 1902.
[16] Cornell, *op. cit.,* p. 237.
[17] New York *Times,* November 16, 1902.

tinued to be held in Scranton, and thereafter its activities were transferred to the federal courthouse in Philadelphia. "I return to Philadelphia in a day or two," Spalding informed Father Hudson on January 1, 1903, "and shall probably be engaged on the work of the Anthracite Commission a month or six weeks longer."[18] Hundreds of witnesses passed before the commission when the hearings resumed on January 9, and the testimony ultimately filled fifty-six volumes. At the conclusion of the hearings, the commissioners adjourned to Washington, where for several weeks they worked in executive sessions on the report of their findings and the specific awards with regard to wages, hours, and other matters germane to the controversy. Finally, on March 18, 1903, the anthracite coal commission laid the full text of its report before the President.[19]

Organized labor expressed general satisfaction with the results, since the miners were granted a 10 per cent wage increase, and even though there was no outright recognition of the United Mine Workers' Union, there were gains important enough for the strikers to regard the settlement as a victory.[20] John Mitchell agreed that the award displayed great practical wisdom, and that it illustrated the tendency of wise men to surrender theoretical prejudices when they come in contact with a real and pressing problem. He refused, however, to discuss the *Report,* which, in his opinion and that of the majority of unions, was a document that had been prepared by fair-minded and intelligent men, and yet had betrayed, he believed, "a lack of appreciation of some of the fundamental principles of unionism."[21] This could be interpreted as a reference to the commission's denial of a principle fundamental to unionism, namely

[18] UND, Hudson Papers, Spalding to Hudson, Peoria, January 1, 1903.

[19] Cornell, *op. cit.,* p. 252.

[20] Reynolds, *op. cit.,* p. 100.

[21] John Mitchell, *Organized Labor* (Philadelphia, 1903), p. 392.

the right of the union to a closed shop.[22] On this question, the *Report* had stated:

The right to remain at work where others have ceased to work or to engage anew in work which others have abandoned, is part of the personal liberty of a citizen that can never be surrendered . . . Our language is the language of a free people, and fails to furnish any form of speech by which the right of a citizen to work when he pleases, and on what terms he pleases, cannot be successfully denied. The common sense of our people, as well as the common law, forbids that this right should be assailed with impunity.[23]

Spalding was, most likely, opposed to the closed shop.[24] The question of the right to work and/or the open shop versus the closed shop was, however, in his view, one that was honeycombed with conditions, and if he had ever hesitated to give formal approval to the concept of the closed shop, there was no doubt as to where his sympathy lay in the resolution of this intricate issue. Only trade unionism could bring relief from the economic ills besetting the American people, he declared shortly after the *Report* had been made public. What labor desired, first of all, was not charity, but justice, since "the cause of labor if rightly understood," he insisted, "is the cause of humanity."[25]

Just one year later, on April 7, 1904, testifying before the Senate Committee on Education and Labor on the bill which sought to create a national arbitration tribunal, Spalding gave evidence "that his social education had advanced beyond the theoretical stage."[26] In a reply to Senator Jonathan Dolliver of Iowa,[27] who was concerned about the power of unions in de-

[22] A. C. Schroll, *The Social Thought of John Lancaster Spalding, D.D.*, Washington, 1944, p. 141.

[23] Cornell, *op. cit.*, pp. 255–256.

[24] Schroll, *op. cit.*, p. 141.

[25] New York *Tribune*, May 3, 1903.

[26] Roohan, *op. cit.*, p. 426.

[27] U.S. Congress, Senate, Committee on Education and Labor, United States Senate, Washington, D.C., April 7, 1904, Senate document, 3259, pp. 34–35 and *passim*.

nying non-union men from working during a strike, Spalding declared that as an abstract question there were no two opinions about the inviolability of the right to work; but, he said, the question must be considered in the concrete. The exercise of the right to work in an actual situation had to be denied in innumerable instances, and unless a union put difficulties in the way of that exercise, it would cease to exist as a union. Whenever there was a strike, whenever there was an attempt to bring in non-union labor, there would be intimidation, picketing, and other means to prevent the success of such efforts. The union's right to maintain itself was a necessary one, even though it would interfere with the individual's right to work, Spalding said. Whether the union's attitude in these cases was justifiable or not was, to his mind, a wholly different question from the abstract question of the right to work. By way of example, Spalding said,

. . . take men such as those in the anthracite coal region. There are 150,000 men, most of whom have become unfitted for any other kind of labor. They have lived in the mines until they have become unsuited for any other kind of work. They say that they have acquired certain equities: that they have helped to develop those properties and have incapacitated themselves for other means of making a livelihood . . . They find that there are reasons for them to strike. Then you send all over the country and bring in professional strikebreakers to prevent . . . success.[28]

Since this procedure would endure whenever strikes occurred, Spalding said, the abstract question of the right to work was not a practical one. "We fail to secure to our laborers that abstract right," he concluded, "and we shall continue to fail as long as organized labor is the mighty force it is." There was no power on earth that could destroy organized labor, he was convinced, and though labor might destroy itself by anarchistic and socialistic tendencies, he had no use for the National Asso-

[28] *Ibid.,* p. 34.

ciation of Manufacturers, headed at the time by David M. Parry, since to Spalding it was an evil movement, "because it starts out to destroy organized labor." Nothing good, he believed, could come from a movement whose obvious purpose was to break the power of the unions.[29] It was perhaps this position that prompted John Mitchell to say of Spalding some years later that, "during the executive sessions of the commission to settle the anthracite coal strike . . . Bishop Spalding fought and pleaded harder to secure the redress of the wrongs of the workingman than any other man on the commission."[30] To Mitchell he was "a true bishop," who stood in the front ranks of all who contended "for the rights of the weak and the poor . . ."[31]

[29] *Ibid.*, p. 35.

[30] *Catholic Citizen* (Milwaukee), July 17, 1909. The writer is indebted to the Reverend Robert J. Cornell, O. Praem., for this reference. The latter told the writer that "this statement seems particularly significant in view of the fact that one member of the commission was E. E. Clark, Grand Chief of the Order of Railway Conductors."

[31] Spalding's concept of the episcopal role was refreshingly broad. Though he disagreed, for example, with the single tax theory of Henry George, he did not hesitate in December, 1897, to speak at the Henry George memorial meeting. It was not necessary, he argued, to accept a man's peculiar views or theories in order to admire and honor him. The great merit of a Henry George was not in the special theory that he had advocated but rather in the spirit in which he had worked, in his love of the people, in his love of justice, and in his heroic defense of what he believed to have been right. He had helped his fellow men "and had made us all feel," Spalding maintained, "that we were not doing our duty by them . . ." *New World* (Chicago), December 11, 1897. At this memorial meeting held in Chicago on December 5, 1897, and attended by 5,000 people, the Bishop spoke without manuscript or notes. Some Catholics had espoused George's theories as propounded in his *Progress and Poverty.* When conservative forces in the American hierarchy sought in 1888 to have George's works placed on the Index of Forbidden Books, the Bishop of Peoria wrote to Rome against any such condemnation (AAB, 84-I-12, O'Connell to Gibbons, Rome, April 17, 1888). The most widely

325

Though his work as a member of the commission took up a considerable amount of time, Spalding had not hesitated in the course of the hearings to accept several invitations to preach and to lecture. "Bishop Spalding's occasional lectures and sermons in this city," commented the *New Century* of Washington, "are one of the few luxuries that we owe to the coal strike."[32] On the same day, for example, that Judge Gray had submitted the full report of the arbitration commission to President Roosevelt, Spalding lectured in the Catholic University of America before an audience that included Archbishop Falconio, the new Apostolic Delegate, college presidents, diplomats, labor leaders, and an overflow crowd that had to stand, so it was reported, in the corridors and stairwells of McMahon Hall that they might listen to "the foremost leader in the religious and educational life of the country."[33] Introduced by

---

known of George's backers was Dr. Edward McGlynn, pastor of St. Stephen's Church, New York. The story of McGlynn's difficulties with Archbishop Corrigan of New York has been told elsewhere. Cf. Ellis, *Gibbons,* I, pp. 547–594. McGlynn was reconciled to the Church on December 23, 1892, by Archbishop Satolli, the first apostolic delegate. One week later, Spalding wrote to Corrigan: "The restoration of McGlynn without penance of apology is a puzzle to all of us out here. . . . Things seem to be going from bad to worse" (AANY, C-44, Spalding to Corrigan, Peoria, December 30, 1892). The difficulty for Spalding was not McGlynn's social thought, but his disobedience. The same spirit that led the Bishop to honor Henry George prompted him to attend the memorial meeting in Chicago in April, 1902, for John P. Altgeld, former Governor of Illinois, where he delivered the moving panegyric, "An Orator and Lover of Justice." Cf. Chapter XIII in *Socialism and Labor and Other Arguments,* pp. 189–200.

[32] *New Century* (Washington, D.C.), March 21, 1903. Cf. also Henthorne, op. cit., pp. 199–202, for the various lectures and sermons which the bishop delivered in Scranton, Philadelphia, and Washington during the course of the hearings.

[33] *Western Watchman* (St. Louis), March 26, 1903.

Bishop Conaty as "one of the University's devoted friends," the Rector asserted that the Bishop of Peoria had never failed in all circumstances "to manifest a vital interest in the development of the Catholic University of America."[34]

Actually, during the years since its opening, Spalding's enthusiasm for the University had waned on several occasions,[35] even if his disillusionment had been only momentary. At the start of Conaty's administration, for example, he had not been in a cheerful mood concerning the institution, and, although he had been urged to do so, he had failed to attend the Rector's installation.[36] Thomas J. Conaty, described as a "quiet peaceful man with no special talents for the position . . . ," had sought

to unify the University community and to restore confidence in the idea of a national Catholic university after the Keane dismissal had caused such serious damage to its prestige and support. But the student body continued to decrease, financial support was inadequate in every way, the faculties were incomplete and the University did not have the interested backing of the Catholic body in the United States.[37]

Finance had always been a major concern of the University's board of trustees, and to stave off an imminent financial crisis in the third year of Conaty's rectorship, the board had voted, in October 1898, to ask Rome to allow Archbishop Keane to return to the United States that he might devote at least a year to the task of collecting much needed funds.[38] Spalding was delighted by the news. "You have heard no doubt that Abp. Keane has consented to return to America," he remarked

[34] *Catholic University Bulletin*, IX (April, 1903), 312.

[35] Cf. Chapter 6, note 69.

[36] *Ibid.*, n. 83.

[37] Colman J. Barry, O.S.B., *The Catholic University of America, 1903–1909, The Rectorship of Denis J. O'Connell* (Washington, 1950), pp. 24–25.

[38] ACUA, MMBT, October 11, 1898. Cf. also, AAB, 96-S-1, Gibbons to Rampolla, Baltimore November 1, 1898, copy.

to Father Hudson, "and give his time to collecting for the University." It was a generous act on Keane's part, Spalding thought, and he hoped that he would meet with success. "The future of the University," he added, is more promising, "and the heads I think begin to see that there is a need of great economy." That was precisely what he wanted to see, namely "a retrenchment."[39]

Not long thereafter, aware, no doubt, of Spalding's renewed hopes, Conaty asked him to give some lectures in Washington in behalf of the University that he had helped to found. Reluctant at first, Spalding told the Rector that the Marquise des Monstiers-Merinville [Mary Gwendolen Caldwell] had strongly urged him to accept the invitation, and since Conaty seemed to think "that I can do some real good," he would make the trip and would give two lectures, which, he thought, would be quite enough. At the same time, he urged Conaty to have Archbishop Keane come home as quickly as possible, since, as he said, "the rich have plenty of money and if the Pope [Leo] were to die, things might change."[40] "Life and Education" was Spalding's theme as he addressed the audience in McMahon Hall on January 13, 1899, when he asked his listeners to be

[39] UND, Hudson Papers, Spalding to Hudson, Peoria, October 28, 1898.

[40] ACUA, Spalding to Conaty, November 15, 1898. The Marquise des Monstiers-Merinville had visited the University on October 30, 1898, and delighted with its progress, she established a scholarship in the School of Divinity in the name of her nephew, Waldemar Conrad Baron von Zedtwitz, "Lina" Caldwell's son, and $10,000 was also provided for the endowment of a fellowship in the divinity faculty. "It was a great consolation and encouragement for us," the rector wrote to Archbishop Corrigan, "to have an opportunity of expressing to her the gratitude of the University for her great act of generosity in the founding of the Divinity Building." AANY, G-28, Conaty to Corrigan, Washington, November 19, 1898.

patient while the work of the Catholic University of America progressed from year to year.[41]

The women of the auxiliary board of regents of Trinity College had also asked Spalding to speak in behalf of their new institution, and Conaty had agreed that the second lecture might be given for the benefit of the Sisters of Notre Dame de Namur and the college that they proposed to open for girls in the national capital. "The effect was momentous," it was said, when the Bishop of Peoria delivered his classic lecture, "Women and the Higher Education," in the Columbian University on January 16. Spalding's eloquence aroused "intense enthusiasm . . . for Trinity College . . . and hope was kindled for the realization of the project which just then . . . ," it was later recalled, "seemed doomed to oblivion."[42] A leading advocate of higher education of women, Spalding had spoken of it frequently, and at a time when it was still regarded as a rather advanced idea. The day would soon come, Spalding hoped, "when Trinity College shall stand beside the Catholic University . . . to lure and illumine . . . all . . . who are drawn to God by the love of truth and goodness and beauty."[43] Trinity College was formally opened on November 7, 1900.

Cheered by Spalding's renewed support for the Catholic University of America, Cardinal Gibbons reported to Keane that the Bishop's lectures had created great interest. Not only was Spalding anxious for Keane to return, but he stood ready to accompany Keane on a collection tour for the institution insofar as his diocesan duties would permit. "There can be no doubt of success," the Cardinal wrote, "and thus our hearts will be cheered by the feeling that our University will enter into the New Century fully endowed, at least in the work in which it

[41] *New World* (Chicago), November 19, 1898.

[42] Sr. M.P. "Trinity College," *CHR*, XI (January, 1926), p. 666.

[43] Spalding, "Women and the Higher Education," in *Opportunity*, p. 67 and *passim*.

is now engaged."[44] Equally sanguine in his hopes for the University's future, Spalding addressed the members of the Association of Catholic Colleges at Chicago in April, 1899, when he told the Catholic educators:

. . . we are privileged to do a great part in building up a high intellectual culture here in America. We must do it. We must have a great center of light and influence, a center to which we can invite whatever able man we can discover anywhere on earth, a center to which we will all look for the best thought on whatever question comes up, a center to which our wealthy men can look with pride and with generous feeling that they are glad to help that work, because they are thereby helping to produce that which is of the highest value. This the Catholic University of America aims to be. Of all the works it is the most promising; it will develop in many ways of which we do not dream.[45]

American Catholics were united in the faith, he maintained, but they were infinitely disunited in almost everything else. There was need for a point of union, because in laboring for parishes and parish interests, Spalding said, "we have become mere parish people," who failed to realize that American Catholicism must become "as big as the country" and built up by men, he said, "who will give us what is best in all the past, and who will live in the future; who feel they belong to God's living power in the world, to that institution against which no power of Earth or hell shall ever prevail."[46]

But the collection tour did not prove to be the success that had been hoped for; soon after, moreover, Keane was named second Archbishop of Dubuque,[47] which prevented him from making further collection tours in behalf of the University. At the trustees' meeting in October, a further depressing note was rendered in the annual report on the state of the University.

[44] AAB, 97-C-1, Gibbons to Keane, Washington, January 26, 1899, copy.

[45] *New World* (Chicago), April 22, 1899

[46] *Ibid.*

[47] Cf. Chapter 8, note 5.

Disheartened by his lack of success on the collection tour, Spalding did not attend the meeting, for, as he told Father Hudson, "I have not had the courage to go to Washington for the University meeting. It is a long journey and little to be done there."[48] Later, he informed Denis O'Connell that the latter's letter had reached Peoria too late to accomplish the purpose for which it was written, since the meeting had already adjourned. "I did not go," Spalding explained, "for I did not know any special business was to come up and I have grown weary of going a thousand miles to do nothing." Furthermore, he grumbled, "if the Professors need my assistance, they know me well enough to inform me in time."[49]

In a brief while, however, there would be special business that Spalding could assist in, which O'Connell's letter had already suggested. By now, the bishop no longer looked on Monsignor O'Connell as the "Machiavelli" of yesteryear, but rather as a friend; moreover, Father Charles Grannan of the University's School of Theology had already begun his campaign to force Conaty's resignation on the completion of his first term, and to urge the succession of O'Connell to the rectorship.

During the Summer of 1901, Grannan met with O'Connell in Switzerland, where they discussed the situation at the University and the need for a new rector. On Grannan's return from Europe, he was highly successful, as the 1901 fall term began, in arousing both Ireland and Spalding to act. "The University is in perilous condition," Ireland reported to O'Connell, ". . . and the next meeting at which Spalding leads will be most important. It must reform things—else, the University goes down."[50]

On November 20, 1901, four days before Thomas J. Conaty

[48] UND, Hudson Papers, Spalding to Hudson, Peoria, October 8, 1900.

[49] ADR, Spalding to O'Connell, Peoria, January 1, 1901.

[50] ADR, Ireland to O'Connell, New York, November 6, 1901.

331

was to be consecrated, the trustees gathered at the University for the annual meeting. Spalding lost no time in moving that Cardinal Gibbons appoint a special committee of inquiry with full authority, as it was said, "to examine into the actual condition, financial and academic, of the University and to report with suggestions to a meeting of the Board of Trustees to be held . . . on April 9th, 1902." The motion was quickly carried and the Cardinal Chancellor thereupon chose Keane, Spalding, and Bishop Camillus Maes of Covington to constitute the investigating team.[51] Grannan boasted soon after the meeting that it had been his idea to leave the Cardinal and the Rector off the committee so that the professors might be able to speak freely about the University. The choice of names, he reported to O'Connell, had been made up beforehand, "so that the cardinal would not have the option in the choice of members." Grannan had also tried to get the trustees to put Archbishop Riordan of San Francisco on the committee as chairman, but Riordan had not been present, and he lived too far away. And while Keane was wedded to his blunders, as Grannan caustically remarked, "yet it is hoped that Spalding and Maes—two good men—will be able to dominate him."[52]

Rumors were plentiful when Spalding and his two colleagues met in Caldwell Hall on February 4, 1902, to begin their investigation. It was whispered, so Grannan had already informed O'Connell, that the Bishop of Peoria, as chairman of the special committee, would recommend "a pretty clean sweep of all the Departments except Theology and Philosophy proper."[53] Sweeping changes were, indeed, imperative, and "retrenchment"

[51] CUA, MMBT, November 20, 1901, p. 95.

[52] ADR, "J-E-S-H-U-R-U-N" to "Dok" [Grannan to O'Connell] (Washington, postmarked, November 24, 1901). Reference has already been made to the use of code names by many of O'Connell's correspondents.

[53] ADR, Same to Same Washington, January 29, 1902.

would be a theme in Spalding's report to the board of trustees; yet it was the same committee, through Spalding's insistence, that furthered the plan whereby the University could extend its academic influence with the establishment in New York of an Institute of Pedagogy. Interest in a pedagogical institute had been aroused by the series of lectures which Father Edward A. Pace, Professor of Philosophy, had given in 1898 in the Cathedral Library Extension Centre in New York, which was then under the direction of Father Joseph H. McMahon.[54] Appointed by the board of trustees in October 1901 to collect funds for the University throughout the country, McMahon had suggested a plan to Conaty for a University extension school in pedagogy, and had asked Spalding's help in support of the proposed teachers' institute.[55] Not unexpectedly, Spalding had warmly endorsed the plan, since inferior teachers, he had insistently maintained, make for inferior schools,[56] and it was chiefly due to his efforts that Catholic normal schools were established for teacher training. Years later, his original outline for a central normal school for teaching sisters served as a model for Father Thomas E. Shields in his plans for the establishment of the Sisters' College at the Catholic University of America.[57]

Immediately after the episcopal committee had completed its investigation, Spalding, Maes, and McMahon went to New York, where they called upon Archbishop Corrigan and secured his approval of the proposed institute.[58] A meeting was then

[54] Hogan, op. cit., p. 83.

[55] CUA, Rector's Report to the Executive Committee on the Institute of Pedagogy, undated, p. 1.

[56] Cf. Spalding, "Normal Schools for Catholics," in Catholic World, LI (April, 1890), pp. 88–97.

[57] On Shields, cf. Justine Ward, Thomas Edward Shields, Biologist, Psychologist, Educator (New York, 1947).

[58] ACUA, Rector's Report . . . on the Institute of Pedagogy, pp. 1–2.

called for February 22 at the Catholic Club on West 59th Street, where Spalding gave the principal address on the nature and the need of an extension school in pedagogy;[59] and on the following day he presided at a special meeting of school superintendents and principals, where the feasibility and the probable difficulties in establishing such an institute were thoroughly discussed. Since the majority opinion of those present strongly favored the University directing such a movement, Spalding asked Bishop Conaty to bring the matter before the academic senate of the University and the executive committee of the board of trustees.[60] "The Right Rev. Chairman of the Committee bids me say," Conaty soon reported to the senate, "that the Committee is unanimous in recommending the Institute, and hopes that the . . . Senate of the University will authorize the work to be commenced at once."[61] The academic senate, notwithstanding, disapproved, and expressed itself as believing that under the existing circumstances the University should neither sponsor nor assume responsibility for the undertaking. It was tersely noted that "the University is not prepared to take charge on an institute of Pedagogy in New York City."[62] Spalding, however, on April 9, 1902, persuaded the executive committee of the board of trustees to override the senate's decision. "The proposed action . . . with regard to the School of Pedagogy . . . was endorsed heartily," the minutes stated, "and considered a very efficient way to bring the work of the Catholic University and its financial needs to the notice of the public."[63] Grannan, newsy as ever, told O'Connell that he was convinced that the trustees had voted for the institute "for

[59] New York *Tribune,* February 23, 1902.

[60] CUA, Rector's Report . . . on the Institute of Pedagogy, p. 2.

[61] *Ibid.,* p. 5.

[62] CUA, Report of the Senate, March 12, 1902.

[63] CUA, MMBT, April 9, 1902, p. 97.

form's sake, and that it will never be realized. . . ."[64] Despite Grannan's prediction, however, the foundation had been laid, and by October 1902, the Institute of Pedagogy had been successfully launched under Pace's direction with a registration, it was reported, of some one hundred and eighteen teachers.[65]

Important as the pedagogical institute was in the expansion of the University's academic life, graver matters confronted the board of trustees at the April meeting when the Bishop of Peoria completed the reading of the "Report of the Special Committee." A document characterized as "masterly in content and style,"[66] it covered a good deal of ground: the work required of a university professor; the need for a native-born English-speaking Sulpician to be president of Divinity College; a new spiritual director for Caldwell Hall, one who, it was said, "would have the power to draw the students to his instructions"; the necessity for a chair of sacred eloquence, since, Spalding noted, "the preaching in Caldwell Hall is said to be distressingly faulty and feeble."[67] Since the success of the University depended chiefly on the rector, who should be at once, he insisted, "the head and heart of the whole organism," there

[64] ADR [Grannan to O'Connell], Washington [April, 1902], unsigned. Grannan was strongly opposed to the Institute of Pedagogy and told O'Connell, "It was the work of Spalding," and added: "Spalding is sure to do something out of the way." Later, he complained that the academic senate was of the opinion that the University should not touch the project under existing circumstances, nor should it assume responsibility for the institute, but "Spalding thought otherwise, and with very much difficulty he succeeded in persuading the Trustees to that effect." They feared to turn him down, Grannan noted, "especially since he was head and ears in the work," and furthermore "It might spoil his ardor." Cf. ADR, Same to Same, Washington, May 30, 1902

[65] Hogan, op. cit., p. 86.

[66] Barry, op. cit., p. 60.

[67] ACUA, Files of the Board of Trustees, "Report of the Special Committee," April 9, 1902.

was need for one who would be "full of a noble enthusiasm, devoted, alert, energetic and untiring." If the rector, Spalding continued, "throws himself unreservedly into the work; if he grasps the purposes and scope of a University; if he refuse no labor, if he think no sacrifice great, if he is deterred by no difficulties," then, he believed, success would be inevitable.[68]

In more trenchant tones, Spalding then discussed the institution's financial management. "There has been not only a lack of business method and competency," he stated bluntly, "but an almost culpable negligence, while in the matter of securing more ample endowments little zeal or ability has been shown."[69] The committee recommended, therefore, that steps be taken at once to provide for the safety of the University's funds. An examination of the securities in which these funds had been invested by Thomas E. Waggaman, who had from the beginning acted as the University's treasurer, had led the committee to the conviction that they were insufficient and in every way unsatisfactory. It was recommended that three members of the board of trustees should constitute a finance committee empowered to take charge of the funds subject to the direction and approval of the entire board.[70] Finally, the report recommended that a more detailed account of receipts and expenditures be presented at the annual board meeting, and that a competent layman be entrusted under the direction of the rector with the current financial affairs of the University. If a

[68] *Ibid.*

[69] *Ibid.*

[70] *Ibid.* Spalding had already indicated to Gibbons what to expect when he wrote: "Dr. Conaty, it seems to me, laks [*sic*] business capacity, though I do not wish to say this to anyone but yourself." He hoped that "the Waggaman business" would be settled in a thoroughly satisfactory manner by the April 9, meeting "as any doubt on this point," he warned "would make anything we might propose futile." AAB, 99-M-6, Spalding to Gibbons, Peoria, March 14, 1902.

true university were chiefly a question of funds and salaries, Spalding reminded the trustees:

it would be absurd for us to think of competing with the more richly endowed institutions of our country. A Croesus, who, it may be, is an agnostic, will at a stroke of the pen, give more money for educational purposes, than we can hope to collect in a generation. If we permit the belief in the sovereign power of Mammon to pervert our minds and hearts, we shall not only fail, but we shall make the Catholic world understand that it had been better had we never attempted a task to which we shall have proven ourselves unequal.[71]

What the Catholic University of America needed first of all and most of all, he concluded, was not the equipment that money could buy, but "the Spirit, the unselfish devotion, the inexhaustible zeal for truth and goodness which nothing but the love of Christ can inspire." Libraries and laboratories were useful, but enlightened, heroic, Christlike men were indispensable to the welfare and progress not only of the university, but of the Catholic Church itself.[72]

The report of the special committee and its recommendations were soon acted upon, and were climaxed when Bishop Conaty was not reelected for a second term and Denis O'Connell was chosen to be the new rector. As Conaty's term came to a close, the trustees met on November 12, 1902, to draw up the *terna* of names to be submitted to Rome.[73] Meanwhile, the campaign for O'Connell had gone into high gear. "Abp. Keane & myself have already taken counsel on the matter," Ireland assured the

[71] *Ibid.*

[72] *Ibid.*

[73] *Ibid.* At the November, 1902 meeting, Spalding read a list of suggestions which were intended to supplement the April report of the special committee. ACUA, FBT, "Document anent Report of the Special Committee, April, 1902, Exhibit F," November 12, 1902. "Unfortunately," Barry stated, "it cannot be proved that he wrote this second report, it is not his style, and it is typewritten." Cf. Barry, *op. cit.*, p. 62, n. 87

337

waiting candidate. "We both of course will stand by you. The battle is on and we ought to win." The Archbishop added that Spalding was soon to come to see him, "and I will indoctrinate him."[74] And Grannan reported, "I have seen Spalding several times. He is all right . . . You can save this place. No one else can . . ."[75] However, upon completion of the balloting for the *terna*, it was found that Conaty had received the votes of all the members present on the first ballot and was named *dignissimus*. In subsequent voting, O'Connell was designated *dignior*, while Father Thomas J. Shahan, professor of ecclesiastical history, was chosen *dignus*. It had already been decided, nevertheless, that no matter what names were placed on the *terna*, O'Connell was to be nominated rector.[76] Cardinal Gibbons was highly pleased, but hardly surprised, therefore, when Cardinal Satolli informed him that on January 3, 1903, Pope Leo XIII had appointed Monsignor O'Connell as third Rector of the Catholic University of America.[77] "O'Connell in Washington—simply impossible," Ireland gloated. "Well, he is here— *Viva l'Americanismo! Viva sempre!*"[78] Spalding, while equally delighted, spoke in more restrained tones. "Mgr. O'Connell, as you know, is the Rector of our University," he informed the

[74] ADR, Ireland to O'Connell, St. Paul, September 7, 1902.

[75] ADR, Grannan to same, Washington, (postmarked, October 6, 1902).

[76] AAB, 100-B-3, O'Connell to Gibbons, Rome, October 6, 1902. O'Connell told the Cardinal that Satolli wanted Conaty's name on the *terna* "and then *un 'altro nome qualunque'* " plus his own, "and yours," insisted Satolli, "yours will come out."

[77] AAB, 100-G-2, Satolli to Gibbons, Rome, January 14, 1903. On January 12, 1903, Pope Leo XIII approved O'Connell's appointment and transferred the University from the jurisdiction of the Congregation de Propaganda Fide to the Congregation of Studies over which Satolli presided.

[78] ADR, Ireland to O'Connell, St. Paul, January 14, 1903.

Abbé Klein, "and we expect much of him." "The future of the University," he added, "looks bright."[79]

The brightened hopes for the University soon failed, however, for the "much" expected of the new rector could hardly be realized in the wake of the financial crisis that soon beset his administration. "The whole trouble is a lack of money," Spalding had written after O'Connell's installation, "and a good start will awaken interest everywhere."[80] O'Connell's proposal for an annual collection to be taken up in all the dioceses in the United States had seemingly awakened interest, and the total returns from the first collection had been satisfying.[81] But there were other factors which overshadowed what had apparently been a good start. On Spalding's insistence, the special committee of investigation had recommended on November 17, 1902, that Thomas Waggaman be instructed to surrender the University funds in his possession to the finance committee.[82] At

[79] ADP, Spalding to Klein, March 11, 1903, copy.

[80] ACUA, Same to O'Connell, Peoria, April 25, 1903. "Above all things," Spalding emphasized, "keep the Paedagogical School in New York at work." O'Connell had been installed as rector on April 22, 1903.

[81] The report of the special committee on April 9, 1902, had already recommended a voluntary annual collection for the support of the university, but at the installation meeting on April 22, 1903, the board of trustees voted for a compulsory collection. Pope Pius X issued a letter of approval which ordered an annual collection. "The Holy Father's letter seemed to me rather weak," Archbishop Riordan complained to Spalding, and "I do not expect great results from this collection." The bishops of the country, he believed, would have to take some efficient means, "of bringing the University and its works to those Catholics who can afford to give a goodly sum of money." Otherwise, he added, "its progress must be very slow." Cf. Archives of the Archdiocese of San Francisco, Riordan to Spalding, San Francisco, November 20, 1903, copy. The writer is grateful to Thomas J. Riley for this reference.

[82] CUA, MMBT, November 17, 1902.

O'Connell's installation, Waggaman had promised that he would soon convert the University's investments into cash and would turn the sum over to the committee. But by the Summer of 1903, the Treasurer had submitted only the principal notes on hand, since he could not at the time, he believed, safely release the collateral. As a consequence, Spalding called an emergency meeting of the special committee at Archbishop Quigley's residence in Chicago on December 3, 1903, where it was resolved that a special session of the board of trustees, to meet at the University the following month, should choose a committee of laymen to handle the financial affairs of the institution.[83] "You will of course get all possible information concerning the value and nature of the real estate notes Waggaman has given the University," Spalding advised O'Connell after the Chicago meeting. "The more authentic information you have on this subject," he said, "the more satisfactory our meeting will be."[84]

The action taken by the trustees on January 28, 1904, was more than satisfactory; it undoubtedly helped to save the Catholic University of America when disaster struck. Sweeping powers were given to a new finance committee which consisted of Michael Jenkins, already a board member, Charles J. Bonaparte of Baltimore, Michael Cudahy of Chicago, Adrian Iselin, Thomas Fortune Ryan, and John McCall of New York, "an imposing line-up of Catholic business and professional talent,"[85] it was noted, who were instructed

... to examine into the condition of the securities of the University in the hands of its Treasurer and to take whatever steps they may deem necessary to secure the interests of the University in its property ... We now authorize and instruct them to take charge of all properties, securities, etc., in the hands of the Treasurer.[86]

83 Barry, *op. cit.* p. 79.
84 ADR, Spalding to O'Connell, Peoria, December 16, 1903.
85 Barry, *op. cit.,* p. 81.
86 CUA, MMBT, January 28, 1904.

"I trust the new committee is already at work," an anxious Spalding remarked to Gibbons on his return to Peoria, "and that things are not as bad as they appear to be." Furthermore, Monsignor O'Connell must not rest until, he added, "everything is safe and in order."[87] But everything was not in order, and upon an examination into the value and nature of the Waggaman notes, the new committee discovered that things were worse than they had first appeared to be, that the financial crisis was of greater scope than had been feared. Finally, in August, 1904, involuntary bankruptcy proceedings were instituted against Waggaman, and the entire financial structure of the Catholic University of America was shaken.[88] The blow long anticipated had at last fallen, Gibbons wrote, and the time had now come for all the members of the board of trustees "to exert themselves in an heroic manner and to preserve their honor and integrity before the world." The salvation of the University itself depended on the early action of the trustees, and, the Cardinal added, "when we meet in November . . . we must give public assurance that the funds left to us will be religiously safeguarded . . ."[89] There was nothing but hard news in November, however, when Bonaparte and the committee's legal counsel reported on the Waggaman bankruptcy proceedings. From here on, as an historian of this crisis has written,

[87] CUA, Spalding to Gibbons, Peoria, February 4, 1904. The Bishop had also enclosed a check for $4,000, the total amount of the first annual collection in the Diocese of Peoria for the support of the University. A comparison of receipts from annual collections can be gathered from a glance at the tables in Barry, *op. cit.*, pp. 260–264. It will be seen that in the period, 1903–1908, the Catholic University of America received greater monetary support from the Diocese of Peoria than from several of the large archdioceses.

[88] Barry, *op. cit.*, p. 89.

[89] ADP, Gibbons to Spalding, Baltimore, August 26, 1904.

... through the remainder of Monsignor O'Connell's administration and for some time thereafter, the University was involved in extensive and complicated litigation to recover what could be saved from the Waggaman notes. It was an ever-present pressure on the administration, forcing economy . . . at a time when expansion and development were at last within possibility . . . the entire monied endowment had dissolved, and the road back was to be slow and hard.[90]

Slow and hard the road might be, but the first painful steps had been taken and the university would survive. When Cardinal Gibbons could later report cheering news, no one was happier than the Bishop of Peoria, who replied: "I wish with all my heart that I were able to be of more assistance."[91]

Personal tragedy had precluded the possibility, however, that Spalding could ever again equal his past performance in active support of the Catholic University of America. Upon the Bishop's arrival in Washington for the November 1904 meeting, he was informed that the Marquise des Monstiers-Merinville, so closely associated with the University's formative years, had left the Church. In a communication to the editor of the Associated Press, the Marquise had stated that it might be of interest to know that the former Miss Caldwell, "who it will be remembered," she noted, "founded the Roman Catholic University some years ago, has entirely repudiated her former creed." Interviewed by the press, the Marquise continued:

Yes, it is true that I have left the Roman Catholic Church. Since I have been living in Europe my eyes have been opened to what the church really is and to its anything but sanctity. But the trouble goes much further back than this. Being naturally religious my imagination was early caught by the idea of doing something to lift the church from the lowly position which it occupied in America so I thought of a university or higher school, where its clergy could be educated, and if

[90] Barry, *op. cit.*, p. 100.

[91] AAB, 102-S-1, Spalding to Gibbons, Peoria, October 20, 1905.

342

possible refined. Of course in this I was merely influenced by Bishop Spalding, who represented it to me as one of the greatest works of the day.[92]

When she was twenty-one, she had turned over one-third of her fortune to establish the University, she added, but for years she had endeavored to rid herself of what she called "the subtle overwhelming influence of a church which pretends, not only to the privilege of being 'the only true church,' but of being alone able to open up the gates of heaven to a sorrowful world." At last, her honest Protestant blood had reasserted itself, she concluded, and she now and forever cast off the yoke of Rome.[93] Questioned by reporters about the Marquise's statement, Spalding simply replied, "It is all a mystery to me."[94] There was no further comment.

But there was a consequence. The combination of the Chicago scandals and their painful *dénouement,* the work of the anthracite coal commission, the Waggaman failure, the Marquise's defection, and a heavy schedule of lectures and sermons—in addition to diocesan duties—had taken a heavy toll. "I was intoxicated with work," Bishop Spalding later exclaimed, "and God saw it and struck me down . . ."[95] On Friday morning, January 6, 1905, Spalding said Mass at the usual time and after breakfast worked in his study throughout the forenoon. At lunch, he mentioned to Father Frank O'Reilly, the chancellor, that he seemed to have a slight attack of neuralgia, but that it did not appear to be serious. Later, he returned to his study on the second floor. Shortly after four o'clock, Bridget Wall, the housekeeper, heard someone fall and hurried upstairs to find

[92] Peoria *Journal,* November 15, 1904.

[93] *Ibid.*

[94] New York *Times,* November 16, 1904.

[95] Interview of Sister Mary Evangela Henthorne, B.V.M., with Miss Maybelle Spalding, June 1929, cited in Henthorne, "The Life and Career of Bishop John Lancaster Spalding," p. 395.

Spalding on the floor, half-unconscious and unable to rise. With help, he was carried to his bedroom, and Dr. Leonard Spalding, his brother, and Dr. Richard Slevin, his nephew, were quickly summoned. For several hours, the Bishop was unable to speak, but "leeches applied to his head" partially restored his speech. The morning newspapers carried the news flash, BISHOP SPAL-DING STRICKEN, and anxious inquiries began to pour into Peoria from friends in all walks of life.[96] From the White House came the message, "The President is much concerned to learn of the illness of Bishop Spalding and would like to be advised as to his condition. William Loeb, Secretary to the President."[97] That President Roosevelt, senators, congressmen, university presidents, labor leaders, and coal miners had telegraphed to inquire about the Bishop and to express their sympathy was evidence, said the Louvain American College *Bulletin,* "of the high and universal esteem in which the Bishop of Peoria is held throughout America."[98]

When Dr. Frank Billings came down from Chicago to examine the patient and give the opinion that he might hope for a complete recovery, Spalding's friends rejoiced. "I have just heard from Peoria that the Bishop's recovery is assured. He is rapidly convalescing," Cardinal Gibbons informed Father George Dougherty, to which he added, "This is a moral and financial gain."[99] Father Riordan relayed the good news to Father Hudson at Notre Dame in some detail:

Before all else let me tell you that I consider the Bp's condition very much improved. He is able to sit up in bed and his physician promises

[96] Peoria, *Journal,* January 7, 1904. "His days for active work are over," Archbishop Riordan wrote to O'Connell, "and of course this will preclude any possible promotion as much dreaded by certain parties." ADR, Riordan to O'Connell, San Francisco, January 10, 1905.

[97] *Ibid.*

[98] *American College Bulletin* (Louvain), III (April, 1905), p. 81.

[99] CUA, Gibbons to Dougherty, January 25, 1905. Dougherty was secretary to Denis O'Connell.

to have him sitting up out of bed in about ten days. Of course he is quite weak but there is a distinct gain each day. He sleeps well and eats with appetite and relish. His mind was perfectly clear and capable of sustained attention. There is still some evidence of his trouble in his face about the corner of his mouth and also in his eyes, and he has no power in his arm which is motionless. His foot and leg are about in the normal condition. They keep him very quiet and few are admitted to the sick room. They learned by experience that he must avoid all excitement.[100]

For that reason it was inadvisable, Riordan believed, to mention to the Bishop that Hudson had omitted a certain passage in correcting the proofs of Spalding's latest book. Since there was nothing to suggest an omission in the corrected proof, "no harm will be done," he was confident, "and the Bishop will know that you used your best judgment." If he could have been consulted, Riordan would have advised it, but that was out of the question and the bishop was most anxious to have the book published at once.[101] Six weeks later, McClurg and Company, of Chicago, Spalding's publishers through the years, announced the publication of *Religion and Art and Other Essays,* his last literary endeavor.[102]

[100] UND, Hudson Papers, Riordan to Hudson, Chicago, January 27, 1905.

[101] *Ibid.*

[102] The book was first published on March 11, 1905, and contained several of the lectures which Spalding had given during the previous Autumn. Especially noteworthy was "The Development of Educational Ideas in the Nineteenth Century," which the bishop had delivered on September 21, 1904, at the St. Louis Purchase Exposition before the International Congress of Arts and Sciences. The lecture first appeared in the *Educational Reveiw,* XXVIII (November, 1904), pp. 335–360. It became Chapter II in *Religion, Art and Other Essays,* pp. 68–111. In words as cogent today as when he spoke them nearly sixty years ago, he asked: "Shall we in our schools set aside days to commemorate some mediocre patriot, poet, or orator, and make it an offence there to do homage to Him who has given His name to our civilization . . . ?" (*ibid.,* p. 105). Spalding warned, interestingly enough, in the light

In due time, Father Riordan accompanied Bishop Spalding to Hot Springs, Arkansas, where he had been advised to rest. The Chicago priest soon heard from Father Frank O'Reilly that the Cardinal of Baltimore was eager for news of Spalding, and he took the liberty, as he put it, to tell Gibbons, "You will be pleased to know that the Bishop shows steady improvement. To me he seems to be gaining every day." He stated that Spalding was carried to the dining room for all his meals and sat at the table unsupported and fed himself. "His mind is perfectly clear," Riordan added, "and there are flashes of wit and humor that bespeak his old self." The left leg was still weak, but it could be moved at will, although the arm showed little improvement. But the doctor's prognosis was favorable, and Spalding himself was in the best of spirits and most hopeful, and, Riordan concluded, he was "greatly touched by the interest you have shown him from the beginning of his illness."[103] Spalding's

---

of the school prayer decision of the Supreme Court (*Engel vs. Vitale*, June 25, 1962), that if the state and the school organized themselves on a purely secular or utilitarian basis, the nation's social and political life would undergo a radical change because, as he said:

> We may increase our commercial efficiency; may so manipulate the natural resources of our continent that the markets of the world shall pay tribute to us, we may heighten the level of intelligence and raise the standard of living for the multitude; but little by little we shall lose the power to believe in the absolute worth of truth and goodness and beauty, of justice and purity and love . . . Existence will cease to have for us a spiritual content, and we shall come to hold that a man's life consists in the abundance of the things he possesses, and not in the faith, hope and righteousness which make him a child of God and a dweller in eternal worlds.

Ibid., pp. 110–111.

[103] AAB, 102-H, Riordan to Gibbons, Hot Springs, April 8, 1905. After the spring meeting of the University's board of trustees, Gibbons wrote to Spalding to convey the board's expression of sympathy at the sad state of his health and the hope of all that he would be with them

health continued to improve, and on his return to Peoria he thanked Gibbons for his continued solicitude. His physicians had assured him that he should recover completely, but he admitted, "the progress has been very slow and I am still much of an invalid unable to do active work." For a man of Spalding's temperament, this was, to be sure, a cross, and, therefore, he begged for the Cardinal's prayers.[104]

Other pressures soon aggravated the burden. "Have you read in this morning's *Herald* the dispatch from Peoria—'Baroness Zedwitz [*sic*] Seeking an Interview with Bp. Spalding'?" Archbishop Ireland asked Denis O'Connell. "I hope no trouble is brewing."[105] "SPALDING'S WARD PENITENT," a Chicago newspaper headlined the story. "BARONESS WHO RENOUNCED CATHOLICISM SEEKS RECONCILIATION. PRELATE DELAYS ACTION."[106] The headlines were, however, only partially true. The Baroness, the former Elizabeth or "Lina" Caldwell, had, in fact, visited Bishop Spalding, but upon her arrival in Chicago on her way to New York, she had issued a statement in which she said:

My sister and I renounced forever the Catholic faith. The decision is irrevocable. We have neither the desire nor the intention of rejoining the Church. I am sorry the impression has been created that we are vacillating in any way . . . My visit to Bishop Spalding was solely a business one. A mistake has been made in the report that he was ever the guardian of my sister or myself. Our relations with him came about

---

once again "to aid and stimulate them," as the Cardinal said, "by that enthusiasm & deep interest which you have always manifested in the University." For himself, Gibbons prayed that Spalding's recovery would be rapid and sure, "that many years will yet be granted you to continue the many good works you have begun, to add even greater luster to the life that has shed so many blessings upon the American Church." AAB, 102-K, Gibbons to Spalding, Baltimore, May 7, 1905, copy.

[104] AAB, 102-S-1, Spalding to Gibbons, Peoria, October 20, 1905.
[105] ADR, Ireland to O'Connell, New York, December 9, 1905.
[106] Chicago *Tribune,* December 9, 1905.

in connection with donations to charities in which he was interested. We were never his wards, for my father never knew him.[107]

When she and her sister had left the Church, she continued, they had left it completely, and had not clung to former friends among the clergy; "to have kept Bishop Spalding as a close friend," she insisted, "would have been like clinging to the corner of the altar cloth." They had merely adjusted a matter that had been unsettled between them, the Baroness concluded, "and so the incident is closed."[108]

Nettled, nevertheless, by reports that continued to imply that she had not completely severed all connection with the Catholic Church, and by what she called "the extremely hostile attitude assumed by the Roman Church . . . and its persistent efforts to, at first, deny and then belittle the sincerity of my renunciation," the

[107] *Ibid.* December 13, 1905. Bishop Spalding had, perhaps, anticipated the Baroness's visit. Together with the United States Trust Company of New York, Spalding had been a co-trustee of a trust fund created under the last will and testament of William S. Caldwell for the benefit of the Marquise des Monstiers-Merinville. On November 27, 1905, Spalding filed a petition in the New York Supreme Court in which he asked to be permitted to resign as co-trustee and showed that he had never acted as trustee nor had any of the property of the said trust in his possession. At a special term of the Supreme Court, Part II, held in and for the County of New York, at the County Court House, on May 15, 1906, Spalding's petition was read and filed. Both the Baroness and the Marquise verified the facts in the petition in a letter to the court, dated May 14, 1906, and it was thus "ordered." Cf. Files of the United States Trust Company of New York, Estate Papers of William S. Caldwell, Estate Papers of Mary G. Caldwell, the Marquise des Monstiers-Merinville, Estate Papers of Elizabeth B. Caldwell, the Baroness von Zedtwitz. The author is grateful to Waldemar von Zedtwitz, the Baroness's son, for the opportunity to view the papers of the Caldwell estate. Cf. also, ADP, Edward W. Sheldon to Spalding, New York, July 5, 1906. Sheldon, an officer of the United Trust Company, informed Spalding that his liability as co-trustee had been terminated.

[108] *Ibid*

Baroness sought, in the Spring of 1906, to convince the world that her decision had been irrevocable and her repudiation final through the publication of a small volume entitled *The Double Doctrine of the Church of Rome*. Generally, the book reiterated popular arguments for anti-Catholicism, but toward the end became more personal, describing a certain "disheartened prelate" who had embarked on the Roman ship only to be shipwrecked in "the bottomless ocean of loneliness and doubt,"[109] his faith shattered and his hope dead. From Peoria, there was only silence; Spalding knew precisely when to say nothing.

Meanwhile, rumors had begun to circulate that Spalding had suffered a second stroke, and that his condition was critical, with little hope for recovery. Annoyed by the newspaper reports, Spalding demanded that the press retract what he called a "canard," since he had simply checked into Milwaukee's Sacred Heart Sanitarium to take a new treatment for his paralysis.[110] Yet it was his progressively declining health that compelled him in the year ahead to tender his resignation to Monsignor O'Connell as a member of the University's board of trustees,[111]

[109] Baroness Von Zedtwitz, *The Double Doctrine of the Church of Rome* (New York, 1906), pp. 15–16.

[110] ADP, Spalding clippings, Peoria *Herald-Transcript,* July 18, 1906.

[111] ADR, Spalding to O'Connell, Hot Springs, March 11, 1907. Archbishop Riordan had strongly urged Spalding to resign from the University's board of trustees. "I wrote him a good strong letter," he told O'Connell, "and I hope it will have its effect" (ADR, Riordan to O'Connell, San Francisco, March 2, 1907). When the trustees accepted Spalding's resignation, Gibbons wrote:

> The Trustees all recognize your great service to the University in the past, and how in a sense you could be considered its founder and its ever constant protector. The Board holds these great merits in grateful memory, and while returning to you its warm thanks for them, likewise expresses the hope that in the course of time, your health being restored, you may be able to resume your accustomed place among us.

ADP, Gibbons to Spalding, Baltimore, April 30, 1907. When Riordan

and to admit to Theodore Roosevelt, as he wrote to acknowledge a gift of the President's published works, that "I have for the last two years now been an invalid. I regret this the more because I imagine had I been well and strong you might have found some useful thing for me to do."[112]

Frequent and long absences from Peoria had given credence to the gossip that Spalding would never be completely well again, and they provided the occasion, moreover, for complaints to Rome that the Diocese of Peoria was in a deplorable state. There was, a group of diocesan priests informed Pope Pius X, an auxiliary bishop who had been the vicar general but who, although "a good man," was "rather inept." Bishop O'Reilly, however, had stayed far away from diocesan affairs, since Spalding had little confidence in his ability. Furthermore, what was termed the "rivalry and antagonism" between the Auxiliary Bishop and the Chancellor, Father Frank O'Reilly, "who *de facto*," the priests stated, "rules the diocese," was a source of scandal and had divided the diocese into two camps. Consequently, the diocese was in chaos and riddled with intrigue, which was fomented by a group of priests who, it was said, "by threats, blandishments and lies always obtained what they wanted." Although the writers of this letter had appealed to Archbishop Falconio, the apostolic delegate, nothing had been

---

heard of the resignation, he wrote to O'Connell: "My letter to Peoria had one of its desired effects; the other effect of it I think will come. I urged both very strongly" (ADR, Riordan to O'Connell, San Francisco, May 4, 1907). Riordan had feared, of course, the disastrous effects of the continued attacks upon Spalding by the Marquise and the Baroness such as in their letters to Jeremiah J. Crowley, quoted in Crowley, *Romanism a Menace to the Nation,* pp. 38–39.

[112] Library of Congress, Roosevelt Papers, Spalding to Roosevelt, Peoria, May 4, 1907. The Abbé Félix Klein visited Spalding late in the summer of 1907 and noted the great contrast in the bishop's appearance since his previous visit four years before. Cf. Klein, *Sans Arrêt,* p. 268.

done to remedy the situation, and they now begged the Holy Father, therefore, for a new bishop, or at least an administrator, for the Diocese of Peoria.[113]

Serious as these charges may have been, other reasons of far graver moment soon prompted the apostolic delegate no longer to postpone action. Well aware of the personal vendetta waged by the Baroness von Zedwitz against the Bishop of Peoria and of her hostile threats to publish a book about the Prelate's personal probity,[114] Archbishop Falconio sought to spare the stricken Prelate further harassment and humiliation. With that in mind, he asked Ireland to talk with Spalding and to obtain his promise to resign his See.[115] Ireland's trip to Peoria was successful, and he soon informed Monsignor O'Connell:

> I wired you from Chicago the result of my interview with my friend. He then promised to resign. I waited before writing to you until I had the matter in writing. This I now have. So all is settled . . . I have myself written to Mgr. Falconio, telling him of the Bishop's letter to me.

[113] ACPF, Lett., Folder 153/1907, no. 77847, "certain priests of Peoria, most humble and unworthy sons," to the "Most Holy Father," United States of America, July 30, 1907. Cf. also, ACPF, Lett. Folder 153/1907, no. 77847, ". . . priests of good will" to His Eminence Cardinal Gotti, United States of America, July 24, 1907.

[114] Ireland and Riordan were both gravely concerned. "You should write at once to Lina," Ireland urged O'Connell, "to have her stop her manoeuverings . . ." He was ready to visit Spalding, he said, as soon as he was assured that action on the Bishop's part would stop all other proceedings. "If the book were still to appear after he had acted," warned Ireland, "we would be worse off than we had heretofore been" (ADR, Ireland to O'Connell, St. Paul, June 27, 1908). Riordan was likewise fearful that the Baroness would bring on a storm in which she would be engulfed as well as others. "I did my best to obtain his resignation from the position which he holds," Riordan noted, "and he yielded to one request but the other he has not as yet." ADR, Riordan to O'Connell, San Francisco, July 13, 1908.

[115] ACPF, Lett., etc., Folder 153/1909, no. 83696, Falconio to Gotti, Washington, September 24, 1908.

351

I must say, I encountered but little opposition. He understands that his health is irreparably shattered & that the work to be done in the diocese demands an active bishop.[116]

Spalding had insisted on secrecy, however, until he was ready to make a personal announcement, and since this might not be done for several weeks, Ireland urged the rector to be most reticent.[117]

"BISHOP SPALDING RESIGNS HIS SEE," announced the daily press on September 10, 1908. "POET, PHILOSOPHER AND ORATOR WEARY AFTER NEARLY THIRD OF A CENTURY OF EFFORTS. DESIRES YOUNGER MAN FOR PLACE. NATION REGRETS DECISION."[118] It was a day chosen, perhaps, by design, for it was the sixtieth anniversary of Martin John Spalding's consecration as coadjutor with the right of succession to Bishop Flaget of Louisville.

He had now been ill for three and a half years, Spalding explained to reporters, and it would be years more before he could hope to resume active duty in the diocese. Now in his sixty-ninth year and crippled by paralysis, after long consideration, he had therefore resolved to submit his resignation to Pope Pius X. For thirty-one years he had served as Bishop of Peoria, and in that time he had witnessed the rapid and prosperous growth of the Catholic Church in the Middle West, but now,

[116] ADR, Ireland to O'Connell, St. Paul, August 7, 1906.

[117] *Ibid.*

[118] Peoria *Journal,* September 10, 1908. The announcement was dated September 9, but the news broke on the following day. William Jennings Bryan, again the presidential nominee of the Democratic Party, was the main speaker at the Democratic State Convention which met on September 9, in Peoria. After Bryan had called on him, Spalding went to the convention where he remained for two and a half hours until the adjournment at the close of Bryan's address. *Ibid.* Years before, during Bryan's free silver campaign, Spalding had written to Bishop Ryan of Alton: "I am sure you are a rabid silverite, but I believe Bryan is an Apaist" (ADP, Spalding to Ryan, Peoria, July 26, 1896, copy).

he continued, "that I am unable to assist actively in the continuation of that growth I believe it is better that I should retire and that some younger and more active prelate be placed in charge."[119]

The irremovable rectors of the diocese disagreed, however, and after a spirited meeting they decided to recommend to the Pope that when the resignation reached him it be refused. "We want you to hold the position," their spokesman told Spalding, "until God calls you."[120] But Spalding was not to be dissuaded, and on September 21, 1908, he forwarded his letter of resignation to the apostolic delegate. It read:

His Holiness Pope Pius X
Most Holy and Reverend Father. My long and serious illness constrains me to tender to you my resignation of the office of Bishop of Peoria which you in your wisdom and goodness will doubtless see your way to accept assigning me at the same time a suitable pension on the diocese in which I have labored for more than thirty years, having the happiness to see my labors blessed most abundantly by the Divine Lord. Kneeling at your feet, I humbly kiss your sacred hands.

J. L. Spalding, Bishop of Peoria[121]

Archbishop Falconio immediately dispatched Spalding's letter of resignation to Cardinal Gotti, Prefect of Propaganda, together with the Bishop's request for an annual pension of $2,000.[122] "For the last two years," the Delegate noted, "Msgr.

[119] Peoria *Journal,* September 10, 1908.

[120] *Ibid.,* September 16, 1908.

[121] ACPF, Lett., etc., Folder 153/1909, no. 83696, Alleg. I, Spalding to Pius X, Peoria, September 21, 1908.

[122] ADP, Falconio to Spalding, Washington, September 24, 1908. The Delegate acknowledged receipt of Spalding's resignation and informed the Bishop that he had been visited by a delegation of priests from the Diocese of Peoria, to which he added, "and I must inform your Lordship that I was edified and delighted with their expression of love and veneration for your Lordship, and their sorrow at the loss of your leadership." *Ibid.*

Spalding has suffered repeated attacks of paralysis which have rendered him unable to govern his diocese nor is there any hope that he can recover." For the good of the Diocese of Peoria, Falconio added, "and also for the peace of mind of the prelate, rendered incapable of administration by the terrible illness which afflicts him," he begged Gotti to recommend to the Pope that the resignation be accepted without delay. He urged action not only for the reasons cited, "but much more for reasons . . . which . . . had been presented to the Sacred Congregation," so he had been informed, "on the occasion of the election of the last Archbishop of Chicago . . ." With regard to the pension, the Holy Father could readily consent to the request, since Peoria's diocesan income, he had been assured, could sustain the burden without grave inconvenience.[123] Finally, Falconio wished to present a letter from a delegation of diocesan priests in which they petitioned the Holy See "to mark the occasion of Bishop Spalding's retirement from active diocesan work after so many years of unrelaxing earnestness and fruitful zeal by some special mark of Apostolic favor."[124] While it seemed to him that a titular archbishopric would be satisfactory, he left it to Gotti's prudence to propose to the Pope whatever he might deem fitting in order to satisfy the desires of the clergy and the people of the diocese. "Certainly some consideration ought to be extended to

[123] ACPF, Lett., etc., Folder 153/1909, no. 83696, Falconio to Gotti, Washington, September 24, 1908.

[124] ACPF, Lett. etc., Folder 153/1909, no. 83696, Alleg. II, Francis J. O'Reilly *et al.,* to Falconio, Peoria, September 21, 1908. Pointing to the distinguishing features of Spalding's career, especially his efforts to bring about an increasing friendliness among Catholics and their separated brethren, the priests wrote that largely through his voice and pen this friendly sentiment had displaced the familiar prejudice and bigotry of previous generations. "This work of conciliation has come more effectively from Bishop Spalding," they maintained, "owing to the fact that his ancestors for more than two centuries have been American of the Americans and not more American than Catholic."

the American people," he concluded, "who recognize in Msgr. Spalding an intellectual man and a distinguished orator."[125]

In an audience held on October 8, 1908, Pope Pius X accepted the resignation of John Lancaster Spalding as Bishop of Peoria, granted him an annual pension of $2,000, and promised to elevate him to the rank of titular archbishop.[126] Notified of this action by Cardinal Gotti, the Apostolic Delegate replied that it was apparent that the Cardinal Prefect had not as yet received his confidential report which had been prompted by Spalding's subsequent insistence on a pension of $4,000 a year.[127] Until the question of the amount of pension had been settled, Falconio wrote, he deemed it inadvisable to inform the Bishop that he would be named a titular archbishop. Furthermore, Gotti had said nothing about the appointment of an administrator for the now vacant diocese, and he wondered, therefore, whether Spalding should retain the administration until a

---

[125] ACPF, Lett., etc., Folder 153/1909, no. 83696, Falconio to Gotti, Washington, September 24, 1908.

[126] ACPF, Udienze di Nostro Signore, October 8, 1908, Folder 153/1909, no. 83696. Hereafter this will be cited as ACPF, Udienze, etc.

[127] ACPF, Lett., etc., Folder 153/1909, no. 83696, Falconio to Gotti, Washington, October 26, 1908. The delegate had already informed Spalding that an annual pension of $4,000 might possibly embarrass his successor. "I am sure that the priests of the Diocese of Peoria who have shown such love and veneration towards you," wrote Falconio, "will not see you in any discomfiture," and "they have even spoken of erecting a new residence for you." ADP, Falconio to Spalding, Washington, October 1, 1908. Previously, Bishop Ryan had written to Spalding: "The least you should have is $5,000.00; nothing else will become you or the Diocese of Peoria, grown to splendor out of the shreds and patches you found it, when you took it in hand more than thirty-one years ago." Spalding should keep in mind, Ryan added, "that grounds must be kept up and that even a new house will need the occasional visits of the plumber, etc.," ADP, Ryan to Spalding, Alton, September 29, 1908.

successor had been appointed, or whether other provisions were to be made. Since as yet he had no answers to these questions, Falconio added, he therefore believed it inexpedient to advise the Bishop that his resignation had been accepted, for the diocese would then be without a head.[128]

The answers were not long delayed. Archbishop Falconio was advised by cablegram that Pope Pius X personally had ordered that Bishop Spalding be told without delay that his resignation had been accepted, and that the Holy See granted him an annual pension of $2,500.[129] The promise of a titular archbishopric was not to be published, however, at least for the present, and the apostolic brief which had nominated the former Bishop of Peoria to the rank of titular Archbishop of Scythopolis, so Gotti added in a covering letter, was to be kept in the custody of the delegate. Furthermore, the Cardinal Prefect empowered the Archbishop of Chicago to appoint an administrator for the Diocese of Peoria, *sede vacante*.[130] When Archbishop Quigley thereupon appointed Bishop Peter J. O'Reilly as administrator, Spalding informed the diocese that his resignation had been accepted by the Holy Father, and he added:

When my severe and long-continued illness compelled me to recognize that it was the will of God that I should withdraw from the active ministry of the Church, that a younger and abler man might assume the burden which infirmity and age had me incapable of longer bearing, the first and keenest pang this sacrifice caused me sprang from the knowledge that my step, which had not been hastily taken, involved separation from the priests and people of the Peoria diocese, who for so many years had been my strength and joy. May God bless them and

128 *Ibid.*

129 ACPF, Udienze, etc., November 5, 1908, Folder 153/1909, no. 83968.

130 ACPF, Lett., etc., Folder 153/1909, no. 83968, Gotti to Falconio, Rome, November 12, 1908. The apostolic brief had been sent to the Delegate on October 30, 1908.

hold them ever within His sheltering arms. Had I not deliberately chosen this course His unfailing messenger, death, would have come to sever the ties of love. May the Heavenly Father watch over you along the one true way to the gates of everlasting life.[131]

Though he was no longer their bishop, Spalding expressed the hope "that I shall be permitted to spend the rest of my days with you," to which he added the plea, "Be mindful of me in your prayers and supplications as one who walked modestly and lovingly among you, doing as best he could the work God gave him to do."[132]

"One thing I beg of the Lord," Spalding had written some forty-seven years before, "this I seek: that I may dwell in the house of the Lord all the days of my life."[133] The seminarian's prayer had not been in vain, because "God . . . struck me down," an aged Archbishop would reminisce, "and gave me all these years to think."[134]

[131] Peoria *Journal*, December 14, 1908. The Bishop's message was read in all the churches of the diocese on Sunday, December 13, 1908.

[132] *Ibid.*

[133] ADP, "Journal of J. Lancaster Spalding," January 20, 1861. It was on the title page of his journal that Spalding, the seminarian, had inscribed this fourth verse of Psalm 26.

[134] Interview of Sister Mary Evangela Henthorne, B.V.M., with Miss Maybelle Spalding, June, 1929, cited in Henthorne, "The Life and Career of Bishop John Lancaster Spalding," p. 395.

10

In the Winter of Age

WITH the announcement that Pope Pius X had accepted his resignation as Bishop of Peoria, John Lancaster Spalding, for the moment at least, had little time to reminisce. "Until my successor shall have been appointed," he had written, "the diocese will be governed by the Rt. Rev. P. J. O'Reilly, whom you know and love."[1] Loyal, amiable Peter J. O'Reilly, the auxiliary for eight years, was the logical choice, some believed, to succeed Bishop Spalding. It was known, however, that the latter preferred Francis J. O'Reilly, his chancellor, as successor. The chancellor, as Bishop Ryan had already commented, "is unquestionably far and away the best fitted."[2] Spalding was greatly pleased, therefore, when the irremovable rectors met with Archbishop Quigley at the cathedral rectory in Peoria on December 10, 1908, and chose Father O'Reilly for first place on the priests' *terna,* while Father John P. Quinn, pastor of St. John's Parish, Peoria, and Father Henry A. O'Kelly, pastor of Immaculate Conception Parish, Streator, were named for the second and third places.[3] Eleven days later, the bishops of the Province of Chicago also designated Father O'Reilly *dignissimus* on their *terna,* but they substituted in place of Quinn and

[1] Peoria *Journal,* December 14, 1908.

[2] ADP, Ryan to Spalding, Alton, September 29, 1908.

[3] Peoria *Journal,* December 11, 1908.

358

O'Kelly the names of Father James Shannon, pastor of St. Mark's Parish, Peoria, and Father Edmund M. Dunne, Chancellor of the Archdiocese of Chicago.[4] Soon thereafter, Spalding informed Bishop Ryan that he had written to the Cardinal of Baltimore "in behalf of Father Frank," but, he feared, "perchance there might be a nigger in the woodpile." Hence, it might be helpful if Ryan would write to the Cardinal, since "Gibbons has, I think, more influence in Rome than anyone else in this country and then he is one of our own whom we know and can trust." Furthermore, since he had been appointed administrator, Spalding added, "Bishop O'Reilly seems now quite contented."[5]

But if the administrator seemed contented, many priests in the Diocese of Peoria were disturbed by the fact that the auxiliary's name had been excluded from both lists of candidates. Sixty priests sent a memorial to Archbishop Falconio in protest against the proposed elevation of the Chancellor to the episcopacy, while Spalding, annoyed by the opposition, went to Chicago to see Archbishop Quigley and to push Father O'Reilly's candidacy.[6] The feature article in a Peoria newspaper on New Year's Day, 1909, which sketched Father O'Reilly's career under the title "Retiring Bishop and His Probable Successor," only

[4] *Ibid.,* September 9, 1909. In March, 1910, Gaetano Cardinal De Lai, Secretary of the Congregation of the Consistory, issued instructions to the effect "that all who were connected in any way with episcopal *ternae* were bound *sub gravi* to keep the information secret. There had been abuse of confidence in some cases and the publication of the names in the newspapers had a tendency to impair the freedom of the Holy See's judgment." AAB, unclassified, De Lai to Gibbons, Rome, March 20, 1910, printed copy, quoted in Ellis *Gibbons,* II, pp. 418, 137.

[5] ADP, Spalding to Ryan, Peoria, December 26, 1908, copy.

[6] Interview of the writer with the Rt. Rev. Patrick O'Culleton, late pastor of St. Patrick's Parish, Peoria, April 27, 1957. The latter informed the writer that he had signed the memorial in protest against Father O'Reilly's candidacy.

359

added to the growing resentment.[7] On April 29, it was announced in Rome that Spalding had been named titular Archbishop of Scythopolis,[8] but there was still no word about his successor; then, on June 30, 1909, the Associated Press carried the news release that Edmund Michael Dunne, Chancellor of the Archdiocese of Chicago, had been appointed the second bishop of Peoria.[9] Questioned by the press, Bishop O'Reilly stated that he had not as yet received official word of Dunne's appointment; Father O'Reilly dismissed the report as mere rumor.[10] Dunne was likewise dubious, and told reporters that he had not been informed of the honor; but, he said,

[7] Peoria *Journal*, January 1, 1909. Father Francis J. O'Reilly was born on February 24, 1862, near Minonk, Illinois, attended St. Viator College in Bourbonnais and St. Joseph's Seminary, Dunwoodie, New York. Ordained a priest in 1885, he was Rector of St. Mary's Cathedral in Peoria from 1897 to 1910, when he became pastor of St. Patrick's Parish, Danville, until his retirement in 1935, after the celebration of his golden jubilee as a priest. Interview of the writer with the Rt. Rev. Francis A. Cleary, late pastor of St. Columba's Parish, Ottawa, Illinois; Peoria Public Library, Peoria, April 23, 1953.

[8] *Acta Apostolicae Sedis, I* (May 15, 1909), p. 435. ". . . *Chiesa titolare arcivescovile di Scitopoli, per Mons. Giovanni Lancaster Spalding, promosso dalla sede cattedrale di Peoria.*" On May 22, 1909, the *New World* (Chicago) declared in its editorial "Hail Archbishop Spalding," that "it is not an empty honor as some of the secular papers are saying. Rome bestows no empty honors. . . . And we take it that there is not a thoughtful man or woman in America, Catholic, Protestant, Jew . . . who will not declare that the famous prelate of Peoria deserves the new honor Rome has put upon him." Following a conciliatory report from Archbishop Falconio, Raffaele Cardinal Merry del Val directed the Delegate to give Spalding the apostolic brief which had named him titular archbishop. ACPF, Lett., Folder 153/1909, no. 40039, Merry del Val to Gotti, The Vatican, October 21, 1909

[9] Peoria *Evening Journal*, June 30, 1909

[10] *Ibid.*

. . . if the press reports should prove incorrect I would be glad to remain here . . . In fact I would rather stay here . . . It would be easier work, probably, in the Diocese of Peoria, but I am not looking for that. I don't know anyone there and I'm not sure the good people of the Diocese of Peoria would be as pleased to have me as they would some of their own . . . I have told my friends that I dislike to leave and I can say that I hope I shall not have to go.[11]

But as it turned out, the press report proved to be accurate, and Bishop O'Reilly received official word on July 5 that Pope Pius X had appointed Dunne to the See of Peoria.[12] The following September, Bishop Dunne was installed as second bishop of Peoria in St. Mary's Cathedral.[13]

Soon after Dunne's installation, Archbishop Spalding moved into the new home that the priests of the diocese had built for him on the bluff overlooking the city.[14] Though he was to live there for the rest of his life, yet the last years were not without incident. Hardly had the archbishop returned to Peoria, in April, 1910, after a visit with relatives in Kentucky, when he hastened to assure Theodore Roosevelt that he was entirely in sympathy with the stand that the ex-President had taken on his recent trip to Rome.[15]

The story was a simple one, despite the commotion that it had caused on both sides of the Atlantic. American Methodists in Rome, not content with their attempts to proselytize Italian Catholics, had antagonized the Vatican by an anticlerical and anti-Catholic campaign which they had waged from their head-

[11] *Ibid.,* July 1, 1909

[12] *Ibid.,* July 5, 1909

[13] *Ibid.* September 8, 1909. Archbishop Quigley was to have been the presiding prelate but illness prevented his attendance at the installation.

[14] *New World* (Chicago), October 2, 1909. It was announced that Spalding's new home on Glen Oak Avenue would be completed by October 15.

[15] Elting E. Morison, (ed.), *The Letters of Theodore Roosevelt* (Cambridge, 1954), VII, pp. 77–78.

361

quarters on the Via Venti Settembre. When Charles W. Fairbanks, Roosevelt's former vice president, had visited Rome early
in 1910, the press had made much of the fact that Fairbanks'
address before the Methodist Association had resulted in the
cancellation of his scheduled audience with the Pope, and had
described the Vatican's action as another instance of Catholic
bigotry and intolerance.[16] The affair had scarcely been forgotten
when Roosevelt, about to set out for Rome after an African sa-
fari, was greeted with the message that the Holy Father would
receive him, but only on the condition that he likewise refrain
from any action such as had made the reception of Fairbanks
impossible. The former President replied that he could not submit to any condition which in any way might limit his "freedom of conduct."[17]

The Vatican then declared that, though Mr. Roosevelt had an
"entire right" to freedom of conduct, still an audience would
not be possible without some concession on the former President's part. Roosevelt then wired the American Ambassador to
Italy, saying that the proposed audience was now, of course, impossible, and that he proposed to make public the reasons why
he had not visited the Vatican. Shortly thereafter, nearly every
newspaper in the U.S. was quoting Roosevelt's now famous
declaration of American religious tolerance. It was a declaration,
however, that was in part also a rebuff to the Vatican, and an
issue that, therefore, greatly divided American Catholics. In
the aftermath, Archbishop Falconio, an American citizen, and
Boston's Archbishop, William Henry O'Connell, defended the
Pope's action; Cardinal Gibbons vetoed a proposal, made by
Robert J. Collier, editor of *Collier's Weekly* and a Catholic,
that he and Roosevelt attend a dinner together; and an erstwhile friend of Roosevelt, Maria Longworth Storer, urged the
formation of an "Anti-Roosevelt League."

[16] Ellis, *Gibbons*, II, p. 510.
[17] Morison, *op. cit.*, VII, pp. 63–64.

362

There was some consternation, therefore, when, in early September 1910, the New York *Times* carried a dispatch to the effect that Theodore Roosevelt had been invited to speak at the annual Columbus Day banquet in Peoria "as the guest of Archbishop Spaulding [*sic*] and the Knights of Columbus."[18] Ten days later, the *Times* reported that Archbishop John J. Glennon of St. Louis had decided to decline the invitation to attend the banquet.[19]

Despite a report that Bishop Dunne was to be "out of town," and a rumor that many of his former diocesan priests would boycott the banquet,[20] Archbishop Spalding was at the Rock Island Depot on October 12, ready to greet his friend. Pressed for a statement, Spalding declared, ". . . Yes, I wrote a personal letter to the colonel to visit Peoria . . . and sent it in care of the American minister at Copenhagen who is the Honorable Maurice Francis Egan." He had never met Roosevelt until his appointment to the arbitration commission to settle the anthracite coal strike, but they had met many times in Washington during the course of those proceedings, and, he said, "the bond of friendship that sprang up between us has been growing stronger ever since." Colonel Roosevelt, he declared "was the most remarkable man that this country has had for years but like all men of his strength and individuality he has many enemies who are as bitter as his friends are enthusiastic." Spalding then predicted that Roosevelt would be next president of the United States, since he had seemingly "transcended all parties." At least, no one could deny, added the Archbishop, that he was the "most interesting personality that we have in America at the present time."[21]

[18] New York *Times*, September 18, 1910.
[19] *Ibid.*, September 28, 1910.
[20] *Ibid.*, September 28, 1910.
[21] Peoria *Journal*, October 12, 1910

Upon his arrival in Peoria, Roosevelt bounced from the train and enthusiastically embraced the Archbishop, whereupon the two were whisked away in a "Glide" to a luncheon for one hundred and fifty guests at the Peoria Country Club.[22] After lunch, Roosevelt spent the remainder of the day at Spalding's residence, until it was time to leave for the Coliseum. "His speech at the banquet was notable," the New York *Times* reported, "for the prediction that in the course of time there would be a Catholic President of the United States," and it was remarked further that it was Roosevelt's "first public utterance to Roman Catholics since the Vatican incident last Spring."[23] There was, of course, no mention of the unpleasant affair, but no one doubted the real meaning of his message. Stressing the Catholic contribution to the development of the United States, he defended his friendship with Catholics and declared that there was no other country in the world where, as he said, "Catholic and Protestant get on as we do here, each treating the other on the basis of our common citizenship and judging him not as to how he worships his creator but on his conduct toward his fellow men, on his own worth as a man."

When he came to speak of his friendship with Archbishop Spalding, however, the Peoria *Journal* reported, Roosevelt was "wildly applauded." "I had rather talk about the Archbishop when he was not here," Roosevelt commented, "but even though he is here, I merely ask you to let me say publicly how much I owe to him, the help he has been to me," and not only, he concluded, by the fact that Spalding had helped in one of the most important tasks of his administration, and had rendered what Roosevelt termed "assistance which no one but himself could

[22] Peoria *Journal-Transcript*, May 24, 1936. A feature article entitled "When 'Teddy' Came to Peoria . . . and Rode in a 'Glide'" identified the latter as a "real made-in-Peoria automobile."

[23] New York *Times*, October 13, 1910.

render."[24] Thus the story of Roosevelt and the Vatican had its cheerful *dénouement* in Peoria. Roosevelt had feared "that some of the Catholics, headed by Archbishop O'Connell of Boston, and Bishop McFawle [*sic*] of New Jersey intend to make a set at me," but, he had warned, "I shall not answer them as long as it seems that I can do best by ignoring them, but if ever it becomes worth my while to attack them, I will give them their bellyfull."[25] Fortunately, an attack proved unnecessary in the aftermath of Roosevelt's Peoria speech, since it led to a seeming *rapprochement*.

Three years later, the Spalding Council of the Knights of Columbus announced that Archbishop Spalding would be the guest of honor at its annual banquet, which would climax the celebration of his golden sacerdotal jubilee. "My friends here insist on celebrating my fiftieth year of priesthood," Spalding had written to Father Hudson, "and I was weak enough to give my consent though I know such things do little or no good."[26] Nonetheless, on November 24, 1913, in St. Mary's Cathedral, assisted to the throne prepared for him beside Bishop Dunne, Spalding presided at the Solemn Pontifical Mass celebrated by Archbishop Quigley, and listened to Archbishop Glennon preach the jubilee sermon.[27]

[24] Peoria *Journal,* October 12, 1910.

[25] Morison, *op. cit.,* VII, p. 83. "McFawle" was James Augustine McFaul, Bishop of Trenton.

[26] UND, Hudson Papers, Spalding to Hudson, Peoria, October 23, 1913.

[27] *New World* (Chicago), November 29, 1913. Spalding had been ordained on December 19, 1863. In July, 1912, he wrote to Monsignor Jules De Becker, Rector of the American College, Louvain: ". . . during my long illness I have been forced to move my books and papers so often that I have lost the record of my ordination date. . . . I was ordained in a large class Dec. 18 or 19, 1863. I shall be fifty years a priest next December a year. If you will please have the matter looked up and let me know the exact date I shall be more than

365

Under God's providence, Glennon began, it had been evident that the first Bishop of Peoria had labored successfully to discharge the special mission that had been entrusted to him, namely "to make, through his genius and his great faith, America Catholic." Though that mission was an ideal still to be realized, the Archbishop had done what he could do and had accomplished much for Church and country because "in the long roll of great men, priests and prelates of our country from Bishop Carroll's day to our own," Glennon asserted,

I have no fear in placing Archbishop Spalding . . . as the one Catholic who has best understood the American mind. He has understood it because in all wherein it was best, it was his own. He has understood it, because he has approached the study in a broad, generous and Catholic way. And knowing it, he did not fear it; and because of the love of it, and because it was his duty he would instruct and elevate it, he would Catholicize it.[28]

In season and out of season, therefore, he had struggled with voice and pen "to edify, enlighten and conquer for Christ the hearts and minds of his fellow countrymen." When at length his strength had given way and his hand could hold the pen no

---

grateful to you." In the same letter, Spalding asked the Rector for information about his nephew's vocation and progress in studies (AAC-L, Spalding to De Becker, Peoria, July 9, 1912). The nephew, Father Martin Spalding, was ordained in 1916 for the Diocese of Peoria and died on April 23, 1960, as pastor of Immaculate Conception Parish, Monmouth, Illinois.

[28] *Ceremonies of the Golden Sacerdotal Jubilee of His Grace John Lancaster Spalding,* p. 17. Present at the cathedral, in addition to Quigley and Glennon, were Bishops Muldoon of Rockford, James Davis of Davenport, Richard Scannell of Omaha, John F. Hennessy of Wichita, and J. Henry Tiehan of Lincoln. From South Bend came Fathers John Cavanaugh, President of the University of Notre Dame, Charles L. O'Donnell, professor of literature in the same institution, and Daniel E. Hudson, editor of *Ave Maria.* Father Daniel Riordan of Chicago was also present (*ibid.,* pp. 22–23).

longer, Archbishop Spalding had been compelled to rest. But the impress that he had made and the good he had accomplished, Glennon believed, were "unequaled in the annals of our American Church . . . ," and they would remain "in [their] unfading richness at once his consolation and his crown."[29]

At the conclusion of the ceremonies at the cathedral, luncheon was served at the country club, but the jubilarian was unable to attend lest the day's excitement endanger his appearance at the evening banquet.[30] Later that evening, as the Archbishop walked out on the stage of the Coliseum, he was given a tremendous ovation as he took his place between Bishop Dunne and Father Frank O'Reilly who once again acted as toastmaster.[31] When it was his turn to speak, Bishop Muldoon thanked the Archbishop for all that he had done for the American Church because, as he said, "If there is less hostility today, if we as Catholics, are better understood in the United States, it was largely through the strength and the voice of the first Bishop of Peoria." Furthermore, many had truths to bring before the American people, but all had not been listened to, Muldoon believed, "but the people did listen to Archbishop Spalding."[32]

The next speaker was Monsignor Thomas J. Shahan, Rector of the Catholic University of America. Recalling the formative years of that institution Shahan remarked:

No one who knows the beginnings of this work will gainsay me when I say that all this is owing to John Lancaster Spalding, that it originated in his heart and mind, and that its first measure of realization was owing to his faith in such an enterprise, his readiness to lead with voice and deed, his power of inspiring the first generous and noble gift that made it possible . . . , and his wisdom and courage in its

[29] *Ibid.*
[30] *Ibid.*, p. 22.
[31] *Ibid.*, p. 27.
[32] *Ibid.*, pp. 30–31.

earliest years, when the new institution that he had called into being, walked, so to speak through the Valley of Dispute, and by the very old law of survival earned its right to go about the business for which it was created by Leo XIII and the Catholic bishops of the United States.[33]

It was in the maturity of his powers and in the fullness of his reputation, Shahan continued, that the Bishop of Peoria became the leader of the movement for a Catholic university, and "perhaps . . . no one else could have arrested the busy workers in so many scattered fields of Catholic endeavor, and compelled them to look up and dwell awhile in the higher regions of the intellect."[34] But Spalding could force a hearing for his cause and thus become "the prophet of Catholic higher education . . . and the moral leader . . . of devoted bishops and priests who found in his utterance the confirmation of their own . . . views and convictions." Without him, the idea of a Catholic university for the United States might have long awaited its champion, since above all Spalding had a great heart overflowing with courage and a mind profoundly convinced "that the time had come for action, and that further delay was equivalent to a defeat . . . from whose consequences the Catholic people would never recover." It was his hope, therefore, that the Archbishop's remaining days would be filled with deep happiness, and with the knowledge that he would leave American Catholicism "on a higher level than it held when he entered its service."[35]

All in all, Spalding was pleased by the jubilee celebration. He had known friends and foes in his lifetime, he had been commended and had been found fault with, he had tasted the delights of home and had breathed the air of strange lands, he had been followed and had been opposed, he had triumphed and had suffered defeat, but now, in "the winter of age," he had

[33] *Ibid.,* p. 44.
[34] *Ibid.,* p. 46.
[35] *Ibid.,* p. 48.

realized before it was too late, he confessed, "how many people there are in this world who love me."[36]

Surrounded by friends and relatives, Spalding spent his remaining days in Peoria, the city that he had come to love, and Lebanon, at Evergreen Bend. His brother, Dr. Leonard Spalding, died in August 1914,[37] and two days after Christmas the Archbishop received news of Archbishop Riordan's death, the truest friend he had. "I loved him ever since I first met him in Louvain more than fifty years ago," Spalding wrote, "a long span of life which has shrunk to a point." In his opinion, Patrick W. Riordan was "one of the best and noblest men" that he had ever known, "high in all his thoughts and aspirations, and thoroughly imbued with the spirit of our Divine Lord and Saviour, in the light and love of whose manifest presence," he said, "I doubt not, he now lives." It was a disappointment to him that his health did not permit him to be in San Francisco for "the last solemn rites over what was in him mortal."[38]

Four months later, Spalding narrowly escaped death when the carriage in which he was sitting was struck by an automobile in Peoria's downtown business district. Thrown from the carriage, which was completely demolished, Spalding was caught under the wreckage. Not badly injured, but in a state of shock, Spalding was taken to his home.[39] It was feared that he might never recover, but he rallied with surprising speed. On June 2, 1915, a delegation of the Spalding Council of the Knights of Columbus waited on the venerable prelate to bring him good wishes and flowers on the occasion of his seventy-fifth birthday.

[36] Interview of Sister Mary Evangela Henthorne, B.V.M., with Miss Maybelle Spalding, June, 1929, quoted in Henthorne, "The Life and Career of Bishop John Lancaster Spalding," p. 432, microfilm copy.

[37] *The Record* (Louisville), September 3, 1914.

[38] *Most Reverend Patrick William Riordan, D.D., Second Archbishop of San Francisco. In Memoriam* (San Francisco, 1915), p. 62.

[39] Peoria *Daily Journal*, May 5, 1915.

As he was assisted into his carriage for his daily ride, Spalding told his well-wishers:

I am feeling exceptionally well on this birthday and you may say to all my friends that my heart is full of gratitude to God for his care and I send out my kindliest greetings to my hosts of friends whose never failing remembrance makes every day of my life bright. One cloud over-shadows us all just now. It is the terrible war that has engulfed half the world. To us who have prayed and worked so long for peace, who have had our visions of that day when human brotherhood should be realized over the whole earth, this war has come as a great shock.[40]

As an American, Spalding said, he was doubly sad because of what he termed the complications that have drawn the United States government into discord with nations formerly our 'friends. "I am sorry we have gone so far." Two days later he left for a holiday at Evergreen Bend.[41]

In the year ahead, it was evident to those close to the Archbishop that for John Lancaster Spalding the end was not far off. "I thought I should like to go back to Kentucky to die," he had said more than once, "but after all, it does not make any difference where one dies."[42] Quietly, on the afternoon of August 25, 1916, the first Bishop of Peoria closed his rich and varied life. Kate Spalding and Mrs. Nathan Putnam, his sisters, were at the bedside as Father Maurice Sammon gave the dying Prelate the last rites of the Church. "He was just simply wasted away," the attending physician reported, "he did not suffer . . . pain, and his passing . . . was as peaceful as any human could expect."[43]

Funeral arrangements were left to Bishop Dunne. "Few prelates were better known throughout the American continent,"

[40] Peoria *Journal,* June 2, 1915.

[41] *Ibid.*

[42] Interview of Sister Mary Evangela Henthorne, B.V.M., with Miss Maybelle Spalding, June, 1929, quoted in Henthorne, *op. cit.,* p. 436, microfilm copy

[43] Peoria *Daily Journal,* August 26, 1916.

he stated to the press. "His versatility as a pulpit orator, essayist and administrator entitle him to undying fame."[44] From Oyster Bay came Theodore Roosevelt's message: "There was no finer citizen in this country, nor a man who represented better what all good Americans should wish to see in their religious leaders than Archbishop Spalding. He was a cultured gentleman and one of the most eminent and patriotic citizens in the United States."[45] Archbishop Ireland told Dunne that he was very sorry that he was unable to leave home to be present at the funeral; Cardinal Gibbons likewise regretted that it was impossible for him to come to Peoria.[46] "So poor, dear Archbishop Spalding has been taken home at last," wrote the gentle Archbishop Keane. "Surely we must be glad of his deliverance from so much suffering. Of course I must manage to get to his funeral at any risk."[47]

On August 29, 1916, Bishop Dunne celebrated the Solemn Pontifical Mass for the repose of the soul of the first Bishop of Peoria.[48] Archbishop George W. Mundelein, who recently had been appointed to the See of Chicago, preached the funeral sermon. He paid a simple tribute to the deceased prelate, whose voice, as he said, "from this pulpit so often thrilled you and fanned to brighter flame your love for God and for your country."[49] The preacher briefly recounted the career of the man whom he characterized as a "militant churchman, a patriotic citizen, a famous educator, a powerful orator, and one of the greatest

[44] Peoria *Star*, August 26, 1916.

[45] *Ibid.*, August 27, 1916.

[46] *Ibid.*, August 29, 1916.

[47] *Ibid.*

[48] Peoria *Daily Journal*, August 29, 1916.

[49] George William Mundelein, *Two Crowded Years. Being Selected Addresses, Pastorals and Letters Issued During the First Twenty-four Months of the Episcopate of the Most Rev. George William Mundelein, D.D., as Archbishop of Chicago* (Chicago, 1918), p. 129.

essayists our country has produced."[50] Mundelein realized how strange it must seem that he, who only lately had come to the Middle West from the "distant East," should have been chosen as the one to pay the last farewell to Peoria's "first citizen." Yet it was fitting that it was so, Mundelein thought, because Archbishop Spalding belonged "not to this city, this diocese, this state alone," but to the entire land where American Catholics had claimed him as their own. Millions had been proud of him, and when the preacher had been but a "tiny boy," he recalled, it had been impressed on his memory that one of the greatest prelates of American's Church was Bishop Spalding of Peoria.[51]

At the end of the Mass, three absolutions were imparted,[52] by Bishop Henry Althoff of Belleville, Archbishops Glennon, and Henry Moeller of Cincinnati, and the fourth by John J. Keane,[53] who had managed at great risk to his health to come to Peoria to say goodbye to an old friend. Archbishop Mundelein gave the final absolution, the antiphon, *In paradisum*, was intoned, and the funeral cortege moved slowly from the cathedral and thence to St. Mary's Cemetery, where the body of John Lancaster Spalding was laid to rest.[54]

[50] *Ibid.*, p. 130.

[51] *Ibid.*, p. 140.

[52] Peoria *Daily Journal*, August 29, 1916.

[53] Cf. Ahern, *Life of John J. Keane*, p. 356. Archbishop Falconio had notified Keane on April 25, 1911, that his resignation from the See of Dubuque had been accepted by the Holy Father. On April 28, Keane was appointed titular Archbishop of Ciana, his fifth episcopal title.

[54] Peoria *Daily Journal*, August 29, 1916. In his last will and testament, dated November 25, 1911, Spalding had stated: "I desire that the Bishop of Peoria shall erect and furnish . . . a Spalding Memorial Chapel not to cost my estate in excess of Ten Thousand ($10,000) Dollars and that the same shall be so constructed as to contain vaults for burial purposes." The total value of the estate when the final report of the executor was made on May 13, 1920, amounted to $77,191.77 (Archives of the County Probate Clerk, Peoria County

While time has been less kind to Spalding the man as writer, humanist, intellectual—the force of his ideas and the brilliance of his oratory good enough and occasionally very good for his own times, but lacking that assured and comprehensive prevision that will remember a man to posterity—while time has neglected Spalding here, it has nevertheless borne out the true quality and stature of many of his ideas and labors. Because of Spalding, education in the United States, and particularly higher education, was changed for ever, and for the best. He was, by determination if not explicitly, a champion of the religious and political pluralism so cherished in our day, and a staunch advocate of intellectual freedom.

Posterity will not record that Spalding of Peoria did for American Catholicism what a Newman had done for the English Church, but even so he is not to be ignored, being neither great nor irrelevant. "But try, I urge, the trying shall suffice," he once wrote. "The aim, if reached or not, makes great the life."[55]

Courthouse, Peoria, Estate Papers of John Lancaster Spalding). The writer is grateful to Reverend Patrick W. Collins of St. Mary's Cathedral, Peoria, Illinois, for the above reference. Since after the estate had been settled, no money was allocated for the mausoleum, each parish in the diocese was assessed to pay for it. Cf. Patrick W. Collins, "The Cathedral of Peoria," unpublished master's dissertation, Seminary of St. Paul, St. Paul, Minnesota, n.p. Spalding's remains were transferred to one of the eight water tight crypts on June 21, 1922. The colonial façade of the new tomb was a miniature replica of Spalding's Glen Oak Avenue residence (ibid).

[55] Spalding, "Culture and the Spirit of the Age," in *Education and the Higher Life,* p. 73. Spalding was here paraphrasing Robert Browning's poem, "Bishop Blougram's Apology," line 492: "But try, you urge," etc.

Abbreviations

Index

375

Rome, 219–224; rumored
for rectorship of Catholic
University of America,
246–248; in Rome, 266–
267; defends Hecker be-
fore Leo XIII, 267; dis-
course at the Gesù (Rome)
on "Education and the
Future of Religion," 267–
273; visits Florence, 273–
274; visits Milan, 275; ar-
rives in Paris, 276; returns
to Peoria, 283; requests
auxiliary, 284; intervenes
in Chicago ecclesiastical
affairs, 288–290; silver jubilee, 294–297; recom-
mended for New York, 298;
recommended for Chicago,
300–304 (and *passim*);
Baroness von Zedwitz im-
pugns character, 308–309;
Riordan advises against
Spalding's appointment to
Chicago, 309; in Washing-
ton, 315–316; appointed to
labor arbitration committee
by Roosevelt, 316–326; suf-
fers stroke, 343–344; va-
cations in Hot Springs,
346–347; resigns see, 351–
352; named titular arch-
bishop of Scythopolis, 356;
retirement, 358 and *pas-
sim;* meets with Roosevelt,
363–365; golden jubilee,
365–369; last days, 369;
death, 370; requiem for,
371–372
2. and American anti-imperial-
ism, 252–256; and Amer-
ican Protective Association,
223–232; and apostolic
delegation in U.S., 142–
145, 212–214; and *Balti-
more Catechism,* 174–175;
and bishops of U.S., 213;
and Cahenslyism, 201–202,
227–228; and Catholic
Church in U.S., 98–99, 182–

187, 224–232; and Cath-
olic University of America,
127–133, 166–170 (*See*
under same); and Church-
state relations in U.S., 124–
127; and Civil War, 66–
67; and colonization of
western U.S., 118–123;
and Columbian Catholic
Congress, 207–210; and
education, 136–139, 145,
185–187, 262–265, 267–
273, 328–330; and German
immigrants, 114–116, 118,
192–194, 244; Gesù dis-
course, French reaction to,
276–280; and Irish immi-
grants, 122–126; and Irish
Catholic Colonization As-
sociation, 119–122, 154;
and Irish independence,
149–150; and Italian im-
migrants, 146–147; and lay
congresses, 188–190, 207–
210; and Negroes of Louisville, 76–78, 92; and on-
tologism, 81–90, 100, 105;
and papal infallibility, 93,
104; and parochial schools,
203–204, 208–210, 216,
228–231; and religious
ownership of property,
165–166, 292–293; and
Second Plenary Council of
Baltimore, 78–80; and se-
cret societies in Church,
237–241; and seminary
education, 136–139; and
temperance, 154–155; and
Ultramontanism, 64–67
Spalding, Kate, 153, 370
Spalding, Leonard, 28–30, 71, 344,
369
Spalding, Martin, 28–29
Spalding, Martin, 366
Spalding, Martin J., 29–30, 34, 42–
46, 48, 58, 60–73, 75, 77,
80–81, 88–92, 94–95, 105–
106, 118, 128–129, 153,
160, 281, 294, 309, 352